Lonely Planet Publications

D0114716

Damien Simonis

Barcelona

The Top Five

1 **La Sagrada Família**
Marvel at Gaudí's incredible work in progress (p106)

2 **La Rambla**
Stroll along Barcelona's famous boulevard (p85)

3 **Museu Picasso**
Be inspired by the early works of this 20th-century master (p96)

4 **Park Güell**
Explore the 'forest' of the Sala Hipóstila (p111)

5 **Camp Nou**
Cheer on FC Barcelona at the team's home stadium (p116)

Contents

Published by Lonely Planet Publications Pty Ltd
ABN 36 005 607 983

Australia Head Office, Locked Bag 1, Footscray,
Victoria 3011, ☎ 03 8379 8000, fax 03 8379 8111,
talk2us@lonelyplanet.com.au

USA 150 Linden St, Oakland, CA 94607,
☎ 510 893 8555, toll free 800 275 8555,
fax 510 893 8572, info@lonelyplanet.com

UK 72–82 Rosebery Ave, Clerkenwell, London,
EC1R 4RW, ☎ 020 7841 9000, fax 020 7841 9001,
go@lonelyplanet.co.uk

© Lonely Planet 2006
Photographs © Krzysztof Dydynski and as listed
(p272) 2006

The Author

Damien Simonis

In 1990, during an early Continental foray from a rain-sodden London, Damien found himself snooping around southwest France. With no particular plan, he wound his way up into the Pyrenees and Andorra. Now what? On a whim he jumped on a bus heading down the mountains to pre-Olympics Barcelona. He had never before set foot in Spain. What was it about this town? The crowded produce markets, the dimly-lit *colmados* (treasure caverns of all sorts of weird and wonderful foods), the gaily noisy terraces where chatter mixed so easily with wine, the Gaudí colours, the mysterious narrow lanes of the Barri Gòtic, the crowded busy hum of the centre, the seaside? Perhaps it was all this and some unifying, undefinable quality that got under his skin. What a place to live! mused our restless Sydney-born, London-based wayfarer. Barcelona was stored away for future reference and slowly slipped into his subconscious.

Years and travels slipped by and it was not until 1998 that Damien turned up in a Rambla-side *pensión* on assignment for Lonely Planet. And that old magic started doing its work again. A chat with a fellow in a bar and he had a room in a top-floor flat in Gran Via. And so Barcelona gradually became a second home. After Gran Via and various old town locations (from St Pere més alt through El Raval to Poble Sec), he finally settled on a typical, tunnel-shaped apartment in l'Eixample. It is from this strategic mid-point that he steps out into the Barcelona night in search of the next bar, the latest restaurant or just one of his old faves for a quiet read of the paper. Barcelona's still got it.

Damien's Top Barcelona Day

A great way to kick-start the day is with everyone else, leaning up against a bar over a *cafè amb llet* (coffee with milk), an orange juice and a pastry (preferably something nice and creamy like a *canya*). A quick read of the paper to find out where we stand on the latest round of squabbling over Catalan autonomy, and it's time to hit the streets. There are few monuments in the world like La Sagrada Família, where it's always worth calling by just to see where they are up to on this unique work in progress. A visit to the Museu Picasso or the CaixaForum, to catch the latest temporary art exhibition, takes care of the day's spiritual nourishment and lunch beckons. I head into the narrow lanes of La Barceloneta for a slap-up meal of fish or finger-licking *mariscos* (seafood). The choice of area has a double purpose, for what's a day in Barcelona without a couple of hours lazing on the beach? Then it's time to go home for a little rest before heading out again for dinner in the grid maze of l'Eixample. From there the night is wide open: what about dancing to dawn at Otto Zutz?

PHOTOGRAPHER
Krzysztof Dydyński

Born and raised in Warsaw, Poland, Krzysztof quickly discovered a passion for travelling, which took him on various trips across Europe, Asia and South America, and finally to Australia, where he now lives. He first visited Spain, including Barcelona, as early as 1974 and has regularly returned to the country ever since. Barcelona is one of his great loves, where he is inspired by its arts and cuisine, the labyrinth of the narrow medieval streets of the Barri Gòtic, and Gaudí's dreamlike architectural creations.

Introducing Barcelona

A Mediterranean metropolis, Barcelona is one of Europe's glittering jewels. Sun-kissed and lapped by the sea, it is a go-ahead city that could hardly be better located. A magnet for art and architecture lovers, with its magnificent medieval and modernista heritage, it is also a place that lives for the here and now. This hedonist's haven bubbles with nightlife and its countless restaurants always seem to be full; their tables groan under the weight of good food and fine wine. In short, Barcelona is a pleasure for all the senses.

Barcelona is and isn't Spain. The second city after Madrid, it is capital of the autonomous region of Catalonia (Catalunya to the locals), only fully (and unwillingly) incorporated into the Spanish state after defeat in battle in 1714. The Catalans speak their own language, and not just literally. Barcelona has long been the engine room of the Spanish economy and its people have always run their own race. It displays a zest for life, artistic genius and a sense of style few cities can rival. It also seems to be in a permanent state of transformation and self-renewal, its skyline constantly being altered and more neglected districts coming in for surgical beauty treatment. Barcelona is often held up as an example of how to go about urban renewal.

Barcelona's medieval period left it with one of the most impressive and varied Gothic legacies in Europe. After a long hiatus came another wave of architectural inspiration with the modernistas. Led by Antoni Gaudí, they cast across Barcelona an Art Nouveau splash unparalleled anywhere else. Some of

the greatest artists of the 20th century put in time here – Picasso and Miró make an impressive duo, and Dalí was born and lived much of his life just up the coast. Today a phalanx of local and international design stars is adding to this impressive heritage with landmark 21st-century buildings.

But Barcelona is not just about monuments and paintings. The city provides all sorts of entertainments, starting with the palate. Catalan cuisine is among Spain's best. Traditional old restaurants will welcome you in from the winter cold, or you can spend long summer afternoons over alfresco seafood meals. And just as the town fathers are unwilling to rest on their laurels, so Barcelona has become a cauldron of culinary activity. Led by Ferran Adrià, a host of new young chefs is taking avant-garde cooking to new heights of inventiveness. In Barcelona you can eat anything from tortilla in a bread roll through traditional seafood rice dishes to the most sophisticated of vapours and essences yet concocted in the world's modern kitchens.

LOWDOWN

Population 1.58 million

Time zone GMT + one hour

Average three-star double room Around €120 to €180

Entrepà/bocadillo (filled bread roll) €3 to €5

Average club admission €15, includes first drink

Metro ticket €1.20 (single ride)

Targeta T-10 (10-ride ticket) €6.65

Greetings A peck (not a slather) on each cheek is the standard greeting between people of the opposite sex – much nicer than a handshake!

What's normal? For years the regional government has encouraged a programme of 'linguistic normalisation'; in other words, encouraging people to speak Catalan rather than Spanish

This happy situation is not restricted to grub. For Barcelona is surrounded by some of the country's finest wine-producing regions. Easily the best known is the nearby Penedès area, home to *cava,* the prized local bubbly, and a broad range of whites and reds.

If you thought it was time to head for bed after a meal that might not have started before 10pm, think again. You've barely begun. The city centre and several other *barris* (neighbourhoods) heave to the joyous rhythms of bar-hoppers. Barcelona leaves much of the rest of Europe for dead with its sheer concentration of bars, cafés and clubs. Again, there is something for all tastes, from exquisitely maintained modernista taverns deep in the old town to the trendiest of *fashionista* dance locations in the chic Zona Alta part of town, from old-time dancehalls converted into clubs to seaside chillout lounges. Those with a penchant for higher-minded nocturnal activities will want to explore the music and opera options. The Gran Teatre del Liceu is one of Europe's grandest opera houses and is complemented by several other major venues.

If you overdo it at night, you can flop the summer days away at the beach. But beware that there is rarely time for dull moments. In summer especially, various parts of the city seem to lose their sanity, giving themselves over to week-long *festes* (festivals). These outdoor parties feature bands, competitions, and traditional parades of *gegants, capgrossos* and *dimonis* (giants, dwarfs and demons). And then there's the madness of *correfoc* (firerunning) through the narrow lanes of the old city with fire-breathing dragons during the September Festes de la Mercè. This latter festival is also a high point on the city's concert calendar, with major bands playing across the city. Barcelona hosts other big music fests, including the summer Sonar electronic music extravaganza.

New bars and cafés continue to appear all over town as the city council keeps up a cracking pace to clean up its most run-down quarters, especially in Ciutat Vella (Old City). Fortunately Barcelona retains some of its rough-diamond flavour, which attracts an earthy working class, a grunge-chic international inner-city set and a growing, colourful community of foreigners from as far afield as Argentina and Pakistan.

Barcelona doesn't exist in a vacuum. From the centre of town you are no more than a few hours' drive from southern France, the Pyrenees (skiing in winter, hiking in summer), the seaside lunacy of Sitges (the gay capital of the *costas,* or coast), Romanesque and Gothic monasteries and churches, the Penedès wine country, and the rugged splendours of the Costa Brava. Old rivals such as medieval Girona (to the north) and Roman Tarragona (south) are easily accessible.

As soaring rent and real-estate prices attest, people are drawn in droves from elsewhere in Spain and beyond to this Mediterranean magnet. Come to 'Barna' and you'll soon see why!

City Life

City Life

BARCELONA TODAY

Spain's most glamorous city is a hive of activity. Like a catwalk model, Barcelona starts with some enviable natural advantages: a beautiful medieval core, the wacky delights of modernista architecture, a splendid seaside location and sunny climate. A magnet for those who enjoy the good life, the city offers a broad palette of fine dining and drinking that local sybarites have long enjoyed and a growing number of guests have more recently discovered. But as any model will say, you have to work at it too, and Barcelona is frenetic with activity, ranging from extensive urban regeneration through an impressive trade-fair calendar to a campaign to turn the city into a hi-tech hot spot. Like any city, Barcelona has its share of problems, but they pale into insignificance beside the cauldron of raw energy that it exudes.

In February 2006 Barcelona hosted the world's biggest annual mobile phone fest, the 3GSM trade fair, reinforcing the Mediterranean port's image as a city opening its arms to the 21st century. Confirming the city's importance as a host of international congresses and fairs, the festival was a powerful symbol for a city that seems indefatigable in its efforts to renew and renovate itself. A couple of weeks later, 150,000 food-industry people flocked in for the Alimentaria fair, which Barcelona hopes to make the biggest in the world by 2008.

Barcelona's make-over began in the late 1980s with the preparations for the 1992 Olympic Games. Possibly nowhere else in the modern history of the Games has benefited from them more than this sparkling city on the sea.

Barcelona, long the bicultural capital of Spain's most entrepreneurial region, is still being transformed, somewhat willy-nilly, into a multicultural metropolis. While the politics of the city can verge on obsessive navel-gazing, Barcelona seems intent on force-marching itself into a pre-eminent position on the European stage.

The astonishing programme of urban renewal (see p22) is the most concrete sign of this. With surgical precision, Barcelona is combining major infrastructural improvements with redevelopment. The Fòrum/Diagonal Mar project, still in progress, gave the city massive new congress space with high-rise hotels, created a new residential district out of nothing and opened a pleasurable new stretch of the coastline (with a protected bathing area and a brand-new marina) that before had been little more than a half-abandoned sewerage outlet. Work on redevelopment around l'Hospitalet de Llobregat and La Sagrera will not only clean up two depressed areas, but double the city's trade-fair space, create a new court district and add a high-speed train terminus and transport interchange. Open to the world, Barcelona remains keen to draft in the planet's best architects to do their best. Among the latest are Jean Nouvel, Toyo Ito and Frank Gehry.

Perhaps the most ambitious long-term project is to convert part of the one-time industrial district of El Poblenou into a cutting-edge home to world-class hi-tech and media companies, the so-called 22@bcn (more commonly known simply as 22@) district. On the subject of hi-tech, Mare Nostrum, Europe's most powerful supercomputer, began ticking over in a deconsecrated chapel in the posh Barcelona suburb of Pedralbes in 2005. It is used for research in fields as wide-ranging as biomedicine and aerospace. Also in 2005, Barcelona was made the administrative HQ for the International Thermonuclear Experimental Reactor research project in France.

All this activity creates temporary inconvenience, and sometimes worse. Work on the saturated airport's new terminal, which will double capacity to 40 million passengers a year, won't be complete until 2008. The high-speed AVE train link to Madrid is years behind schedule and work on its railway line into Barcelona has interrupted the already poor transport links between the city and airport. A new Metro line that will connect the city with the airport and trade fairs is also well behind schedule. Work on it ground to a complete halt for a while after tunnelling for the extension of another line caused the collapse of several blocks of flats in the working-class suburb of El Carmel in January 2005. Miraculously, no-one was killed.

Critics of the Socialist-led city and regional governments abound, but there is no doubt that things are moving in Barcelona. Within months of Spain's national parliament legalising gay marriages in mid-2005, enterprising companies were promoting Barcelona as a gay wedding destination. A nationwide antismoking law in January 2006 was a first step in eliminating clouds of smoke from restaurants and bars bigger than 100 sq metres. They claim to have lost 20% of their custom as a result, so it is not surprising that most of the smaller establishments opted to keep their ashtrays in action. The Catalan government, however, would like to go one step further than Madrid and emulate the Italian decision to ban smoking in *all* enclosed public spaces. Wrangling between the authorities and business associations in Barcelona continues. Barcelona is one step ahead in another area: since 2005, four Barcelona hospitals and 60 pharmacies have been dispensing marijuana capsules to patients with painful illnesses, from multiple sclerosis to cancer. New rules granting Catalan male public servants up to four weeks' paternity leave were also approved in 2005.

The city remains a European favourite for holidaymakers and a rapidly growing expatriate community. It is not hard to see why: the bright lights of new restaurants and bars continue to twinkle and spread; beaches of every possible kind spread up and down the coast in and beyond the city; some of Spain's most noteworthy wines are made within 40km of central Barcelona; the climate is enviable and the lifestyle relaxed. But even in the business of pleasure, the locals don't just rest on their laurels. Some of the most exciting novelties in avant-garde cooking are taking place here. Iconic Catalan chef Ferran Adrià and some of his protégés, like Sergi Arola, have rocketed to international cooking stardom.

It is other issues, however, that preoccupy the local media. In 2005 the Catalan government sent a radical new draft autonomy statute (the Estatut), aimed at greatly increasing its autonomy from central government in Madrid, to the national parliament for discussion and approval. Among the more controversial clauses was one explicitly recognising Catalonia as a 'nation' and others that would have shifted a great part of tax-collecting prerogatives in Catalonia to Barcelona.

The right-wing Partido Popular (PP), which since its national electoral defeat in March 2004 seems incapable of anything but fear-mongering and political histrionics, demanded the proposal be rejected out of hand. That the prime minister, José Luis Rodríguez Zapatero, was determined to negotiate a compromise was, for the PP, tantamount to 'dismembering Spain'. Even some fellow socialist leaders accused Catalonia of not wanting to share its wealth with poorer Spanish regions. As far as many Catalans are concerned, their region has been contributing more than its fair share for far too long. Just as lamentable as PP politicking was the promotion of a boycott of Catalan bubbly *(cava)* in the rest of Spain, which in 2005 caused a drop in sales of 6% and a corresponding rise in imports of French champagne! Tension has increased as a result of all this, and a survey in early 2006 showed

HOT CONVERSATION TOPICS

- Will the prospect of a €300 fine discourage people from using Barcelona's streets as a toilet?
- Patriotism has a price: the new Catalonia-specific Web domain suffix '.cat' costs four times as much as domains ending in '.com' or '.es' (for Spain).
- Will Pasqual Maragall be able to win back power in regional elections after the referendum on Catalonia's new autonomy statute caused his tri-party government to fall?
- Depending on whom you listen to, the use of Spanish *and* Catalan are both in mortal danger in Catalonia. Someone must be exaggerating!
- Just what did the genius of avant-garde cooking, Ferran Adrià, mean when he said that in 2008 he wants to 'return to cooking'? Was it code for retiring?
- The Ministry of Defence will only hand over Castell de Montjuïc to the city of Barcelona (as promised by the government in 2005) if the latter guarantees to keep the Spanish flag flying over it. Will the polemics never end?
- Barcelona is the most expensive Spanish city in which to buy property. How can anyone afford to live here?
- The annual world 3GSM trade fair is big business for Barcelona, to the tune of €100 million in just four days. The only hitch in 2006 was that many delegates found they could not place calls from their mobiles in the fairground area!

half of Catalans thought Catalonia should be a state, either fully independent (14.8%) or as part of a loose Spanish federation (32.4%). After all the grandstanding, a heavily watered down version of the new Estatut was approved in Madrid and confirmed by referendum in Catalonia in June. It ranges from increased fiscal power for Catalonia (up to half of income tax collected in Catalonia will stay in Catalonia), a seven-year period of heightened central government investment in the region, and various articles that open the way to easier access to abortion and the possibility of euthanasia.

The PP was equally vocal on another subject: rejecting long-standing Catalan demands that historic archives removed from Barcelona to a national archive in Salamanca after the Civil War be returned. Barcelona could finally celebrate victory on this score with the return of the 'Salamanca papers' in early 2006.

CITY CALENDAR

If your idea of fun is to party the nights away, Barcelona is plenty of fun any time of the year. But the city also has a rich calendar of events worth seeing and/or participating in. Many are steeped in colourful tradition, while others are more modern affairs focused on concerts, theatre cycles and sport. Some envelop the entire city; other local *festes* (festivals) are limited to a particular *barri* (neighbourhood).

Events take place throughout much of the year, although there is more activity in the warmer months. It is a good idea to time a trip with one eye on the events and the other on the weather charts (see p256). December to February is the coldest period; July and August are the hottest months of the year and make you understand why air conditioning was invented. Locals like to get out, especially in August, when an eerie quiet descends on the normally cacophonous streets of Barcelona. Many restaurants close and offices run in neutral.

For a list of official public holidays in Barcelona, see p259.

JANUARY

ANY NOU/AÑO NUEVO (NEW YEAR'S DAY)

Like Cap d'Any/Noche Vieja (New Year's Eve) anywhere, this occasion can create but not always fulfil expectations. Many locals arrange parties in their homes as restaurants, bars and clubs fill to bursting and charge like wounded bulls. All await the 12 *campanadas* (bell chimes) that mark midnight, when they try to stuff 12 grapes (one for each chime) into their mouths (not easy to do – especially if there are pips in your grapes!) and make a wish for the new year.

REIS/REYES

Epifanía (the Epiphany) on 6 January is also known as the Dia dels Reis Mags/Día de los Reyes Magos (Three Kings' Day), or simply Reis/Reyes, perhaps the most important day on a Barcelona kid's calendar. Traditionally young Spaniards wait until the Epiphany for presents (Santa Claus is an import). If they've been bad they get lumps of *carbón* (coal). Well, nowadays even the coal is sweet and you can see piles of the stuff in pastry stores. The holiday itself is quiet, but on 5 January children delight in the Cavalcada dels Reis Mags (Parade of the Three Kings). Three local personalities dress up as the three kings (or three wise men) and, after landing in Port Vell, head off in a colourful parade of floats and music from Parc de la Ciutadella, along Via Laietana and on to the Palau Nacional in Montjuïc via Plaça de Catalunya and Carrer de Sepúlveda. The parade starts at 6.30pm and ends at 9pm. All along the route the wise men and their helpers hurl volleys of boiled

TOP FIVE UNUSUAL EVENTS

- Carnestoltes/Carnaval (opposite) Parades, floats and the burial of the sardine greet the approach of spring.
- Divendres Sant/Viernes Santo (Good Friday; opposite) A touch of Andalucía with an emotive religious procession.
- Festes de la Mercè (p13) The city's biggest knees-up marks the end of the summer.
- L'Ou com Balla (p12) A curious local festival of bobbing egg shells to mark Corpus Christi.
- Reis/Reyes (Epiphany; left) The Three Kings shower kids with sweets as they parade through the city.

sweets into the crowds – even adults have trouble resisting the temptation to scramble for them! Afterwards everyone heads home to open their presents.

FESTES DELS TRES TOMBS

A key part of the district festival of Sant Antoni Abat (17 January) is this Feast of the Three Circuits, a parade of horse-drawn carts through parts of l'Eixample, around Ronda de Sant Antoni to Plaça de Catalunya, down Via Laietana and on to Parc de la Ciutadella. Sant Antoni Abat (St Anthony the Abbot) is the patron saint of domestic and carriage animals. The *festa* has been celebrated since the mid-19th century.

FEBRUARY

BARCELONA VISUALSOUND

www.bcnvisualsound.org
Since 2004 this three-week festival has brought together young audiovisual creators in a celebration of emerging stars in the making of anything from video to multimedia art. Exhibitions are held in cultural centres around town.

BARNASANTS

Each year the city's main live-music venues host a bevy of Spanish and Latin American singer-songwriters for concerts spread over a period from the end of January until about mid-March.

CARNESTOLTES/CARNAVAL

Celebrated in February or March, this festival involves several days of fancy-dress parades and merrymaking, ending on the Tuesday 47 days before Easter Sunday. The Gran Rua (Grand Parade) takes place on the Saturday evening from 5.30pm, starting on or near Plaça d'Espanya and proceeding west along Carrer de la Creu Coberta. All sorts of floats and carriages participate to welcome the Carnival King. The festivities culminate in the Enterrament de la Sardina (Burial of the Fish), often on Montjuïc, on the following Wednesday. This marks the beginning of Lent.

Down in Sitges (p238) a much wilder version takes place. The gay community stages gaudy parades and party-goers keep the bars and clubs heaving to all hours for several days running.

FESTES DE SANTA EULÀLIA

www.bcn.es/santaeulalia
Coinciding roughly with Carnival, this is the feast of Barcelona's first patron saint, Eulàlia (or 'la Laia' for short). The Ajuntament (town hall) organises a week of cultural events, from concerts through to performances by *castellers* (human-castle builders; see p196) and the appearance of *mulasses* (dragons) in the main parade. Pick up a programme from the Palau de la Virreina arts information office (p264).

MARCH & APRIL

DIVENDRES SANT/VIERNES SANTO (GOOD FRIDAY)

Although not celebrated with the verve it is accorded further south in Spain, you get a taste of this occasion with the Procesión del Padre Jesús del Gran Poder (Procession of Father Jesus of the Great Power) and the procession of the Virgen de la Macarena from the Església de Sant Agustí in El Raval on Good Friday. It starts at 5pm and ends in front of La Catedral three hours later.

Accompanying the huge image of the Virgin are solemn bands and members of *cofradías* (religious fraternities) dressed in robes and *capilotes* (tall conical hoods), who look alarmingly like members of the Ku Klux Klan. Most striking are the barefoot women penitents dressed in black and dragging heavy crosses and chains around their ankles. Emotional bystanders shed a tear while the less inhibited may be heard to cry out to the Virgin '*¡Guapa, guapa, guapa!*' (Beautiful, beautiful, beautiful!).

DIA DE SANT JORDI

Catalonia celebrates the feast of its patron saint (St George) on 23 April. At the same time, the Dia del Llibre (Day of the Book) is observed – men give women a rose, women give men a book, publishers launch new titles, the Premi Sant Jordi is awarded to the year's winning Catalan writer and La Rambla and Plaça de Sant Jaume fill with book and flower stalls.

FERIA DE ABRIL DE CATALUNYA

Andalucía comes to town with this traditional southern festival staged by and for the city's big Andalucian population. It lasts for about a week from late April and recently has been held in the Fòrum. People crowd into the *casetas* (tent stands) to sip sherry and munch on tapas.

MAY

L'OU COM BALLA

A curious tradition with several centuries of history, the 'Dancing Egg' is an empty shell that bobs on top of the flower-festooned fountain in the cloister of La Catedral. This spectacle is Barcelona's way of celebrating Corpus Christi (the Thursday after the eighth Sunday after Easter Sunday). Other dancing eggs can be seen on the same day in the courtyard of the Casa de l'Ardiaca and various other fountains in the Barri Gòtic.

FESTA DE SANT PONÇ

To commemorate the patron saint of beekeepers and herbalists, on 11 May locals fill Carrer de l'Hospital in El Raval with the chatter and bustle of a street market.

PRIMAVERA SOUND

www.primaverasound.com
For three days late in May (or early June) the Auditori Fòrum and other locations around town become the combined stage for a host of international DJs and musicians.

JUNE

SÓNAR

www.sonar.es
Sónar is Barcelona's celebration of electronic music and said to be Europe's biggest such event. Get into the latest house, hip-hop, trip-hop, eurobeat and any other new styles on offer, presented by local and international acts. Locations and dates change each year.

FESTIVAL DEL GREC

www.barcelonafestival.com
Many theatres shut down for summer, but into the breach steps this eclectic programme of theatre, dance and music, which lasts until well into August. Performances are held all over the city, not just at the Teatre Grec (Map pp304–5; Passeig de Santa Madrona; Ⓜ Espanya) amphitheatre on Montjuïc from which the festival takes its name.

DIA DE SANT JOAN/DÍA DE SAN JUAN BAUTISTA (FEAST OF ST JOHN THE BAPTIST)

The night before this feast day (24 June), the people of Barcelona hit the streets or hold parties at home to celebrate the Berbena de Sant Joan (St John's Night), which involves drinking, dancing and fireworks. The latter can be seen in districts all over town (and across Catalonia), which is why the evening is known as La Nit del Foc (Fire Night). The traditional pastry to eat on this summer solstice is a dense candied cake known as *coca de Sant Joan.*

DIA PER L'ALLIBERAMENT LESBIÀ I GAI

This is a gay and lesbian festival and parade that takes place on the Saturday nearest 28 June. The boisterous parade kicks off in the evening from Plaça de l'Universitat.

AUGUST

FESTA MAJOR DE GRÀCIA

www.festamajordegracia.org
This local festival, which takes place over about nine days around 15 August, is one of the biggest in Barcelona. More than a dozen streets in Gràcia are decorated by their inhabitants as part of a competition for the most imaginative street. Locals set up tables and benches to enjoy feasts, but people from all over the city pour in to participate. In squares (particularly Plaça del Sol) and intersections all over the *barri,* bands compete for attention. Snack stands abound and numerous bars open onto the streets to sell rivers of drink. Local residents who hope to get any sleep in this week tend to stay with friends or leave town!

FESTA MAJOR DE SANTS

The district of Sants launches its own weeklong version of decorated mayhem, held around 24 August, hard on Gràcia's heels.

SEPTEMBER

DIADA NACIONAL DE CATALUNYA

Catalonia's national day commemorates, curiously, Barcelona's surrender on 11 September 1714 to the Bourbon monarchy of Spain at the conclusion of the War of the Spanish Succession (see p63).

FESTES DE LA MERCÈ
www.bcn.es/merce

This four-day period of festivities sparks a final burst of prewinter madness, with the bulk of the activities taking place in the centre of town. Nostra Senyora de la Mercè (whose image lies in the church of the same name on Plaça de la Mercè) was elevated to co-patron of the city after she single-handedly beat off a plague of locusts in 1637! Then in 1714, as Barcelona faced defeat in the War of the Spanish Succession, town elders appointed her commander in chief of the city's defences (an eloquent expression of hopelessness if ever there was one).

This is the city's *festa major*. There's a swimming race across the harbour, a fun run, an outstanding series of free concerts organised under the auspices of Barcelona Acció Musical (BAM; www.bcn.es/bam), and a bewildering programme of cultural events. Adding to the local colour are all the ingredients of a major Catalan *festa: castellers, sardanes* (traditional Catalan folk dancing), parades of *gegants* and *capgrossos* (giants and big heads) and a huge *correfoc* (fire race). The latter is a pyromaniac's dream. It's held on the last night (a Sunday), and crowds hurl themselves through the streets before fire-spurting demons (not to mention kids armed with high-calibre firecrackers) who have been released from the Porta de l'Infern (Gate of Hell) near La Catedral.

Parade of capgrossos, Festes de la Mercè (above)

MOSTRA DE VINS I CAVES DE CATALUNYA
An excellent chance to taste a wide range of Catalan wine and *cava*, this expo is usually held at Maremàgnum over four days towards the end of September.

FESTA MAJOR DE LA BARCELONETA
Barcelona's party-goers have only a short wait until the next opportunity for merry-making. Although on a small scale, La Barceloneta's gig (to celebrate the local patron saint, Sant Miquel, on 29 September) lasts about a week and involves plenty of dancing and drinking (especially down on the beach).

OCTOBER
FESTIVAL DE CINE ERÓTICO
One of Europe's biggest porn-film fairs takes place in L'Hospitalet de Llobregat, between Barcelona and the airport, over about five days in early October. Barcelona is one Europe's biggest porn production centres. Whatever you make of this business, there's no doubting it attracts a lot of attention!

NOVEMBER
FESTIVAL INTERNACIONAL DE JAZZ DE BARCELONA
www.the-project.net

For most of the month (and sometimes the beginning of December too) the big venues (from the Auditori down) across town host a plethora of international jazz acts (such as the Dave Brubeck Quartet in 2005). Tickets cost between €15 and €50. At the same time, a more home-spun jazz fest takes place for about a month in bars across the old city. The Festival de Jazz de Ciutat Vella can run from late October or into December. Many of the performances are free.

DECEMBER
NADAL/NAVIDAD (CHRISTMAS)
Christmas is a fairly quiet family affair. Catalans tend to have their main Christmas dinner on Christmas Eve, although many have another big lunch the following day. An odd event to mark the occasion is the annual 200m swimming dash from Maremàgnum to the Moll de les Drassanes. Hundreds of hardy swimmers dive into the none-too-warm water for the race on what really should be a day for dealing with hangovers.

POO-POOING CHRISTMAS

One of the oddest things about Christmas is the *pessebres* (nativity scenes) that families set up at home (a giant one goes up in Plaça de Sant Jaume too) – you can see a display of them in an annex of the **Església de Betlem** (p85). These cribs are common throughout the Catholic world, and particularly in the Mediterranean. What makes them different here is the surprisingly scatological presence, along with the baby Jesus, Mary, Joseph and the three kings, of the *caganer* (crapper), a chap who has dropped his pants and is doing number twos (a symbol of fertility for the coming year). In 2005 one *caganer*-maker produced a version of Crown Prince Felipe and his wife Letizia in this position. No offence meant or taken apparently. On a similar note, the *caga tió* (poop log) is a wooden beast that 'lives' in the kitchen or dining room in the run-up to Christmas and has to be 'fed' (traditionally things like dry bread and water) so that on Christmas day it will *cagar* (shit) gifts. Once they were sweets. In some families they tend to be more substantial nowadays. The whole thing developed from a country tradition of placing a huge tree trunk (the *tió*) in the fireplace – its gifts in the misty past were simply the benefits of heat and light in the cold days of Christmas. Somewhere along the line the story became more, shall we say, sophisticated. You can buy your own *caganers* and let kids have a go hitting a *caga tió* with a stick to get a present at the Fira de Santa Llúcia, a Christmas market in front of La Catedral, in the weeks leading up to Christmas.

CULTURE

IDENTITY

Spain's second city, Barcelona counts 1.58 million souls, while the region of which it is capital, Catalonia (Catalunya) has 6.7 million. The bulk of them (five million) are crammed into Barcelona province, and frequently people talk of a greater Barcelona area taking in neighbouring towns to make a total population of around 4.5 million.

The Catalans are known as an entrepreneurial lot with a strong work ethic. Not as voluble as Spaniards from the south, the Catalans are not as tight-lipped as the taciturn central Castilians either. Indeed, like any port-city dwellers, they are a gregarious lot with a love of fine food and wine. They are particularly attached to groups and are inveterate joiners. Starting with the family, Catalans have a tendency to divide a lot of their lives into groups and clubs. Walking clubs, swimming clubs, chess clubs, you name it, they have one. No wonder FC Barcelona has such a huge membership: it epitomises the Catalan ethic of *fer pinya* (to pull together). This very clubiness can make the locals a little impervious to outside influences. Penetrating Catalan social circles requires time and patience!

While much of the rest of the region is largely Catalan in identity, Barcelona and its province is a mixed bag. Massive internal migration in the 1950s and 1960s brought 1.5 million Spaniards from other parts of the country to the capital and surrounding areas. The city still attracts people from other parts of the country and has long lost any uniformly Catalan feel. Although second and subsequent generations have come to speak Catalan, in many families Spanish (Castilian) remains the primary language.

The more affluent parts of the city and some central districts have a predominantly Catalan flavour, but things are again changing fast. Rapidly increasing immigration from abroad is altering the city's face. Almost 15% of the officially resident population are foreigners, and 35% in Ciutat Vella (Old City).

SWEET LITTLE BALLS

Wherever you come from, you have probably at some point sucked on one of Barcelona's best-known products. That's right, those little round boiled sweets on sticks, Chupa Chups, were invented right here. Enric Bernat (1923–2003), grandson of the first producer of *caramels* (sweets) in all Spain, went one better when he came up with the idea for the suckable sweet in 1958. Bernat had inherited an Asturian sweets factory and one of its products, which sold in those days for one peseta, struck him as having potential. Bernat modified the lolly and dubbed it Chups. A little ditty urged young 'uns to *'chupa Chups'* (suck on Chups). The song itself was such a success that Bernat had to change the name of the lollies to match, and later Salvador Dalí designed the logo. Seeing he had a winner on his hands, Bernat began to export the sweet associated with bald TV character Kojak, and later produced it all over the world, even in Russia and China. Today, 90% of sales are abroad.

The new arrivals have added a splash of colour to the urban panorama. The overwhelming majority are South Americans (especially from Ecuador and, more recently, Argentina), but there are also sizable contingents from Morocco and Pakistan (mostly living in El Raval). No-one really knows how many unregistered illegal immigrants *(clandestinos)* live in the city.

Nominally, most Catalans are Catholics, although one study says that more than half of young Catalans declare themselves nonreligious. Barcelona's working class has, since the 19th century, given the city a reddish political hue. The traditionally close association of the Church with centralist governments in Madrid and especially Franco has done little to endear much of Barcelona's population to priests. Church-burning was a recurring pastime from the Setmana Tràgica in 1909 to the Civil War. The region's principal lay movement, the Liga por la Laicidad, campaigns to have religious studies (which costs Catalan taxpayers €25 million a year) dropped from public school programmes, much to the annoyance of the clergy.

Immigrants have brought with them other religions to Barcelona. Most numerous are Protestants, Jehovah's Witnesses and Muslims. Much smaller groups include Jews, Buddhists, Hindus, Sikhs, Orthodox, Bahai, Adventists and Taoists.

LIFESTYLE

Barcelonins come in many different sizes and flavours. The affluent folk of La Zona Alta, often descendents of the industrial barons of the 19th century, or in some other way tied to the business, political, legal and media elite, live the high life. The richest luxuriate in mansions surrounded by gardens and love nothing better than to parade around the clubs and restaurants north of Avinguda Diagonal. The true arbiters of power meet for dinner, drinks and dancing in the Círculo Equestre (Equestrian Club) on the right (north) side of Avinguda Diagonal.

Some members of this tribe, universally known as *pijos,* venture south of that line, especially to sample the eateries and shops in the Quadrat d'Or (Golden Sq) – the blocks on either side of Passeig de Gràcia. They have a predilection for designer labels, plastic surgery, sports cars and 4WDs, and usually sport a perma-tan. Most have at least one getaway residence on the Costa Brava and probably a sprawling *masia* (farmhouse) in the Alt Empordà (northern Catalonia). And winter weekends wouldn't be quite right without the occasional chichi ski trip to Baqueira-Beret in the Pyrenees.

A rather more mixed crowd of long-standing middle-class folk, modest professionals who have worked hard to ensure a comfortable if not spectacular lifestyle, inhabits much of the l'Eixample grid section of town. Their typical apartments are long, tunnel-like affairs, often around 100 sq metres, with windows on the street and on to the block's internal courtyard. Some giant flats of 200 sq metres or more survive, but soaring prices since the late 1990s have led increasingly to subdivision. And everyone longs to have a private *terrassa* (terrace), great for breakfast in the sun and rooftop dinner parties.

Other tribes live in other parts of town. Catalans are increasingly abandoning Ciutat Vella to foreigners, whether to South American, Pakistani and North African migrants in the more crowded and once slummy areas such as El Raval and around the Mercat de Santa Caterina, or to cashed-up Europeans with romantic visions who choose to live in the heart of the medieval Barri Gòtic or über-trendy El Born.

Gràcia, on the other hand, remains relatively intact as a middleclass enclave of younger Catalans with a slightly self-consciously boho leaning. Its restaurants and bars and lack of tourist-attracting sights make up for its noisy, narrow streets.

Locals love to head out in gregarious bands to *tapear* (eat tapas in one bar after another) or dine in the city's thousands of restaurants. Dinner at home with friends, long a minority activity, has become more popular in recent years as the price of going out has sky-rocketed. One happy piece of news to report is that, hard-working or not, Catalans have not abandoned the tradition of the long lunch.

After dinner, it's off to one of the seemingly endless bars splashed across the city. Few Barcelonins allow themselves to get blind drunk. They love a tipple – and the tipples are generous – but keep it under control. After all, many have to last until the next dawn and the object is enjoyment, not making themselves ill in as short a time as possible.

FASHION

Barcelona's fashion industry was dealt a blow in 2006 when the Generalitat (regional Catalan government) finally decided to pull the plug on the city's Pasarela Gaudí fashion show. The Catalan catwalk had for years been competing with Madrid's Pasarela Cibeles show and was lagging far behind the big shows in Paris, Milan and London. For years up to 80% of its funding had come from public funds.

When the going gets tough, the tough get going and so a clutch of top Barcelona designers opted to create a new show, Pasarela Barcelona. The likes of Custo Barcelona, perhaps motivated by a sudden flair of local patriotism, led the way. The government funding may have been cut, but not all the news is bad. The successful Berlin Bread & Butter urban streetwear show, first staged in the German capital in 2000, started staging a Barcelona edition in 2005, with a great deal more success than the Pasarela Gaudí. Its promoters are so pleased that they have committed to staging summer and winter events here until at least 2008.

Another local stalwart who signed on for the Pasarela Barcelona is Joaquim Verdú, who has been making men's and women's clothes since 1977. He was joined by Antonio Miró, born in nearby Sabadell and also well established on the international circuit. He designed the Spanish team's uniforms for the 1992 Olympic Games and even does a line in designer furniture.

Further local names or Barcelona-based designers to watch include David Valls, Josep Font, Armand Basi, Purificación García, Konrad Muhr, Sita Murt and TCN.

In the *prêt-a-porter* department, Mango is a big Barcelona success story. Based outside the city in the Vallès area, it has more than 900 stores throughout the world (in locations as far-flung as Vietnam and London's Oxford St), and has come a long way since opening its first store on Passeig de Gràcia in 1984. Mango is now one of Spain's largest textile exporters, specialising in women's fashion.

With so much talent around them, it is hardly surprising that Barcelonins like to dress in style. They have no shortage of outlets to look for their favourite designers. The city's premier shopping boulevards, Passeig de Gràcia and Avinguda Diagonal, are lined with all the international and Spanish rag-trade names. If l'Eixample is the classy shopping mecca for fashion victims, there's plenty more in the old town. The Barri Gòtic and El Born are peppered with shops sporting all sorts of youthful fashion, unfettered by convention or macroeconomic considerations. For grunge and secondhand clothing, people gravitate towards Carrer de la Riera Baixa in El Raval.

MUCHO GUSTO, MR CUSTO

Custo (actually Custodio Dalmau) and his brother David, from Lleida and now based in Barcelona, have become hot fashion property since breaking into the tough US women's fashion market in the early 2000s. Indeed, the light and breezy brand has become something of a cult obsession with women around the world. Their ever-cosmopolitan, inventive and often provocative mix of colours, especially in their hallmark tops, are miles away from the more conservative, classic fashion tastes that still dominate some sectors of Barcelona high society. Maybe that's why the Dalmau brothers concentrated their initial efforts on the USA. Although they cover most angles of feminine clothing, they're keeping the emphasis on their over-the-top tops.

SPORT

Football

Football in Barcelona has the aura of religion about it. It pervades the air and, for much of the city's population, support of its premier side, FC Barcelona, is taken for granted as an article of faith. The reality is a little different because the city has another hardy, if less illustrious, side, Espanyol. If FC Barcelona is traditionally associated with the Catalans and even Catalan nationalism, Espanyol is often identified with Spanish immigrants from other parts of the country.

It all started on 29 November 1899, when Swiss Hans Gamper founded FC Barcelona (Barça) four years after English residents had first played the game here. His choice of club colours, the blue and maroon of his home town, Winterthur, have stuck. The following year Espanyol was formed. It distinguished itself from the other sides, ironically, by being formed solely of Catalans and other Spaniards. Most other sides, including FC Barcelona, were made up mostly of foreigners.

By 1910 FC Barcelona was the premier club in a rapidly growing league. The first signs of professionalism emerged – paid transfers of players were recorded and Espanyol's management charged spectators. Barça had 560 members (about 130,000 today), who were all chuffed at the team's victory at that year's national championship.

City Life CULTURE

A match at Camp Nou (p116) can be a breathtaking event. Although games here do not generate the hooligan trouble associated with some teams in, for instance, the UK, FC Barcelona is not completely exempt from the problem. Els Boixos Nois (Mad Boys) are a rowdy minority of roughnecks who, when they get in, usually gather behind the northern goal. The police generally keep a close watchful eye on them. For more on how to see a game, see p195.

After several years in the desert, FC Barcelona found its form again under charismatic Dutch trainer Frank Rijkaard and won the 2004–05 premiership. The following season they seemed invincible and, in spite of a slippery patch late in the proceedings, seized the premiership well in front of nearest rivals Real Madrid and Valencia. If the city was delirious with joy at the premiership victory, it was positively beside itself when the dream team went on to win the European Champion's League trophy in a tight game with London's Arsenal. Meanwhile, the city's cinderella team, Espanyol, also took accolades by defeating Zaragoza to take the Copa del Rey, the equivalent of the UK's FA Cup, in 2006.

Barça is one of only three teams (the others are Real Madrid and Athletic de Bilbao) never to have been relegated to the second division. Since the league got fully under way in 1928, Barça has emerged champion 17 times, second only to archrivals Real Madrid (with 29 victories). Between them the two have virtually monopolised the game – only seven other teams have managed to come out on top (three of them only once or twice) in almost 70 years of the competition.

Bullfighting

Hemingway called it death in the afternoon and, like so many things in Barcelona, it is a subject of controversy and political demagogy. In 2004 the city council narrowly voted for a symbolic declaration that Barcelona was anti-bullfighting. Animal rights groups, who oppose la lidia (bullfighting), were delighted. But there was more to the vote than meets the eye. Promoted by the Esquerra Republicana de Catalunya (ERC, Republican Left of Catalonia) independence party, the declaration stands in line with the common claim that bullfighting is a Spanish cultural imposition on Catalonia, largely loathed by right-thinking Catalans.

There is little doubt that this spectacle of bravado, often described by its followers as a noble art, is quintessentially Spanish. But it is equally a part of tradition in Portugal and parts of southern France. And the first bullfight in Barcelona was held in 1387, long before Catalonia was subordinated to Castilian overlordship.

Catalans may or may not be less enthusiastic about bullfighting than other Spaniards (vegetarian anarchists banned it during the Civil War years in Barcelona), but this doesn't stop them from staging a season at the Plaça de Braus Monumental bullring on the corner of Carrer de la Marina and Gran Via de les Corts Catalanes, usually on Sunday afternoons in spring and summer.

On an afternoon ticket there are generally six bulls and perhaps three star matadors (those bullfighters who do most of the fighting and then kill the bull at the end). The matador leads a *cuadrilla* (team) of other fighters who make up the rest of the colourful band that appears in the ring. It is a complex business, but in essence the matadors aim to impress the crowd and jury with daring and graceful moves as close to an aggressive, fighting bull as possible. While the death of the bull is generally inevitable (its meat is later sold), this in no way implies the bullfighter always gets off scot-free. It is a genuinely dangerous business, and being gored and tossed by several hundred kilos of bull is no fun.

While few modern fighters match the courage and skill of former greats such as Luis Miguel Dominguín (1926–96) or Rafael Ortega (1921–97), there are some stars to look out for. They include Jesulín de Ulbrique, Julián 'El Juli' López, 'Joselito' (José Miguel Arroyo) and El Cordobés (Manuel Díaz). Local *toreros* include Manolo Porcel and Serafín Marin.

For information on how to see a bullfight in Barcelona, see p195.

Basketball

FC Barcelona's basketball players are top-notch, winning 14 premier league competitions since 1946. It has also taken a host of other trophies, including the Copa del Rey (18 times) and two European titles. For information on how to see a game, see p195.

LANGUAGE

Barcelona is a bilingual city. The mother tongue of born-and-bred locals is Catalan, which belongs to the group of Western European languages that grew out of Latin (Romance languages), including Italian, French, Spanish and Portuguese. By the 12th century it was a clearly established language with its own nascent literature. The language was most closely related to *langue d'oc*, the southern French derivative of Latin that was long the principal tongue in Gallic lands. The most conspicuous survivor of *langue d'oc* is the now little-used Provençal. Catalan followed its speakers' conquests and was introduced to the Balearic Islands and Valencia. It is also spoken in parts of eastern Aragón, and was for a while carried as far afield as Sardinia (where it still survives, just, in Alghero).

Alongside Catalan, Spanish is also an official (and for many non-Catalans the only) language. Since 1980 Catalan regional governments have done everything in their power to reintroduce Catalan as the main idiom of daily life. To what degree this campaign, referred to as *normalització lingüística* (linguistic normalisation), has been successful depends largely on whom you ask, and is the subject of unending polemics.

MESSAGE IN THE MEDIUM

Much of the Spanish media makes little effort to hide its political affiliations. The respected national daily, *El País*, born out of the early days of democracy in the 1970s, is closely aligned to the PSOE (Spanish Socialist Workers' Party). Many Catalans find its political coverage overwhelmingly biased towards the PSOE. *ABC*, on the other hand, is a long-standing organ of the conservative right and readily identified with the Partido Popular. Catalans, by their choice of paper, make political statements. Reading the local Spanish-language and slightly conservative *La Vanguardia* is a clear vote for local product, while *Avui*, a loss-maker that is backed by the Generalitat, is stridently Catalan nationalist. See also p261.

It is not much different in the electronic media. The most important local stations, such as the Catalan government's TV-3 and Canal 33, while they sometimes have interesting programming, push an almost constant Catalan line. Documentaries on the Civil War, the horrors of the Franco period and so forth abound, while investigative journalism on some of the dodgier sides of Catalan government since 1980 are noticeable by their strict absence. See also p263.

WAR OF WORDS

Since Barcelona was crushed in the War of the Spanish Succession in 1714, the use of Catalan has been repeatedly banned. Franco was the last of Spain's rulers to clamp down on it.

People in the country and small towns largely ignored the bans, but intellectual circles in Barcelona and other cities only 'rediscovered' Catalan with the Renaixença at the end of the 19th century (see p65). Franco loosened the reins a little from the 1960s on, but all education in Catalan schools remained exclusively in Spanish until after the dictator's demise in 1975.

Since the first autonomous regional parliament was assembled in 1980, the Generalitat (Catalan government) has waged an unstinting campaign to 'normalise' the use of Catalan. The Generalitat reckons about 95% of the population in Catalonia understand Catalan and nearly 70% speak it. In Valencia, about half the population speak it, as do 65% in the Balearic Islands. The big problem is that not nearly as many can write it. Even in Catalonia only about 40% of the population write Catalan satisfactorily.

In Catalonia today it is impossible to get a public-service job without fluency in Catalan. New regulations to be approved in 2006 will make fluency in Catalan a favourable factor (but not prerequisite) for judges wishing to transfer to Catalonia. It's not so easy in the private sector either. And just as Franco had all signs in Catalan replaced, Spanish road signs, advertising and the like are now harder to find.

About 80% of primary education is in Catalan, and about 50% of secondary. A law passed in 2002 provides professors who teach in Catalan with financial incentives. Complex content rules mean that certain radio and TV stations must include a minimum fixed percentage of programming in Catalan (including even music played). On certain chat programmes you'll occasionally strike hosts speaking Catalan, with their interlocutors answering in Spanish. On the other hand, movies dubbed or subtitled in Catalan are virtually nonexistent. The Catalan government hailed the decision in 2005 allowing the use of Catalan in EU institutions as 'historic'.

A 1998 law provides for fines to be applied in certain situations, for example where companies do not label products or put up signs in Catalan (as well as Spanish if they so choose). That law has rarely been applied with any vigour, but the head of the right-wing Partido Popular, Mariano Rajoy, declared in early 2006 that Spanish was being pushed underground in the same way Catalan had been under Franco – a fairly silly assertion rejected even by some of his Catalan party colleagues.

ECONOMY & COSTS

Barcelona has a reputation for being a hard-working industrial and mercantile city. The roots of its trading culture lie in the days of Mediterranean empire-building, but industry first stirred to life in the small-scale textile factories that emerged during the 18th century.

More than 25% of Spanish exports come from the greater metropolitan area of Barcelona – more than Madrid, Bilbao and Valencia put together! Three-quarters of Catalan industry is in or near the capital. Although Barcelona is increasingly concerned by Madrid's place as the hub of finance and business in Spain, there are plenty of signs that Barcelona remains strong. Some 44% of all inward investment in Spain poured into Catalonia in 2005, most of it in Barcelona (which is reckoned to be the sixth biggest recipient of foreign investment among European cities). National inflation (4.2%) is relatively high, and higher still in Catalonia (4.6%), but unemployment in Catalonia is down to 6.6%, the lowest since 1978. The national rate is 8.7%.

Across Catalonia about 60% of the working population is employed in the services sector, 36% in industry and 4% in agriculture. Alongside traditional industries like textiles, leather goods, chemicals, pharmaceuticals, car production (the Volkswagen-owned Seat plant in nearby Martorell) and cosmetics, the regional government and city council are making a concerted effort to project Barcelona into the front rank of hi-tech industries. The new biomedical research park in La Barceloneta is emblematic, and the region aims to see more than 100 new biomedical companies created by 2020. El Poblenou is being revamped as the 22@bcn district for concentrating hi-tech and media companies. The Generalitat must be frustrated that private investment in R&D dropped from 2.4% of Catalan GDP in 2001 to 2.1% in 2004. The official goal is that it should reach 5.2% by 2008.

One of the main pillars of Barcelona's economy is tourism. It represents around 15% of the city's GDP, and 4.6 million visitors came to the city in 2005. More than one million cruise ship passengers dock in Barcelona each year. New facilities completed in 2005 made it the biggest cruise-ship port in Europe, and the most popular. For the first time ever, the Queen Mary 2 included Barcelona (and other Mediterranean ports) on its New York–Europe run in 2005. A growing number of tourists are coming to Barcelona as a starting point for Mediterranean cruises. The container port will double in size by 2008 and have direct rail links by 2011 (which should cut truck traffic considerably).

Barcelona is not the cheap city it once was, but still more so than many other major European destinations. A midrange hotel double room can cost anything from €60 to €180, and a quality meal €30 to €40. On the other hand, simple, filling lunchtime set meals can cost under €10, and many museums have free admission days (they are noted in the Sights chapter).

HOW MUCH?

1L of mineral water in a supermarket €0.35

1L of unleaded petrol €0.95

330mL bottle of Estrella Voll Damm beer €2.50 to €4

A tapa €1.50 to €3

Cocktail €6 to €8

Entrance to La Sagrada Família €8

Good midrange meal €30 to €40

La Vanguardia newspaper €1

Postage for a normal letter (up to 20g) within Europe €0.57

Souvenir T-shirt €10 to €24

GOVERNMENT & POLITICS

Political life in Barcelona has been dominated since 2005 by the inflammatory negotiations to reform the 1979 devolution statute that sets out the degree of Catalonia's regional autonomy. The new statute, the result of a compromise package hammered out by the national parliament in Madrid, went into effect in mid-2006.

At a national level, the right-wing opposition Partido Popular (PP) has accused the government, led by José Luis Rodríguez Zapatero, of setting Spain on the road to self-destruction. This policy of fomenting national tension has marked the PP's time in opposition since being ousted from office in March 2004 by Zapatero's Partido Socialista Obrero Español (PSOE, Spanish Socialist Workers' Party).

A little background: the Generalitat de Catalunya (the regional Catalan government) was resurrected by royal decree in 1977. Its power as an autonomous government is enshrined in the statutes of the Spanish constitution of 1978, and by the Estatut d'Autonomia (devolution statute). The Govern (executive) is housed in the Palau de la Generalitat on Plaça de Sant Jaume. The Generalitat has wide powers over matters such as education, health, trade, industry, tourism and agriculture.

Jordi Pujol's nationalist, right-of-centre Convergència i Unió (CiU) coalition remained in power in Catalonia from 1980 to 2003. Pujol's successor, Artur Mas, won the most votes at the November 2003 elections but failed to ward off an unsteady left-wing coalition headed by Pasqual Maragall, leader of the Partit Socialista de Catalunya (PSC, the Catalan branch of the PSOE) and popular former mayor of Barcelona, Josep

The Ajuntament (p88), Plaça de St Jaume

Lluís Carod-Rovira's ERC and the green party, Joan Saura's Iniciativa Verds-Esquerra Unida (Green Initiative-United Left).

Things are quieter in the Ajuntament (town hall), which stands opposite the Palau de la Generalitat in Plaça de St Jaume and has traditionally been a Socialist haven. Joan Clos, Maragall's PSC successor as mayor in 1997, narrowly won his electoral challenge in 2003 and in any case is unlikely to be replaced by anyone other than another PSC candidate in future polls.

Elections to the Ajuntament and Generalitat take place every four years. They are free and by direct universal suffrage. The members of each house thus elect then vote for the president of the Generalitat and the mayor.

Barcelona is divided into 10 *districtes municipals* (municipal districts), each with its own *ajuntament*.

ENVIRONMENT

THE LAND

Barcelona spreads along the Catalan coast in what is known as the Pla de Barcelona (Barcelona Plain), midway between the French border and the regional frontier with Valencia. The plain averages about 4m above sea level. Mont Taber, the little elevation upon which the Romans built their town, is 15m above sea level. To the southwest, Montjuïc is 173m high.

Urban sprawl tends to be channelled southwest and northeast along the coast, as the landwards side is effectively blocked off by the Serralada Litoral mountain chain, which between the Riu Besòs and Riu Llobregat is known as the Serra de Collserola. Tibidabo is the highest point of this chain at 512m, with commanding views across the whole city.

Badalona to the northeast and L'Hospitalet to the southwest mark the municipal boundaries of the city – although, as you drive through them, you'd never know where they begin and end. To the north, the Riu Besòs (so successfully cleaned up in recent years that otters have been spotted in it for the first time since the 1970s!) in part marks the northern limits of the city. The Riu Llobregat, which rises in the Pyrenees, empties into the Mediterranean just south of L'Hospitalet. On the southern side of the river is El Prat de Llobregat and Barcelona's airport.

GREEN BARCELONA

Serious concentrations of green are few and far between in Barcelona, but there are some exceptions. Closest to the town centre is the Parc de la Ciutadella, with the regional parliament and zoo. Tacked on to the northeast flank of La Ribera, the park can make a pleasant escape from the pressure-cooker effect of the city.

The main green lung is the hill of Montjuïc, which rises behind the port. Extensive landscaped gardens surround the Olympic stadium, swimming pools, art galleries, museums, cemeteries and the fort, making it a wonderful spot for walks.

The city is bordered to the west by the Serra de Collserola, which serves as another smog filter and is laced with walks and bicycle paths. Declared a Natural Park in September 2006, it is however under increasing pressure from urban development around and in part within it. Experts warn that it will soon be cut off from other green areas beyond Barcelona, which would be a disaster for the local fauna.

About 35% of the trees that line Barcelona's streets and parks are plane trees. Others include acacias and nettle trees.

ENVIRONMENTAL ISSUES

A 2006 report by the Ministry for the Environment stated that Barcelona was among the cities in Spain with the worst air pollution, although the levels have more than halved since 1980. The single biggest source (85%) of unhealthy air is private vehicles. In reaction, parking and traffic restrictions in central Barcelona have been tightened and the city's buses are being progressively replaced by new models powered by compressed natural gas. Three experimental hydrogen-powered buses are also in service.

Barcelona is leading the way in research on photovoltaic energy. In 2004 a huge photovoltaic panel was set up in the Fòrum near the Riu Besòs and another, double in size, will be in place by late 2007. The panels will be used also for solar energy research. In 2005 Barcelona was chosen as the administrative centre for the international ITER thermonuclear research plant being built in France.

Although much depends on the goodwill of citizens, rubbish disposal is not too bad. Large, brightly coloured containers have been scattered about the city for the separated collection of paper, glass and cans, and they are emptied daily.

Every night the city streets are hosed down, but every day they wind up dirty again. Some areas (such as much of Ciutat Vella) are worse than others (such as l'Eixample). Countless dogs make an unpleasant contribution to the walkways, while at night not a few humans add to the stench with rivers of pee (hopefully the new €300 fines introduced in 2006 for this activity will bring relief).

Noise pollution is also a problem, again especially in parts of the old city (notably around El Born and in El Raval). Rowdy traffic, late-night rubbish collection, day-long construction and roadworks, and the screaming and shouting of revellers, all contribute to insomnia. Residents of areas such as El Born can put all the signs they want on their balconies demanding quiet, but it seems to make little difference. For many, double or even triple glazing is the only answer (not much help in summer).

URBAN PLANNING & DEVELOPMENT

The eminent British architect and town planner, Lord Richard Rogers, declared in 2000 that Barcelona was 'perhaps the most successful city in the world in terms of urban regeneration'.

That process, which got under way in earnest with the 1992 Olympic Games, thunders ahead. No sooner is one area given a new look, than another becomes the subject of modernisation. The number and dimension of the projects underway is staggering.

The recent €2.5 billion Diagonal Mar plan focused on the Fòrum area along the northeast stretch of coast up to the Riu Besòs. High-rise hotels and apartment blocks, a sprawling shopping centre, sculpted parks, a marina, convention centres and solar panels are part of the package. The zoo will eventually be moved here too. This mini-Manhattan-by-the-sea has completely transformed the city skyline, which with a few exceptions was resolutely low-rise. For more on the key buildings on the site, see p45.

The Ajuntament is turning parts of El Poblenou (117 blocks to be precise) into the hi-tech 22@bcn precinct. One former factory that takes up a whole block of Avinguda Diagonal near Plaça de les Glòries Catalanes will become the Parc Barcelona Mèdia, a huge audiovisual centre. Hi-tech companies are being encouraged to move into the phallic Torre Agbar (p102). To the north, the Sagrera area will be transformed by the new high-speed railway station and transport interchange, complemented by a series of buildings with Frank Gehry's signature.

To the southwest along Gran Via, a whole new trade-fair complex is being developed, along with the new Ciutat Judicial (a complex that houses approximately 200 courtrooms, along with shops and other businesses) in l'Hospitalet.

Further funds have been released for the renovation of the city centre. Slowly, parts of the Barri Gòtic, La Ribera and El Raval that were depressed and abandoned are being brought back to life. In El Raval a new boulevard, La Rambla del Raval, was opened in 2001 and is finally attracting attention. The streets around it remain dodgy, but plans are in place for a new hotel (designed by local doyen of architecture Oriol Bohigas) and shopping complex.

Arts

Arts

Few places are humming in Spain the way Barcelona is. After decades of torpor in the Franco years, it is like a permanent bottle of *cava* bubbling forth. This is as true in the world of the arts as in other aspects of the city's life. Although not always world class, the city's cultural scene is nothing if not busy.

The city has had a bit of a stop-start history, however. At the height of its power in the Middle Ages, the city and Catalonia were a cauldron of activity in painting and sculpture. By the time the Renaissance filtered across from Italy, however, the region's stark decline seemed to shut off much of its creative talent too. Only in the 19th century was there something of a reawakening, but an uneven one. Alongside a small coterie of good but not world-class artists emerged three of the geniuses of the 20th century: Picasso, Dalí and Miró. Since their eclipse, a bevy of artists has been at work, and an eager new generation is coming through.

With literature, it was much the same. Important works in medieval Catalan survive, and then a centuries-long void was only broken in the 19th century. Some of Spain's top writers are Catalans. Many today write in Spanish (Castilian), which is understandable, given that their potential readership is much greater than in Catalan! That has not stopped the emergence of literature in Catalan in the past few decades. Theatre, on the other hand, is more often than not presented in Catalan, generally in translation of foreign works but with a component of original home-grown material too.

TOP FIVE MUSEUMS

- Museu Barbier-Mueller d'Art Pre-Colombí (p95)
- Museu d'Història de la Ciutat (p87)
- Museu Marítim (p92)
- Museu-Monestir de Pedralbes (p113)
- Museu Nacional d'Art de Catalunya (p121)

The region's pop and rock bands have fewer qualms about singing in their regional tongue, and the scene is busy. In general, the Iberian contribution to great classical music has been thin, but an unusually high proportion of the Spain's leading composers and opera figures hail from Catalonia. Catalonia may not seem like classic flamenco country, but a surprising number of its stars were born in Catalonia.

Various Catalan filmmakers are busy at work, but rarely has a film made in Catalan met with much success.

PAINTING & SCULPTURE

THE MIDDLE AGES

Many anonymous artists left their work behind in medieval Catalonia, mostly in the form of frescoes, altarpieces and the like in Romanesque and Gothic churches. But a few leading lights managed to get some credit. Gothic painter Ferrer Bassá (c 1290–1348) was one of the region's first recognised masters. Influenced by the Italian school of Siena, his few surviving works include murals with a slight touch of caricature in the Monestir de Pedralbes (p113).

Bernat Martorell (1400–52), a master of chiaroscuro who was active in the mid-15th century, was one of the region's leading exponents of International Gothic. As the Flemish school gained influence, painters such as Jaume Huguet (1415–92) adopted its sombre realism, lightening the style with Hispanic splashes of gold, as in his *Sant Jordi* in the Museu Nacional d'Art de Catalunya (p121). Another of his paintings hangs in the Museu Frederic Marès (p88).

In the latter museum you may be overwhelmed by the collection of medieval wooden sculpture. Mostly anonymous sculptors were busy throughout Catalonia from at least the 12th century, carving religious images for the growing number of churches. Although saints and other characters sometimes figured, by far the most common subjects were Christ crucified and the Virgin Mary with the Christ child sitting on her lap.

Another source of exquisite sculpture lies in VIP sarcophagi. Examples range from the alabaster memorial to Santa Eulàlia in La Catedral (p84) to the pantheon of count-kings in the Reial-Monestir de Santa Maria de Poblet (see the boxed text, p245) outside Barcelona.

TOP FIVE GALLERIES

- CaixaForum (p118)
- Fundació Antoni Tàpies (p104)
- Fundació Joan Miró (p120)
- Museu d'Art Contemporani de Barcelona (p92)
- Museu Picasso (p96)

FORTUNY'S CENTURY

It is fair to say that little of greatness was achieved in the field of Catalan painting and sculpture from the end of the Middle Ages to the 19th century. Barcelona neither produced nor attracted any El Grecos, Velázquezs, Goyas, Zurbaráns or Murillos.

By the mid-19th century, however, Realisme was the modish medium on canvas, reaching something of a zenith with the work of Marià Fortuny (1838–74). The best known (and largest) of his paintings is the 'official' version of the *Batalla de Tetuán* (Battle of Tetuán; 1863), depicting the rousing Spanish victory over a ragtag Moroccan enemy in North Africa. Fortuny, whom many consider the best Catalan artist of the 19th century, left his native turf for Italy in 1857, where he died in Rome aged just 36. He had lived for a time in Venice, where his lodgings now constitute a gallery of his works.

MODERNISME & NOUCENTISME

As the years progressed, painters developed a greater eye for intimate detail and less enthusiasm for epic themes; this led painters into Anecdotisme, out of which emerged a fresher generation of artists – the modernistas of the turn of the 20th century. Influenced by their French counterparts (Paris was seen as Europe's artistic capital), the modernistas allowed themselves greater freedom in interpretation than the Realists. They sought not so much to portray observed 'reality' as to interpret it subjectively and infuse it with flights of their own fantasy. Ramón Casas (1866–1932) and Santiago Rusiñol (1861–1931) were the most important exponents of the new forms of art in Barcelona. The former was a wealthy dilettante of some talent, the latter a more earnest soul who ran a close second. Both were the toast of the bohemian set in turn-of-the-20th-century Barcelona, but neither was destined for greatness. The single best collection of works by these two artists is on show in the Museu Nacional d'Art de Catalunya.

In a similar class was Josep Llimona (1864–1934), the most prolific and prominent sculptor of the late 19th century and on into the 1930s. His works can be seen scattered about town today, ranging from the statue to Ramon Berenguer el Gran on the square of the same name just off Via Laietana to friezes on the Monument a Colom (p86). Although often classed as a modernista, his style was nevertheless in constant development across a long career.

Museu Nacional d'Art de Catalunya (p121), Montjuïc

From about 1910, as modernisme fizzled, the more conservative cultural movement Noucentisme (loosely '20th centuryism'!) sought, in general, to advance Catalonia by looking backwards. The Noucentistas demanded a return to a 'healthier' classicism, clarity and 'Mediterranean light' after the 'excesses' of the modernistas. From about 1917, a second wave of Noucentistas challenged these notions, which had begun to feel like an artistic straitjacket.

Among the Noucentistas, Joaquim Sunyer (1874–1956) and Isidre Nonell (1876–1911) were clearly influenced by the likes of Cézanne; some of their works can be seen in the Museu Nacional d'Art de Catalunya. They were soon to be overshadowed by true genius.

20TH-CENTURY MASTERS

Pablo Picasso

Born in Málaga in Andalucía, Pablo Ruiz Picasso (1881–1973) was already sketching by the age of nine. After a stint in La Coruña (in Galicia), he landed in Barcelona in 1895. His father had obtained a post teaching art at the Escola de Belles Artes de la Llotja (housed in the stock exchange building) and had his son enrolled there too. It was in Barcelona and Catalonia that Picasso matured, spending his time ceaselessly drawing and painting.

After a stint at the Escuela de Bellas Artes de San Fernando in Madrid in 1897, Picasso spent six months with his friend Manuel Pallarès in bucolic Horta de Sant Joan, in western Catalonia – he would later claim that it was there he learned everything he knew. In Barcelona Picasso lived and worked in the Barri Gòtic and El Raval (where he was introduced to the seamier side of life in the Barri Xinès).

By the time Picasso moved to France in 1904, he had explored his first highly personal style. In this so-called Blue Period, his canvases have a melancholy feel heightened by the trademark dominance of dark blues. Some of his portraits and cityscapes from this period were created in and inspired by what he saw in Barcelona. Plenty of pieces from this period hang in the Museu Picasso (p96).

This was followed by the Pink (or Rose) Period, in which Picasso's subjects became merrier and the colouring leaned towards light pinks and greys.

Picasso was a turbulent character and gifted not only as a painter but as a sculptor, graphic designer and ceramicist. Down the years, his work encompassed many style changes. With *Les Demoiselles d'Avignon* (Ladies of Avignon; 1907), Picasso broke with all forms of traditional representation, introducing a deformed perspective that would later spill over into cubism. The subject was supposedly taken from the Carrer d'Avinyó in the Barri Gòtic, in those days populated with a series of brothels.

By the mid-1920s he was dabbling with surrealism. His best-known work is *Guernica* (in Madrid's Centro de Arte Reina Sofia), a complex painting portraying the horror of war, inspired by the German aerial bombing of the Basque town Gernika in 1937.

Picasso worked prolifically during and after WWII and he was still cranking out paintings, sculptures, ceramics and etchings until the day he died in 1973.

Joan Miró

By the time the 13-year-old Picasso arrived in Barcelona, his near contemporary, Joan Miró (1893–1983), was cutting his teeth on rusk biscuits in the Barri Gòtic, where he was born and would spend his younger years. Indeed, he passed a third of his life in his hometown. Later in life he divided his time between France, the Tarragona countryside and the island of Mallorca, where he ended his days.

Like Picasso, Miró attended the Escola de Belles Artes de la Llotja. He was a shy man

Fundació Joan Miró (p120), Montjuïc

STREET TREATS

Barcelona hosts an array of street sculpture, from Miró's 1983 *Dona i Ocell* (Map pp296–7), which stands in the park dedicated to the artist, to *Peix* (Fish; Map pp302–3), Frank Gehry's shimmering, bronze coloured headless fish facing Port Olímpic. Halfway along La Rambla, at Plaça de la Boqueria, you can walk all over Miró's *Mosaïc de Miró*. Picasso left an open-air mark with his design on the façade of the Col.legi de Arquitectes (Map pp298–9) building opposite La Catedral in the Barri Gòtic.

Others you may want to keep an eye out for are *Barcelona's Head* (Map pp302–3) by Roy Lichtenstein at the Port Vell end of Via Laietana and Fernando Botero's characteristically tumescent *El Gat* (Map pp298–9) on Rambla del Raval.

Perhaps the weirdest monument is what looks like a pile of square rusty containers with windows leaning precariously, like so many dice, on Platja de Sant Sebastià. Made in 1992 by Rebecca Horn, it is called *Homenatge a la Barceloneta* (Homage to La Barceloneta; Map pp302–3). A little further south is the 2003 *Homenatge als Nedadors* (Homage to Swimmers), a complex metallic rendition of swimmers and divers in the water by Alfredo Lanz. Odder is Antoni Tàpies' 1983 *Homenatge a Picasso* (Homage to Picasso, also known as L'Estel Ferit, the Wounded Star; Map pp302–3) on Passeig de Picasso, a glass cube set in a pond and filled with, well, junk.

Antoni Llena's *David i Goliat* (Map pp302–3), a massive sculpture of tubular and sheet iron, in the Parc de les Cascades near Port Olímpic's two skyscrapers, looks like an untidy kite inspired by Halloween. Beyond, Avinguda d'Icària is lined by architect Enric Miralles' so-called *Pergoles*, bizarre, twisted metal contraptions that look like they might well take flight.

And who is taking the mickey at the bottom end of Rambla de Catalunya? The statue of a thinking bull is simply called *Meditation* (Map pp298–9), but one wonders what Rodin would make of it.

Perhaps one of the best known pieces of public art whimsy is Xavier Mariscal's *Gamba* (Prawn, although it is actually a crayfish; Map pp302–3) on Passeig de Colom. Stuck here in 1987 on the roof of the Gambrinus bar, when this strip was lined by popular designer bars (which unfortunately disappeared in the late 1990s), it became the object of a public tussle over ownership after the bar's closure. At one point it was rumoured that a Japanese association wanted to purchase it. In the end, Mariscal ceded the outsize 'prawn' to the city of Barcelona, which duly had it restored in 2004.

For a comprehensive look at street art (and much more), go to the city of Barcelona's main website (www.bcn.es) and click on Art Públic. Here you will find a host of files on public sculpture, modern and older, along with a host of other categories of art and architecture.

and initially uncertain about his artistic vocation – in fact he studied commerce. In Paris from 1920, he mixed with Picasso, Hemingway, Joyce and friends, and made his own mark, after several years of struggle, with an exhibition in 1925. The masterpiece from this, his so-called realist period, was *La Masia* (Farmhouse).

It was during WWII, while living in seclusion in Normandy, that Miró's definitive leitmotifs emerged. Among the most important images that appear frequently throughout his work are women, birds (the link between earth and the heavens), stars (the unattainable heavenly world, the source of imagination), and a sort of net entrapping all these levels of the cosmos. The Miró works that most people are acquainted with emerged from this time – arrangements of lines and symbolic figures in primary colours, with shapes reduced to their essence.

In the 1960s and '70s Miró devoted more of his time to creating sculpture and designing textiles, largely employing the same kinds of symbolic figures. He lived in Mallorca, home of his wife Pilar Juncosa, from 1956 until his death in 1983. The Fundació Joan Miró (p120) in Montjuïc has the single largest collection of Miró's work in the world.

Salvador Dalí

Although he spent precious little time in Barcelona, and nothing much of his can be seen in the city today, it would be churlish to leave Salvador Dalí i Domènech (1904–89) out of the picture. He was born and died in Figueres, where he left his single greatest artistic legacy, the Teatre-Museu Dalí (p232).

Prolific painter, showman, shameless self-promoter or just plain weirdo, Dalí was nothing if not a character – probably a little too much for the conservative small-town folk of

Figueres. By 1922 his name had appeared in Barcelona's press as an up-and-coming artist. Little did they know what was coming!

Every now and then a key moment arrives that can change the course of one's life. Dalí's came in 1929 when the French poet Paul Éluard visited Cadaqués with his Russian wife Gala. The rest, as they say, is histrionics. Dalí shot off to Paris to be with Gala and plunged into the world of surrealism.

In the 1930s Salvador and Gala returned to live at Port Lligat on the north Catalan coast, where they played host to a long list of fashionable and art-world guests until the war years – the parties were by all accounts memorable.

They started again in Port Lligat in the 1950s. The stories of sexual romps and Gala's appetite for young local boys are legendary. The 1960s saw Dalí painting pictures on a grand scale, including his 1962 reinterpretation of Marià Fortuny's *Batalla de Tetuán*. On his death in 1989 he was buried (according to his own wish) in the Teatre-Museu he had created on the site of the old theatre in central Figueres, which now houses the single greatest collection of Dalí's work.

THE PRESENT

Artistic life did not come grinding to a halt with the demise of Miró and Dalí. Barcelona has for decades been a minor cauldron of activity, dominated by the figure of Antoni Tàpies (1923–), by now a venerable elder statesman of Catalan contemporary art. Early in his career (from the mid-1940s onwards) he seemed keen on self-portraits, but also experimented with collage using all sorts of materials from wood to rice. Check out his Fundació Antoni Tàpies (p104).

Perhaps the best-known images of Joan Brossa (1916–72) are photos of him sitting in his office surrounded by mountains of paper. A prolific poet, Brossa was a multifaceted artist who combined his verse with all sorts of experimental art, often centred on simple objects such as gloves, or pencils in a pencil case.

Joan Hernández Pijuan (1931–2005) was one of the most important 20th century abstract painters to come out of Barcelona. Having studied, like Picasso and Miró, at the Llotja, he produced work concentrating on natural shapes and figures, often using neutral colours on different surfaces.

Susana Solano (1946–) is a painter and sculptor, considered one of the most important at work in Spain today and certainly one of Barcelona's best. She uses stainless steel in some of her latest sculptures, like *Huella Desnuda Que Mira* (Naked Trace Looking) and also does video installations like her one-hour 2003 loop, *Amb Noms* (With Names).

Barcelona-born Jaume Plensa (1955–) is possibly Spain's best contemporary sculptor. His work ranges from sketches, through sculpture, to video and other installations that have been shown around the world. Between 1999 and 2004 he was especially busy doing stage sets, in particular for Barcelona's madcap La Fura dels Baus theatre company. The sculptural work from these have since become centrepieces in some of his international exhibitions.

Jordi Colomer (1962–) makes heavy use of audiovisual material in his artworks, creating highly imaginative spaces and three-dimensional images. Somewhat hallucinatory videos like *Simo* and *Pianito* shot him to fame in the late 1990s, but his latest work embraces sculpture (of a sort) with *Prototipos,* a selection of what look like weird white classic cars.

Another promising young artist is Joanpere Massana (1968–), born in the province of Lleida but educated in Barcelona. Some of his paintings are a little reminiscent of Tàpies, with his use of different materials and broad brushstrokes to create striking images. He also does installation art and in recent years has begun exhibiting abroad, as well as across Catalonia and the rest of Spain. David Casals (1976–), who only finished his degree at the University of Barcelona in 1999, already has behind him an impressive series of exhibitions for his paintings, which include thoughtful landscapes done in acrylic on paper or wood.

To see the work of these and other artists head first to the Museu d'Art Contemporani de Barcelona (Macba; p92), where you will get a good introductory look at what is happening in contemporary local art. CaixaForum (p118) is another excellent public gallery.

The private commercial gallery scene has traditionally been concentrated on and around Carrer del Consell de Cent, between Passeig de Gràcia and Carrer d'Aribau. A handful of classic galleries operate in the Barri Gòtic, of which the Sala Parés (p204) is the most interesting if you want to tap into shows by a broad range of Catalan artists working today.

LITERATURE

A good deal of modern Spanish literature pours from the pens of Barcelonins and other Catalans, whether based in the city or beyond. The city continues to be the heartland of Spanish publishing. All the literary big-hitters, such as Tusquets Editores, Seix-Barral, Anagrama, Planeta and Quaderns Crema, are based in the Catalan capital.

Although local literary production in Catalan has grown since the demise of Franco in 1975, the bulk of Barcelona's and Catalonia's best-known writers have by and large continued to write in Spanish, thus reaching a far greater audience.

TOP FIVE BOOKS

- *Homage to Catalonia*, George Orwell
- *La Ciudad de los Prodigios* (The City of Marvels), Eduardo Mendoza
- *La Sombra del Viento* (The Shadow of the Wind), Carlos Ruiz Zafón
- *La Verdad Sobre el Caso Savolta* (The Truth About the Savolta Case), Eduardo Mendoza
- *Plaça del Diamant* (The Time of the Doves), Mercè Rodoreda

FROM LAW CODES TO THE SEGLE D'OR

The earliest surviving documents written in Catalan date from the 12th century. Most are legal, economic, historical and religious texts. The oldest of them is a portion of the Visigothic law code, the *Liber Iudicorum* (Book of Laws), rendered in the vernacular. The oldest original text in Catalan is the *Homilies d'Organyà*, a religious work.

The first great Catalan writer was Ramon Llull (1235–1315), who eschewed the use of both Latin and Provençal in literature. His two best-known works are *El Llibre de les Bèsties* (Book of Beasts) and *El Llibre d'Amic i Amat* (Book of the Friend and the Loved One), the former an allegorical attack on feudal corruption and the latter a series of short pieces aimed at daily meditation – both inspired in part by Islamic works.

The count-king Jaume I was a bit of a scribbler himself, writing a rare autobiographical work called *Llibre dels Feyts* (Book of Deeds) in the late 13th century. Ramon Muntaner (1265–1336), more of a propagandist than anything else, spent a good deal of his life eulogising various Catalan leaders and their deeds in his *Crónica* (Chronicle).

Everyone seems to have a 'golden century', and for Catalan writers it was the 15th. Ausiàs March (1400–59), from Valencia, announced he had abandoned the style of the troubadours and went ahead to forge a Catalan poetic tradition. His style is tormented and highly personal, and continues to inspire Catalan poets to this day.

Several European peoples like to claim responsibility for producing the first novel. The Catalans claim it was Joanot Martorell (c 1405–65), with *Tirant lo Blanc* (Tirant the White Knight), which was made into a movie in 2006 (see p35). Cervantes himself thought it the best book in the world. Martorell was a busy fighting knight and his writing tells of bloody battles, war, politics and sex. Some things don't change!

RENAIXENÇA

Catalan literature declined rapidly after the 15th century and suffered a seemingly mortal blow when the Bourbon king, Felipe V, banned its use after his victory in the War of the Spanish Succession in 1714.

As Catalonia began to enjoy a burgeoning economy in the 19th century, however, there was sufficient leisure time for intellectuals, writers and artists to take a renewed interest in all things Catalan. The revival of Catalan literature is commonly dated to 1833, when homesick Carles Aribau (1798–1862) penned the rather saccharine poem *A la Pàtria* (To the Homeland) in Madrid. Unkind cards remark that Aribau couldn't have been all that homesick, since he quite cheerfully remained most of his life in Madrid!

From 1859, when Catalan intellectuals reintroduced Catalan-language poetry competitions, the Jocs Florals (Floral Games), a steady stream of material generally fit to be ignored started to dribble out of the tap. True quality in poetry came with the appearance in 1877 of country pastor Jacint Verdaguer (1845–1902), whose *L'Atlàntida* is an epic that defies easy description. To the writer's contemporaries it confirmed Catalan's arrival as a 'great' language. Verdaguer's death in a farmhouse outside Barcelona (which you can visit today, see p115) was greeted as a national tragedy and the streets of Barcelona filled for his funeral.

Modernisme's main literary voice of note was the poet Joan Maragall (1860–1911). Also noteworthy is the work of Víctor Català (1873–1966), actually Caterina Albert. As was typical of the time she had to pretend to be a man to get somewhere. Her principal work, *Solitud* (Solitude), charts the awakening of a young woman whose husband has taken her to live in the Pyrenees.

INTO THE 20TH CENTURY

What Verdaguer was to poetry, Josep Pla (1897–1981) was to prose. He wrote in Catalan and Spanish and his work ranged from travel writing (after Franco's victory in 1939 he spent many years abroad) to histories and fiction. His complete works total 46 volumes.

Mercè Rodoreda (1909–83) had her first success with the novel *Paloma* (1938), which tells the story of a young girl seduced by her brother-in-law. After the Spanish Civil War Rodoreda went into exile and, in 1962, published one of her best-known works, *Plaça del Diamant* (The Time of the Doves), which recounts life in Barcelona before, during and after the civil war, as seen through the eyes of a struggling working class woman.

In the 1930s George Orwell (1903–50) was one of many idealistic leftists who flooded into Barcelona to join the fight against Franco's Nationalist forces. He was sorely disappointed, both by the desultory fighting and plight of the divided Republican forces on the front line, and by the infighting he witnessed in Barcelona as the communists crushed and disarmed rival Trotskyite and anarchist groups. His account of those difficult days, *Homage to Catalonia*, has become a classic.

Juan Goytisolo (1931–), who lives in Marrakech, started off in the neo-Realist camp but his more recent works, such as the trilogy made up of *Señas de Identidad* (Marks of Identity), *Reivindicacion del Conde Don Julián* (Count Julian) and *Juan sin Tierra* (John the Landless), are decidedly more experimental and by far his most powerful writings. Much of his work revolves around sexuality, as he equates sexual freedom (he is bisexual) with political freedom. In *Juan sin Tierra* he sets homosexuality and heterosexuality in conflict with one another, while in *Reivindicacion del Conde Don Julián* he gives reign to his disgust with traditional, conservative Spain, attacking it through its own great literature.

Goytisolo's contemporary, Jaime Gil de Biedma (1929-90), was one of the 20th century's most influential poets in Catalonia and indeed across Spain.

Montserrat Roig (1946–91) crammed a lot of journalistic and fiction writing (largely in Catalan) into her short life. Her novels include *Ramon Adéu* (Goodbye Ramon), *El Temps de les Cireres* (The Time of the Cherries) and *L'Hora Violeta* (Purple Hour).

Jorge Semprún (1923–), who lost his home and family in the civil war, ended up in a Nazi concentration camp for his activities with the French Resistance in WWII. He writes mostly in French. His first novel, *Le Grand Voyage* (The Long Voyage), is one of his best. It is his account of the agonising journey of a young Spaniard who had fought with the French Resistance on his way to the Buchenwald concentration camp – it is his own story. *Quel Beau Dimanche!* (What a Beautiful Sunday!) is the follow-up, covering the years from 1944 until 1964, when he was expelled from the Spanish Communist Party.

Manuel Vázquez Montalbán (1939–2003) was one of the city's most prolific writers, best known for his Pepe Carvalho detective novel series and a range of other thrillers. Montalbán shared with his character Pepe a predilection for the semiobscurity of El Raval, where he ate frequently at Casa Leopoldo (p146) and drank at the district's bars. He didn't restrict his activity to Pepe and, in 2002, he published *Erec y Enide* (Eric and Enide), a modern love story inspired by the Chrétien de Troyes treatment of King Arthur. Among his works available in English are thrillers such as *Murder in the Central Committee* and *Galíndez*. The latter is about the capture, torture and death of a Basque activist in the Dominican Republic in the 1950s. It was made into a moderately interesting film, *El Misterio Galíndez* (The Galíndez File), starring Harvey Keitel, in 2002.

One of Montalbán's contemporaries, Juan Marsé (1933–) is another iconic figure on the Barcelona literature scene. Among his outstanding novels are *Motocicleta* (Motorbike), *Últimas Tardes con Teresa* (Last Evenings with Teresa) and *El Embrujo de Shanghai* (The Shanghai Spell). The latter, set in Gràcia, was brought to the screen in a memorable film by Fernando Trueba in 2002. The story revolves around characters struggling along in the wake of the civil war and a 14-year-old's timid discovery of love.

THE PRESENT

Eduardo Mendoza (1943–) is one of Barcelona's finest contemporary writers. His *La Ciudad de los Prodigios* (The City of Marvels) is an absorbing and at times bizarre novel set in the city in the period between the Universal Exhibition of 1888 and the World Exhibition of 1929. It is one of the must-read novels set in Barcelona. Another wacky yarn set in Barcelona is *La Verdad Sobre el Caso Savolta* (The Truth About the Savolta Case), about a man who leaves a psychiatric ward to solve a mystery in a tearfully funny story. Mendoza was back in 2006 with another Barcelona novel, *Mauricio o las Elecciones Primarias*, which tells the story of Barcelona in the run up to the 1992 Olympics, an event that helped turn the city on its head.

Enrique Vila-Matas (1948–) has won fans way beyond his native Barcelona and his novels have been translated into a dozen languages. In *Paris No Se Acaba Nunca* (Paris Never Ends; 2003), Vila-Matas returns to the 1970s, when he rented a garret in Paris from Marguerite Duras and penned his first novel. It is a curious mix of fiction and autobiography from a writer whose trademark has always been a blurring of lines and genres.

The runaway success story in the bookstore in recent times has been *La Sombra del Viento* (The Shadow of the Wind), by Barcelona-born, US-based Carlos Ruiz Zafón (1964–). This engaging, multi-layered mystery story plays out over several periods in Barcelona's 20th-century history and is fascinating for anyone who has spent time in the city. For those who haven't, the tale itself is worth the investment. Hot on Zafón's tail is Ildefonso Falcones (1945–), lawyer by profession, with his *La Catedral del Mar* (Cathedral of the Sea), a historical novel set in medieval Barcelona and telling the story of construction of the Església de Santa Maria del Mar in La Ribera, a Gothic beauty raised in record-, and for many of its workers, back-breaking time.

Quim Monzó (1952–) is perhaps the highest profile author writing in Catalan today. He churns out a prolific stream of short stories, columns and essays. His wide-ranging work is marked by a mordant wit and an abiding interest in pornography. He revised the best of his stories and published them under one volume, *Vuitanta-sis Contes* (Eighty-six Short Stories), in 1999.

Albert Sánchez Piñol (1965–), who has tried everything from studying Pygmies as an anthropology student to selling insurance, had almost instant success with *La Pell Freda* (Cold Skin), the first part of a terror trilogy that has been so successful that it's been translated into Spanish and now is sold in 20 countries.

MUSIC
CONTEMPORARY

After his album *Clandestino* (1998), a highly personal creation, became the sensation of the moment as the century turned, Paris-born Manu Chao (of a Galician father and a Basque mother) decided to head down to Barcelona for a while. He's still there, although he won't make any predictions about the future. Manu likes his freedom – and the rumours about him running a bar in Barcelona are utterly unfounded.

The musical world of Barcelona that attracted Manu Chao is a variegated one. At one end of the spectrum is the grand daddy of Catalan pop, probably its best-known name, Lluís Llach (1948–). A singer-songwriter of the ilk of Bob Dylan, Llach emerged as a voice of protest in the dying stages of the Franco era. He still produces new material and performs in Barcelona, although he has announced that he will retire from the concert circuit in 2007. Joan Manuel Serrat (1943–) is another mythical figure for locals. Born in Barcelona's Poble Sec district, this poet-singer is equally at ease in Catalan and Spanish. He has repeatedly shown that record sales are not everything to him. In 1968 he refused to represent Spain at the Eurovision song contest if he were not allowed to sing in Catalan. Accused of being anti-Spanish, he was banned from performing in Spain. In the 1970s he managed to attract similar wrath from various Latin American governments for his forthright condemnation of the death penalty and 'officially sanctioned violence'. Yet another singer-songwriter who came to prominence in the Franco years and remains a favourite with Catalans is Raimon (1940–).

For a pleasing combination of rock and folk, Mesclat is a group to watch out for and particularly popular on their home turf. Band members come from all over Catalonia. They have cut a couple of CDs, *Mesclat* and *Manilla*.

A specifically local strand of rock has emerged since the 1980s. *Rock Català* (Catalan rock) is not essentially different from rock anywhere else, except that it is sung in Catalan by local bands that appeal to local tastes. Among the most popular and long-lived bands are Sau and Els Pets (one of the region's top acts) from Tarragona. Until they broke up in 2001, Girona's Sopa de Cabra made a big regional name with hits such as *L'Empordà*. Barcelona brothers David and José Muñoz (aka Estopa) have enjoyed national success with their mix of rock, rumba and pop, and recently made something of a comeback after dropping off the map for a while. The king of local rock since the 1980s has been Loquillo (and his band Trogloditas), born in the Barcelona district of El Clot. He sings in Spanish and recently brought out a compilation CD and DVD pack called *Hermanos de Sangre*.

Since 1998 the annual summer Senglar Rock concert has been *the* date for Catalan rock music, usually spiced up with some international acts. In 2005 it was held over three days in Lleida, but the dates and location tend to change. In April 2006 a local feature film on the history of Catalan rock, *Rock & Cat*, came out. Directed by Jordi Roigé, it is a good introduction to the entire home-grown rock scene.

LONGING FOR CUBA

The strongest musical tradition to have survived to some degree in popular form in Catalonia is that of the *havaneres* (from Havana) – nostalgic songs and melancholy sea shanties brought back from Cuba by Catalans who lived, sailed and traded there in the 19th century. Even after Spain lost Cuba in 1898, the *havanera* tradition continued and today it is enjoying a revival. In some coastal towns, such as Calella on the Costa Brava, you can turn up for an evening's *cantada de havaneres*.

An attractive new boy-girl duo on the Barcelona scene is Nena Daconte. Kim (the boy from Barcelona, guitar) and Mai (originally from Madrid, vocals) produce a clear, melodious ray of light in the contemporary Spanish music industry. Their CD, *He Perdido los Zapatos* (I Lost My Shoes) is loaded with deceptively simple tracks. Dol Beltrán's soft lyrics have made her trio, Pastora, one of the latest popular hits of mainstream Spanish pop. Check out their latest CD, *Vida Moderna* (Modern Life).

Girona-born Albert Pla (1966–) is one of the most controversial singer-songwriters on the national scene. Swinging between his brand of rock lyrics and stage and cinema, he is a multifaceted maestro.

Badalona boy Ángel Molina is possibly the most sought-after DJ in Spain, not just his near-native Barcelona. As his latest CD, *Pasada Profesional,* shows, he is what you might call a thinking person's DJ, mixing all sorts of sounds and indulging in a little experimentation rather than pounding a techno board.

CLASSICAL, OPERA & BAROQUE

Spain's contribution to the world of classical music has been modest, but Catalonia has produced a few exceptional composers. Best known is Camprodon-born Isaac Albéniz (1860–1909), a gifted pianist who later turned his hand to composition. Among his best-remembered works is the *Iberia* cycle.

THE POWER OF PAU

Pau Casals (1876–1973) was one of the greatest cellists of the 20th century. Born in El Vendrell, in southern Catalonia, he was playing in the orchestra of the Teatre del Liceu by the age of 20 and in 1899 he debuted in London and Paris, the beginning of his international career. He only returned to live in Barcelona in 1919, but chose exile in southern France after Franco's victory in the Civil War. In 1946 he declared he would not play in public any more as long as the Western democracies continued to tolerate Franco's regime, a decision he stuck to for many years. He continued to teach, direct and participate in various functions in festivals around Europe, and in 1956 moved to Puerto Rico. One of the most moving moments of his career came when he accepted a request to play before the UN General Assembly in New York in 1958. The concert was transmitted by radio around the world and that same year he was a candidate for the Nobel Peace Prize. In his later years he worked increasingly as a conductor. He was also a prolific composer of operatic songs, although the bulk of his works remain unpublished. Among the best known pieces is *El Pessebre* (The Nativity Scene), whose final version he completed in 1960. He died in Puerto Rico in 1973, and his remains were brought back to El Vendrell in 1979.

Lleida's Enric Granados i Campina (1867–1916) was another fine pianist. He established Barcelona's conservatorium in 1901 and composed a great many pieces for piano, including *Danzas Españolas, Cantos de la Juventud* and *Goyescas*.

Other Catalan composers and musicians of some note include Eduard Toldrà (1895–1962) and Frederic Mompou (1893–1987).

Montserrat Caballé is Barcelona's most successful voice. Born in Gràcia in 1933, the soprano made her debut in 1956 in Basel (Switzerland). Her home-town launch came four years later in the Gran Teatre del Liceu (p83). In 1965 she performed to wild acclaim at New York's Carnegie Hall and went on to become one of the world's finest 20th-century sopranos. Her daughter, Montserrat Martí, is also a singer and they occasionally appear together.

Catalonia's other world-class opera star is the renowned tenor Josep (José) Carreras (1946–).

Jordi Savall (1941–) has assumed the task of rediscovering a European heritage in music that predates the era of the classical greats. He and his wife, soprano Montserrat Figueras, have, along with musicians from other countries, been largely responsible for resuscitating the beauties of medieval, Renaissance and baroque music. In 1987 Savall founded La Capella Reial de Catalunya and two years later he formed the baroque orchestra Le Concert des Nations. You can sometimes catch their recitals in such atmospheric locations as the Església de Santa Maria del Mar (p95).

DANCE
CONTEMPORARY

Barcelona is the capital of contemporary dance in Spain and Ramon Oller is the city's leading choreographer, working with one of the country's most established companies, Metros (www.metrosdanza.com), which he created in 1986. Its dance is rooted in a comparatively formal technique. His modern adaptation of *Carmen* has been a big success, and his troupe has been touring with it since 2004.

Other dance companies worth keeping an eye out for are Cesc Gelabert (www.gelabert azzopardi.com, run by the choreographer of the same name), Mudances (www.margarit -mudances.com, Àngels Margarit), Lanònima Imperial (www.lanonima.com, Juan Carlos García) and Mal Pelo (www.malpelo.org, Maria Muñoz and Pep Ramis). All tend to work from a base of 'release technique', which favours 'natural' movement, working from the skeleton, over a reliance on muscular power. Sol Picó (www.solpico.com) is a younger company that does provocative dance sets on a big scale, while Marta Carrasco (www.marta carrasco.com) does dance that spills over more heavily into theatre. Butoh style aficionados should check out the work of Andrés Corchero and Rosa Muñóz. Smaller independent companies include Búbulus, Nats Nus, Alexis Eupierre, Senza Tempo and Iliancan.

FLAMENCO

For those who think that the passion of flamenco is the preserve of the south, think again. The *gitanos* (Roma people) get around, and some of the big names of the genre come from Catalonia. They were already in Catalonia long before the massive migrations from the south of the 1960s, but with these waves came an exponential growth in flamenco bars as Andalucians sought to recreate a little bit of home.

First and foremost, one of the greatest *bailaoras* (flamenco dancers) of all time, Carmen Amaya (1913–63) was born in what is now Port Olímpic. She danced to her father's guitar in the streets and bars around La Rambla in pre–civil war years. Much to the bemusement of purists from the south, not a few flamenco stars today have at least trained in flamenco schools in Barcelona – dancers Antonio Canales (1962–) and Joaquín Cortés (1969–) are among them. Other Catalan stars of flamenco include *cantaores* (singers) Juan Cortés Duquende (1965–) and Miguel Poveda (1973–), a boy from Badalona. He took an original step in 2006 by releasing a flamenco album, *Desglaç*, in Catalan. Another interesting flamenco voice in Catalonia is Ginesa Ortega Cortés, (1967–), actually born in France. She masters traditional genres ably but loves to experiment. In her 2002 album, *Por los Espejos del Agua* (Through the Water's Mirrors), she does a reggae version of flamenco and she has sung flamenco versions of songs by Joan Manuel Serrat and Billie Holliday.

An exciting combo formed in Barcelona in 1996 and which defies classification is the seven-man, one-woman group Ojos de Brujo (Wizard's Eyes), who meld flamenco and rumba with rap, ragga and electronic music. Their latest CD, *Techari,* is the smoothest and most exciting yet.

See p193 for information on where to see flamenco performances.

SARDANA

The Catalan dance *par excellence* is the *sardana,* whose roots lie in the far northern Empordà region of Catalonia. Compared with flamenco it is a sober sight indeed, but is not unlike a lot of folk dances seen in various other parts of the Mediterranean.

The dancers hold hands in a circle and wait for the 10 or so musicians to begin. The performance starts with the piping of the *flabiol,* a little wooden flute. When the other musicians join in, the dancers begin – a series of steps to the right, one back and then the same to the left. As the music 'heats up' the steps become more complex, the leaps are higher and the dancers lift their arms. Then they return to the initial steps and continue. If newcomers wish to join in, space is made for them as the dance continues and the whole thing proceeds in a more or less seamless fashion.

For information on where and when to see locals indulging in their traditional two-step, see p194.

CINEMA

In 1932 Francesc Macià, president of the Generalitat, opened Spain's first studios for making 'talkies' and a year later Metro Goldwyn Mayer had a dubbing studio in Barcelona. Prior to the civil war, *El Fava d'en Ramonet* (Little Ramon's Bean) was about the only cinematic hit in Catalan. In the wake of Franco's victory, pretty much all cinematic production happened in Madrid and was, in any case, largely a mix of propaganda and schmaltz. In 1956 the so-called

Arts

CINEMA

Escola de Barcelona began to produce experimental stuff, and some important filmmakers such as Vicente Aranda (his biggest recent production was *Juana la Loca,* Mad Love, about the 15th-century Spanish queen shoved aside for her alleged madness) cut their teeth here.

But Madrid has remained the centre of Spanish cinema and it has been slow going in the Catalan film world. José Juan Bigas Luna (1946–) is one of the region's better-known directors, responsible for the hilarious *Jamón, Jamón* (1992). His latest flick, *Yo Soy la Juani* (I am Juani; 2006), takes us into the life of a modern young woman in the tough world of Spanish outer suburbs.

Ventura Pons (1945–) is a veteran of Catalan theatre and film-making. *Animales Heridos* (Wounded Animals; 2006) is his 18th movie. Three stories of love and the lack thereof in different social contexts make up the fibre of this film.

After a stunning career in publicity, Gràcia-born Isabel Coixet (1960–) got a directing break with her quirky *Cosas Que Nunca Te Dije* (Things I Never Told You; 1996), filmed in English and set in Oregon. She has continued on this international path and won four Goyas for *Vida Secreta de las Palabras* (The Secret Life of Words; 2005), in which a taciturn nurse arrives on a moribund North Sea oil platform to take care of a burns patient. She turns out to be a torture victim of the wars in ex-Yugoslavia. The twists and turns are utterly unpredictable.

A local name to watch is Àlex Pastor (1981–), whose *La Ruta Natural* won the prize for best short at the Sundance festival in the US in 2006.

Vilanova i la Geltrú's Sergi López (1965–) has asserted himself as a prominent and versatile actor across Europe in films like Stephen Frears' *Dirty Pretty Things* (2002), a bizarre murder story set in the illegal immigrant scene in London. He plays a nasty fellow who meets an unpleasant end.

Joves (Young Ones; 2005), touching on the life (and excesses) of young Catalans, is perhaps most interesting because it was made in Catalan, a rarity. Its producers complained that, to get sufficient screening across the city's cinemas, they had to dub half the opening night copies into Spanish.

Vicente Aranda was back in 2006 with a surprising blockbuster based on the medieval tome *Tirant Lo Blanc*. His film follows the life, loves and battles of the knight Tirant, and stars Casper Zafer as the knight, Victoria Abril and Leonor Watling.

WILL BOLLYWOOD COME TO BARNA?

In the spring of 2006, an Indian businessman by the name of Shankar Kishani Lal (who migrated to Spain in the 1980s) secured a deal for a permanent slot to show Bollywood movies regularly at a classic old Barcelona cinema, the Maldà. It was a first in Spain and possibly a lifesaver for the struggling cinema, which otherwise has a niche name as a home to Berlin cabaret in Barcelona! With more than 10,000 Pakistanis alone living in the Catalan capital, Kishani Lal shouldn't have trouble attracting customers. But his big dream, along with mayor Joan Clos, is to turn Barcelona into a regular set for Indian movies. Clos has been to India selling his town to the Bollywood barons, so watch this space…

THEATRE

Barcelona rivals Madrid as a centre of theatrical production in Spain. Purely Catalan theatre was revived amid the rhetoric of the Renaixença in the late 19th century. Playwright and impresario Frederic Soler (1839–95), who went by the pseudonym Serafí Pitarra, and Canary Islands–born Catalan-nationalist dramatist Àngel Guimerà (1845–1924) were the revival's principal driving force.

The bulk of dramatic theatre on Barcelona's stages is done in Catalan, whether local fringe stuff or interpretations of Ibsen and Shakespeare.

Several outstanding local theatre companies have a far wider appeal. One of the world's wackiest theatre companies is La Fura dels Baus (www.lafura.com). These guys turn theatre spaces (often warehouses) into a kind of participatory apocalypse – 60 minutes of at times spine-chilling performance. Tricicle (www.tricicle.com) is a three-man mime team easily enjoyed by anyone. Els Comediants (www.comediants.com) and La Cubana (www.lacubana.es) are highly successful comedy groups that owe a lot to the impromptu world of street theatre. Els Joglars (www.elsjoglars.com) are not afraid to create pieces full of social critique, while Dagoll Dagom (www.dagolldagom.com) is Catalonia's very own bells-and-whistles musical theatre company. Lavish and somewhat all-over-the-place performances are their speciality, with lots of kitschy high drama. They switch been home-grown material and original interpretations of Broadway classics.

See p192 for theatrical locations.

Architecture ∎

Architecture

How odd it is that the many weird and wonderful buildings that attract planeloads of tourists to Barcelona every day barely raised an eyebrow among locals until the 1990s. As seaside tourism took off in Spain from the 1960s, Barcelona was ignored by all. The bulk of its modernista (Catalan Art Nouveau) masterpieces lay buried under decades of grime, neglected by locals and unknown to outsiders. Barcelona was sitting on a goldmine but nobody realised it!

Gaudí was already vaguely known abroad for his unfinished architectural symphony, La Sagrada Família. But no-one gave a fig for La Pedrera, his gracefully curvaceous piece of whimsy on Passeig de Gràcia, or the still more outlandish Casa Batlló on the same street.

How things have changed. Gaudí stood at the pinnacle of modernisme, which since the Olympic Games of 1992 has been re-discovered across Europe for the burst of joyous creativity its architects brought to construction in Barcelona from the late 1800s to the 1920s.

The modernistas produced an extraordinary opus. Barcelona's last such building boom had come at the height of the Middle

TOP 10 NOTABLE BUILDINGS
▪ Casa Amatller (p103)
▪ Casa Batlló (p103)
▪ Edifici Fòrum (p102)
▪ Església de Santa Maria del Mar (p95)
▪ Hospital de la Santa Creu i de Sant Pau (p105)
▪ La Pedrera (p105)
▪ La Sagrada Família (p106)
▪ Palau de la Música Catalana (p97)
▪ Pavelló Mies van der Rohe (p122)
▪ Torre Agbar (p102)

Ages, when its great Gothic churches, mansions and shipyards were raised, together creating what survives to this day as one of the most extensive Gothic old city centres in Europe.

Although the medieval wrecking balls put paid to most of it, there was architecture before Gothic. On the site of the original Roman town rose a busy centre full of Romanesque monuments. Some evidence of both periods can still be admired today.

ROMAN REMNANTS

What Caesar Augustus and friends called Barcino was a fairly standard Roman rectangular town. The forum lay more or less where Plaça de Sant Jaume is today, and the whole place covered little more than 10 hectares.

Today there remain some impressive leftovers of the 4th-century walls that once comprised 70 towers. In the basement of the Museu d'Història de la Ciutat (p87) you can inspect parts of a tower and the wall, as well as a whole chunk of the Roman town unearthed during extensive excavations. Elsewhere in the immediate vicinity, on the edge of what was the forum, stand columns of the temple raised for emperor worship. A little further north along what was once one of the roads leading out of the Roman town, sarcophagi of modest Roman tombs (p90) are visible.

ROMANESQUE

Unfortunately, little remains of Barcelona's Romanesque past – it was torn down to make way for what were considered greater Gothic spectacles as the city moved into its golden age. If you have the opportunity, a tour through the northern reaches of Catalonia should more than satisfy your curiosity as to what form the Catalan version of this first great wave of Christian-European architecture took.

Lombard artisans from northern Italy first introduced the Romanesque style of building to Catalonia. It is characterised by a pleasing simplicity. The exteriors of most early Romanesque edifices that have not been tampered with are virtually bereft of decoration. Churches tend to be austere, angular constructions, with tall, square-based bell towers. There were a few notable concessions to the curve – almost always semicircular or semicylindrical. These included the barrel vaulting inside the churches, the apse (or apses – as the style developed, up to five apses might be tacked on to the 'stern' of a church) and arches atop all the openings.

The main portal and windows are invariably topped with simple arches. If builders were feeling daring, they might adorn the main entrance with several arches within one another. From the late 11th century, stonemasons began to fill the arches with statuary.

In Barcelona you can see only a few Romanesque remnants. In La Catedral the 13th-century Capella de Santa Llúcia (p85) survives, along with part of the cloister doors. The 12th-century former Benedictine Església de Sant Pau del Camp (p92) is also a good example, especially the cloisters.

Other scattered reminders in the old city include the Capella d'En Marcús (p94) and a few elements of the Església de Santa Anna (p127). They have all been much interfered with in subsequent centuries. If Romanesque is your thing and you want to see a little more without really leaving Barcelona, catch the FGC train north to Sant Cugat del Vallès (p124). Although much was incorporated into a later Gothic construction, the 12th-century cloister is a fine example of Romanesque design, as is the Lombard bell tower.

The counterpoint to Romanesque architecture was the art used to decorate so many of the churches and monasteries built in the style. In this respect Barcelona is the place to be, as the best of Romanesque art from around Catalonia has been concentrated in the Museu Nacional d'Art de Catalunya (p121).

GOTHIC

This soaring form of architecture took off in France in the 13th century and spread across Europe. Its emergence coincided with Jaume I's march into Valencia and the annexation of Mallorca and Ibiza, accompanied by the rise and rise of a trading class and a burgeoning mercantile empire. The enormous cost of building the grand new monuments could thus be covered by the steady increase in the city's wealth.

The style of architecture reflected the development of building techniques. The introduction of buttresses, flying buttresses and ribbed vaulting in ceilings allowed engineers to raise edifices that were loftier and seemingly lighter than ever before. The pointed arch became a standard characteristic, and great rose windows were the source of light inside these enormous spaces. Think about the little hovels that most labourers on such enormous projects lived in, the precariousness of wooden scaffolding and the primitive nature of building materials available, and you get an idea of the degree of awe the great cathedrals, once completed, must have inspired in people. Gothic churches were not built in a day. It took more than 160 years to finish La Catedral (p84), which was a fairly typical time frame. Its rival in beauty and size, the Església de Santa Maria del Mar (p95), was one for the record books, taking only 59 years to raise!

Vault detail of the Església de Santa Maria del Mar (p95), La Ribera

Catalan Gothic did not follow the same course as the style typical of northern Europe. Decoration here tends to be more sparing and the most obvious defining characteristic is the triumph of breadth over height. While some northern European cathedrals reach for the sky, Catalan Gothic has a tendency to push to the sides, stretching its vaulting design to the limit.

The Saló del Tinell (p87), with a parade of 15m arches (among the largest ever built without reinforcement) holding up the roof, is a perfect example of Catalan Gothic. Another is the present home of the Museu Marítim, the Drassanes (p92), Barcelona's enormous medieval shipyards. In their churches, too, the Catalans opted for a more robust shape and lateral space – step into the Església de Santa Maria del Mar or the Església de Santa Maria del Pi (p89) and you'll soon get the idea.

Another notable departure from what you might have come to expect of Gothic north of the Pyrenees is the lack of spires and pinnacles. Bell towers tend to terminate in a flat or nearly flat roof. Occasional exceptions prove the rule – the main façade of Barcelona's Catedral, with its three gnarled and knobbly spires, does vaguely resemble the outline that confronts you in cathedrals in Chartres or Cologne. But then it was a 19th-century addition, admittedly to a medieval design.

Perhaps the single greatest building spurt came under Pere III. This is odd in a sense because, as Dickens might have observed, it was not only the best of times, but also the worst. As the Mediterranean empire had spread, Barcelona's coffers had been filled but, by the mid-14th century, when Pere III was in command, the city had been pushed to the ropes by a series of disasters: famine, repeated plagues and pogroms.

Maybe he didn't notice. He built, or began to build, much of La Catedral, the Drassanes, the Llotja stock exchange, the Saló del Tinell, the Casa de la Ciutat (which now houses the Ajuntament, or town hall) and numerous lesser buildings, not to mention part of the city walls. The churches of Santa Maria del Pi and Santa Maria del Mar were completed by the end of the 14th century. The last of these is considered by many to be the finest of Barcelona's great Gothic monuments.

Gothic had a longer use by date in Barcelona than in many other European centres. It seemed that with this style the city had found the expression of its soul. By the early 15th century the Generalitat still didn't have a home worthy of its name, and architect Marc Safont set to work on the present building on Plaça de Sant Jaume (p88). Even renovations carried out a century later were largely in the Gothic tradition, although some Renaissance elements eventually snuck in – the façade on Plaça de Sant Jaume is a rather disappointing result.

Carrer de Montcada (p94), in La Ribera, was the result of a late-medieval act of town planning – a street laid out by design rather than by simple evolution. Eventually, mansions belonging to the moneyed classes of 15th- and 16th-century Barcelona were erected along it. Many now house museums and art galleries. Although these former mansions appear quite austere and forbidding on the outside, their interiors often reveal another world altogether, of pleasing courtyards and decorated external staircases. They mostly went through a gentle baroque make-over in later years, but retain the basic Gothic feel.

Most of Barcelona's Gothic heritage lies, predictably enough, within the boundaries of Ciutat Vella, but a few examples can be found beyond it, notably the Museu-Monestir de Pedralbes (p113) in the district of Sarrià, which until 1921 was a separate village.

OH, HOW AWFULLY GOTHIC!

The lofty Gothic churches and other buildings of medieval Europe inspire awe and admiration in their modern visitors. But as early as the 16th century, when Renaissance artists and architects turned to the clean lines of Classical Antiquity for inspiration, suddenly all things medieval began to look crude, rough and, well, frankly barbarian, just like the ancient Germanic tribes of Goths that had stormed across Europe centuries before. To label something Gothic became the ultimate insult, something akin to 'that is so yesterday', with bells on. This attitude spread across much of Europe. In Barcelona many private homes built in Gothic style would get a baroque make-over later on, but thankfully most of the major monuments were left alone. Not until the 19th century did this extraordinary heritage again begin to awaken admiration in its beholders, to such an extent that in some north European countries in particular it led to a wave of Gothic revival building.

RENAISSANCE TO NEOCLASSICISM

The strong Barcelonin affection for Gothic, coupled with a decline in the city's fortunes that led to a decrease in urban development, seems to have largely closed Barcelona to the Renaissance and baroque periods that later blossomed elsewhere in Europe (and in other parts of Spain). Such modest examples of baroque as can be found in Barcelona are generally purely decorative, rather than structural, and are usually additions to pre-existing Gothic structures.

Among the more important but restrained baroque constructions in Barcelona are the Església de la Mercè (p129), home to the medieval sculpture of Mare del Déu de la Mercè (Our Lady of Mercy; Barcelona's copatron with Sant Eulàlia), the Església de Sant Felip Neri (p127) and the Jesuits' Església de Betlem (p85), largely destroyed in the civil war and since rebuilt. Also worth a look is the courtyard of the Palau de Dalmases (p94), in Carrer de Montcada, which has been reworked from the original Gothic structure. Much the same can be said of the other fine mansions on this strip (including those that constitute the Museu Picasso).

The Palau de la Virreina (p85), just across Carrer del Carme from the Església de Betlem, is, depending on which expert you read, a rococo or neoclassical building built in the 1770s. If anything, it is hybrid. More definitely neoclassical and raised around the same time is Palau Moja (p86), across La Rambla.

THE MODERNISTAS

The big urban expansion programme known as l'Eixample, designed to free the choking population from the city's bursting medieval confines, coincided with an extraordinary blossoming of unfettered thinking in the arts. Nowhere was this more apparent than in architecture. The feverish speculation and building that took place on all the land suddenly opened up between Barcelona and Gràcia in the late 19th and early 20th centuries ensured architects had plenty of work. What the developers could not have predicted was the calibre of those architects.

Leading the way was Antoni Gaudí i Cornet (1852–1926). Born in Reus and initially trained in metalwork, he obtained his architecture degree in 1878. Gaudí personifies, and in large measure transcends, a movement in architecture that brought a thunderclap of innovative greatness to an otherwise middle-ranking European city. This startling wave of creativity subsided just as quickly – the bulk of the modernistas' work was done from the 1880s to about 1910.

What the Catalans called modernisme emerged as a trend in the arts in Barcelona in the 1880s in the context of the Catalan Renaixença, a rebirth or rediscovery of Catalan heritage by a certain intellectual elite. This rebirth expressed itself in many ways, from the founding of Catalan-nationalist political pressure groups that sought the re-establishment of autonomous rights for the region through to the conscious resurrection of Catalan as an active literary language – embodied in the poetry of Jacint Verdaguer (p30). The good and the great of Barcelona felt, too, that their town was emerging onto the world stage. After all, it had been the first city in Spain to stage a Universal Exhibition (all the rage in Europe at that time), in 1888.

The avowed aims (especially in literature) of modernisme's followers were perhaps outlandish and even pretentious, but

Casa Batlló (p103), l'Eixample

THREE GENIUSES

Gaudí and the two architects who most closely followed him in talent, Lluís Domènech i Montaner (1850–1923) and Josep Puig i Cadafalch (1867–1957), were all Catalan nationalists. Puig i Cadafalch, in fact, was a senior politician and president of the Catalan Mancomunitat (a shadow parliament that demanded Catalan autonomy) from 1916 to 1923.

The political associations are significant, for while elsewhere in Europe Art Nouveau may have been merely a matter of *Zeitgeist* and creative caprice, in Barcelona it became something of a means of expression for Catalan identity. Modernisme barely touched the rest of Spain; where it did one frequently finds the involvement of Catalan architects.

A quick comparison of work by Gaudí, Domènech i Montaner and Puig i Cadafalch is enough to illustrate the difficulty in defining what exactly constitutes modernisme. It is marked, if anything, by its rule-breaking eclecticism.

As Gaudí became more adventurous he increasingly appeared as a lone wolf. With age he became almost exclusively motivated by stark religious conviction and devoted much of the latter part of his life to what remains Barcelona's call sign – the unfinished La Sagrada Família (p106). His inspiration in the first instance was Gothic. But he also sought to emulate the harmony he observed in nature. Straight lines were out. The forms of plants and stones were in. Gaudí used complex string models weighted with plumb lines to make his calculations (you can see examples in the upstairs mini-museum in La Pedrera, p105). The architect's work is at once a sublime reaching-out to the heavens, and yet an earthy appeal to the sinewy movement.

This is as much the case in La Sagrada Família as in other key works by Gaudí, like La Pedrera and Casa Batlló (p103), where all appears a riot of the unnaturally natural, or the naturally unnatural. Not only are straight lines almost eliminated, but the lines between real and unreal, sober and dream drunk, 'good sense' and play are all blurred.

For contrast, just look from Casa Batlló to Puig i Cadafalch's Casa Amatller (p103) next door, where the straight line is very much in evidence. This architect also looked to the past and to foreign influence (the gables are borrowed from the Dutch), and created a house of startling beauty and invention. Domènech i Montaner, too, clearly looked into the Gothic past, but never simply copied, as shown by the Castell dels Tres Dragons (built as a café-restaurant for the Universal Exhibition in 1888 and now home to the Museu de Zoologia, p96) or the Hospital de la Santa Creu i de Sant Pau (p105). In these buildings, Domènech i Montaner put his own spin on the past, in both decoration and structure. In the case of the Castell dels Tres Dragons, the main windows are more of a neoclassical borrowing, and Islamic touches can be made out in the detail. Domènech i Montaner seems to come closest to Gaudí's ideas in the Palau de la Música Catalana (p97). The structure may be linear, but the décor is as curvaceous as a Gaudí doorway.

the urge to seek innovation in artistic expression was genuine and coincided with a period of generalised optimism in Barcelona and throughout much of Western Europe. In spite of the loss of Cuba and the Philippines in 1898 and the spread of violence in the city in the first decade of the 20th century, Barcelona also experienced something of Europe's *belle époque*.

Indeed, modernisme did not appear in isolation in Barcelona. To the British and French the style was Art Nouveau; to the Italians, Lo Stile Liberty; the Germans called it Jugendstil (Youth Style); and their Austrian confreres, Sezession (Secession). Its vitality and rebelliousness can be summed up in those epithets: modern, new, liberty, youth and secession! A key uniting element was the sensuous curve in art and design. The curve implies movement, lightness and vitality, and this idea informed a great deal of Art Nouveau thinking across Europe, in part inspired by long-standing tenets of Japanese art.

For all that, there is something misleading about the name modernisme. It suggests 'out with the old, in with the new'. In a sense, nothing could be further from the truth. From Gaudí down, modernista architects looked to the past for inspiration. Gothic, Islamic and Renaissance design all had something to offer. At its most playful, modernisme was able to intelligently flout the rule books of all these styles and create new and exciting cocktails. Even many of the materials used by the modernistas were traditional – the innovation came in their application. All the ingredients were already there: what was new was how they were thrown together to create new flavours.

As many as 2000 buildings in Barcelona and throughout Catalonia display at least some modernista traces. And Gaudí and his contemporaries also undertook a handful of projects

Materials & Decoration

All three of the 'greats', and a whole gaggle of lesser-known figures of the modernista style, relied heavily on the skills of artisans that have now been all but relegated to history. There were no concrete pours for these guys (contrary to what is being done at La Sagrada Família today). Unclad brick, stone, exposed iron and steel frames, and copious use of glass and tiles in decoration were all features of the new style – and indeed it is often in the décor that modernisme is at its most flamboyant.

The craftsmen required for these tasks were the heirs of the guild masters and had absorbed centuries of know-how about just what could and could not be done with these materials. Forged iron and steel were newcomers to the scene, but the approach to learning how they could be used was not dissimilar to that adopted for more traditional materials. Gaudí, in particular, relied on these old skills and even ran schools in La Sagrada Família workshops to keep them alive.

Iron came into its own in this period. Nowhere is this more evident than in Barcelona's great covered markets: Mercat de la Boqueria (p86), Mercat de Sant Antoni and Mercat de la Llibertat (p110), just to name the main ones. Their grand metallic vaults not only provided shade over the produce, but were also a proclamation both of Barcelona's dynamism and the success of 'ignoble' materials in grand building.

The Rome-trained sculptor Eusebi Arnau (1864–1934) was one of the most popular figures called upon to decorate Barcelona's modernista piles, inside and out. The appearance of the Hospital de la Santa Creu i de Sant Pau is one of his legacies and he was heavily involved in the design and embellishment of monuments in the Parc de la Ciutadella (p97). He also had a hand in the Palau de la Música Catalana, the Hotel España (p216) restaurant in El Raval, and Casa Amatller, among others.

Other decorators were quick to jump onto the modernista bandwagon. Casa Quadros on La Rambla, with its Chinese dragon and impossible cladding of umbrellas, remains a dreamy example of daring shopfront design. Less obvious but just as clearly modernista are the many surviving shopfronts of, above all, pharmacies (for example, Carrer de València 256 and Carrer de Mallorca 312) and bakeries (for example, Antiga Casa Figueras, La Rambla 83).

Digging For Modernista Gems

Barcelona bubbles with modernista traces. A separate guidebook would be needed to detail all of them. The Walking Tours chapter presents a selective tour of some of the main modernista sights (see p131), and a number of intriguing lesser sights are mentioned in passing. All of the major modernista buildings are discussed in more detail in the Sights chapter.

Tourist offices can provide pamphlets and other materials with detailed maps that cover a greater range of modernista sights. Remember that many of these modernista buildings are still private houses and/or offices, so it is often difficult to see inside them. The city has organised a Ruta del Modernisme (www.rutadelmodernisme.com), a planned route that takes you to many of the major sights and some lesser known ones; see p105 for details.

beyond Catalonia. Everything from rich bourgeois mansion blocks to churches, from hospitals to factories, went up in this 'style', a word too constraining to adequately describe the flamboyant breadth of eclecticism inherent in it.

It is one thing to have at hand an architect of genius – it is still more remarkable that several others of considerable talent should have been working at the same time. But the proliferation of their work was due, above all, to the availability of hard cash – as with most great artists, genius required both a muse and a patron. Gaudí and friends had no shortage of orders. That is where the l'Eixample urban expansion project came in, providing a new playing field where, potentially, anything went. And money for building was also available. As the landmark efforts of Gaudí and others went up and their owners preened themselves with pride at their own startling modernity, a cash-rich keeping-up-with-the-Joneses reaction took place. For a couple of decades, there probably wasn't an architect worth his salt in Barcelona who didn't try his hand at a little inspired innovation in order to satisfy clients.

AFTER MODERNISME

As quickly as the fad had gathered pace, so it was swept aside. By the time Gaudí died in 1926, he had been left behind and alone in his creative 'craziness'. In the aftermath of WWI especially, modernisme seemed stale, self-indulgent and somehow unwholesome.

While other movements replaced modernisme in fine arts and literature, architecture took a nose dive. From the 1920s until the civil war, a host of sober neoclassical and neobaroque edifices went up. A wander along Via Laietana provides plenty of examples. At the same time, the 1930s was a period of timid experimentation inspired by the Bauhaus school of thought. Surprising angular, utilitarian blocks of flats and public buildings popped up in ad hoc fashion around the city.

In the aftermath of the civil war there was little money, time or willingness for architectural fancywork. Apartment blocks and offices, designed with a realism and utilitarianism that to most mortals now seem deadly dull, were erected instead. One of the greatest urban-planning crimes was the erection of the incredibly ugly town hall office block just behind the Ajuntament, smack in the middle of the oldest part of the city. In the opening years of the 21st century, the top few floors were gingerly dismantled to at least palliate the awful effect of this monstrosity's presence in the old city. A project of enormous import to the city was Camp Nou (p116) football stadium, built between 1954 and 1957.

The 1960s and 1970s were the years of sprawl, when rank upon rank of anonymous apartment blocks were planted like corn crops across great swathes of peripheral Barcelona to absorb the massive waves of internal migration from all over Spain. A lot of it ain't pretty, as a drive through l'Hospitalet or along Avinguda de la Meridiana will quickly confirm. Indeed, the incessant hunger for land has kept the developers in business to this day.

There were some highlights, however. In 1971 Barcelona-born Josep Lluís Sert (1902–83) built the light, white Fundació Joan Miró (p120) on Montjuïc as a central exhibition space for his artist friend's works.

BARCELONA TODAY

The title of Llàtzer Moix's study of architecture and design in modern Barcelona, *La Ciudad de los Arquitectos* (The City of Architects), could just as well serve as an epithet for the city.

In 2006 an exhibition on architecture and design in Spain at New York's Museum of Modern Art (MOMA) featured two new emblematic Barcelona landmarks that were completed in 2005: Jean Nouvel's ovoid Torre Agbar and the Mercat de Santa Caterina by local boy Enric Miralles. Barcelona continues to be an architect's playground.

Barcelona's latest architectural revolution began in the 1980s. The appointment then of Oriol Bohigas (1925–), regarded as something of an elder statesman for architecture in Barcelona, as head of urban planning by the ruling socialist party marked a new beginning. The city set about its biggest phase of urban renewal since the heady days of l'Eixample in the late 19th century.

In the run-up to the 1992 Olympics, more than 150 architects were working away on almost 300 building and design projects! The Port Vell waterfront was transformed with the creation of the Maremàgnum shopping and entertainment complex (p206). The long road to resurrecting Montjuïc took off with the refurbishment of the Olympic stadium and the creation of such landmarks as Arata Isozaki's (1931–) Palau Sant Jordi and Santiago Calatrava's (1951–) Torre Calatrava. Work on and around the mount continued long after, with such key works as the recreated Pavelló Mies van der Rohe (p122) and the creation of the CaixaForum art gallery (p118) in a former modernista factory.

The Port Olímpic area was also transformed, with the creation of a busy yacht harbour and two skyscrapers, one of them arguably the hottest hotel address in Barcelona, the Hotel Arts (p219).

In the hangover after 1992, things slackened off a little, but landmark buildings still went up in strategic spots. Rarely was one built without the ulterior motive of trying to pull the surrounding area up by its bootstraps. Two of the most emblematic of these projects are the gleaming white, undulating Museu d'Art Contemporani de Barcelona (Macba; p92), which opened in 1995, and the nearby Centre de Cultura Contemporània de Barcelona (CCCB; p92).

Ricard Bofill's (1939–) team designed the Teatre Nacional de Catalunya (p192) – a mix of neoclassical and modern design. Across the road, Madrid-based Rafael Moneo's (1937–) l'Auditori (p191) has become one of the city's top venues for classical music.

Henry Cobb's (1926–) World Trade Center, at the tip of a quay jutting out into the waters of Port Vell, is like a cruise ship ready to weigh anchor. With its offices, luxury hotel (completed in 2002) and restaurant, it has become an attractive portside business hub.

One of the biggest recent projects is Diagonal Mar. A whole city quarter has been built (some work continues) in the northeast coastal corner of the city where before there was a void. The Ajuntament (town hall) came up with a world event to justify the activity, the Fòrum Universal de les Cultures 2004. This months-long culture fest was not as successful as hoped but the urban legacy is considerable: skyscraper apartment blocks have gone up in a city where such towers were once a rarity. They are joined by waterfront office towers and five-star hotels, a sprawling shopping centre and two key structures. One is the blue, triangular Edifici Fòrum (p102) by Swiss architects Herzog & de Meuron. The other is Josep Lluís Mateo's (1949–) Centre de Convencions Internacional de Barcelona (CCIB; p102), said to be Europe's biggest convention centre. Add a tree-lined marina, the future zoo, swimming areas, green zones along the nearby Riu Besòs and a new marina across the river in Sant Adrià del Besòs and the extent of the project becomes clear.

In 2005 the most visible addition to the skyline was completed. The shimmering, cucumber-shaped Torre Agbar (p102) is a product of the imagination of French architect Jean Nouvel (1945–), a big step in the regeneration of the area around Plaça de les Glòries Catalanes in the city's northeast.

The heart of La Ribera has also been given a fresh look with its brand-new Mercat de Santa Caterina (p95). The market is quite a sight with its wavy ceramic roof and tubular skeleton, designed by one of the most promising names in Catalan architecture until his premature death, Enric Miralles (1955–2000). Around the market, much new housing (some in questionable taste) has been thrown up in an effort to decongest this part of the old city.

Torre Agbar (p102), El Poblenou

…AND BARCELONA TOMORROW

In La Barceloneta, two landmark buildings are nearing completion. Miralles' Edifici de Gas Natural adds a tall tower to the city's waterfront. While only 100m high, the glass tower complex is extraordinary for its mirrorlike surface and weirdly protruding adjunct buildings, which could be giant glass cliffs bursting from the main tower's flank. The nearby beachside Parc de Recerca Biomèdica de Barcelona (PRBB, Barcelona Biomedical Research Park), designed by Manel Brullet and Albert de la Pineda, is intended as a European centre of research excellence. Its central building, just back from the beach, is an eye-catching elliptical affair.

Due for completion in 2007 is the ambitious new Fira M2 (trade fair) centre (Map pp290–1), designed by Japanese architect Toyo Ito (1941–), along Gran Via de les Corts Catalanes. Its star buildings (due for completion in 2009) will be two twisting towers (one a hotel, the other offices) that will look something like branchless sci-fi oaks. Together with the old fairground at Montjuïc, this breathtaking project will make Barcelona, already a key player on the trade-fair circuit, one of the biggest in Europe.

Later down the track will come the complete overhaul of the Plaça de les Glòries Catalanes roundabout and surrounding area. They will be transformed in a series of projects by MBM (Martorell, Bohigas & Mackey). Their design museum, which will contain several of the city's collections, is a daring project that looks something like a tip-truck. Beneath the roundabout they will create a Cripta del Tresor (Treasure Crypt) as part of the museum space. Zaha Hadid (1950–) will chime in with her redesign of Plaça de les Arts in front of the Teatre Nacional de Catalunya.

Further away from the centre, in the until now much neglected district of La Sagrera, construction of a major transport interchange for the high-speed AVE train from Madrid, metro and buses will be complemented by a characteristically out-there project from Frank Gehry (1929–), who will finally get to leave a more substantial mark on the city than his Peix sculpture at the Port Olímpic with five twisting steel and glass towers.

Food & Drink ■

Food & Drink

In Barcelona, food can be as fun or as serious as you want it to be. For some years those noted lovers of fine dining north of the Pyrenees, the French, have been singing the culinary praises of Barcelona and Catalonia. There is every reason to. Catalonia has a rich gastronomical tradition, and its cuisine is considered, alongside that of the Basque Country to the west, to be the best Spain has to offer. With the traditional variety of seafood and hearty meals from the interior, a whole new culture of inventive gourmet dining has mushroomed since the 1990s, catapulting the city into the limelight. Local chefs, led by the inimitable Ferran Adrià and disciples like Sergi Arola have become international cooking icons. And what is a great meal without fine wine to accompany it? No problem. Aside from being the main producer of bubbly in Spain, Catalonia is rich in wine districts producing everything from the dark and heavy reds of El Priorat to light whites from the Penedès. Catalonia's vineyards are among the nation's best and most varied.

Food terminology throughout this book is given in Catalan/Spanish (Castilian) or Catalan alone, except in the few cases where the Spanish term is used in both languages. Rather than descend into the murky depths of linguistic polemics, the idea is to reflect what you are most likely to see and hear in the restaurants and bars of Barcelona.

HISTORY & CULTURE

The Romans didn't just bring straight roads, a large temple and a functional sewerage system to the little town of Barcino. They also brought with them their culinary habits, which included such fundamentals as olives and grapes, and that produce's conversion into olive oil and wine. We can perhaps be grateful that another Roman favourite, *garum* (a kind of tart fish paste that could survive long sea voyages), did not survive the demise of the empire.

Catalan cooking is one of several regional Spanish cuisines, all of which have been influenced to a greater or lesser degree by common factors. A particular spin comes from the country's long history of Muslim occupation, reflected in the use of spices such as saffron and cumin and, in desserts, the predominance of honeyed sweets. The high place accorded to almonds and fruit also betrays a lasting Muslim influence. The other major source of culinary influence was South America, whence came everyday staples such as potatoes and tomatoes (not to mention coffee and chocolate).

At the heart of Catalan cooking is a diversity of products and tradition. Some dishes are referred to as *mar i muntanya* (surf and turf), a mix of seafood and meats, and this perhaps best sums up the situation. Barcelona sits on the sea and has always been enamoured of edible marine inhabitants (Roman annals suggest big, juicy local oysters were once a common item on ancient menus). But the Catalan hinterland, especially the Pyrenees, has long been the hearth of a much chunkier, heartier cooking tradition. From wintry mountain stews to an array of sausages and the general craziness for charcuterie, as well as venison, the Catalan countryside contributes much to the dinner table. To these raw materials the Catalans add a rich array of sauces, betraying a French influence on their habits over the hob.

But there's more. Barcelona has long attracted migrants, at first from the rest of Spain and, since the 1990s, from all over the world. And so the city is jammed with Galician seafood restaurants and Basque tapas bars.

And now, look what's happening – alongside the designer food, mixed Mediterranean, *nueva cocina* (new cuisine) and other food genres that have become common fare in large Western cities, ethnic food has arrived. While cheap and cheerful Chinese establishments have always been here, until the early 1990s you could count Japanese, Thai and Indian restaurants on the fingers of one hand. All this has changed. Suddenly *pizzerie* (pizzerias), sushi on the go, tandoori temptations, Thai, Korean and kebabs are everywhere. The number of foreign (ie non-Spanish) restaurants in Barcelona has more than quadrupled since the opening of the

21st century. Vegetarians, and especially vegans, can have a hard time in Spain, but in Barcelona a growing battery of vegetarian restaurants offers welcome relief to meat-loathers.

You name it, Barcelona's got it. It might all seem old hat to veteran foodies arriving from London, Paris, New York or Sydney, but here in Spain the new ethnic eateries are a remarkable addition to what was already a remarkable local scene. *Bon profit!*

HOW BARCELONINS EAT

You may not arrive in Barcelona with jet lag but, due to the different Spanish eating habits, your tummy will think it has abandoned all known time zones.

Esmorzar/desayuno (breakfast) is generally a no-nonsense affair taken at a bar on the way to work. A *cafè amb llet/café con leche* (coffee with milk) with a *pasta* (pastry) is the typical breakfast. You may get a croissant or some cream-filled number such as a *canya*. Some people prefer a savoury start – you could go for the oddly named *bikini*, which is nothing more or less than a classic toasted ham and cheese sandwich. A *torrada/tostada* is simply buttered toast (you might order something to go with it).

Dinar/comida (or *almuerzo*; lunch time) is basically from 2pm to 4pm and is generally the main meal of the day, although modern work and living habits are changing this for some people. Many workers opt for the generally cheap and cheerful, set-price *menú del día* at lunch. Some restaurants offer more elaborate versions both at lunch and dinner time.

A simpler version still is the *plat combinat/plato combinado* (combined dish), basically a meat-and-three-veg dish that will hardly excite taste buds, but will have little fiscal impact. So you can eat solidly and economically at lunch and then splash out at dinner!

On the subject of *sopar/cena* (dinner), locals wouldn't even start thinking about it much before 9pm. Most kitchens close by midnight, if not a little before. A full meal can comprise an *entrant/entrante* (starter), *plat/plato principal* (main course) and *postre* (dessert). In some places the first two are referred to as the *primer plat/primer plato* (first course) and *segon plat/segundo plato* (second course). You will generally be asked what you would like *de primer* (for your first course) and then *de segon* (for your second course). You can skip the starter without causing offence.

Instead of heading for a sit-down meal, some locals prefer to *tapear* or *ir de tapeo* (go on a tapas crawl, also known as *picar* or *pica-pica*). This is the delightful business of standing in bars and choosing from a range of tasty little goodies. You can stay in one place or move from one to another. You basically keep munching and drinking until you've had enough.

A plate of tapas

The origin of the *tapa* appears to lie in the old habit of serving drinks with a lid *(tapa)* on the glass, perhaps to keep out pesky bugs. The *tapa* might have been a piece of bread and at some point a couple of morsels on the *tapa* became par for the course – usually salty items bound to work up a greater thirst. In some bars in Barcelona you will still get a few olives or other free snacks with your beer, but since tapas were always more a southern Spanish thing, it is not overly common. In Barcelona, if you want something, you pay for it.

A *tapa* is a tiny serving; if you particularly like something you can have a *media ración* or even a full *ración*. Two or three of the latter, depending on what they are, can easily constitute a full meal.

The Basques have been present in Barcelona for a long time, but since the mid-1990s the number of Basque tapas bars has increased exponentially. They generally work like this: you order drinks (try the slightly fizzy Basque white wine, *txacolí*) and ask for a plate. Many of the tapas (*pintxos* to the Basques) are *montaditos* (a sort of canapé), which might range from a creamy Roquefort cheese and walnut combination to a chunk of spicy sausage. They all come with toothpicks. These facilitate their consumption, but serve another important purpose too: when you're ready to leave, the toothpicks are counted up and the bill presented.

If the local opening times have your tummy in a panic, don't worry. Plenty of restaurants in more touristy parts of town open early for foreigners – clearly you pay for this with often mediocre food and the almost exclusive company of other tourists. Many bars and restaurants serving tapas and *raciones* have them out before and after the appointed main meal times, which means you can almost always pick up something to eat.

Many bars and other establishments offer some form of solid sustenance. This can range from *entrepans/bocadillos* (filled rolls), tapas and *raciones* to full meals served in *menjadors/comedores* (sit-down restaurants) out the back. *Tavernes/tabernas, cerveserias/ cervezerías* (beer bars) and *cellers/bodegas* (wine cellars) are some of the establishments in this category.

For a full meal you will most frequently end up in a restaurant/*restaurante*, but other names will pop out at you. A *marisquería* specialises in seafood, while a *mesón* (a 'big table') might (but will not necessarily) indicate a more modest eatery.

ETIQUETTE

Grabbing the attention of waiters can be a time-consuming business in some restaurants, although in smarter places they are usually pretty quick to attend. Generally diners order a bottle of wine and water – separate glasses for each are provided (in Spain the larger glass is generally for the water). In midsummer (mostly at lunch time) you might also ask for some Casera (lemonade) to mix with and dilute your heavy red wine and make *tinto de verano* (summer red).

In many simpler restaurants you will keep the same knife and fork throughout the meal. Once your order is taken and the first course (which could range from a simple *amanida/ensalada rusa* – a cold vegetable salad thick with potatoes and mayonnaise – to an elaborate seafood item) is in place, you may find the level of service accelerates disconcertingly. This especially becomes the case as you reach the end of any given course. Hovering waiters (where were they when you wanted to see the menu?) swoop like eagles to swipe your unfinished dish or lift your glass of wine, still tinged with that last sip you wanted to savour. '*Encara no he terminat*'/'*Todavía no he terminado*' ('I haven't finished yet') you may point out; you'll be flashed a cheerful smile and your waiter will be off and leave you to finish in peace.

Dessert is a mixed bag. Many of the better restaurants go to great lengths to tempt you into enormous sins of gluttony. At simpler eateries, especially at lunch, dessert might simply be a choice of fruit, *flan* (crème caramel) or *gelat/helado* (ice cream). If you opt for ice cream, don't be surprised to shown a list of manufactured goodies of the sort you'd grab at the beach.

Spain is a smokers' paradise and restaurants seem to be a favourite place for this activity. Not only do Spaniards smoke with satisfaction at the conclusion of a filling meal, many smoke between courses, regardless of whether their co-diners have finished or not. A law introduced in 2006 provided some relief by obliging all establishments bigger than 100 sq metres to become nonsmoking (with the option of setting up costly, separately ventilated, smokers' areas). All the smaller places were given the choice of becoming smoking or non-smoking. No prizes for guessing which choice most of them went for.

Don't jump out of your seat if people coming and going past your table address you with a hearty *'bon profit!'/'¡buen provecho!'* They're just saying 'enjoy your meal!'

STAPLES

The basics are simple enough: bread and olive oil. And lots of garlic. No Catalan would eat a meal without bread, and olive oil seems to make its way into just about every dish. There are many local brands, but one of the best is Borges. In business in Tàrrega, in Lleida province, since 1896, it produces olive oils, including extra virgin oil using Arbequina olives. Spices, on the other hand, are generally noticeable by their absence. If you're told something is *picante* (spicy, hot) you can generally be sure it is little more than mild.

A typical *carta* (menu) begins with starters such as *amanides/ensaladas* (salads), *sopes/sopas* (soups) and *entremeses* (hors d'oeuvres). The latter can range from a mound of potato

---

CATALAN FAVOURITES

Here are some typical Catalan dishes.

Starters

- **Amanida catalana** (Catalan salad) Almost any mix of lettuce, olives, tomatoes, hard-boiled eggs, onions, chicory, celery, green peppers and garlic, with fish, ham or sausage, and mayonnaise or an oil and vinegar dressing.
- **Calçots amb romesco** *Calçots* are a type of long spring onion, delicious as a starter with *romesco* sauce and only in season in late winter/early spring. This is when Catalans get together for a *calçotada,* the local version of a BBQ. The *calçots* are the amusing part of the event, as the black ash in which they are cooked is rubbed into your neighbour's face! This is usually followed by an enormous meal with countless meat and sausage courses.
- **Escalivada** Red peppers and aubergines (sometimes onions and tomatoes too), grilled, cooled, peeled, sliced and served with an olive oil, salt and garlic dressing.
- **Esqueixada** Salad of *bacallà/bacalao* (shredded salted cod) with tomatoes, red peppers, onions, white beans, olives, olive oil and vinegar.

Main Courses

- **Arròs a la cassola/arroz a la catalana** Catalan paella, cooked in an earthenware pot, without saffron.
- **Arròs negre** Rice cooked in black cuttlefish ink. It sounds awful, but it's good.
- **Bacallà a la llauna** Salted cod baked in tomato, garlic, parsley, paprika and wine.
- **Botifarra amb mongetes** Pork sausage with fried white beans.
- **Cargols** Snails, almost a religion to some, often stewed with *conill/conejo* (rabbit) and chilli.
- **Escudella** A meat, sausage and vegetable stew, the sauce of which is mixed with noodles or rice and served as a soup, with the rest served as a main course known as *carn d'olla*. It's generally available in winter only.
- **Fideuá** Similar to paella, but using vermicelli noodles as the base, it is usually served with tomato and meat and/or sausage or fish. You should also receive a little side dish of *allioli* (pounded garlic with olive oil, often with egg yolk added) to mix in as you wish – if you don't, ask for it.
- **Fricandó** A pork and vegetable stew.
- **Sarsuela/zarzuela** Mixed seafood cooked in *sofregit* (fried onion, tomato and garlic sauce) with seasonings.
- **Suquet de peix** A kind of fish and potato hotpot – there are all sorts of variations on this theme, depending on what seafood you toss in.
- **Truita de botifarra** Sausage omelette, a particularly Catalan version of the famous Spanish tortilla.

Desserts

- **Crema catalana** A cream custard with a crisp, burnt-sugar coating.
- **Mel i mató** Honey and fresh cream cheese – simple but delicious.
- **Music** A serving of dried fruits and nuts, sometimes mixed with ice cream or a sweetish cream cheese and served with a glass of sweet muscatel.

GOURMET GLOSSARY

Here is a brief glossary of some food terms that could come in handy. Items listed below are in Catalan/Spanish (Castilian) where they start with the same letter. Where the two terms start with different letters, or where only the Catalan or the Spanish term is provided, they are listed separately and marked (C) for Catalan or (S) for Spanish. If an entry is not marked at all, it is because it takes the same form in both languages.

aceite (S)	oil	helado (S)	ice cream
aigua/agua	water	huevos (S)	eggs
alcachofa (S)	artichoke	llagosta/langosta	lobster
ametlla/almendra	almond	llamàntol (C)	a type of lobster common on local menus
anyell or xai (C)	lamb		
arròs/arroz	rice	llenties/lentejas	lentils
bacallà/bacalao	salted cod	menjador (C)	dining room, sit-down restaurant
bogavante (S)	a type of lobster common on local menus		
		menú del día (S)	fixed-price meal, mostly available at lunch time
boquerons/boquerones	white anchovies in vinegar		
		montaditos (S)	canapés
botifarra	Catalan pork sausage	nueva cocina	new cuisine
		oli (C)	oil
cafè amb llet/ café con leche	coffee with milk	ous (C)	eggs
		paella (S)	rice, seafood and meat dish
caldereta	a seafood stew	patates braves/ patatas bravas	potato chunks bathed in a slightly spicy tomato sauce
carxofa (C)	artichoke		
cava	Catalan version of champagne	pebre/pimienta	pepper
		peix/pescados	fish
ceba/cebolla	onion	queso (S)	cheese
cervesa/cerveza	beer	rap/rape	monkfish
chupito	a shot (small glass of spirits)	ratafia (C)	a local, high-octane liquor
cordero (S)	lamb	ternera (S)	beef
costella/chuleta	cutlet	torrada/tostada	open toasted sandwich
cranc/cangrejo or centollo	crab	trucha (S)	trout
formatge (C)	cheese	truita (C)	omelette/tortilla, trout
gambes/gambas	prawns	vedella (C)	beef
gelat (C)	ice cream	vi/vino	wine

salad with olives, asparagus and anchovies to an array of cold meats, slices of cheese and olives. The more upmarket the restaurant, the more imaginative the offerings.

The basic ingredients of later courses can be summarised under the general headings of *pollastre/pollo* (chicken), *carn/carne* (meat), *mariscos* (seafood), *peix/pescado* (fish) and *arròs/arroz* (rice). Meat may be subdivided into *porc/cerdo* (pork), *vedella/ternera* (beef) and *anyell/cordero* (lamb). If you want a *guarnicí/guarnición* (side order), you may have to order it separately. This may be the only way to get a decent serve of *verdures/verduras* (vegetables), which for many locals seem to be anathema.

If you opt for *tapes/tapas*, it is handy to identify some of the common items: *boquerons/ boquerones* (white anchovies in vinegar – delicious and tangy); *mandonguilles/albóndigas* (meatballs); *pebrots/pimientos de Padrón* (little green peppers from Galicia – some of which are hot); *patates braves/patatas bravas* (potato chunks bathed in a slightly spicy tomato sauce, sometimes mixed with mayonnaise); *gambes/gambas* (prawns, either done *al all/al ajillo*, with garlic, or *a la plantxa/plancha*, grilled); *chipirons/chipirones* (baby squid); *calamars/calamares a la Romana* (deep-fried calamari rings)…the list goes on.

SPECIALITIES

The essence of Catalan food lies in its sauces for meat and fish. These sauces are so ubiquitous in more traditional eateries that they may not be mentioned on menus. There are five main types: *sofregit* (fried onion, tomato and garlic); *samfaina* or *chanfaina* (*sofregit* plus red pepper and aubergine or courgette – but be aware that these names are applied to a lot of different items around Spain); *picada* (based on ground almonds, usually with garlic, parsley, pine nuts or hazelnuts, and sometimes breadcrumbs); *allioli* (pounded garlic with olive oil, often with egg yolk added to make more of a mayonnaise); and *romesco* (an almond, red pepper, tomato, olive oil, garlic and vinegar sauce, also used as a salad dressing).

Catalans find it hard to understand why other people put butter on bread when *pa amb tomàquet/pan con tomate* (bread sliced then rubbed with tomato, olive oil, garlic and salt) is so much tastier!

The Catalan version of the pizza is the *coca*, often made in the shape of a long, broad tongue. There are many variations on this theme, savoury or sweet. The former can come with tomato, onion, pepper and sometimes sardines. The sweet version, often almond-based, is more common and is a standard item at many a *festa* (festival) such as Dia de Sant Joan in June (see p12). Catalans also like pasta, and *canelons* (similar to Italian cannelloni) is a common dish.

Bolets (wild mushrooms) are a Catalan passion – people disappear into the forests in autumn to pick them. There are many, many types of *bolets;* the large succulent *rovellons* are a favourite. A trip to the Boqueria market in central Barcelona around October will reveal their abundant variety.

The main centres of cheese production in Catalonia are La Seu d'Urgell, the Cerdanya district and the Pallars area in the northwest. Although some traditional cheeses are becoming less common, you can still come across things like *formatge de tupí* (goat's cheese soaked in olive oil).

You will also find all sorts of sausages, most using pork as a base. Some generic names include *botifarra, fuet* (a thin, whip-like dried pork sausage) and *llonganissa*. The names often seem to apply to very different sausages, depending on where you buy them. Some are spicier than others.

Of course fish and seafood are major components of the region's cuisine. Only 15% of Catalonia's needs are fished in Catalan waters: much of what ends up on Catalan tables comes from northern Spain, France, the UK and even as far off as South Africa (cod in particular in the last case)! Apart from the more standard approaches, such as serving up steamed, baked or fried fish, the Catalans like to mix it up a little, especially in their fish soups and stews. *Suquet* is the best known, combining several types of fish with potatoes in a warming seaside stockpot. Richer in its variety of fish ingredients and missing the potatoes is *sarsuela*. Other themed stews often go by the name of *caldereta*, where one item (preferably lobster) is the star ingredient.

DRINKS

ALCOHOLIC

One rule of drinking etiquette to observe closely in bars: never ask for or suggest having one last drink. Catalans always order the *penúltima* (next but last), even if it really is the last drink of the evening. To mention the *última* (last) is bad luck, since it sounds like one's last drink on earth. Of course, the problem with ordering a *penúltima* is that frequently it ends up being just that…

Wine

Spain is a wine-drinking country and *vi/vino* (wine) accompanies almost every meal (although even most Spaniards draw the line at drinking at breakfast). Spanish wine, whether *blanc/blanco* (white), *negre/tinto* (red), or *rosat/rosado* (rosé) tends to have some kick, in part because of the climate and in part because of grape varieties and production methods. That said, the long-adhered-to policy of quantity over quality has for some time given way to a subtler approach in many wine-making regions, and none more so than in Catalonia. It is still possible to find cheap, kick-arse stuff that makes your mouth pucker and which a disparaging local would write off as *garrafón* (plonk). But the palette of wine styles has become much more sophisticated in recent decades.

At the bottom end of the market (apart from true *garrafón* in the form of almost give-away Tetrabriks), an entirely drinkable bottle of *vi de taula/vino de mesa* (table wine) can easily enough be had for around €3 to €5 in supermarkets and wine merchants (especially the old kind, a slowly dying breed, where they will fill your bottle from giant casks). The same money in a restaurant won't get you far, however. Apart from *vi/vino de la casa* (house wine), which is commonly ordered at lunch time by the litre or half-litre, you will pay an average of €10 to €15 for a reasonable bottle, and considerably more for something classier.

You can also generally order wine by the *copa* (glass) in bars and restaurants, although the choice will be more limited.

As in the other major wine-producing countries of the EU, there are two broad categories: table wine and quality wine. The former ranges from the basic *vi de taula/vino de mesa* to *vi de la terra/vino de la tierra*, a wine from an officially recognised wine-making area. If a region meets certain strict standards, it receives DO *(denominación de origen)* status. Outstanding wine regions get DOC *(denominación de origen calificada)* status. The number of DO regions is growing (12 at last count in Catalonia), although some may cover little more than a few vineyards.

Classifications are not always a guarantee of quality, unfortunately, and many drinkers of Spanish wine put more faith in the name and reputation of certain producers or areas than in the denomination labels.

In Catalonia the bulk of DO wines are made from grapes raised in the Penedès area, which pumps out almost two million hectolitres a year. The other DO wine-making zones (spread as far apart as the Empordà area around Figueres in the north and the Terra Alta around Gandesa in the southwest) together have an output of about half that produced in Penedès. The wines of the El Priorat area, which tend to be dark, heavy reds, have been promoted to DOC status, an honour shared only with those of the Rioja (which have been so categorised since 1926). Prices have accordingly shot up and most locals in that part of Catalonia can no longer afford their own wine!

Most of the grapes grown and used in Catalonia are native to Spain and include White Macabeo, Garnacha and Xarel.lo (for white wines), and Black Garnacha, Monastrell and Ull de Llebre (Hare's Eye) red varieties. Increasingly, foreign varieties (such as Chardonnay, Riesling, Chenin Blanc, Cabernet Sauvignon, Merlot and Pinot Noir) are also used.

The bulk of production in and around the Penedès area is white. Of these the best-known drop is *cava*, the regional version of champagne. The two big names in bubbly are Freixenet and Codorníu, both of which have extensive export markets. Connoisseurs tend not to get too excited by the big boys, however, preferring the output of smaller and lesser-known vintners. The main name in Penedès still wines is Miguel Torres – one of its stalwart reds is *Sangre de Toro*. See p240 for some tips on wineries to visit in the Penedès area.

There is plenty of wine to look out for beyond Penedès. Raïmat, in the Costers del Segre DO area in Lleida province, produces some fine reds and a couple of notable whites. Good fortified wines come from around Tarragona (p242) and some nice fresh wines are also produced in the Empordà area in the north.

Beer

The most common way to order *cervesa/cerveza* (beer) is to ask for a *canya*, which is a small draught beer *(cervesa/cerveza de barril)*. A larger beer (about 300mL) is sometimes called a *tubo* (which comes in a straight glass). A pint is a *gerra/jarra* and is usually relevant only in pseudo-Irish pubs. A small bottle of beer is called a *flascó/botellín*. A 200mL bottle is called a *quinto* (fifth) and 330mL is a *tercio* (third). If you just ask for a *cerveza* you may get bottled beer, which tends to be marginally more expensive.

The main Catalan brewery is Damm, established by Alsatian immigrants in the 19th century. Their lager-style Estrella Damm is the most common beer in Barcelona (other Damm variants include the potent and flavoursome malt Voll Damm). San Miguel, founded in Lleida in the 1940s, is also widely drunk and the company (which has several breweries around Spain) is owned by the Mahou beer conglomerate. Damm company produces 15% of all Spain's beer, as does San Miguel.

A *clara* is a shandy – a beer with a hefty dash of lemonade (or lemon Fanta).

Other Drinks

Sangría is a red wine and fruit punch (usually with lemon, orange and cinnamon), sometimes laced with brandy. It's refreshing going down, but can leave you with a

DRINKS

BARCELONA'S NEW OLD BEER

Moritz is back! This crisp lager, once Barcelona's most popular beer and brewed since 1856 by a company founded by Louis Moritz, an Alsatian brewer, was back in the bars in 2004 after a hiatus of nearly 30 years. The Barcelona brewery went belly-up in 1978 but now the descendants of Moritz (who kept the brand) are back in action. The old brewery buildings at Ronda Sant Antoni 39-43 (Map pp298–9) are being turned into a cultural centre (under the direction of French architect Jean Nouvel), with restaurant, small-scale public demonstration brewery and museum, in addition to the company headquarters. The reborn beer first started appearing in bars in mid-2004. Curiously, although sold as a wholly Catalan product (the company claims with Font d'Or mineral water from Montseny, north of Barcelona), it is actually made at La Zaragozana brewery in Zaragoza (Aragón), a point that has irritated some local punters. Why they should be so upset is something of a mystery as the beer itself is really quite a tasty drop.

sore head. Indeed, the origins of the drink go back to the days when wine quality was not always what one might have hoped and the vinegary taste needed a sweetener to make it palatable. Another version you might come across is *sangría de cava,* the same drink made with sparkling white. *Tinto de verano* is a mix of wine and Casera, a brand of *gaseosa* (like lemonade).

There is no shortage of imported and local top-shelf stuff – *coñac* (brandy) is popular. Larios is a common brand of gin (but it doesn't get too many rave reviews from resident Brits!).

You will on occasion be asked if you'd like a *chupito* to round off a meal. This is a little shot of liqueur or liquor; the idea is to help digestion. Popular and refreshing Spanish *chupitos* are *licor de manzana verde* (green apple liqueur) and *licor de melocotón* (peach liqueur), both transparent, chilled and with around 20% alcohol.

A popular drink across Spain that swings between sweet liqueur and something a little harder is Ponche Caballero. If you wander into a Galician restaurant you might come across their version of grappa, a clear firewater made with crushed grapes and called *orujo*. The Catalan firewater is *ratafia,* a particularly Pyrenean drop tasting vaguely similar to Kahlua.

South American cocktails such as the Brazilian cachaça-based *caipirinha* and the Cuban rum-based *mojito* are especially popular – many bars will whip these up for you.

SOMETHING GOOD BURNING

With Catalan impresarios making money hand over fist in sugar plantations in Cuba and other South American colonies from the late 18th century, it is hardly surprising they developed a taste for one of its by-products, *rom/ron* (rum). In 1818 the Pujol liquor company set up a rum distillery in Catalonia, and since then Ron Pujol has been one of the dominant local brands for this sweetish firewater. Today it produces all sorts of rum and rum-based drinks, including the classic Ron Pujol (42%), Pujol & Grau (38%, a lighter, white rum) and Ron 1818, based on the original recipe made in the Antilles. Closer to the Brazilian Cachaça is Caña Pujol (50%). The great Catalan drink, especially popular in summer festivals, is *rom cremat* (burned rum). Litres of rum are poured into a shallow ceramic bowl, to which is added 100 grams of sugar per litre, strips of lemon zest (half a lemon) and a stick of cinnamon. The lot is then set alight and constantly *remanat* (stirred and ladled) for about 20 to 30 minutes. About 30% of the alcohol is burned off. When the surface appears to be completely *tot foc* (alight), with no *llunes* (spaces), your rum is well burned and ready. A small cup of good coffee is poured into the mix to extinguish (this takes some minutes). If you then have to put on a lid to put out remaining flames, you've stuffed it and haven't burned the rum properly!

NONALCOHOLIC

For tap water in restaurants you could ask for *aigua de l'aixeta/agua de grifo,* but you're bound to get a funny look. People rarely opt for Barcelona tap water (and with good reason; it's bloody awful). *Aigua/agua mineral* (bottled water) comes in innumerable brands, either *amb gas/con gas* (fizzy) or *sense gas/sin gas* (still).

Coffee, Tea & Hot Chocolate

The coffee in Spain is strong and slightly bitter. A *cafè amb llet/café con leche* (generally drunk at breakfast only) is about half coffee, half hot milk. Ask for *grande* or *doble* if you want a large cup, *en got/vaso* if you want a smaller shot in a glass, or a *sombra* if you want lots of milk. A *cafè sol/café solo* (usually abbreviated to just *un solo*) is a short black or espresso; *un (cafè) tallat/(café) cortado* is a short black with a little milk (more or less the same as a *macchiato* in Italy). For iced coffee, ask for *cafè amb gel/café con hielo;* you'll get a glass of ice and a hot cup of coffee, to be poured over the ice – which, surprisingly, doesn't all melt straight away! If you want to skip the caffeine, ask for a *cafè descaféinat/café descaféinado* (decaf). If you want it supercharged, say with a shot of Baileys (very popular), ask for a *cigaló/carajillo.*

Barcelonins prefer coffee, but you can also get many different styles of *té* (tea) and *infusiones* (herbal teas such as camomile). Locals tend to drink tea black. If you want milk, ask for it to come *a part/a parte* (separately) to avoid ending up with a cup of tea-flavoured watery milk.

A cup of *xocolata calenta/chocolate caliente* (hot chocolate) is an invitation for sticky fingers – it is a thick, dark sweet-tooth's dream and could easily be classed as a food.

Fruit & Soft Drinks

Suc de taronja/zumo de naranja (orange juice) is the main freshly squeezed juice available, often served with sugar. To make sure you are getting the real thing, ask for the juice to be *natural,* otherwise you run the risk of getting a puny bottle of runny concentrate. Unfortunately, *natural* also means room temperature in these parts, so if you are proffered a bottle when asking for *natural* you'll need to explain that you want it *espremut/exprimido* (squeezed).

Refrescos (cool drinks) include the usual international brands of soft drinks, local brands such as Kas, and, in summer, *granissat/granizado* (iced fruit crush).

A *batut/batido* is a flavoured milk drink or milk shake. *Orxata/horchata* is a Valencian drink of Islamic origin. Made from the juice of *chufa* (tiger nuts), sugar and water, it is sweet and tastes like soy milk with a hint of cinnamon. You'll come across it both fresh and bottled (but this is a drink that should be consumed freshly made). A naughtier version is a *cubanito,* made by adding a fat dollop of chocolate ice cream.

History

History

THE RECENT PAST

In 2006 a curious, slim volume appeared on Catalan book shelves, *L'Endemá de la Inde-pendència* (The Day After Independence), in which 10 leading Catalan media personalities present a series of essays, ranging from fiction to political analysis, on the subject of the possible independence of Catalonia from Spain.

The views expressed in the book are widely divergent, but what is·most interesting is that the independence theme has become so prominent. Since 2003 the political heat in Catalonia and Spain has risen considerably.

The debate has always formed a substratum of Catalan life, but the rise in prominence of Josep Lluís Carod-Rovira's independence-seeking Esquerra Republicana de Catalunya (ERC, Republican Left of Catalonia) since 2003 has added a new urgency. With a new socialist-led government in the seat in Madrid since March 2004, the Socialist-led coalition Tripartit (Triparty) Catalan government thought the moment opportune to reopen the old debate of its autonomy statutes. The proposed new Estatut sent by Barcelona to parliament in Madrid for consideration (see p9) was in some ways in the grand tradition of long-time former Catalan president Jordi Pujol, who in his 23 years in power had constantly chipped away at the central edifice, seeking greater rights for Catalonia.

In early 2006 Prime Minister José Luis Rodríguez Zapatero's governing Partido Social-ista Obrero Español (PSOE, Spanish Socialist Workers' Party) and the Catalan right-wing nationalist coalition party, Convergència i Unió (CiU), agreed to approve a modified ver-sion of the Estatut. Pasqual Maragall, Catalan president and head of the Partit Socialista de Catalunya (PSC, the Catalan branch of the PSOE), went along with this plan, but found himself caught in an uncomfortable bind. His ERC allies protested they would not be party to such a deal and forced Maragall to dissolve the Catalan parliament and call new elections for autumn 2006.

Many Catalans weary of the seemingly unending political wrangling and in 2004 the city staged an enormous festival, the Fòrum de les Cultures (Forum of the Cultures), a strange event largely conceived to justify the enormous Diagonal Mar urban redevelopment project. For five months in spring and summer the city hosted a parade of world-music festivals, talk fests with international VIPs of the ilk of former Soviet leader Mikhail Gorbachev and other cultural events. It was a strange business and not an enormous financial success, but the transformation of the northeastern coastal corner of the city is staggering.

FROM THE BEGINNING

SIGNS FROM THE DISTANT PAST

The area around present-day Barcelona was certainly inhabited prior to the arrival of the Romans in Spain in 218 BC. By whom, and whether or not there was an urban nucleus, is open to debate.

Pre-Roman coins found in the area suggest the Iberian Laietani tribe may have settled here. As far back as 35,000 BC the tribe's Stone Age predecessors had roamed the Pyrenees and begun to descend into the lowlands to the south. In 1991 the remains of 25 corpses were found in Carrer de Sant Pau in El Raval – they had been buried around 4000 BC. It has been speculated that, in those days, much of El Raval was a bay and that the hillock that is Plaça de Sant Jaume may have been home to a Neolithic settlement.

TIMELINE	c 4000 BC	218 BC
	Neolithic settlement believed to have thrived around the present-day Plaça de Sant Jaume	Roman troops land at Empúries and take control of coastal areas of modern Catalonia

Other evidence hints at a settlement established around 230 BC by the Carthaginian conqueror (and father of Hannibal) Hamilcar Barca. It is tempting to see in his name the roots of the city's own name. Archaeologists believe that any pre-Roman town must have been built on the hill of Montjuïc.

ROMANS, VISIGOTHS & ISLAM

The heart of the Roman settlement of Barcino (much later Barcelona) lay within what would later become the medieval city – now known as the Barri Gòtic. At its core is a barely discernible rise, Mont Taber, where the temple was raised. Remains of city walls, temple pillars and graves all attest to what would eventually become a busy and lively town. Barcino was not a major centre, however. Tarraco (Tarragona) to the southwest and the one-time Greek trading centre of Emporion (Empúries) to the north were more important. In 15 BC, however, Caesar Augustus was magnanimous enough to grant the town the title of Colonia Julia Augusta Faventia Pia. The Latin poet Ausonius paints a picture of contented prosperity – Barcino lived well off the agricultural produce in its hinterland and from fishing. Oysters, in particular, appeared regularly on the Roman menu in ancient times. Wine, olive oil and *garum* (a rather tart fish paste and favourite staple of the Romans) were all produced and consumed in abundance.

As the Roman Empire wobbled, Hispania (as the Iberian Peninsula was known to the Romans) felt the effects. It is no coincidence that the bulk of Barcelona's Roman walls, vestiges of which remain today, went up in the 4th century AD. Marauding Franks had visited a little death and destruction on the city in a prelude to what was to come – several waves of invaders flooded across the country like great Atlantic rollers. By 415 the comparatively Romanised Visigoths had arrived and, under their leader Athaulf (a narrow lane in the Barri Gòtic is named after him), made a temporary capital in Barcino before moving on to Toletum (Toledo).

In 711 the Muslim general Tariq landed an expeditionary force at present-day Gibraltar (Arabic for Tariq's Mountain). He had no trouble sweeping across the peninsula all the

Roman tombs (p90), Barri Gòtic

AD 415	718
Visigoths establish Barcino as temporary capital	Barcelona falls to Muslim troops from North Africa

way into France, where he and his army were only brought to a halt in 732 by the Franks at Poitiers.

Barcelona fell under Muslim sway but they seem not to have been overly impressed with their prize. The town is mentioned in Arabic chronicles but it seems the Muslims resigned themselves early on to setting up a defensive line along the Riu Ebro to the south. Louis the Pious, the future Frankish ruler, retook Barcelona from them in 801.

The *comtes* (counts) installed here as Louis' lieutenants hailed from local tribes roaming on the periphery of the Frankish empire. Barcelona was a frontier town in what was known as the Frankish or Spanish March – a rough-and-ready buffer zone south of the Pyrenees.

AN EMPRESS IN BARCINO

Galla Placidia (AD 390–450), daughter of the Roman (Spanish-born) emperor Theodosius I (347–395), could never have imagined under what circumstances she herself would wind up in Spain. In the wake of her father's death, the Visigoths under Alaric invaded Italy and sacked Rome in 410. They took Galla prisoner and set off across Italy into Gaul, where Galla managed the trick of converting herself from hostage into the wife of Athaulf, Alaric's brother and successor. She was with him when the Visigoths arrived in Barcino in 414. There she had a son, who died in infancy. One year later Athaulf was killed and Galla was shipped back to Rome. There, her half-brother Honorius forced her to marry his co-emperor Constantius III. Their son, Valentinian III (419–55), was one of the last of the western Roman emperors. Galla Placidia died in Rome and is buried in Ravenna. A square is named after her in Barcelona.

A HAIRY BEGINNING

The plains and mountains to the northwest and north of Barcelona were populated by the people who by then could be identified as 'Catalans' (although surviving documentary references to the term only date from the 12th century). Catalan, the language of these people, was closely related to the *langue d'oc*, the post-Latin lingua franca of southern France (of which Provençal is about the only barely surviving reminder).

The March was under nominal Frankish control but the real power lay with local potentates (themselves often of Frankish origin, however) who ranged across the territory. One of these rulers went by the curious name of Guifré el Pelós, or Wilfred the Hairy. This was not a reference to uneven shaving habits: according to legend, old Guifré had hair in parts most people do not (exactly which parts was never specified!). He and his brothers gained control of most of the Catalan counties by 878 and Guifré entered the folk mythology of Catalonia. If Catalonia can be called a nation, then its 'father' was the hirsute Guifré.

Guifré and his immediate successors continued, at least in name, to be vassals of the Franks. In reality, his position as 'Comte de Barcelona' (Count of Barcelona; even today many refer to Barcelona as the *ciutat comtal*, or city of counts) was assured in his own right.

THE COMTES DE BARCELONA

By the late 10th century, the Casal de Barcelona (House of Barcelona) was the senior of several counties (whose leaders were all related by family ties) that would soon be a single, independent principality covering most of modern Catalonia except the south, plus Roussillon (today in France).

This was the only Iberian Christian 'state' not to fall under the sway of Sancho III of Navarra in the early 11th century. The failure of the Franks to come to Barcelona's aid when it was plundered by the Muslims under Al-Mansur in 985 led the counts to reject Frankish suzerainty. So a new entity – Catalonia – acquired tacit recognition across Europe.

Count Ramon Berenguer I was able to buy the counties of Carcassonne and Béziers, north of Roussillon, and Barcelona would maintain ambitions in France for two more centuries – at one point it held territory as far east as Provence. Under Ramon Berenguer III (1082–1131) sea trade developed and Catalonia launched its own fleet.

801	1137
Frankish king, Louis the Pious, wrests Barcelona from Muslims	Ramon Berenguer IV betrothed to Petronilla, creating a new state, the Corona de Aragón

A system of feudal government and law evolved that had little to do with the more centralised and absolutist models that would emerge in subsequent centuries in Castilla, reconquered from the Muslims. A hotchpotch of Roman-Visigothic laws combined with emerging feudal practice found its way into the written bill of rights called the 'Usatges de Barcelona' from around 1060.

Justice in those days was a little rough by modern standards: '...let them (the rulers) render justice as it seems fit to them: by cutting off hands and feet, putting out eyes, keeping men in prison for a long time and, ultimately, in hanging their bodies if necessary.' Was there an element of misogyny in the Usatges? 'In regard to women, let the rulers render justice by cutting off their noses, lips, ears and breasts, and by burning them at the stake if necessary...'

MARRIAGE OF CONVENIENCE?

In 1137 Ramon Berenguer IV clinched what must have seemed an unbeatable deal. He was betrothed to Petronilla, heiress to the throne of Catalonia's western neighbour Aragón, thus creating a joint state that set the scene for Catalonia's golden age. This state, known as the Corona de Aragón (Crown of Aragon), was ruled by *comtes-reis* (count-kings, ie counts of Barcelona and kings of Aragón). The title enshrined the continued separateness of the two states, and both retained many of their own laws. The arrangement was to have unexpected consequences as it tied Catalonia to the destiny of the rest of the peninsula in a way that ultimately would not appeal to many Catalans.

MEDITERRANEAN EMPIRE

Not content to leave all the glory of the Reconquista to the Castilians, Jaume I (r 1213–76) set about on his own spectacular missions. At only 21 years of age, he set off in 1229 with fleets from Tarragona, Barcelona, Marseilles and other ports. His objective was Mallorca, which he won. Six years later he had Ibiza and Formentera. Things were going so well that, prodded by the Aragonese, for good measure he took control of Valencia (on the mainland) too. This was no easy task and was only completed in 1248 after 16 years of grinding conquest. All this activity helped fuel a boom in Barcelona and Jaume raised new walls that increased the size of the enclosed city tenfold.

The empire-building shifted into top gear in the 1280s. Jaume I's son Pere II (1240–85) took Sicily in 1282. The easternmost part of the Balearics, Menorca, fell to Alfons II in 1287 after prolonged blood-letting. Most of its people were killed or enslaved and the island remained largely deserted throughout its occupation. Malta, Gozo and Athens were also briefly taken. A half-hearted attempt was made on Corsica but the most determined and ultimately fruitless assault began on Sardinia in 1324. The island became the Corona de Aragón's Vietnam.

In spite of the carnage and the expense of war, this was Barcelona's golden age. It was the base for what was now a thriving mercantile empire and the western Mediterranean was virtually a Catalan lake.

THE RISE OF PARLIAMENT

The rulers of the Casal de Barcelona and then the *comtes-reis* of the Corona de Aragón had a habit of regularly absenting themselves from Barcelona. Initially, local city administration was in the hands of a viscount, but in the course of the 12th and 13th centuries local power began to shift.

In 1249 Jaume I authorised the election of a committee of key citizens to advise his officials. The idea developed and, by 1274, the Consell dels Cent Jurats (Council of the Hundred Sworn-In) formed an electoral college from which an executive body of five *consellers* (councillors) was nominated to run city affairs.

1348	1484
Outbreak of plague	Inquisition established in Barcelona, leading to flight of Jews and crippling of the city's economy

TOP FIVE BOOKS ON THE HISTORY OF BARCELONA

- *Barcelona,* Robert Hughes (1996) – A witty and passionate study of the art and architecture of the city through history. It is neither flouncing artistic criticism nor dry history, rather a distillation of the life of the city and people and an assessment of its expression. He followed up with the briefer, more personal *Barcelona the Great Enchantress* in 2004.
- *Barcelona – A Thousand Years of the City's Past,* Felipe Fernández-Armesto (1991) – A fascinating history of the city from medieval days to the 20th century, organised not in chronological order but rather by themes such as Barcelona and the Sea and Barcelona and Europe.
- *Homage to Barcelona,* Colm Tóibín (1990) – An excellent personal introduction to the city's modern life and artistic and political history by an Irish journalist who has lived there.
- *Homage to Catalonia,* George Orwell (1938) – Orwell's classic account of the first half of the 1936–39 Spanish Civil War as he lived it in Barcelona and on the front line in Catalonia, moving from the euphoria of the early days in Barcelona to disillusionment with the disastrous infighting on the Republican side.
- *Historia de Barcelona,* María Pomés and Alicia Sánchez (2001) – Spanish readers will appreciate this straightforward, chronological account of the city, which presents plenty of curious social history alongside the usual political events.

In 1283 the Corts Catalanes met for the first time. This new legislative council for Catalonia (equivalent bodies sat in Aragón and Valencia) was made up of representatives of the nobility, clergy and high-class merchants to form a counterweight to regal power. The Corts Catalanes met at first annually, then every three years, but had a permanent secretariat known as the Diputació del General or Generalitat. Its home was, and remains, the Palau de la Generalitat.

The Corts and Council increased their leverage as trade grew and their respective roles in raising taxes and distributing wealth became more important. As the *comtes-reis* required money to organise wars and other enterprises, they increasingly relied on impresarios who were best represented through these two oligarchic bodies.

Meanwhile, Barcelona's trading wealth paid for the great Gothic buildings that bejewel the city today. La Catedral, the Capella Reial de Santa Àgata and the churches of Santa Maria del Pi and Santa Maria del Mar were all built in the late 13th or early 14th centuries. King Pere III (1336–87) created the breathtaking Reials Drassanes (Royal Shipyards) and extended the city walls again, this time to include the El Raval area.

DECLINE & CASTILIAN DOMINATION

Preserving the empire began to exhaust Catalonia. Sea wars with Genoa, resistance in Sardinia, the rise of the Ottoman Empire and the loss of the gold trade all drained the coffers. Commerce collapsed. The Black Death and famines killed about half of Catalonia's population in the 14th century. Barcelona's Jewish population suffered a pogrom in 1391.

After the last of Guifré el Pelós' dynasty, Martí I, died heirless in 1410, a stacked council elected Fernando (Ferran to the Catalans) de Antequera, a Castilian prince of the Trastámara house, to the Aragonese throne. This Compromiso de Caspe (Caspe Agreement) of 1412 was engineered by the Aragonese nobility, who saw a chance to reduce Catalan influence.

Another Fernando succeeded to the Aragonese throne in 1479 and his marriage to Isabel, queen of Castilla, united Spain's two most powerful monarchies. Just as Catalonia had been hitched to Aragón, now the combine was hitched to Castilla.

Catalonia effectively became part of the Castilian state, although it jealously guarded its own institutions and system of law. Rather than attack this problem head on, Fernando and Isabel sidestepped it, introducing the hated Inquisition to Barcelona. The local citi-

1670	1714
Bullfights held in Barcelona for the first time	Barcelona loses all autonomy after surrendering to Felipe V on 11 September at the end of the War of the Spanish Succession

zenry implored them not to do so as what was left of business life in the city lay largely in the hands of *conversos* (Jews at least nominally converted to Christianity) who were a particular target of Inquisitorial attention. The pleas were ignored and the *conversos* packed their bags and shipped out their money. Barcelona was reduced to penury. Their successors, the Habsburg Holy Roman Emperor Carlos V (Carlos I of Spain), and his son, Felipe II, tightened Madrid's grip on Catalonia, although the region long managed to retain a degree of autonomy.

Impoverished and disaffected by ever-growing financial demands from the crown, Catalonia revolted in the 17th century in the Guerra dels Segadors (Reapers' War; 1640–52) and declared itself to be an independent 'republic' under French protection. The countryside and towns were devastated, and Barcelona was finally besieged into submission.

WAR OF THE SPANISH SUCCESSION

By the beginning of the 18th century Spain was on the skids. The last of the Habsburgs, Carlos II, died in 1700 with no successor. France imposed a Bourbon, the absolutist Felipe V, but the Catalans preferred the Austrian candidate, Archduke Carlos, and threw in their lot with England, Holland, some German states, Portugal and the House of Savoy to back Austria. In 1702 the War of the Spanish Succession broke out. Catalans thought they were onto a winner. They were wrong and in 1713 the Treaty of Utrecht left Felipe V in charge in Madrid. Abandoned by its allies, Barcelona decided to resist. The siege began in March 1713 and ended on 11 September 1714.

There were no half measures. Felipe V abolished the Generalitat, built a huge fort (the Ciutadella) to watch over Barcelona, and banned writing and teaching in Catalan. What was left of Catalonia's possessions were farmed out to the great powers.

Memorial of the seige of 1713–14

A NEW BOOM

After the initial shock, Barcelona found the Bourbon rulers to be comparatively light-handed in their treatment of the city. Indeed, its prosperity and productivity was in the country's interest. Throughout the 18th century the Barcelonins concentrated on what they do best – industry and commerce.

The big break came in 1778 when the ban on trade with the Spanish American colonies was lifted. Since the Conquistadors opened up South America to Spanish trade, Barcelona had been sidelined in a deliberate policy to favour Seville and its satellite ports, deemed as loyal to Madrid. That ban had been formalised after the defeat of 1714. Some enterprising traders had already sent vessels across the Atlantic to deal directly in the Americas – although this was still technically forbidden. Their early ventures were a commercial success and the lifting of the ban stimulated business. In Barcelona itself, growth was modest but sustained. Small-scale manufacturing provided employment and profit. Wages were rising

1810	1869
Catalan is made the official language of Catalonia in an attempt to endear the Catalans (under French occupation) to Napoleon	Antoni Gaudí, 17 years old, arrives in Barcelona from Reus

and the city fathers even had a stab at town planning, creating the grid-based workers' district of La Barceloneta.

Before the industrial revolution, based initially on the cotton trade with America, could really get underway, Barcelona and the rest of Spain had to go through a little more pain. A French revolutionary army was launched Spain's way (1793–95) with limited success, but when Napoleon turned his attentions to the country in 1808 it was another story. Barcelona and Catalonia suffered along with the rest of the country until the French were expelled in 1814 (Barcelona was the last city in the hands of the French, who left in September).

By the 1830s Barcelona was beginning to ride on a feel-good factor that would last for most of the century. Wine, cork and iron industries developed. From the mid-1830s onwards, steamships were launched off the slipways. In 1848 Spain's first railway line was opened between Barcelona and Mataró.

Creeping industrialisation and prosperity for the business class did not work out so well down the line. Working-class families lived in increasingly putrid and cramped conditions. Poor nutrition, bad sanitation and disease were the norm in workers' districts, and riots, predictably, resulted. As a rule they were put down with little ceremony – the 1842 rising was bombarded into submission from the Montjuïc castle. Some relief came in 1854 with the knocking down of the medieval walls but the pressure remained acute.

In 1869 a plan to expand the city was begun. Ildefons Cerdà designed l'Eixample (the Enlargement) as a grid, broken up with gardens and parks and grafted onto the old town, beginning at Plaça de Catalunya. The plan was revolutionary. Until then it had been illegal to build in the plains between Barcelona and Gràcia, the area being a military zone. As industrialisation got under way this building ban also forced the concentration of factories in Barcelona itself (especially in La Barceloneta) and surrounding towns like Gràcia, Sant Martí, Sants and Sant Andreu (all of which have subsequently been swallowed up by the burgeoning city).

L'Eixample became (and to some extent remains) the most sought-after chunk of real estate in Barcelona – but the parks were mostly sacrificed to an insatiable demand for housing and undisguised land speculation. The flourishing bourgeoisie paid for lavish, ostentatious buildings, many of them in the unique, modernista style.

SPAIN'S FIRST WOMAN DOCTOR

It took guts and determination for a certain Dolors Aleu i Riera (1857–1913) to carry out her life's ambition, to enter the exclusive men's club of doctors. At 22, she completed her degree in medicine at the University of Barcelona. If she had been allowed to come so far, no-one thought she would have the gall to actually want to practise! Wrong, gentlemen. A feminist before her time, Aleu fought against the decision to block access to her diploma, which was finally grudgingly awarded in 1882. A year later her thesis was finally published. She thus became the first woman in Spain with a degree in medicine and went on to practise as a gynaecologist and paediatrician for the next 25 years. Hers was a conscious fight against a social injustice.

There seemed to be no stopping this town. In 1888 it hosted a Universal Exhibition, in spite of almost going broke in the process. Little more than a year before, work on the exhibition buildings and grounds had not even begun, but they were all completed only 10 days late. Although the exhibition attracted more than two million visitors, it did not get the international attention some had hoped for.

Still, changing the cityscape had become habitual in modern Barcelona. La Rambla de Catalunya and Avinguda del Paral.lel were both slammed through in 1888. The Monument a Colom and Arc de Triomf, rather odd monuments in some respects (Columbus had little to do with Barcelona and tangible triumphs were in short supply) also saw the light of day that year.

1895	1898
Young Pablo Picasso arrives in Barcelona with his family	The year of 'disaster'; the loss of Spain's remaining colonies to the US deals a heavy blow to Barcelona businesses

DIVE, DIVE, DIVE

It could have been the Spanish Navy's V2, a late-19th-century secret weapon. But the admirals turned their noses up at a prodigious invention, a working submarine.

Narcís Monturiol i Estarriol (1819–85), part-time publisher and all-round utopian, was fascinated by the deep blue sea. In 1859 Monturiol launched a wooden, fish-shaped submarine, the *Ictíneo*, in Barcelona. Air shortages made only brief dives possible but Monturiol became an overnight celebrity. He received, however, not a jot of funding.

Undeterred, he sank himself further into debt by designing *Ictíneo II*. This was a first. Seventeen metres long, its screws were steam driven and Monturiol had devised a system for renewing the oxygen inside the vessel. Nothing like it had been built before. It was trialled in 1864 but again attracted no finance from the navy or private industry. By 1868 his creditors had lost patience and had the vessel broken up for scrap, a blow from which Monturiol never really recovered.

Now if the Spaniards had had a few of these when they faced the US Navy off Cuba and in the Philippines in 1898, perhaps things might have turned out differently!

BARCELONA REBORN

Barcelona was comparatively peaceful for most of the second half of the 19th century but far from politically inert. The relative calm and growing wealth that came with commercial success helped revive interest in all things Catalan.

The Renaixença (Renaissance) reflected the feeling in Barcelona of renewed self-confidence. The mood was both backwards- and forwards-looking. Politicians and academics increasingly studied and demanded the return of former Catalan institutions and legal systems. The Catalan language was readopted by the middle and upper classes and new Catalan literature emerged as well.

In 1892 the Unió Catalanista (Catalanist Union) demanded the re-establishment of the Corts in a document known as the *Bases de Manresa*. In 1906 the suppression of Catalan newssheets was greeted by the formation of Solidaritat Catalana (Catalan Solidarity, a nationalist movement). Led by Enric Prat de la Riba, it attracted a broad band of Catalans, not all of them nationalists.

Perhaps the most dynamic expression of the Catalan Renaissance occurred in the world of art. Barcelona was the home of modernisme, Catalan Art Nouveau. While the rest of Spain stagnated, Barcelona was a hotbed of artistic activity, an avant-garde base with close links to Paris. The young Picasso spread his artistic wings here and drank in the artists' hang-out, Els Quatre Gats (p143).

An unpleasant wake-up call came with Spain's short, futile war with the US in 1898, in which it lost not only its entire navy, but its last colonies (Cuba, Puerto Rico and the Philippines). The blow to Barcelona's trade was enormous.

MAYHEM

Barcelona's proletariat was growing fast. The total population grew from 115,000 in 1800 to over 500,000 by 1900 and over one million by 1930 – boosted, in the early 19th century, by poor immigrants from rural Catalonia and, later, from other regions of Spain. All this made Barcelona ripe for unrest.

The city became a swirling vortex of anarchists, Republicans, bourgeois regionalists, gangsters, police terrorists and hired *pistoleros* (gunmen). One anarchist bomb at the Liceu opera house on La Rambla in the 1890s killed 20 people. Anarchists were also blamed for the Setmana Tràgica (Tragic Week) in 1909 when, following a military call-up for Spanish campaigns in Morocco, rampaging mobs wrecked 70 religious buildings and workers were shot on the street in reprisal.

1917	1936
Thirty-two die in violent clashes during general strike	Spanish Civil War breaks out; George Orwell arrives in Barcelona to join the Republican forces

In the post-WWI slump, unionism took hold. This movement was led by the anarchist Confederación Nacional del Trabajo (CNT), or National Confederation of Work, which embraced 80% of the city's workers. During a wave of strikes in 1919 and 1920, employers hired assassins to eliminate union leaders. The 1920s dictator General Miguel Primo de Rivera opposed bourgeois-Catalan nationalism and working-class radicalism, banning the CNT and even closing Barcelona football club, a potent symbol of Catalanism. But he did support the staging of a second world fair in Barcelona, the Montjuïc World Exhibition of 1929.

Rivera's repression only succeeded in uniting, after his fall in 1930, Catalonia's radical elements. Within days of the formation of Spain's Second Republic in 1931, leftist Catalan nationalists of the ERC (Esquerra Republicana de Catalunya), led by Francesc Macià and Lluís Companys, proclaimed Catalonia a republic within an imaginary 'Iberian Federation'. Madrid pressured them into accepting unitary Spanish statehood but after the leftist Popular Front victory in the February 1936 national elections, Catalonia briefly won genuine autonomy. Companys, its president, carried out land reforms and planned an alternative Barcelona Olympics to the official 1936 games in Nazi Berlin.

But things were racing out of control. The left and the right across Spain were shaping up for a showdown.

THE CIVIL WAR

On 17 July 1936 an army uprising in Morocco kick-started the Spanish Civil War. Barcelona's army garrison attempted to take the city for General Franco but was defeated by anarchists and police loyal to the government.

Franco's Nationalist forces quickly took hold of most of southern and western Spain; Galicia and Navarra in the north were also his. Most of the east and industrialised north stood with Madrid. Initial rapid advances on Madrid were stifled and the two sides settled in for almost three years of misery.

For nearly a year Barcelona was run by anarchists and the Partido Obrero de Unificación Marxista (POUM; the Marxist Unification Workers' Party) Trotskyist militia, with Companys as president only in name. Factory owners and rightists fled the city. Unions took over factories and public services, hotels and mansions became hospitals and schools, everyone wore workers' clothes (in something of a foretaste of what would later happen in Mao's China), bars and cafés were collectivised, trams and taxis were painted red and black (the colours of the anarchists) and one-way streets were ignored as they were seen to be part of the old system.

The anarchists were a disparate lot ranging from gentle idealists to hardliners who drew up death lists, held kangaroo courts, shot priests, monks and nuns (over 1200 of whom were killed in Barcelona province during the civil war), and also burnt and wrecked churches – which is why so many of Barcelona's churches are today oddly plain inside. They in turn were shunted aside by the communists (directed by Stalin from Moscow) after a bloody internecine battle in Barcelona that left 1500 dead in May 1937.

Barcelona became the Republicans' national capital in autumn 1937. The city was first bombed from the air the following March. In the first three days 670 people were killed; after that, the figures were kept secret. The Republican defeat in the Battle of the Ebro in southern Catalonia in summer 1938 left Barcelona undefended. It fell to the Nationalists on 25 January 1939. That first year of occupation was a strange hiatus before the full machinery of oppression began to weigh in. Within two weeks of the city's fall, a dozen cinemas were in operation and the following month Hollywood comedies were being shown between rounds of Nationalist propaganda. The people were even encouraged to dance the *sardana*, Catalonia's national dance, in public (the Nationalists thought such folkloric generosity might endear the people of Barcelona to them).

(Continued on page 75)

1938	1939
First air raids carried out by Fascist Italian bombers on Barcelona	In January Barcelona falls to Franco's Nationalist forces; two months later the war ends

1 Patrons watch the passing parade of people along La Rambla (p85) 2 Taking a break on a tiled bench in Gaudí's enchanting Park Güell (p111) 3 Locals dance the *sardana* (p34), Catalonia's traditional two-step

1 *The Museu Picasso (p96) displays a unique collection of the early works of the art* **2** *Murals of the Saló de les Croniques in the Ajuntamen (p88)* **3** *The façade of Gaud hallucinogenic Casa Batlló (p103)* **4** *The richly decorate auditorium of the Palau de Música Catalana (p97)* **5** *A bailaora dances the fier flamenco (p34)* **6** *Sculpture the Fundació Joan Miró (p1 Montjuïc* **7** *Sharks are the s of the show at L'Aquàrium (p100)*

1 *The Palau de la Generalitat (p88), the seat of Catalonia's regional government*
2 *The modernista Arc de Triomf (p98), La Ribera*
3 *The 1st-century columns of Temple Romà d'Augusti (p90), Barri Gòtic*

1 The mesmerising light-and-music show of La Font Màgica (p120), Montjuïc
2 The tranquil Romanesque cloister of Església de Sant Pau del Camp (p92), El Raval
3 The Gothic-inspired Palau del Baró Quadras (p109), home to the Casa Asia cultural centre

1 Barcelona's very own cucumber-shaped tower, the Torre Agbar (p102), El Poblenou 2 The soaring interior of La Catedral (p84) 3 The Plaça de Braus Monumental bullring hosts bullfights and is home to the Museu Taurí (p109)

1 *The rippling façade of Gaudí's La Pedrera (p105), l'Eixample* 2 *A distinctive pointed turret of Casa de les Punxes (p104), Avinguda Diagonal* 3 *The Palau Reial de Pedralbes (p114) houses the Museu de Ceràmica and the Museu de les Arts Decoratives*

1 *Decorations on Platja de la Mar Bella celebrate the Festes de la Mercè (p13)* **2** *The pleasure-boat marina at Port Vell (p99)* **3** *Sunbathers flock to Barcelona's beaches (p101)*

On the other hand, the city presented an exhausted picture. The Metro was running but there were no buses (they had all been used on the front). Virtually all the animals in the city zoo had died of starvation or wounds. There were frequent blackouts, and would be for years.

By 1940, with WWII raging across Europe, Franco had his regime more firmly in place and things turned darker for many. Up to 35,000 people were shot in purges, and the executions continued into the 1950s. Lluís Companys was arrested in France by the Gestapo in August 1940, handed over to Franco, and shot on 15 October on Montjuïc. He is reputed to have died with the words 'Visca Catalunya!' ('Long live Catalonia!') on his lips. Locals reacted in different ways. Most accepted the situation and tried to get on with living, while some leapt at opportunities, occupying flats abandoned by 'Reds' who had been forced to flee. Speculators and industrialists in bed with Franco began to make money hand over fist while most people barely managed to keep body and soul together.

FROM FRANCO TO PUJOL

Franco had already abolished the Generalitat in 1938. Companys was succeeded as the head of the Catalan government-in-exile in Mexico by Josep Irla and, in 1954, by the charismatic Josep Tarradellas, who remained its head until after Franco's demise.

Franco, meanwhile, embarked on a programme of Castilianisation. He banned public use of Catalan and had all town, village and street names rendered in Spanish (Castilian). Book publishing in Catalan was allowed from the mid-1940s, but education, radio, TV and the daily press remained in Spanish.

In Barcelona, the Francoist Josep Maria de Porcioles became mayor in 1957, a post he held until 1973. That same year he obtained for the city a 'municipal charter', which expanded the mayor's authority and the city's capacity to raise and spend taxes, manage urban development and, ultimately, widen the city's metropolitan limits to absorb neighbouring territory. He was responsible for such monstrosities as the concrete municipal buildings on Plaça de Sant Miquel in the Barri Gòtic. His rule marked a grey time for Barcelona. Decades of grime accumulated on the face of the city, hiding the delightful flights of architectural fantasy that today draw so many visitors.

By the 1950s opposition to Franco had turned to peaceful mass protests and strikes. In 1960 an audience at the city's Palau de la Música Catalana concert hall sang a banned Catalan anthem in front of Franco. The ringleaders included a young Catholic banker, Jordi Pujol, who would later rise to pre-eminence in the post-Franco era. For his singing effort he wound up in jail for a short time.

Under Franco a flood of 1.5 million immigrants from poorer parts of Spain, chiefly Andalucía, Extremadura and the northwest, poured into Catalonia (750,000 of them to Barcelona) in the 1950s and '60s looking for work. Many lived in appalling conditions. While some made the effort to learn Catalan and integrate as fully as possible into local society, the majority came to form Spanish-speaking pockets in the poorer working-class districts of the city and in a ring of satellite towns. Even today, the atmosphere in many of these towns is more Andalucian than Catalan. Catalan nationalists will tell you it was all part of a Francoist plot to undermine the Catalan identity.

Two years after Franco's death in 1975, Josep Tarradellas was invited to Madrid to hammer out the Catalan part of a regional autonomy policy. Eighteen days later, King Juan Carlos I decreed the re-establishment of the Generalitat and recognised Josep Tarradellas as its president. Twenty years after his stint in Franco's jails, Pujol was elected Tarradellas' successor at the head of the CiU coalition in April 1980. A wily antagonist of the central authorities in Madrid, he waged a quarter-century war of attrition, eking out greater fiscal and policy autonomy and vigorously promoting a re-Catalanisation programme, with uneven success.

1957	1980
Francoist Josep Maria de Porcioles becomes mayor of Barcelona and remains in charge until 1973	Right-wing Catalan nationalist Jordi Pujol elected president of resurrected Catalan government; he remains in power until 2003

Politics aside, the big event in post-Franco Barcelona was the successful 1992 Olympics, planned under the guidance of the Socialist mayor, Pasqual Maragall. The Games spurred a burst of public works and brought new life to areas such as Montjuïc, where the major events were held. The once-shabby waterfront was transformed with promenades, beaches, marinas, restaurants, leisure attractions and new housing.

A LEFTWARDS LURCH & NATIONALIST NOISES

Pujol remained in power until 2003, when he stepped aside to make way for his designated successor, party colleague Artur Mas. Things didn't quite go according to plan, as Pasqual Maragall managed to pip Mas at the post and form an unsteady three-party coalition government in November 2003.

Maragall's PSC is the major partner, seconded by Joan Saura's Iniciativa Verds-Esquerra Unida (Green Initiative-United Left) and, more controversially, ERC. The Tripartit coalition is the first Catalan left-wing government since free regional elections first took place in post-Franco Spain in 1980. Tensions have never been far from the surface and two months after taking office, Maragall sacked Carod-Rovira from the government after the latter held (not so) secret meetings with Euskadi Ta Askatasuna (ETA; Basque Homeland and Liberty) Basque terrorists. Such meetings are considered taboo by the democratic mainstream in Spain.

More surprises lay around the corner. The PSOE's narrow victory at the national elections three days after the Madrid terror bombings of 11 March 2004 (in which 190 people died as Muslim terrorists blew up a series of commuter trains in the capital) surprised everyone. And ERC received votes from no fewer than 650,000 Catalans, taking it from just one seat in Madrid to eight (and making it the fourth party on the national level). The stage was thus set for more parliamentary fireworks.

1992	2006
Barcelona hosts highly successful summer Olympic Games	Catalan government negotiates new autonomy statute with central government in Madrid

Sights ■

Sights

For the people of Barcelona, the *barri* (*barrio* in Spanish), or local district, is everything. It is with these areas that people truly identify. Those born and raised in them are proud to say *'Soc del barri!'* ('I am from this neighbourhood!'). A *barri* has little to do with official municipal boundaries (Barcelona is officially divided into 10 districts and contemplating reordering them); in fact, it can often be a vague term that might mean just the surrounding few streets. This chapter is broken down into a broad palette of *barris* as locals see them and you will discover them.

We start in the Barri Gòtic and La Rambla, the medieval heart of the municipal district known as Ciutat Vella (Old City), which also covers the succeeding two *barris*, El Raval and the lively La Ribera. El Raval stretches southwest of La Rambla, Spain's best-known boulevard. The southern half of La Ribera was the financial district of medieval Barcelona and is now a busy nightlife centre bursting with bars. La Ribera was amputated from the 'Gothic Quarter' by the creation of the rumbling traffic corridor of Via Laietana in 1907.

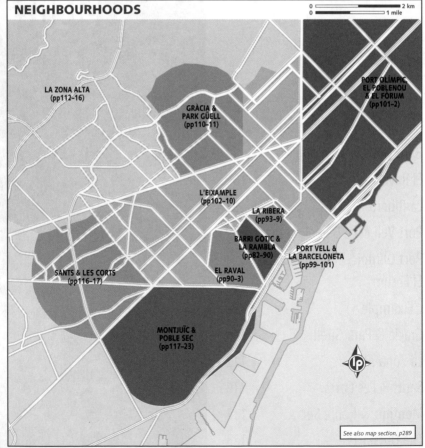

NEIGHBOURHOODS

LA ZONA ALTA (pp112–16)

GRÀCIA & PARK GÜELL (pp110–11)

PORT OLÍMPIC, EL POBLENOU & EL FÒRUM (pp101–2)

L'EIXAMPLE (pp102–10)

LA RIBERA (pp93–9)

BARRI GÒTIC & LA RAMBLA (pp82–90)

PORT VELL & LA BARCELONETA (pp99–101)

SANTS & LES CORTS (pp116–17)

EL RAVAL (pp90–3)

MONTJUÏC & POBLE SEC (pp117–23)

See also map section, p289

BARCELONA FOR FREE

Entry to some sights is free on occasion, most commonly on the first Sunday of the month. Free days are noted throughout the listings in this chapter. Among those most likely to attract your attention are:

- CaixaForum (p118) All the time.
- Estadi Olímpic (p120) All the time.
- Jardins del Laberint d'Horta (p113) Wednesdays and Sundays.
- Museu Barbier-Mueller d'Art Pre-Colombí (p95) First Sunday of the month.
- Museu de la Xocolata (p96) First Monday of the month.
- Museu d'Història de Catalunya (p100) First Sunday of the month.
- Museu d'Història de la Ciutat (p87) 4pm to 8pm first Saturday of the month.
- Museu Frederic Marès (p88) Wednesday afternoons and first Sunday of the month.
- Museu Marítim (p92) 3pm to 8pm first Saturday of the month.
- Museu Picasso (p96) First Sunday of the month.
- Palau Reial de Pedralbes (p114) First Sunday of the month.
- Park Güell (p111) All the time.
- Temple Romà d'Augusti (p90) All the time.

The old town is fronted by Port Vell and La Barceloneta. The 'Old Port' is a combination of pleasure-boat marina and leisure zone with restaurants, cinemas and bars. A brief, sunny stroll takes you into the narrow lanes of the one-time working-class zone of La Barceloneta, a cauldron of seafood eateries with clear signs of gentrification. Beyond the narrow streets, the Mediterranean laps the city's central beaches.

Where La Barceloneta beach ends, a new chapter in Barcelona's urban history begins. Port Olímpic, El Poblenou and El Fòrum reflect contemporary Barcelona's drive to renew and improve itself. The Olympic Port was built for the 1992 Olympics, as were the apartments that stretch behind it in the southwest edge of the city's former factory district, El Poblenou. In recent years this long-neglected area has received attention from the town fathers and locals looking for housing bargains. The first hi-tech tenants are moving into new buildings raised in the heart of Poblenou, the first stages of the remake of this extensive district. Far from the concerns of bio-technicians, crowds flock to the nearby beaches that stretch northeast of Port Olímpic. They peter out in the Fòrum, a residential, business and pleasure district created out of nothing in the first years of the 21st century.

The last time Barcelona went on such an extraordinary urban planning drive was towards the end of the 19th century, with the creation of l'Eixample. Filled out with apartment blocks and mansions in the last decades of the 19th century and well into the 20th, it became *the* place to be in Barcelona. Its modernista treasures, from La Pedrera to La Sagrada Família, attract hordes of appreciative visitors to its grid streets. The creation of l'Eixample filled the gap between Barcelona and Gràcia and Park Güell. Originally a separate town, with its sinuous, narrow lanes and web of lively squares, Gràcia retains an atmosphere utterly its own. Park Güell is a Gaudí fantasy to the north of Gràcia. Here the city rises up towards the hills of Collserola. The slopes of Barcelona in the district of Sarrià-St Gervasi are known to locals as La Zona Alta (the High Zone) and take in sought-after Pedralbes and Tibidabo, with its amusement park. More down-to-earth are the *barris* of Sants and Les Corts, home to the Camp Nou stadium. Finally, we visit Montjuïc, Barcelona's Olympic hill and green lung, and working class Poble Sec.

ITINERARIES

One Day

Start with the medieval core, the Barri Gòtic. You can wander down La Rambla (p85) from Plaça de Catalunya, a convenient junction of Metro stops and taxi ranks. About halfway down La Rambla, head down Carrer de Ferran to Plaça de Sant Jaume, fronted by the Ajuntament and the Gothic Palau de la Generalitat (p88). Once the Roman forum, this is the heart of town. From here you can stroll around La Catedral (p84) and surrounding monuments, including segments of the Roman wall and the fascinating **Plaça del Rei**, which is now part of the **Museu d'Història de la Ciutat** (p87). Across Via Laietana, stroll down Carrer de l'Argenteria to confront the most beautiful church in the city, the Catalan Gothic **Església de Santa Maria del Mar** (p95). The area around it, El Born, is loaded with restaurants and bars where you can take a load off. Art fans will want to set aside a couple of hours for the nearby **Museu Picasso** (p96). To finish off the day, jump on the Metro and head to Gaudí's extraordinary work in progress, **La Sagrada Família** (p106).

> ## TOP FIVE FOR CHILDREN
>
> - Beaches (p101)
> - L'Aquàrium (p100)
> - Museu de la Xocolata (p96)
> - Tibidabo & Parc d'Atraccions (p115)
> - Transbordador Aeri (p101)

Three Days

The One Day route is an excellent way to get your bearings. Fans of Gaudí could easily spend a day wandering in search of his curious architectural efforts. Start in the old town with one of his earliest projects, the **Palau Güell** (p93). Then move north to l'Eixample to explore two of his wackiest contributions to the cityscape, the **Casa Batlló** (p103) and **La Pedrera** (p105).

Need a little Zen time? Head for **Park Güell** (p111), yet another Gaudí gem. Here you can take a refreshing stroll among the trees and weird modernista touches, and admire the splendid views back over the city. Day three could be dedicated to Montjuïc. There is loads to discover here, from the **Fundació Joan Miró** (p120) to the myriad gardens, **Museu Nacional d'Art de Catalunya** (p121) and **Castell de Montjuïc** (p119).

One Week

A week is more like it. You can relax the pace of the above itineraries, or take in more of the city and throw in some day trips beyond town.

Several nerve centres of art will attract buffs. They include the ever-changing displays at **CaixaForum** (p118), the **Fundació Antoni Tàpies** (p104) and the mecca of contemporary goings-on, the **Museu d'Art Contemporani de Barcelona** (p92). You could spend a pleasant half-day wandering the **Parc de la Ciutadella** (p97), perhaps including a visit to its zoo for the kids. Cross the road for another kids' treat, the **Museu de la Xocolata** (p96).

It's also hard to resist a day trip out of town. A quick train ride southwest lies the beachside town of **Sitges** (p238), renowned for its nightlife, while to the north await the riverside medieval city of **Girona** (p228) and, a half-hour further on, the city of Dalí, **Figueres** (p231).

DISCOUNTS

Students generally pay a little over half adult admission prices, as do children aged under 12 and senior citizens (aged 65 and over) with appropriate ID.

Possession of a **Bus Turístic** ticket (see p251) entitles you to discounts to some museums.

Articket (www.articketbcn.org) gives you admission to seven important art galleries for €20 and is valid for six months. The galleries are the Museu Picasso, Museu Nacional d'Art de Catalunya (MNAC), the Museu d'Art Contemporani de Barcelona (Macba), the Fundació Antoni Tàpies, the Centre de Cultura Contemporània de Barcelona (CCCB), the Fundació Joan Miró and La Pedrera. You can pick up the ticket through **Tel-Entrada** (☎ 902 101212; www.telentrada .com), at the tourist offices on Plaça de Catalunya, Plaça de Sant Jaume and Sants train station, or at selected branches of the Caixa de Catalunya bank.

If you want to get around Barcelona fast and visit multiple museums in the blink of an eye, the **Barcelona Card** might come in handy. It costs €23/28/31/34 (a little less for children aged four to 12) for two/three/four/five days. You get free transport (and 20% off the Aerobús) and discounted admission prices (up to 30% off) or free entry to many museums and other sights, as well as minor discounts on purchases at a small number of shops, restaurants and bars. The card is available at the tourist offices; you should have a look at the pamphlet first to see whether the discounted sights are what you are hoping to see.

The **Ruta del Modernisme pack** (p105) is well worth looking into.

ORGANISED TOURS

While Barcelona is easy enough to get to know under your own steam, organised tours allow you to take a different angle. They range from walking tours of the Barri Gòtic or Picasso's Barcelona to organised spins by bicycle around the centre.

BARCELONA GUIDE BUREAU

☎ 93 268 24 22; www.bgb.es; Via Laietana 54
This organisation places professional guides at the disposal of groups for tailor-made tours of the city. Several languages are catered for.

BARCELONA WALKING TOURS Map pp298-9

☎ 93 285 38 34; Plaça de Catalunya 17-S; Ⓜ Catalunya
The Oficina d'Informació de Turisme de Barcelona organises a series of guided walking tours. One explores the Barri Gòtic (adult/child €9/3; English 10am daily, Spanish and Catalan noon Saturday), another follows in Picasso's footsteps and winds up at the Museu Picasso, to which entry is included in the price (adult/child €11/5; English 10.30am Tuesday to Sunday, Spanish and Catalan 11.30am Saturday) and a third takes in the main jewels of modernisme (adult/child €9/3; English 4pm Friday and Saturday, Spanish 4pm Saturday, all tours at 6pm June to September). It also offers a 'gourmet' tour of traditional purveyors of fine foodstuffs, from chocolate to sausages, across the old city (adult/child €11/5; English 11am Friday and Saturday, Spanish and Catalan 11am Saturday). It includes a couple of chances to taste some of the products. All tours last 1½ to two hours and start at the tourist office.

BCN SKYTOUR Map pp290-1

☎ 93 224 07 10; www.cathelicopters.com; Heliport, Passeig de l'Escullera; tour €80; ☒ 10am-7pm
A 10-minute thrill at 800m above the city in helicopter will give a truly bird's-eye view of the city. You can take the Golondrina tour boat (right) to the Heliport.

BUS TURÍSTIC Map pp298-9

☎ 010; www.tmb.net; adult/child 1 day €18/11, 2 consecutive days €22/14; ☒ 9am-7.45pm except Christmas Day & New Year's Day
This hop-on hop-off service links virtually all the major tourist sights. See p251 for more information.

GOLONDRINA EXCURSION BOATS Map pp302-3

☎ 93 442 31 06; www.lasgolondrinas.com; Moll de les Drassanes; adult/under 4yr/4-10yr €7.50/free/?; Ⓜ Drassanes
For a trip around the harbour, board a golondrina (swallow) from Moll de les Drassanes in front of Monument a Colom. The one-hour round trip takes you to Port Olímpic, the Fòrum and back again. The number of departures depends largely on the season and demand. As a rule, the trips are only available from March to November. You can also get a combined ticket for this trip that includes entry to the nearby Museu Marítim (p92; adult/under 4yr/4-10yr/senior & student €12.50/free/6.30/8.50). If you just want to pootle around the port, you can opt for a 35-minute excursion to the break-water and back (adult/child under four years/child aged four to 10 years €4/free/2).

LA CASA ELIZALDE Map pp294-5

☎ 93 488 05 90; www.casaelizalde.com; Carrer de València 302; Ⓜ Passeig de Gràcia
This cultural organisation runs several Barcelona walks (which generally occupy a morning and cost €5 per person) and one-day or weekend excursions outside the city. The tours are generally aimed at locals, but if you can deal with Catalan (you may find this the majority language), they can be informative.

MY FAVOURITE THINGS

☎ 637 265405, 678 542753; www.myft.net; tours €26-32; times vary
These people offer tours of no more than 10 participants based on numerous themes, anything from design to food, from Rollerblading tours to sailing trips. Some of the more unusual activities cost more.

ORSOM Map pp290-1

☎ 93 441 05 37; www.barcelona-orsom.com; Moll de les Drassanes; adult/4-10yr/11-18yr €12/6/9; Ⓜ Drassanes
Similar trips to Golondrina Excursion Boats are on a giant catamaran. There are up to three departures a day. The third, leaving at 6pm, includes a jazz band and costs a little more (€14.50/6.50/10). Whether or not there are sailings depends on how busy it is and whether or not the catamaran is booked for private trips, so call in advance before making a specific trek to the port for this.

SABOROSO.COM

☎ 667 770492, 647 390134; www.saboroso.com
Gastronomes can wander around the old town on a guided eating tour. You will visit various intriguing food stores, munch on tapas and so on. The cost depends on the content of the walking tour, which can last up to four hours (not all walking!). You should expect to pay €80 to €150 a head including food.

UN COTXE MENYS Map pp302–3

☎ 93 268 21 05; www.bicicletabarcelona.com; Carrer de l'Esparteria 3; tours €22; ☑ office 10am–2pm Mon-Fri; Ⓜ Jaume I
This company organises three-hour bike tours around the old city, La Barceloneta, La Sagrada Família and Port Olímpic. There is no need to book unless you have a group of 15 or more. Tours take place at 11am daily throughout the year and at 4.30pm Friday to Monday from April to mid-September. The price includes a drink stop. Turn up to the meeting spot outside the tourist office on Plaça de Sant Jaume.

BARRI GÒTIC & LA RAMBLA

Drinking & Nightlife p165; Eating p142; Shopping p202; Sleeping p214

La Rambla is doubtless the most talked-about boulevard in Spain. It certainly packs a lot of colour into a short walk, with bird stalls, flower stands, grand historic buildings, a pungent produce market, a little loose and louche night fauna around its bottom end and a ceaselessly changing parade of people from all possible walks of life. Once a river and sewage ditch on the edge of medieval Barcelona, it still marks the southwest flank of the Barri Gòtic, the nucleus of old Barcelona.

BARRI GÒTIC & LA RAMBLA TOP FIVE

- La Catedral (p84)
- La Rambla (p85)
- Museu d'Història de la Ciutat (p87)
- Museu Frederic Marès (p88)
- Plaça de Sant Jaume (p88)

The medieval city was constructed on the Roman core, which in succeeding centuries slowly spread north, south and west. The Barri Gòtic is a warren of narrow, winding streets and unexpected little squares, and home to a dense concentration of budget hotels, bars, cafés and restaurants. Few of its great buildings date from after the early 15th century – the decline Barcelona went into at that time curtailed grand projects for several centuries.

Orientation

An early port of call for new visitors to Barcelona is Plaça de Catalunya, which roughly marks the northern boundary of the Barri Gòtic. A couple of Metro lines and the airport train and bus all converge here and the main tourist office is at the southeast corner.

The square hums for much of the day. South American bands often set up at its La Rambla end, and other buskers can be seen hard at work in front of the punters sipping coffee at Cafè Zurich. Shoppers stream in and out of El Corte Inglés and the El Triangle shopping centre, while hordes of locals and tourists charge down from here into La Rambla.

La Rambla proceeds 1.2km southeast gently downhill towards the waterfront. Yes, it's clichéd, but it is a lively introduction to the city. Human statues compete for the attention of passers-by with newsstands seemingly burdened with half the city's porno magazine supply. Flower stands and bird stalls succeed one another. Among the sober 18th-century mansions are scattered overpriced eateries and bars, Dunkin' Donuts and Burger King, and the enticing Mercat de la Boqueria. The highbrow Liceu opera house is theatre within…and without. Around here at night the local transvestite population comes out to play, vying for attention with female prostitutes further down La Rambla. As night wears on, revellers cascade up, down and across the boulevard, in search of the next bar or perhaps one of the rare available taxis.

Try to imagine the northeast side of La Rambla lined by a brooding medieval wall. Inside it lies the labyrinth of the Barri Gòtic. To penetrate quickly to its core, follow Carrer de Ferran, an early-19th-century scar driven through the city, to Plaça de Sant Jaume, lined on either side by the seats of city and regional governments. A step

TRANSPORT

With three Metro lines, FGC trains and *rodalies* trains all arriving at Plaça de Catalunya, not to mention airport buses and trains, and night buses and taxis, there is no problem arriving at the north end of the Barri Gòtic. Other strategic Metro stops include Liceu and Drassanes on Línia 3 and Jaume I on Línia 4.

away stand the remaining columns from the city's Roman temple and further north is its successor, La Catedral.

Southeast of Carrer de Ferran there is a noticeable change. Although much has been improved since the early 1990s, the streets around Plaça Reial still exude a slight whiff of lawlessness. Pickpockets are on the move and a crew of substance abusers congregates around the triangular Plaça de George Orwell. Bars aplenty populate this area, and the acrid smell of urine in the streets late at night is testimony to the roaring trade they do.

CASA DE LA PIA ALMOINA (MUSEU DIOCESÀ) Map pp298-9

☎ 93 315 22 13; www.arqbcn.org; Avinguda de la Catedral 4; adult/under 7yr/senior & student €3/free/1.50; 🕑 10am-2pm & 5-8pm Tue-Sat, 11am-2pm Sun; Ⓜ Jaume I

Barcelona's Roman walls ran across present-day Plaça de la Seu into what subsequently became the Casa de la Pia Almoina. The city's main centre of charity was located here in the 11th century, although the much-crumbled remains of the present building date to the 15th century. Today it houses the Museu Diocesà (Diocesan Museum), where a sparse collection of medieval religious art is on display, usually supplemented by a temporary exposition.

DALÍ ESCULTOR Map pp298-9

Carrer dels Arcs 5; admission €8; 🕑 10am-10pm; Ⓜ Liceu

One of the best things about this collection is its superb location in the Reial Cercle Artístic (Royal Art Circle) building near La Catedral. This somewhat hyped display offers 60-odd little-known sculptures by a man renowned for his painting. Sketches, photos and documents by and on the artist complete the picture. If you can't visit his museum-mausoleum in Figueres (p232),

this is no substitute but does provide some clues to the life and work of the moustachioed maestro.

ESGLÉSIA DE SANTS JUST I PASTOR Map pp298-9

☎ 93 301 74 33; Plaça de Sant Just 5; admission free; 🕑 10am-1pm & 5-8pm Mon-Sat; Ⓜ Liceu

This somewhat neglected, single-nave church was built in 1342 in Catalan Gothic style, with chapels on either side of the buttressing. Inside this church, reputed to be the site of the oldest parish church in Barcelona but now mostly dating from the 14th century, you can admire some fine stained-glass windows. In front of it is what is claimed to be the city's oldest Gothic fountain.

On the morning of 11 September 1924, Antoni Gaudí was arrested as he attempted to enter the church to attend Mass. In those days of the dictatorship of General Primo de Rivera, it took little to ruffle official feathers, and Gaudí's refusal to speak Spanish (Castilian) earned him the better part of a day in the cells until a friend came to bail him out.

GRAN TEATRE DEL LICEU Map pp298-9

☎ 93 485 99 00; www.liceubarcelona.com; La Rambla dels Caputxins 51-59; admission €4; 🕑 guided tour 10am, unguided visits 11.30am, noon & 1pm; Ⓜ Liceu; ♿

You may not be able to catch a night at the opera, but you can still have a look around one of Europe's greatest opera houses, known to locals simply as the Liceu. Smaller than Milan's La Scala but bigger than Venice's La Fenice, it can seat up to 2300 people in its grand horseshoe auditorium.

Built in 1847, the Liceu launched such Catalan stars as Josep (aka José) Carreras and Montserrat Caballé (see p33). Fire virtually destroyed it in 1994, but city authorities were quick to get it back into operation. Carefully reconstructing the 19th-century auditorium and installing the latest in theatre technology, technicians brought the Liceu back to life in October 1999. You can take a quick turn around the main public areas of the theatre or join one of two guided tours.

On the standard tour (adult/child under 10 years/student €6/free/4) you are taken to the grand foyer, with its thick pillars and sumptuous chandeliers, and then up the marble staircase to the **Saló dels Miralls** (Hall of Mirrors). These both survived the 1994 fire and the latter was traditionally where theatre-goers mingled during intermission. With mirrors, ceiling frescoes, fluted columns and high-and-mighty phrases in praise of the arts, it all exudes a typically neobaroque richness worthy of its 19th-century patrons. You are then led up to the 4th-floor stalls to admire the theatre itself.

The longer tour (adult/child under 10 years/student €9/free/7) takes in all of the above and a collection of modernista art, El Cercle del Liceu, which contains some works by Ramon Casas.

LA CATEDRAL & AROUND Map pp298-9

☎ 93 342 82 60; Plaça de la Seu; admission free, special visit €4; ☉ 8am-12.15pm & 5.15-7.30pm, special visit 1-5pm; Ⓜ Jaume I

Approached from the broad Avinguda de la Catedral, Barcelona's central place of worship presents a magnificent image. The richly decorated main (northwest) façade, laced with gargoyles and the stone intricacies you would expect of northern European Gothic, sets it quite apart from other churches in Barcelona. The façade was actually added in 1870 (and is receiving a serious round of restoration, at the time of writing not due for completion before early 2007), although it is based on a 1408 design. The rest of the building was built between 1298 and 1460. The other façades are sparse in decoration, and the octagonal, flat-roofed towers are a clear reminder that, even here, Catalan Gothic architectural principles prevailed.

The interior is a broad, soaring space divided into a central nave and two aisles by lines of elegant, slim pillars. The cathedral was one of the few churches in Barcelona spared by the anarchists in the civil war, so its ornamentation, never overly lavish, is intact.

In the first chapel on the right from the northwest entrance, the main Crucifixion figure above the altar is **Sant Crist de Lepant**. It is said Don Juan's flagship bore it into battle at Lepanto and that the figure acquired its odd stance by dodging an incoming cannonball. Further along this same wall, past the southwest transept, are the wooden **coffins** of Count Ramon Berenguer I and his wife Almodis, founders of the 11th-century Romanesque predecessor to the present cathedral. Left from the main entrance is the baptismal font where,

according to a story owing more to myth than hard research, six North American Indians brought to Europe by Columbus after his first voyage of accidental discovery were bathed in holy water.

In the middle of the central nave is the late-14th-century, exquisitely sculpted timber **coro** (choir stalls; admission €1.50). The coats of arms on the stalls belong to members of the Barcelona chapter of the Order of the Golden Fleece. Emperor Carlos V presided over the order's meeting here in 1519. Take the time to look at the workmanship up close – the Virgin Mary and Child depicted on the pulpit are especially fine.

A broad staircase before the main altar leads you to the **crypt**, which contains the tomb of Santa Eulàlia, one of Barcelona's two patron saints and more affectionately known as Laia. The reliefs on the alabaster sarcophagus, executed by Pisan artisans, recount some of her tortures and, along the top strip, the removal of her body to its present resting place.

For a bird's-eye view (mind the poop) of medieval Barcelona, visit the cathedral's **roof** and tower by taking the lift (€2) from the Capella de les Animes del Purgatori near the northeast transept.

From the southwest transept, exit by the partly Romanesque door (one of the few remnants of the present church's predecessor) to the leafy **claustre** (cloister), with its fountains and flock of 13 geese. The geese supposedly represent the age of Santa Eulàlia at the time of her martyrdom and have, generation after generation, been squawking here since medieval days. They

MANIC MONDAYS

While many of Barcelona's attractions shut their doors on Monday, some remain open. Among those that will welcome you on the first day of the working week are Casa-Museu Gaudí (Park Güell), Centre d'Art Santa Mònica, Fundació Fran Daurel, Fundació Francisco Godia, Galeria Olímpica, Gran Teatre del Liceu, Jardí Botànic, La Catedral, La Pedrera, La Sagrada Família, Monument a Colom, Museu d'Art Contemporani de Barcelona (Macba), Museu de Cera, Museu de l'Eròtica, Museu de la Xocolata, Museu del Futbol Club Barcelona, Museu del Perfum, Museu Egipci, Museu i Centre d'Estudis de l'Esport Dr Melchior Colet, Museu Marítim, Museu Taurí, Palau de la Música Catalana and the Pavelló Mies van der Rohe.

make fine watchdogs! One of the cloister chapels commemorates 930 priests, monks and nuns martyred during the civil war.

Along the northern flank of the cloister you can enter the **Sala Capitular** (Chapter House; admission €1.50; 🕙 10am-12.15pm & 5.15-7pm Mon-Sat, 10am-12.45pm & 5.15-7pm Sun). Although it's bathed in rich red carpet and cosseted by fine timber seating, the few artworks gathered here are of minor interest. Among them figure a pietà by Bartolomeo Bermejo. A couple of doors down in the northwest corner of the cloister is the **Capella de Santa Llúcia**, one of the few intact reminders of Romanesque Barcelona. Walk out the door on to Carrer de Santa Llúcia and turn around to look at the exterior – you can see that, although incorporated into La Catedral, it is a separate building.

Upon exiting the Capella de Santa Llúcia, wander into the 16th-century **Casa de l'Ardiaca** (Archdeacon's House; 🕙 9am-9pm Mon-Fri, 9am-2pm Sat) opposite, which serves as an archive. You may stroll around the supremely serene courtyard, cooled by trees and a fountain. Climb the stairs to the next level, from where you can look down into the courtyard and across to La Catedral. Inside the building itself, parts of the **Roman wall** are visible.

You may visit La Catedral in one of two ways. In the morning or afternoon, entrance is free and you can opt to visit any combination of the choir stalls, chapter house and roof you choose. If you want to visit all three, it costs less (and is less crowded) to enter for the so-called 'special visit' between 1.30pm and 5pm.

Across Carrer del Bisbe Irurita is the 17th-century **Palau Episcopal** or Palau del Bisbat (Bishop's Palace). Virtually nothing remains of the original 13th-century structure. The Roman city's northwest gate stood here, and you can see the lower segments of the Roman towers that stood on either side of the gate at the base of the Palau Episcopal and Casa de l'Ardiaca. In fact, the lower part of the entire northwest wall of the Casa de l'Ardiaca is of Roman origin – you can also make out part of the first arch of the one-time Roman aqueducts.

Across Plaça Nova from La Catedral your eye may be caught by childlike scribblings on the façade of the **Col.legi de Arquitectes** (Architectural College). It is, in fact, a giant contribution by Picasso done in 1962.

LA RAMBLA Map pp298-9

Ⓜ **Catalunya, Liceu or Drassanes**

Flanked by narrow traffic lanes and plane trees, the middle of La Rambla is a broad pedestrian boulevard, crowded every day until the wee hours with a cross section of Barcelonins and out-of-towners. Dotted with cafés, restaurants, kiosks and newsstands, and enlivened by buskers, pavement artists, mimes and living statues, La Rambla rarely allows a dull moment.

La Rambla gets its name from a seasonal stream (*raml* in Arabic) that once ran here. From the early Middle Ages on it was better known as the Cagalell (Stream of Shit) and lay outside the city walls until the 14th century. Monastic buildings were then built and, subsequently, mansions of the well-to-do from the 16th to the early 19th centuries. Unofficially, La Rambla is divided into five sections – this explains why, to many people, the boulevard goes by the name of Las Ramblas.

The initial stretch heading south from Plaça de Catalunya is known as **La Rambla de Canaletes**, named after a turn-of-the-20th-century **drinking fountain**, the water of which supposedly emerges from what were once known as the springs of Canaletes. It used to be said of people who lived in Barcelona that they 'drank the waters of Les Canaletes'. Nowadays people say that anyone who drinks from the fountain will return to Barcelona, which is not such a bad prospect.

The second stretch, **La Rambla dels Estudis** (from below Carrer de la Canuda to Carrer de la Portaferrissa) is also called La Rambla dels Ocells (birds) because of its twittering bird market.

Just north of Carrer del Carme, the **Església de Betlem** was constructed in baroque style for the Jesuits in the late 17th and early 18th centuries to replace an earlier church destroyed by fire in 1671. Fire was a bit of a theme for this site: the church was once considered the most splendid of Barcelona's few baroque offerings, but leftist arsonists torched it in 1936.

La Rambla de Sant Josep, named after a former monastery dedicated to St Joseph, runs from Carrer de la Portaferrissa to Plaça de la Boqueria and is lined with verdant **flower stalls**, which give it the alternative name La Rambla de les Flors.

The **Palau de la Virreina** (La Rambla de Sant Josep 99) is a grand 18th-century rococo

La Rambla (p85)

mansion (with some neoclassical elements) housing an arts/entertainment information and ticket office run by the Ajuntament. Built by the then corrupt captain-general of Chile (a Spanish colony that included the Peruvian silver mines of Potosí), Manuel d'Amat i de Junyent, it is a rare example of such postbaroque building in Barcelona.

Across La Rambla at No 118 is an equally rare example of a more pure neoclassical pile, **Palau Moja**, which houses government offices, the Generalitat's bookshop and exhibition space. Its clean, classical lines are best appreciated from across La Rambla.

Next, you are confronted by the bustling sound, smell and taste-fest of the **Mercat de la Boqueria**. It is possibly La Rambla's most interesting building, not so much for its modernista-influenced design (it was actually built over a long period, from 1840 to 1914, on the site of the former St Joseph monastery) as for the action of the food market (see p141).

At Plaça de la Boqueria, where four side streets meet just north of Liceu Metro station, you can walk all over a Miró – the colourful **Mosaïc de Miró** in the pavement, with one tile signed by the artist.

La Rambla dels Caputxins (aka La Rambla del Centre), named after another now non-existent monastery, runs from Plaça de la Boqueria to Carrer dels Escudellers. The latter street is named after the potters' guild, founded in the 13th century, whose members lived and worked here (their raw materials came principally from Sicily). On the western side of La Rambla is the **Gran Teatre del Liceu** (see p83).

Further south on the eastern side of La Rambla dels Caputxins is the entrance to the palm-shaded **Plaça Reial**. Below this point La Rambla gets seedier, with strip clubs and peep shows. The final stretch, **La Rambla de Santa Mònica**, widens out to approach the **Monument a Colom** (below) overlooking Port Vell. La Rambla here is named after the Convento de Santa Mònica, which once stood on the western flank of the street and has since been converted into an art gallery and cultural centre, the **Centre d'Art Santa Mònica** (☎ 93 316 28 10; La Rambla de Santa Mònica 7; admission free; ◷ 11am-8pm Tue-Sat, 11am-3pm Sun & holidays; Ⓜ Drassanes).

MONUMENT A COLOM Map pp298-9

☎ 93 302 52 24; Plaça del Portal de la Pau; lift adult/under 4yr/senior & 4-12yr €2.30/free/1.50; ◷ 9am-8.30pm May-Oct, 10am-6.30pm Nov-Apr; Ⓜ Drassanes

High above the swirl of traffic on the roundabout below, a pigeon-poop–coiffed Columbus keeps permanent watch, pointing vaguely out to the Mediterranean (to his home town of Genoa?). Built for the Universal Exhibition in 1888, the monument allows you to zip up 60m in the lift for bird's-eye views back up La Rambla and across the ports of Barcelona. It was in Barcelona that Columbus allegedly gave the delighted Catholic monarchs a report of his first discoveries in the Americas after his voyage in 1492. In the 19th century it was popularly believed here that Columbus was one of Barcelona's most illustrious sons. Some historians still make the claim today.

MUSEU DE CERA Map pp298-9

☎ 93 317 26 49; www.museocerabcn.com; Passatge de la Banca 7; adult/child €6.65/3.75; ⊕ 10am-1.30pm & 4-7.30pm Mon-Fri, 11am-2pm & 4.30-8.30pm Sat, Sun & holidays; Ⓜ Drassanes; ♿

Inside this grand late-19th-century pile stand, sit and lounge about 300 wax figures. Yasser Arafat is here, along with a rather awkward-looking Prince Charles with Camilla. As if to show us what she feels, Princess Di is elsewhere giving Mother Teresa a hand. *Star Wars* characters prance in sci-fi style, making poor old Don Quixote look a little forlorn. Dalí had to be in the crowd, along with more exotic figures like Ali Bey, the 18th-century Barcelona-born spy in Mecca. There is also a hall of horror (how could there not be?).

MUSEU D'HISTÒRIA DE LA CIUTAT Map pp298-9

☎ 93 315 11 11; www.museuhistoria.bcn.es; Carrer del Veguer; adult/student €4/2.50 (incl Museu-Monestir de Pedralbes & Park Güell Centre de Acollida), 4-8pm 1st Sat of month free, temporary exhibitions €3.50/1.50; ⊕ 10am-2pm & 4-8pm Tue-Sat, 10am-3pm Sun Oct-May, 10am-8pm Tue-Sat, 10am-3pm Sun Jun-Sep; Ⓜ Jaume I

Leap back into Roman Barcino with a subterranean stroll and then stride around parts of the former Palau Reial Major (Grand Royal Palace), among the key locations of medieval princely power in Barcelona, in what is one of Barcelona's most fascinating museums.

Enter through **Casa Padellàs**, just south of Plaça del Rei. Casa Padellàs was built for a 16th-century noble family in Carrer dels Mercaders and moved here, stone by stone, in the 1930s. It has a courtyard typical of Barcelona's late-Gothic and baroque mansions, with a graceful external staircase up to the 1st floor. Today it leads to a restored Roman tower and a section of Roman wall. Below ground is a remarkable walk through excavated Roman and Visigothic Barcelona – complete with sections of a Roman street, Roman baths, wine stores and remains of a Visigothic basilica and baptismal pool. The route extends underneath the cathedral, where traces of the earlier Romanesque structure can be seen.

Once through, you emerge at a hall and ticket office set up on the northern side of Plaça del Rei. To your right is the **Saló del Tinell**, the banqueting hall of the royal palace and a fine example of Catalan Gothic (built between 1359 and 1370). Its broad arches and bare walls give a sense of solidity and solemnity that would have made an appropriate setting for Fernando and Isabel to hear Columbus' first reports of the New World. The hall is sometimes used for temporary exhibitions, which may cost extra, and mean that your peaceful contemplation of its architectural majesty is somewhat obstructed.

As you leave the Saló you come to the **Capella Reial de Santa Àgata**, the palace chapel, also built in the 14th century. Outside, a spindly bell tower rises from the northeast side of Plaça del Rei. Inside all is bare except for the 15th-century altarpiece and the magnificent *techumbre* (decorated timber ceiling). The altarpiece is considered to be one of Jaume Huguet's finest surviving works.

Head down the fan-shaped stairs from Plaça del Rei and bear right to the entrance to the multitiered **Mirador del Rei Martí** (lookout tower of King Martin), built in 1555, long after the king's death! It is part of the museum and leads you to the gallery above the square. If restoration work is complete, you can climb to the top of the tower, which rewards you with excellent views over the city.

MUSEU DE L'ERÒTICA Map pp298-9

☎ 93 318 98 65; www.erotica-museum.com; La Rambla de Sant Josep 96; adult/senior & student €7.50/6.50; ⊕ 10am-midnight Jun-Sep, 11am-9pm Oct-May; Ⓜ Liceu; ♿

Observe what naughtiness people have been getting up to since ancient times in this Erotica Museum – lots of Kamasutra and 1920s flickering porn movies. The museum caters to all tastes. For those red-faced about entering such a scurrilous place, there really is lots of sound historical material, such as Indian bas-reliefs showing various aspects of Tantric love, 18th-century wood carvings depicting Kamasutra positions (can normal people really engage in all these gymnastics?), Japanese porcelain porn and the like. An array of modern, vaguely erotic artwork also lends intellectual weight to the exercise. Altogether more fun are the 18th-century S&M torture room, the rather complicated, dildo-equipped 'pleasure seat' and early-20th-century skin flicks.

MUSEU FREDERIC MARÈS Map pp298-9

☎ 93 310 58 00; www.museumares.bcn.es; Plaça de Sant Iu 5-6; adult/senior & student €3/1.50, Wed afternoons & 1st Sun of month free; ☺ 10am-7pm Tue-Sat, 10am-3pm Sun & holidays; Ⓜ Jaume I; ♿

This eclectic collection is housed in what was once the medieval Palau Reial Major, on Carrer dels Comtes de Barcelona. Frederic Marès i Deulovol (1893–1991) was a rich sculptor, traveller and obsessive collector. He specialised in medieval Spanish sculpture, huge quantities of which are displayed in the basement and on the ground and 1st floors – including some lovely polychrome wooden sculptures of the Crucifixion and the Virgin.

The top two floors hold a mind-boggling array of knick-knacks, from toy soldiers and cribs to scissors and 19th-century playing cards, from early still cameras to pipes, from fine ceramics to a room that once served as Marès' study and library, but is now crammed with sculpture. The shady courtyard houses a pleasant summer café.

PALAU DEL LLOCTINENT Map pp298-9

Carrer dels Comtes de Barcelona; admission free; Ⓜ Jaume I

The southwest side of Plaça del Rei is taken up by this palace, built in the 1550s as the residence of the Spanish *lloctinent* (viceroy) of Catalonia. The building is somewhat run-down, but boasts a fine wooden ceiling and pleasing courtyard. Until 1993 it housed the Arxiu de la Corona d'Aragón, a unique archive documenting the history of the kingdom prior to unification under Fernando and Isabel. When you walk outside, have a look at the walls of La Catedral. See all the grooves cut into the stone? The viceroy's soldiers, it is said, used the church walls to sharpen their weapons.

PLAÇA DEL REI Map pp298-9

Ⓜ Jaume I

Plaça del Rei is the courtyard of what was the Palau Reial Major, the palace of the counts of Barcelona and monarchs of Aragón. It's surrounded by centuries-old buildings, most of which are open to visitors as the **Museu d'Història de la Ciutat** (see p87). The square is frequently the scene of organised or impromptu concerts and is one of the most atmospheric corners of the Gothic city.

PLAÇA DE SANT JAUME Map pp298-9

Ⓜ Jaume I

In the 2000 or so years since the Romans settled here, the area around this square (often remodelled), which started life as the forum, has been the focus of Barcelona's civic life. Facing each other across it are the Palau de la Generalitat (seat of Catalonia's regional government) on the north side and the Ajuntament (Town Hall) to the south. Both have fine Gothic interiors, which, unhappily, the public can enter only at limited times.

Founded in the early 15th century on land that had largely belonged to the city's by-then defunct Jewish community to house Catalonia's government, the **Palau de la Generalitat** (☺ free guided visit 10am-1pm 2nd & 4th Sun of month plus 23 Apr, 11 Sep & 24 Sep) was extended over the centuries as its importance (and bureaucracy) grew.

Marc Safont designed the original Gothic main entrance on Carrer del Bisbe Irurita. The modern main entrance on Plaça de Sant Jaume is a late-Renaissance job with neoclassical leanings. If you wander by in the evening, squint up through the windows into the **Saló de Sant Jordi** (Hall of St George) and you will get some idea of the sumptuousness of the interior.

If you *do* get inside, you're in for a treat. Normally you will have to enter from Carrer de Sant Sever. The first rooms you pass through are characterised by low vaulted ceilings. From here you pass upstairs to the raised courtyard known as the **Pati dels Tarongers**, a modest Gothic orangery (opened occasionally to the public for concert performances of the palace's chimes; see p190). The 16th-century **Sala Daurada i de Sessions**, one of the rooms leading off the patio, is a splendid meeting hall lit up by huge chandeliers. Still more imposing is the Renaissance Saló de Sant Jordi, whose murals were added last century – many an occasion of pomp and circumstance takes place here. Finally, you descend the staircase of the Gothic **Pati Central** to leave by what was, in the beginning, the building's main entrance.

Facing the Palau de la Generalitat, and otherwise known as the Casa de la Ciutat, the **Ajuntament** (☎ 010; admission free; ☺ 10am-1pm Sun) has been the seat of city power for centuries. The Consell de Cent, from medieval times the city's ruling council, first sat here in the 14th century, but the building has lamentably undergone many changes since the days of Barcelona's Gothic-era splendour.

Only the original, now disused, entrance on Carrer de la Ciutat retains its Gothic ornament. The main 19th-century neoclassical façade on the square is a charmless riposte to the Palau de la Generalitat. Inside, the **Saló de Cent** is the hall in which the town council once held its plenary sessions. The broad vaulting is pure Catalan Gothic and the *artesonado* (intricately joined wooden) ceiling demonstrates fine work. In fact, much of what you see is comparatively recent. The building was badly damaged in a bombardment in 1842 and has been repaired and tampered with repeatedly. The wooden neo-Gothic seating was added at the beginning of the 20th century, as was the grand alabaster *retablo* (retable, or altarpiece) at the back. To the right you enter the small **Saló de la Reina Regente**, built in 1860, where the Ajuntament now sits. To the left of the Saló de Cent you reach the **Saló de les Croniques** – the murals here recount Catalan exploits in Greece and the Near East in Catalonia's empire-building days.

PLAÇA DE SANT JOSEP ORIOL & AROUND Map pp298-9

Ⓜ Liceu

This small plaza, not far from La Rambla, is the prettiest in the Barri Gòtic. Its bars and cafés attract buskers and artists and make it a lively place to hang out. It is surrounded by quaint little streets, many of them dotted with other appealing cafés, restaurants and shops.

Looming over the plaza is the **Església de Santa Maria del Pi** (🕒 8.30am-1pm & 4.30-9pm Mon-Sat, 9am-2pm & 5-9pm Sun & holidays), a Gothic church built in the 14th to 16th centuries. The beautiful rose window above its entrance on Plaça del Pi is claimed by some to be the world's biggest. The interior of the church was gutted when leftists ransacked it in the opening months of the Civil War in 1936 and most of the stained glass is modern. The third chapel on the left is dedicated to Sant Josep Oriol, with a map showing the places in the church where he worked numerous miracles. According to legend, a 10th-century fisherman discovered an image of the Virgin Mary in a *pi* (pine tree) he was intent on cutting down to build a boat. Struck by the vision, he instead built a little chapel, later

to be succeeded by this Gothic church. A pine still grows in the square.

PLAÇA REIAL Map pp298-9

Ⓜ Liceu

Just south of Carrer de Ferran, near its La Rambla end, Plaça Reial is a traffic-free plaza whose 19th-century neoclassical façades hide numerous eateries, bars and nightspots. It was created on the site of a convent, one of several destroyed along La Rambla (the strip was fairly teeming with religious institutions) in the wake of the Spain-wide disentailment laws that stripped the Church of much of its property. The lampposts by the central fountain are Antoni Gaudí's first known works.

Residents here have a rough time of it, with noise a virtual constant as punters crowd in and out of restaurants, bars and *discotecas* (clubs) at all hours. Downright dangerous until the 1980s, the square retains a restless atmosphere, where un-suspecting tourists, respectable citizens, ragged buskers, down-and-outs and sharp-witted pickpockets come face to face. Don't be put off, but watch your pockets.

The southern half of Barri Gòtic is imbued with the memory of Picasso, who lived as a teenager with his family in Carrer de la Mercè, had his first studio in Carrer de la Plata (now a rather cheesy restaurant) and was a regular visitor to a brothel at Carrer d'Avinyó 27. That experience may have inspired his 1907 painting *Les Demoiselles d'Avignon*.

Plaça Reial (above)

ROMAN TOMBS Map pp298-9

Plaça de la Vila de Madrid; Ⓜ Catalunya

Along Carrer de la Canuda, a block east of the top end of La Rambla, is a sunken garden where a series of Roman tombs lie exposed. The burial ground stretched along either side of the road leading northwest out of Barcelona's Roman predecessor, Barcino.

ROMAN WALLS Map pp298-9 & pp302-3

Ⓜ Jaume I

From Plaça del Rei it's worth taking a detour northeast to see the two best surviving stretches of Barcelona's Roman walls. One is on the southwest side of Plaça Ramon de Berenguer el Gran, with the Capella Reial de Santa Àgata atop them. The square itself is dominated by a statue of Ramon de Berenguer el Gran done by Josep Llimona in 1880. The other is a little further south, by the northern end of Carrer del Sotstinent Navarro. The Romans built and reinforced these walls in the 3rd and 4th centuries AD, after the first attacks by Germanic tribes from the north.

SINAGOGA MAJOR Map pp298-9

☎ 93 317 07 90; www.calldebarcelona.org; Carrer de Marlet 5; admission free; ◷ 11am-2pm & 4-7pm Tue-Sat, 11am-2pm Sun; Ⓜ Liceu

When an Argentine investor bought a run-down electrician's store with an eye to converting it into central Barcelona's umpteenth trendy bar, he could hardly have known he had stumbled onto the remains of the city's main medieval synagogue. Remnants of medieval and Roman-era walls remain in the small vaulted space that you enter from the street. Also remaining are tanners' wells installed in the 15th century. The second chamber has been spruced up and is again used as a synagogue. A remnant of late-Roman-era wall here, given its orientation facing Jerusalem, has led some to speculate that there was a synagogue here even in Roman times. This was one of four synagogues in the city, but after the pogroms of 1391 it was Christianised by the placing of an effigy of St Dominic on the building. A guide will explain the significance of the site in various languages.

The area between Carrer dels Banys Nous and Plaça de Sant Jaume was the heart of the city's medieval Jewish quarter, the Call, until the Jews were expelled in the late 15th century. Even before their expulsion, Jews were not exactly privileged citizens. As in many medieval centres, they were obliged to wear a special identifying mark on their garments and had trouble getting permission to expand their ghetto as the Call's population increased.

TEMPLE ROMÀ D'AUGUSTI Map pp298-9

Carrer del Paradis; admission free; ◷ 10am-2pm Mon-Sat; Ⓜ Jaume I

Opposite the southeast end of La Catedral, narrow Carrer del Paradis leads towards Plaça de Sant Jaume. Inside No 10 are four columns and the architrave of Barcelona's main Roman temple, dedicated to Caesar Augustus and built to worship his imperial highness in the 1st century AD. You are now standing on the highest point of Roman Barcino – Mont Taber. A plaque outside insists it is 16.9m above sea level. You may well find the door open outside the listed hours. Just pop in.

EL RAVAL

Drinking & Nightlife p166; Eating p144; Shopping p204; Sleeping p215

Long one of the most rough-and-tumble parts of Barcelona, El Raval is becoming so hip in a grungy, inner-city way that they've even invented a verb for rambling around El Raval – *ravalejar*.

El Raval (an Arabic word referring to the suburbs beyond the medieval walls that long lined La Rambla) has had a chequered history. Its bottom half is better known as the Barri Xinès, a seedy red-light zone that even today, after decades of efforts to clean the area up, retains a touch of its dodgy feel.

For centuries the area has been home to prostitutes, louche lads and, at times, a bohemian collection of interlopers. In the 1920s and '30s especially, it was a popular playground with Barcelonins of many classes,

---

EL RAVAL TOP FIVE

- Antic Hospital de la Santa Creu (opposite)
- Centre de Cultura Contemporània de Barcelona (CCCB; p92)
- Església de Sant Pau del Camp (p92)
- Museu d'Art Contemporani de Barcelona (Macba; p92)
- Palau Güell (p93)

busy at night with the rambunctious activity in taverns, *cafés concerts*, cabarets and brothels. Carrer Nou de la Rambla, where Picasso lived for a while, was particularly lively. By the 1960s many of the brothels and bars had shut down, but there was still plenty of activity, especially when the American fleet came to town. This was also the haunt of Pepe Carvalho, the dissolute star in Barcelona writer Manuel Vázquez Montalbán's much-loved detective stories (see p30).

Recent waves of immigration have changed the makeup of El Raval, which has become the main centre for the city's busy Pakistani population and a North African contingent. Just as great an impact has come from the explosion of bars and restaurants. While it may never attain the popularity of El Born (see p93), El Raval has arrived on the map. Suddenly swarms of more adventurous locals and curious visitors have opened up the area to joyous exploration, especially by night.

Orientation

Bounded by La Rambla in the east and Ronda de Sant Antoni, Ronda de Sant Pau and Avinguda del Paral.lel to the west and south, El Raval started life as a higgledy-piggledy suburb of medieval Barcelona.

Carrer de l'Hospital, named after the city's 15th-century hospital and once the road to Madrid, roughly divides the area in two. The northern half has an almost respectable air about it. It is certainly full of diversity. From the Meridien hotel on expensive Carrer del Pintor Fortuny you are a couple of blocks away from the colourful Mercat de la Boqueria produce market and a feast of contemporary art at the Museu d'Art Contemporani de Barcelona (Macba).

Students flock from class in buildings along Carrer de Valldonzella and Plaça de Joan Coromines to bars along Carrer de Joaquín Costa, joined by others from the Escola Massana dance school on Carrer de les Egipciaques and bookworms who spend the day crouched over tomes in the national library.

Carrer de l'Hospital marks a crossroads. Home to an unassuming mosque (virtually opposite the national library), the street fills with male Muslims around lunch time on Friday. The western end of the street has been largely taken over by Pakistanis and North Africans, who have opened cafés,

www.lonelyplanet.com

TRANSPORT

El Raval is encircled by three Metro lines. Línies 1, 2 and 3 stop at strategic points right around the district, so nothing is far from a Metro stop. The Línia 3 stop at Liceu is the most strategic exit point.

halal butcher shops and barber shops. In La Rambla del Raval, which replaced a whole slum block in 2000, Pakistanis sometimes play cricket, while a youthful set of hedonists explores new bars opening up on and around it.

ANTIC HOSPITAL DE LA SANTA CREU Map pp298-9

☎ 93 270 23 00; Carrer de l'Hospital 56; Ⓜ Liceu

Behind Mercat de la Boqueria stands what was, in the 15th century, the city's main hospital. The restored Antic Hospital de la Santa Creu (Former Holy Cross Hospital) today houses the **Biblioteca de Catalunya** (National Library of Catalonia; admission free; ☿ library 9am-8pm Mon-Fri, 9am-2pm Sat), as well as the **Institut d'Estudis Catalans** (Institute for Catalan Studies).

The library is the single most complete collection of documents (estimated at around three million) tracing the region's long history. The hospital, which was begun in 1401 and functioned until the 1930s, was considered one of the best in Europe in its medieval heyday.

Today you can freely visit the most impressive part of the library, the grand reading rooms beneath broad Gothic stone arches, where you can also see temporary displays of anything from old records to medieval monastic hymnals.

Otherwise, it is possible to join a tour on 23 April (Sant Jordi) and one day late in September (the date changes), when the entire building throws itself open for guided visits.

The visit takes you through the library's public areas and others usually closed to the public, such as the **Museu del Llibre Frederic Marès**, a former private ward in the hospital whose bright tile decoration of the stations of the cross was done in the 17th century. Marès donated 1500 documents and books to the library, some of which are on display. He also sculpted the medallions of great figures of Catalan culture. Antoni Gaudí wound up in the Via Crucis ward in 1926 after being run over by a tram. He died here.

Sights

EL RAVAL

The **capella** (chapel; ☎ 93 442 71 71; www.bcn.es/virreinaexposicions; admission free; ☯ noon-2pm & 4-8pm Tue-Sat, 11am-2pm Sun & holidays) of the former hospital is also worth poking your nose into and is often a venue for temporary exhibitions.

CENTRE DE CULTURA CONTEMPORÀNIA DE BARCELONA (CCCB) Map pp298-9

☎ 93 306 41 00; www.cccb.org; Carrer de Montalegre 5; adult/student €6/4.40; ☯ 11am-8pm Tue-Sat, 11am-3pm Sun & holidays 21 Jun-21 Sep, 11am-2pm & 4-8pm Tue, Thu & Fri, 11am-8pm Wed & Sat, 11am-7pm Sun & holidays 22 Sep-20 Jun; Ⓜ Universitat; ♿

A complex of auditoriums, exhibition spaces and conference halls opened here in 1994 in what had been an 18th-century hospice, the Casa de la Caritat. The expansive courtyard, with a vast glass wall on one side, is spectacular. With 4500 sq metres of exposition space in four separate areas, the centre hosts a constantly changing programme of exhibitions, film cycles and other events.

CONVENT DELS ÀNGELS Map pp298-9

☎ 93 301 77 75; Plaça dels Àngels; Ⓜ Universitat; ♿

The 400-year-old convent was renovated as exposition space by FAD (Foment de les Arts Decoratives), an umbrella group of design associations that has been busy in the city since 1903. It opens only when a show is on, and admission prices vary depending on the exhibition. Although largely gutted, the Gothic framework has been left intact.

ESGLÉSIA DE SANT PAU DEL CAMP Map pp298-9

☎ 93 441 00 01; Carrer de Sant Pau 101; admission free; ☯ cloister 10am-2pm; Ⓜ Paral.lel

Back in the 9th century, when monks founded the monastery of Sant Pau del Camp (St Paul in the Fields), it was a good walk from the city gates amid fields and gardens. Today the church and cloister, erected in the 12th century, are surrounded by dense inner-city housing. The doorway to the church bears some rare Visigothic sculptural decoration, predating the Muslim invasion of Spain. Inside, the beautiful

Romanesque cloister is the main reason for dropping by.

MUSEU D'ART CONTEMPORANI DE BARCELONA (MACBA) Map pp298-9

☎ 93 412 08 10; www.macba.es; Plaça dels Àngels 1; admission €7, Wed €3; ☯ 11am-7.30pm Mon & Wed-Fri, 10am-8pm Sat, 10am-3pm Sun & holidays; Ⓜ Universitat; ♿

The ground and 1st floors of this great white bastion of contemporary art are given over to exhibitions from the gallery's own collections. You may see works by Antoni Tàpies, Joan Brossa, Paul Klee, Miquel Barceló and a whole raft of international talent, depending on the theme of the ever-changing exposition. The gallery also presents temporary exhibitions and has an extensive art bookshop. Outside, the spectacle is as intriguing as in. While skateboarders dominate the space south of the museum, you may well find Pakistani kids enjoying a game of cricket in Plaça de Joan Coromines.

MUSEU MARÍTIM Map pp298-9

☎ 93 342 99 20; www.museumaritimbarcelona .org; Avinguda de les Drassanes; admission €6, 3-8pm 1st Sat of month free; ☯ 10am-8pm; Ⓜ Drassanes; ♿

Venice had its Arsenal and Barcelona the Reials Drassanes (Royal Shipyards), from which Don Juan of Austria's flagship galley was launched to lead a joint Spanish-Venetian fleet into the momentous Battle of Lepanto against the Turks in 1571.

These mighty Gothic shipyards are not as extensive as their Venetian counterpart but an extraordinary piece of civilian architecture nonetheless. Today the broad arches shelter the Museu Marítim, the city's seafaring-history museum and one of the most fascinating in town.

The shipyards were, in their heyday, among the greatest in Europe. Begun in the 13th century and completed by 1378, the long, arched (the highest arches reach 13m) bays once sloped off as slipways directly into the water – which lapped the seaward side of the Drassanes until at least the end of the 18th century.

The centre of the shipyards is dominated by a full-sized replica (made in the 1970s) of Don Juan of Austria's flagship. A clever audiovisual display aboard the vessel brings to life the ghastly existence of the slaves, prisoners and volunteers(!) who at full steam could haul this vessel along at 9 knots. They remained chained to their seats, four to an oar, at all times. Here they worked, drank (fresh water was stored below decks, where the infirmary was also located), ate, slept and went to the loo. You could *smell* a galley like this from miles away.

Fishing vessels, old navigation charts, models and dioramas of the Barcelona waterfront make up the rest of this engaging museum.

Outside and partly obscured by rampant vegetation on the Avinguda del Paral.lel side of the building are the most significant remnants of the city walls erected here in the 13th century and later extended under count-king Pere el Ceremoniós (1336–87).

PALAU GÜELL Map pp298–9

☎ 93 317 39 74; Carrer Nou de la Rambla 3-5;
Ⓜ Drassanes

Welcome to the early days of Gaudí's fevered architectural imagination. This extraordinary modernista mansion, one of the few major buildings of that era raised in Ciutat Vella, gives an insight into its maker's prodigious genius. He built it just off La Rambla in the late 1880s for his wealthy and faithful patron, the industrialist Eusebi Güell. Although a little sombre compared with some of his later whims, it is still a characteristic riot of styles (Gothic, Islamic, Art Nouveau) and materials. After the civil war, the police occupied it and tortured political prisoners in the basement.

Up two floors you reach the main hall and its annexes. The hall is a parabolic pyramid – each wall an arch stretching up three floors and coming together to form a dome that reaches the ceiling. The roof is a mad Gaudían riot of tiled colour and fanciful design in the building's chimney pots.

Picasso – who, incidentally, hated Gaudí's work – began his Blue Period in 1902 in a studio across the street at Carrer Nou de la Rambla 10. Begging to differ with Sr Picasso, Unesco declared the Palau, together with Gaudí's other main works (La Sagrada Família, Casa Batlló, La Pedrera, Park Güell, Casa Vicenç and Colònia Güell crypt) a World Heritage site.

At the time of writing Palau Güell was closed for renovation until 2007.

LA RIBERA

Drinking & Nightlife p169; Eating p147; Shopping p205; Sleeping p217

By the beginning of the 13th century, two busy communities had developed in the fields just northeast of Barcelona's then city walls: Vilanova de Sant Pere, clustered around the convent of Sant Pere de les Puelles, and Vilanova de la Mar, huddled around the Romanesque predecessor to the present Església de Santa Maria del Mar. Between the two, a busy tradesmen's district thrived around Carrer dels Corders (Ropemakers' St). Many streets in this part of town were named after the trades exercised along them for centuries.

Vilanova de la Mar (later known as La Ribera, a name that later referred to the whole area), from where merchants carried out their vital trade across the Mediterranean, became the richest part of the city. Carrer de Montcada was laid to link the tradesmen's workshops with the then waterfront merchants and soon became the address. Its rich legacy of Gothic and baroque mansions attests to its primacy until well into the 18th century, when the creation of the Ciutadella swept away a whole chunk of La Ribera and trade focus shifted to Port Vell. Passeig del Born was the centre of activity, with jousts, executions and other public entertainments on the menu. Not far away, one of Europe's first stock exchanges came to life at La Llotja.

After a long period of relative neglect, El Born has, since the mid-1990s, become the trendiest (and, neighbours complain, the noisiest) nightlife district in the old city, if not all Barcelona. Where in the early 1990s there were a few dowdy bars and eateries, the place is now jammed with trendy restaurants, packed bars and endless local fashion outlets, with the likes of Custo Barcelona leading the way. It is a heterodox, cosmopolitan jumble in a magnificent Middle Ages setting.

LA RIBERA TOP FIVE

- Església de Santa Maria del Mar (p95)
- Museu Barbier-Mueller d'Art Pre-Colombí (p95)
- Museu Picasso (p96)
- Palau de la Música Catalana (p97)
- Parc de la Ciutadella (p97)

Orientation

Via Laietana, a rumbling, traffic-choked thoroughfare that connects the waterfront with the east side of l'Eixample, marks the southwest side of La Ribera, while the Parc de la Ciutadella closes off its northeast flank. To the south, parallel ribbons of main road and highway cut it off from the sea and La Barceloneta, and the grid streets of l'Eixample round it off to the north.

Carrer de la Princesa, ramrod straight between Via Laietana and the park, was laid in the 1820s and neatly cuts La Ribera in half. The gentrified southern half is generally known as El Born, after the busy, bar-lined pedestrian boulevard of the same name. Capped at one end by the magnificent Gothic Església de Santa Maria del Mar, it runs into the former Mercat del Born.

Several important streets feed south into El Born. From the Jaume I Metro stop, restaurant-lined Carrer de l'Argenteria (whose name dates to the 16th century, when it was lined with silversmiths) leads directly to the Església de Santa Maria del Mar. Carrer de Montcada, with its majestic houses (now mostly occupied by the Museu Picasso, other museums and art galleries), reaches El Born from Carrer de la Princesa.

North of Carrer de la Princesa, the area's physiognomy changes rapidly. A mess of untidy streets wiggles northwards around the brand-new Mercat de Santa Caterina and on towards the modernista jewel that is the Palau de la Música Catalana. Much messy urban remaking keeps the area in a state of flux. North African and South American immigrant communities call this part of La Ribera home.

The expanse of the Parc de la Ciutadella is a rare gift in a city so densely packed and lacking in serious greenery, but it started life as an ominous 18th-century citadel, of which little more than the name remains.

TRANSPORT

Metro Línia 4 coasts down the southwest flank of La Ribera, stopping at Urquinaona, Jaume I and Barceloneta. Línia 1 also stops nearby, at Urquinaona and Arc de Triomf (the nearest stop for the Parc de la Ciutadella).

CARRER DE MONTCADA Map pp302–3

Ⓜ Jaume I

An early example of deliberate town planning, this medieval high street was driven down towards the sea from the road that in the 12th century led northeast from the city walls. It would, in time, become the snootiest address in town for the city's merchant class, and the bulk of the great mansions that remain intact today date back to the 14th and 15th centuries (although they were often tampered with later). This area was the commercial heartland of medieval Barcelona.

Five of the mansions on the east side of the street have been linked to house the Museu Picasso (p96). Across the road, others house the Museu Barbier-Mueller d'Art Pre-Colombí (opposite) and Museu Tèxtil i d'Indumentària (p97). Several other mansions on this street are now commercial art galleries where you're welcome to browse. The biggest is the Galeria Maeght (No 25; see p206) in the 16th-century Palau dels Cervelló. If you can peek into the baroque courtyard of the originally medieval Palau de Dalmases (No 20) – now a hideously expensive place to sip wine – do so, as it is one of the finest on the strip.

At the corner of Carrer dels Corders and the northern end of the street, just beyond the 19th century Carrer de la Princesa, stands a much meddled with Romanesque chapel, the Capella d'En Marcús, which acted as a stop on the main road northeast out of medieval Barcelona.

ESGLÉSIA DE SANT PERE DE LES PUELLES Map pp302–3

Plaça de Sant Pere s/n; admission free; Ⓜ Arc de Triomf

Not a great deal remains of the church or convent that, in one form or another, have stood here since early medieval times. The church's pre-Romanesque Greek-cross floor plan survives, as do some Corinthian columns beneath the 12th-century dome and a much-damaged Renaissance vault leading into a side chapel. It was around this church that the first settlement began to take place in La Ribera beyond the original city walls. In 985 a Muslim raiding force under Al-Mansur attacked Barcelona and largely destroyed the convent, killing or capturing the nuns.

ESGLÉSIA DE SANTA MARIA DEL MAR Map pp302-3

☎ 93 319 05 16; Plaça de Santa Maria del Mar; admission free; 9am-1.30pm & 4.30-8pm; M Jaume I

At the southwest end of Passeig del Born stands the apse of Barcelona's finest Catalan Gothic church, Santa Maria del Mar (Our Lady of the Sea). Built in the 14th century, Santa Maria was lacking in superfluous decoration even before anarchists gutted it in 1909 and 1936. This only serves to highlight its fine proportions, purity of line and sense of space. Built with, for the time, record-breaking alacrity (it took just 59 years), the church is remarkable for its architectural harmony. While many grand European churches betray several styles because they took so long to build, Santa Maria del Mar benefited aesthetically from the haste. The main body is made up of a central nave and two flanking aisles separated by slender octagonal pillars, creating an enormous sense of lateral space.

Keep an eye out for music recitals, often baroque and classical, here. The acoustics aren't the best, but the setting more than makes up for it.

Just opposite the southern flank of the church an eternal flame burns brightly over an apparently anonymous sunken square. This was once **El Fossar de les Moreres** (the Mulberry Cemetery, named after the mulberry trees that once grew here), where

Catalan resistance fighters were buried after the siege of Barcelona ended in defeat in September 1714.

MERCAT DE SANTA CATERINA Map pp302-3

www.mercatsantacaterina.net; Avinguda de Francesc Cambó 16; 8am-2pm Mon, 8am-3.30pm Tue, Wed & Sat, 8am-8.30pm Thu & Fri; M Jaume I;

Come shopping for your tomatoes at this extraordinary-looking produce market, built by Enric Miralles and Benedetta Tagliabue to replace its 19th-century predecessor. Finished in 2005, it is distinguished by its kaleidoscopically weird wavy roof, held up above the bustling produce stands, cafés and bars by twisting slender branches of what look like grey steel trees.

The multicoloured ceramic roof (with a ceiling made of warm, light timber) recalls the modernista tradition of *trencadís* decoration (eg in Park Güell). Indeed, its curvy design, like a series of Mediterranean rollers, seems to plunge back into an era when Barcelona's architects were limited only by their (vivid) imagination (the market roof bares an uncanny resemblance to that of the Escoles de Gaudí at La Sagrada Família).

The market's 1848 predecessor had been built over the remains of the demolished (and by all accounts grand) 15th-century Gothic Monestir de Santa Caterina, a powerful Dominican monastery. A small section of the uncovered foundations have been glassed over in one corner as an archaeological reminder.

MUSEU BARBIER-MUELLER D'ART PRE-COLOMBÍ Map pp302-3

☎ 93 310 45 16; www.barbier-mueller.ch; Carrer de Montcada 12-14; adult/under 16yr/student €3/free/1.50, 1st Sun of month free; 11am-7pm Tue-Fri, 10am-7pm Sat, 10am-3pm Sun & holidays; M Jaume I;

Inside the medieval Palau Nadal you plunge into the world of centuries-old South American art and crafts. The artefacts on show are part of the treasure-trove of pre-Columbian art collected by Swiss businessman Josef Mueller (who died in 1977) and his son-in-law Jean-Paul Barbier, who directs the Musée Barbier-Mueller in the heart of old Geneva in Switzerland. Together, the museums form one of the most prestigious collections of such art in the world.

Stained-glass window, Església de Santa Maria del Mar (above), La Ribera

In blacked-out rooms the eerily illuminated artefacts flare up in the gloom. South American gold jewellery introduces the collection, followed by rooms containing ceramics, jewellery, statues, textiles and other objects.

MUSEU DE GEOLOGIA Map pp302-3

☎ 93 319 69 12; www.bcn.es/museuciencies; Passeig de Picasso; admission incl Museu de Zoologia €3; ☯ 10am-2.30pm Tue, Wed & Fri-Sun, 10am-6.30pm Thu; Ⓜ Arc de Triomf

Together with the nearby Museu de Zoologia, this museum also goes by the more grandiose name of Museu de Ciències Naturals de la Ciutadella. Most people would have to have rocks in their heads to spend much time in here, but then again, budding geologists may well want to examine the seemingly endless cabinets of stones, minerals and fossils.

MUSEU DE LA XOCOLATA Map pp302-3

☎ 93 268 78 78; http://pastisseria.com; Plaça de Pons i Clerch s/n; admission €3.80, 1st Mon of month free; ☯ 10am-7pm Mon & Wed-Sat, 10am-3pm Sun & holidays; Ⓜ Jaume l; ♿

Chocoholics have a hard time containing themselves in this museum dedicated to the fundamental foodstuff. How not to launch yourself at the extraordinary scale models made out of chocolate? A little salivation for sweet teeth is inevitable as you trawl around the displays (in part of the former Convent de Sant Agustí) that trace the origins of chocolate, its arrival in Europe and the many myths and images that surround it. Among the informative stuff (with panels in various languages) are chocky models of buildings such as La Pedrera and La Sagrada Família, along with characters such as Winnie the Pooh. It's enough to have you making for the nearest lolly shop, but you don't have to – they sell plenty of chocolate right here! Kids and grown-ups can join guided tours or take part in chocolate-making sessions.

MUSEU DE ZOOLOGIA (CASTELL DELS TRES DRAGONS) Map pp302-3

☎ 93 319 69 12; Passeig de Picasso; admission incl Museu de Geologia €3; ☯ 10am-2.30pm Tue, Wed & Fri-Sun, 10am-6.30pm Thu; Ⓜ Arc de Triomf

The Castle of the Three Dragons is a product of the imagination of Domènech i

Montaner, who put the castle trimmings on a pioneering steel frame. The coats of arms are all invented and the whole building exudes a teasing, playful air. It was used as a café-restaurant during the Universal Exhibition of 1888 and now houses the Zoology Museum. If you like stuffed animals, model elephants and the inevitable skeletons of huge creatures, this rather fusty institution is the place for you. The bulk of the permanent collection is on the 1st floor.

MUSEU DEL REI DE LA MAGIA Map pp298-9

☎ 93 319 73 93; www.elreydelamagia.com; Carrer de l'Oli 6; admission €3, with show €7; ☯ 6-8pm Thu, with show 6pm Sat & noon Sun; Ⓜ Jaume l

This little museum is a timeless curio. Run by the same people who have the nearby magic shop on Carrer de la Princesa (p206), it is the scene of magic shows, home to collections of material that go back to the 19th-century origins of the shop and the place for budding magicians of all ages to enrol in courses. Seeing is believing.

MUSEU PICASSO Map pp302-3

☎ 93 319 63 10; www.museupicasso.bcn.es; Carrer de Montcada 15-23; adult/child/student €6/free/3, 1st Sun of month free; ☯ 10am-8pm Tue-Sun & holidays; Ⓜ Jaume l; ♿

The setting alone, in five contiguous medieval stone mansions, makes the Museu Picasso, one of the city's most visited sights, worth the detour (and the probable queues). The pretty courtyards, galleries and staircases preserved in the first three of these buildings are as delightful as the collection inside is unique. One word of warning: the collections here concentrate on the artist's formative years, making it unique but sometimes disappointing for those hoping for a feast of his better-known later works (best found in Paris!).

The permanent collection is housed in the first three houses, **Palau Aguilar**, **Palau del Baró de Castellet** and **Palau Meca**, all dating to the 14th century. The 18th-century **Casa Mauri**, built over medieval remains (even some Roman leftovers have been identified), and the adjacent 14th-century **Palau Finestres** accommodate the temporary exhibitions.

The collection, which includes more than 3500 artworks, is strongest on Picasso's earliest years, up until 1904, but there is enough material from subsequent periods to give you a deep impression of the man's versatility and genius. Above all, you feel that Picasso is always one step ahead of himself, let alone anyone else, in his search for new forms of expression.

A visit starts with sketches and oils from Picasso's earliest years in Málaga and La Coruña – most of it done around 1893 to 1895. Some of his self-portraits and the portraits of his father, which date from 1896, are evidence enough of his precocious talent. *Retrato de la Tía Pepa* (Portrait of Aunt Pepa), done in Málaga in 1897, is a key painting and the enormous *Ciència i Caritat* (Science and Charity) is proof to doubters that Picasso fully mastered the academic techniques of portraiture. In Room 10 hang paintings from his first Paris sojourn while Room 11 is dedicated to the first significant new stage in his development, the Blue Period. His nocturnal blue-tinted views of *Terrats de Barcelona* (Rooftops of Barcelona) and *El Foll* (The Madman) are cold and cheerless, yet somehow alive.

A few Cubist paintings pop up in Rooms 13 and 14. From 1954 to 1962 Picasso was obsessed by the idea of researching and 'rediscovering' the greats, in particular Velázquez. In 1957 he made a series of renditions of the latter's masterpiece, *Las Meninas*, displayed in Rooms 16 and 17. It is as though Picasso has looked at the original Velázquez painting through a prism reflecting all the styles he had worked through until then. The last rooms contain some 40 pieces of ceramics done in the latter years of his unceasingly creative life.

MUSEU TÈXTIL I D'INDUMENTÀRIA Map pp302-3

☎ 93 319 76 03; www.museutextil.bcn.es; Carrer de Montcada 12-14; admission €3.50, 1st Sun of month free; ☉ 10am-6pm Tue-Sat, 10am-3pm Sun & holidays; Ⓜ Jaume I; ♿

The theme is threads at the Textile & Costume Museum. It occupies the 13th-century Palau dels Marquesos de Llió and part of the Palau Nadal next door (both buildings underwent repeated alterations into the 18th century). Its 4000 items range from 4th-century Coptic textiles to 20th-century local embroidery, but best is the big collection of clothing from the 16th century to the 1930s. Take a load off in the tranquil courtyard café.

PALAU DE LA MÚSICA CATALANA Map pp298-9

☎ 902 442882; www.palaumusica.org; Carrer de Sant Francesc de Paula 2; adult/child/student incl guided tour €8/free/7; ☉ 50min tours every ½hr 10am-7pm Jul & Aug, 10am-3.30pm Sep-Jun; Ⓜ Urquinaona

This concert hall is a high point of Barcelona's modernista architecture. It's not exactly a symphony, more a series of crescendos in tile, brick, sculpted stone and stained glass.

Built by Lluís Domènech i Montaner between 1905 and 1908 for the Orfeo Català musical society, with the help of some of the best Catalan artisans of the time, it was conceived as a temple for the Catalan Renaixença (Renaissance). The palace was built in the cloister of the former Convent de Sant Francesc, and since 1990 it has undergone several major changes, the latest of which was completed in 2004 and greatly improved its facilities as well as adding an outdoor café and increasing performance space.

The Palau, like a peacock, shows off much of its splendour on the outside. Take in the principal façade with its mosaics, floral capitals and the sculpture cluster representing Catalan popular music. Wander inside the foyer and restaurant areas to admire the spangled, tiled pillars. Best of all, however, is the richly colourful auditorium upstairs, with its ceiling of blue-and-gold stained glass and shimmering skylight that looks like a giant crystalline nipple. Above a bust of Beethoven on the stage towers a wind-blown sculpture of Wagner's Valkyries (Wagner was top of the Barcelona charts at the time). This can only be savoured on a guided tour or by attending a performance – either of which is highly recommended.

The original modernista creation, now a World Heritage sight, did not meet with universal approval in its day. The doyen of Catalan literature, Josep Pla, did not hesitate to condemn the structure as quite simply 'horrible', but few share his sentiments today. Montaner himself was also in a huff. He failed to attend the opening ceremony in response to unsettled bills.

PARC DE LA CIUTADELLA Map pp302-3

Passeig de Picasso; ☉ 8am-6pm Nov-Feb, 8am-8pm Oct & Mar, 8am-9pm Apr-Sep; Ⓜ Arc de Triomf

Come for a stroll, a picnic, a visit to the zoo or to inspect Catalonia's regional parliament, but don't miss a visit to this, the most central green lung in the city. Just East of La Ribera and north of La Barceloneta, Parc de la Ciutadella is perfect for a little winding down (or getting over a hangover).

After the War of the Spanish Succession (p63), Felipe V razed a whole swathe of La Ribera to build a huge fortress (La Ciutadella) whose main object was to keep watch over Barcelona. It became a loathed symbol of everything Catalans hated about Madrid and the Bourbon kings, and was later used as a political prison. Only in 1869 did the central government allow its demolition, after which the site was turned into a park and used for the Universal Exhibition of 1888.

The monumental **cascada** (waterfall) near the Passeig de Pujades park entrance, created between 1875 and 1881 by Josep Fontsère with the help of an enthusiastic young Gaudí, is a dramatic combination of statuary, rugged rocks, greenery and thundering water. All of it perfectly artificial! Nearby, hire a rowboat to paddle about the small lake – potentially good therapy for recalcitrant kids.

To the southeast, in what might be seen as an exercise in black humour, the fort's former arsenal now houses the **Parlament de**

Catalunya (☎ 93 304 66 45; www.parlament -cat.net; ☙ free guided visit in Catalan 4-6pm 1st Fri of month). A symbol of Catalan identity, the regional parliament also opens to the public on 11 and 12 September. Head up the sweeping Escala d'Honor (Stairway of Honour) and through several solemn halls to the Saló de Sessions, the semicircular auditorium where parliament sits. At the centre of the garden in front of the Parlament is a statue of a seemingly heartbroken woman, *Desconsol* (Distress; 1907), by Josep Llimona.

The Passeig de Picasso side of the park is lined by several buildings constructed for, or just before, the Universal Exhibition. The medieval-looking caprice at the top end is the most engaging. Known as the Castell dels Tres Dragons (Castle of the Three Dragons), it houses the **Museu de Zoologia** (p96). To the south is **L'Hivernacle**, an arboretum or mini botanical garden with a pleasant café in its midst. Next come the **Museu de Geologia** (p96) and **L'Umbracle**, another arboretum. On Passeig de Picasso itself is Antoni Tàpies' typically impenetrable **Homenatge a Picasso.** Water runs down the panes of a glass box full of bits of old furniture and steel girders.

Northwest of the park, Passeig de Lluís Companys is capped by the modernista **Arc de Triomf** (Map pp290–1), designed by Josep Vilaseca as the main exhibition entrance, with unusual, Islamic-style brickwork. Josep Llimona did the main reliefs. Just what the triumph was eludes us, especially since the exhibition itself was a commercial failure. It is perhaps best thought of as a bricks-and-mortar embodiment of the city's general *fin de siècle* feel-good factor.

PASSEIG DEL BORN Map pp302-3
Ⓜ **Barceloneta**

This hip, bar-lined boulevard was Barcelona's main square from the 13th to the 18th centuries, a plaza where jousting tournaments took place in the Middle Ages and which was the hub of the city's vital maritime trade. Barcelonins used to say '*roda el món i torna al Born*' ('go around the world and return to the Born'), and the merchants and ship owners who lived and dealt around here no doubt saw it as the navel of their world. Nowadays visitors are lucky if they can get around the square with so many distractions along the way, for the area has been, ahem, spectacularly reborn since the mid-1990s, and has become the most popular part of the old city.

Parlament de Catalunya (above), Parc de la Ciutadella

Excavation in 2001 at the former Mercat del Born, a late-19th-century produce market built of iron and glass, unearthed great chunks of one of the city districts flattened to make way for the much-hated Ciutadella (see p97). Historians found intact streets and the remains of houses dating as far back as the 15th century. Excitement was such that plans to locate a new city library in the long-disused market were dropped. Instead, the archaeological site will become part of a museum and cultural centre (at the time of writing it was due for completion in 2007). The site (admission free; ☾ 10am-8pm Sat, 10am-3pm Sun Jun-Sep, 10am-3pm Sat & Sun Oct-May), with raised platforms, was opened to visitors in May 2004. Guided visits (☎ 93 319 02 22; €3) take place on the weekends (no set timetable) and can be booked during the week (10am to 2pm Monday to Friday, plus 4pm to 6pm Tuesday and Thursday) through the Museu d'Història de la Ciutat (p87).

ZOO DE BARCELONA Map pp302-3

☎ 93 225 67 80; www.zoobarcelona.com; adult/under 4yr/senior/4-12yr €14.50/free/7.50/8.75; ☾ 10am-7pm Jun-Sep, 10am-6pm Mar-May & Oct, 10am-5pm Nov-Feb; Ⓜ Barceloneta
The zoo can make a fun distraction for kids although the comparatively limited space makes it a bit of a squeeze for the 7500 critters, everything from geckos to gorillas, crammed in here. A new site is being built on the coast of the Fòrum site northeast of the city centre, but opening is a few years off yet.

PORT VELL & LA BARCELONETA

Drinking & Nightlife p170; Eating p149; Shopping p206; Sleeping p218

Barcelona's old port at the bottom of La Rambla, once such an eyesore that it caused public protests, has been transformed beyond recognition since the 1980s. Abandoned warehouses and general junk are a distant memory, replaced by chic shopping, harbourside munching, movies on the sea, discos and Irish pubs, parking for yachts and a huge aquarium.

La Barceloneta is a mid-18th-century fishermen's quarter laid out by military engineer Juan Martín Cermeño to replace housing destroyed to make way for the building of La Ciutadella. The cute little houses along

narrow streets were later subdivided into four separate 30-sq-metre abodes and subsequently converted into six-storey slums. The attentive eye will pick out some of the few remaining original houses.

By the 19th century La Barceloneta had become an industrial slum, home to the city's gas company, the Nueva Vulcano shipyards and La Maquinista ironworks and steam engine plant (which shut in 1965). What remains of Barcelona's fishing fleet, about 70 vessels and 400 fishermen who land 10 tonnes of fish a day, ties up along the Moll del Rellotge, south of the history museum.

The area is rapidly gentrifying, but retains a sea-salty authenticity about it, especially in the numerous seafood eateries scattered about its labyrinthine web of back streets – it is estimated there is a bar or restaurant for every 120 local residents!

Orientation

Port Vell is at the waterside end of La Rambla. It is not only a haven for yachts: Maremàgnum, a multistorey mall of shops, cheerful chain restaurants, bars, cinemas and clubs, was built out of what had been nasty old docklands. Virtually opposite, the new World Trade Center, designed by Henry Cobb, juts out like the prow of a cruise ship into the harbour. To the southwest stretch the ferry docks for boats to the Balearic Islands and Italy, while a second arm of Port Vell, another chic yachties' hang-out, is backed by the tight streets of La Barceloneta.

On La Barceloneta's seawards side are Platja de Sant Sebastià and Platja de la Barceloneta, the first of Barcelona's beaches. Once dirty and unused, they have now been cleaned up and are popular on summer days. Passeig Marítim de la Barceloneta, a 1.25km promenade from La Barceloneta to Port Olímpic – through an area formerly full of railway sidings and warehouses – makes for a pleasant stroll if you manage to dodge the in-line skaters.

www.lonelyplanet.com

Sights

PORT VELL & LA BARCELONETA

TRANSPORT

Metro Línia 3 takes you to Port Vell (Drassanes stop), while the yellow Línia 4 is best for La Barceloneta. Several buses also converge on La Barceloneta, such as the No 64 that charges down Carrer de Muntaner and Avinguda del Paral.lel, Passeig de Colom and finally Passeig de Joan de Borbó.

ESGLÉSIA DE SANT MIQUEL DEL PORT Map pp302-3

☎ 93 221 65 50; Plaça de la Barceloneta; admission free; ☻ 7am-1.30pm Mon-Fri, 8am-1.30pm Sat; Ⓜ Barceloneta

Finished in 1755, this sober baroque church was the first building completed in La Barceloneta. Built low so that the cannon in the then Ciutadella fort could fire over it if necessary, it bears images of St Michael (Miquel) and two other saints considered protectors of the Catalan fishing fleet: Sant Elm and Santa Maria de Cervelló. Just behind the church is the bustling marketplace, worth an early morning browse. Ferdinand Lesseps, the French engineer who designed the Suez Canal, did a stint as France's General Consul in Barcelona and lived in the house to the right of the church.

L'AQUÀRIUM Map pp302-3

☎ 93 221 74 74; www.aquariumbcn.com; Moll d'Espanya; adult/under 4yr/4-12yr/over 60yr €15/free/10/12; ☻ 9.30am-11pm Jul & Aug, 9.30am-9.30pm Jun & Sep, 9.30am-9pm Mon-Fri & 9.30am-9.30pm Sat & Sun Oct-May; Ⓜ Drassanes; ♿

It is hard to help a slight shudder at the sight of a shark gliding above you, displaying its full munching apparatus. But this, the 80m shark tunnel, is the grand highlight of one of Europe's largest aquariums. Opened in 1995, it has the world's best Mediterranean collection and plenty of gaudy fish from as far off as the Red Sea, the Caribbean and the Great Barrier Reef. All up, some 11,000 fish (including about a dozen sharks) have taken up residence here.

Back in the shark tunnel, which you reach after passing a series of themed fish tanks with everything from bream to seahorses, various species of shark flit above and around you, along with a host of other deep-sea critters, from splendid flapping rays to huge, bloated sun fish. An interactive zone, Planeta Agua, is host to a family of Antarctic penguins and a tank of rays that you watch close up.

Divers with a valid dive certificate can dive (€300; ☻ 9am-2pm Wed, Sat & Sun) in the main tank with the sharks.

MAREMÀGNUM Map pp302-3

Ⓜ Drassanes

At the centre of the redeveloped Port Vell is the Moll d'Espanya, a former quay linked to Moll de la Fusta (Wood Quay) by a futuristic wave-shaped footbridge, the Rambla de Mar, which rotates to let yachts glide in and out of the marina behind it. The quay has been converted into a multi-use mall-on-sea. It's a busy, chirpy place (although rather artificial-feeling) with shops, restaurants, cinemas and bars. The biggest attractions are L'Aquàrium (left) and the Imax Port Vell big-screen 3D cinema.

MUSEU D'HISTÒRIA DE CATALUNYA Map pp302-3

☎ 93 225 47 00; www.mhcat.net; Plaça de Pau Vila 3; admission €3, 1st Sun of month free; ☻ 10am-7pm Tue & Thu-Sat, 10am-8pm Wed, 10am-2.30pm Sun & holidays; Ⓜ Barceloneta; ♿

The Palau de Mar building facing the harbour once served as warehouses (Els Magatzems Generals de Comerç), but was transformed in the 1990s into something quite different. Below the seaward arcades is a string of good restaurants. Inside is the Museum of Catalonian History, something of a local patriotic statement, but interesting nonetheless.

The permanent display covers the 2nd and 3rd floors, taking you, as the bumf says, on a 'voyage through history' from the Stone Age through to the early 1980s. It is a busy hodgepodge of dioramas, artefacts, videos, models, documents and interactive bits: all up, an entertaining exploration of 2000 years of Catalan history. See how the Romans lived, listen to Arab poetry from the time of the Muslim occupation of the city, peer into the dwelling of a Dark Ages family in the Pyrenees, try to mount a knight's horse or to lift a suit of armour. When you have had enough of all this, descend into a civil-war air-raid shelter or head upstairs to the rooftop restaurant and café.

PAILEBOT DE SANTA EULÀLIA Map pp302-3

Moll de la Fusta; adult/child €2.40/1.20, with Museu Marítim ticket free; ☻ noon-5pm Tue-Fri, 10am-5pm Sat & Sun; Ⓜ Drassanes

Along the palm-lined promenade Moll de la Fusta is moored a 1918 three-mast schooner restored by the Museu Marítim. You can see it perfectly well without going aboard, and there's not an awful lot to behold below decks. On occasion it sets sail for demonstration trips up and down the coast.

TRANSBORDADOR AERI Map pp290-1
Passeig Escullera; one way/return €7.50/9;
🕘 11am-8pm mid-Jun–mid-Sep, 10.45am-7pm
Mar–mid-Jun & mid-Sep–late Oct, 10am-6pm late
Oct–Feb; M Barceloneta or 🚌 17, 39 or 64
This cable car (also known as the *funicular aeri*) strung across the harbour to Montjuïc provides a bubble-eye view of the city. The cabins float between Miramar (Montjuïc) and the Torre de Sant Sebastià (in La Barceloneta), with a midway stop at the Torre de Jaume I in front of the World Trade Center. At the top of the Torre de Sant Sebastià is a spectacular restaurant, Torre d'Alta Mar (p151).

PORT OLÍMPIC, EL POBLENOU & EL FÒRUM

Drinking & Nightlife p179; Eating p151; Sleeping p218

Port Olímpic was built for the 1992 Olympic sailing events and is now a classy marina surrounded by bars and restaurants. Behind it, the southwest end of El Poblenou, a one-time industrial workers' district dubbed Barcelona's Manchester in the 19th century, was converted into the Vila Olímpica. The accommodation was sold off as apartments after the event.

The heart of El Poblenou is being developed as a hi-tech zone, 22@bcn. Just to the north, Barcelona's most spectacular modern architectural icon, the Torre Agbar, was finished in 2005. Further northeast, the long abandoned coastal corner of the city around the Riu Besòs has been transformed into a high-class residential area, at whose heart is the extensive congress and leisure area known as Fòrum.

Orientation

On the approach to Port Olímpic from La Barceloneta is the giant copper *Peix* (Fish) sculpture by Frank Gehry. The area behind

Port Olímpic – dominated by two lone skyscrapers, the luxury Hotel Arts Barcelona and Torre Mapfre office block – is the Vila Olímpica.

To the northeast, beaches stretch towards the Riu Besòs (which marks the city's northeast boundary), Fòrum and the Diagonal Mar residential district. Behind Platja de Bogatell runs the leafy main boulevard of El Poblenou, La Rambla del Poblenou.

BEACHES Map pp290-1
M Ciutadella, Bogatell, Llacuna or Selva de Mar or
🚌 36 or 41
A series of pleasant beaches stretches northeast from Port Olímpic marina. The southernmost, Platja de Nova Icària, is the busiest. Behind it, across the Avinguda del Litoral highway, is the Plaça dels Champions, site of the rusting three-tiered platform used to honour medallists in the sailing events of the 1992 Games. Much of the athletes' housing-turned-apartments is in the blocks immediately behind Carrer de Salvador Espriu.

Just in from the next beach, Platja de Bogatell, is the Cementiri de l'Est (Eastern Cemetery; ☎ 902 076902; Carrer de Taulat 2; 🕘 8am-6pm), created in 1773. It was positioned outside the then city limits for health reasons. Its central monument commemorates the victims of a yellow-fever epidemic that swept across Barcelona in 1821. The cemetery is full of bombastic family memorials, but an altogether disquieting touch is the sculpture El Petó de la Mort (The Kiss of Death), in which a winged skeleton kisses a young, kneeling but lifeless body.

Platja de la Mar Bella (with its brief nudist strip) and Platja de la Nova Mar Bella follow, leading into the new residential and commercial waterfront strip, the Front Marítim, that is still being developed as part of the Diagonal Mar project.

FÒRUM
M El Marseme Fòrum
A work still in progress, this northeast corner of the city has been transformed beyond recognition. Where before there was little more than wasteland, half-abandoned factories and a huge sewage-treatment plant, there are now high-rise apartment blocks, luxury hotels, a brand-new marina (Port Forum), a massive shopping centre and a major conference centre.

TRANSPORT

Metro Línia 4, approaching from the city, traverses the area with key stops in Ciutadella-Port Olímpic for the first of the beaches and Maresme Fòrum for the Fòrum area. An alternative that passes the Torre Agbar is the T4 tram, which starts at Ciutadella-Port Olímpic, also stops at Fòrum and terminates on the north side of the Riu Besòs in Sant Adria de Besòs.

BURYING THE PAST

Buried beneath the concrete, congress centre, bathing zone and marina created in the Fòrum lies the memory of more than 2000 people executed in the fields of the Camp de la Bota between 1936 and 1952, most of them under Franco from 1939 on. To their memory, *Fraternitat* (Brotherhood), a sculpture by Miquel Navarro, now stands on Rambla de Prim.

By far the most striking architectural element is the eerily blue, triangular *2001: A Space Odyssey*–style **Edifici Fòrum** (Map pp290–1) building by Swiss architects Herzog & de Meuron. The navy blue raised façades look like sheer cliff faces, with angular crags cut into them as if by divine laser. Grand strips of mirror create a series of fragmented reflections of the sky, bringing splotches of heavenly movement to play.

Next door, Josep Lluís Mateo's **Centre de Convencions Internacional de Barcelona** (CCIB; Map pp290–1) is said to be Europe's biggest convention centre, with capacity for 15,000 delegates. The huge space around the two buildings is used for major outdoor events, such as concerts (eg during the Festes de la Mercè) and the Feria de Abril (p11).

About a 300m stroll east from the Edifici Fòrum is the **Zona de Banys**, a long, tranquil seawater swimming area won from the sea by the creation of massive cement-block dykes. At its northern end, like a great rectangular sunflower, an enormous photovoltaic panel turns its face up to the sun to power the area with solar energy. Just behind it spreads the enormous **Port Forum**, Barcelona's brand-new (and third) marina. The whole area is unified by an undulating esplanade and walkways that are perfect for walking, wheelchair access, bikes and skateboards.

One hundred metres southwest of the CCIB is the **Parc del Diagonal**, designed by Enric Miralles and containing pools, fountains, an educational botanical walk (with more than 30 species of tree and plant) and modern sculptures.

TORRE AGBAR Map pp290-1
Avinguda Diagonal 225; Ⓜ **Glòries;** ♿
Barcelona's very own cucumber-shaped tower, Jean Nouvel's luminous Torre Agbar (the city water company's headquarters) is the most daring addition to Barcelona's skyline since the first towers of the Sagrada

Família went up. A little less adventurous than Sir Norman Foster's Swiss Re Tower in London, it stands out all the same. Completed in 2005, it shimmers in shades of midnight blue and lipstick red, especially at night. At the time of writing it was only possible to wander into the foyer, but by the end of 2006 you should be able to head to a panoramic viewing floor and restaurant high up in the building.

L'EIXAMPLE

Drinking & Nightlife p180; Eating p151; Shopping p206; Sleeping p219

In the 1820s, ranks of trees were planted on either side of the road linking Barcelona (from the Portal de l'Àngel) and the busy town of Gràcia. Thus was born the Passeig de Gràcia, a strollers' boulevard. A regular horse-drawn coach service linked the city and town. All around the boulevard were fields and market gardens, prime real estate. In time, gardens were built along the Passeig, along with snack stands and outdoor theatres. It must have been very pleasant, given the overcrowding in Barcelona.

For the city was bursting at the seams. As the 1850s approached, industrialisation fed a population boom. A progressive government bit the bullet and had the medieval walls knocked down between 1854 and 1856. In 1859 a competition was held to design l'Eixample (Extension) of the city.

Work on l'Eixample began in 1869 on a design by architect Ildefons Cerdà, who specified a grid of wide streets with diamond intersections formed by their chamfered (cut-off) corners. Each block was supposed to have houses on just two sides, open space on the others and parkland in between, but speculators were soon building houses on all four sides of each block. Cerdà's greenery failed to survive the intense demand for l'Eixample real estate. Building continued until well into the 20th century. Wealthy bourgeois families snapped up prime plots

L'EIXAMPLE TOP FIVE

- Casa Batlló (opposite)
- Fundació Antoni Tàpies (p104)
- La Pedrera (p105)
- La Sagrada Família (p106)
- Museu Egipci (p109)

TRANSPORT

Four Metro lines crisscross l'Eixample, three stopping at Passeig de Gràcia for the Manzana de la Discòrdia. Línia 3 stops at Diagonal for La Pedrera, while Línies 2 and 5 call in at Sagrada Família. FGC lines from Plaça de Catalunya take you one stop to Provença, in the heart of the l'Eixample and close to La Pedrera. Numerous buses also ply the roads, so there is always an alternative for tired feet.

along and near Passeig de Gràcia, erecting fanciful buildings in the eclectic style of the modernistas.

Orientation

Along l'Eixample's grid of straight streets are the majority of the city's most expensive shops and hotels, a range of eateries and several nightspots. The main sightseeing objective is modernista architecture, the best of which – apart from La Sagrada Família – is clustered on or near the main shopping avenue, Passeig de Gràcia.

For its inhabitants, l'Eixample is several *barris* in one. La Dreta de l'Eixample (the right side of l'Eixample), stretching northeast from Passeig de Gràcia to Passeig de Sant Joan, contains some of the most sought-after real estate. Beyond, it takes on a dowdy feel, even around La Sagrada Família, a *barri* unto itself. L'Esquerra de l'Eixample (the left side of l'Eixample), running southwest from Passeig de Gràcia, changes character several times. As far as Carrer d'Aribau is also prime land. Indeed, the whole area between Carrer d'Aribau, Passeig de Sant Joan, Avinguda Diagonal and the Ronda de Sant Pere has been known since the early 20th century as the Quadrat d'Or (Golden Sq) is jammed with pricey shops purveying everything from teak furniture to designer clothes.

At night the left side of l'Eixample has its own flavour. Carrer d'Aribau becomes a busy nightlife axis, with an assortment of bars north of Carrer de Mallorca. Closer to the Universitat is the heart of the 'Gaixample', a cluster of gay and gay-friendly bars and clubs in an area bounded by Carrer de Balmes and Carrer de Muntaner. The former also perks up at night as various music bars, largely frequented by a rowdy, juvenile set, fling open their doors. Just to add a little spice, streetwalkers come out to play along Rambla de Catalunya, while

more discreet goings-on take place in the girlie bars and massage parlours nonchalantly sprinkled about the area.

CASA AMATLLER Map pp294-5
☎ 93 487 72 17; www.amatller.org; Passeig de Gràcia 41; admission free; ☺ 10am-8pm Mon-Sat, 10am-3pm Sun; Ⓜ Passeig de Gràcia

Doubtless one of Puig i Cadafalch's most striking bits of modernista fantasy, Casa Amatller combines Gothic window frames with a stepped gable borrowed (deliberately) from Dutch urban architecture. But the bust and reliefs of dragons dripping off the main façade are pure caprice on the part of Cadafalch. The pillared foyer and staircase lit by stained glass are like the inside of some romantic castle. The building, renovated in 1900 for the chocolate baron and philanthropist Antoni Amatller (1851–1910), is one of the three houses on the block between Carrer del Consell de Cent and Carrer d'Aragó that gave it the playful name Manzana de la Discòrdia or 'Apple (Block) of Discord' (see boxed text, p104). The others are Gaudí's **Casa Batlló** (below) and Domènech i Montaner's **Casa Lleó Morera** (p104). They were all renovated between 1898 and 1906 and show how eclectic a 'style' modernisme was. Casa Amatller may at some point soon be at least partly opened to the public, so keep an eye out for queues! For the time being, you can wander through the foyer and visit temporary exhibitions out the back.

CASA BATLLÓ Map pp294-5
☎ 93 216 03 06; www.casabatllo.es; Passeig de Gràcia 43; adult/student & senior €16.50/13; ☺ 9am-8pm; Ⓜ Passeig de Gràcia

This is Gaudí at his hallucinogenic best, and one of the strangest residential buildings in Europe. The façade, sprinkled with bits of blue, mauve and green tile and studded with wave-shaped window frames and balconies, rises to an uneven blue tiled roof with a solitary tower.

Locals know it variously as the *casa dels ossos* (house of bones) or *casa del drac* (house of the dragon). It's easy enough to see why. The balconies look like the bony jaws of some strange beast and the roof represents Sant Jordi and the dragon. If you stare long enough at the building, it seems almost to be a living being. It is by far the weirdest contribution to the Manzana de la

HOW DO YOU LIKE THEM APPLES?

Despite the Catalanisation of most Barcelona names in recent decades, the Manzana de la Discordia has kept its Spanish name to preserve a pun on *manzana*, which means both 'block' and 'apple'. According to Greek mythology, the original Apple of Discord was tossed onto Mt Olympus by Eris (Discord), with orders that it be given to the most beautiful goddess, sparking jealousies that helped start the Trojan War. The pun won't transfer into Catalan, whose word for block is *illa*, and for apple, *poma*.

Discordia. Before going inside, take a look at the pavement. Each paving piece carries stylised images of an octopus and a starfish, Gaudí designs originally cooked up for Casa Batlló.

Owned by the family that runs the Chupa Chups lollipop empire, the 1st floor of the building has been open to visitors since 2002. It is worth every cent of the admission. Traditionally, or until recent decades at any rate, the 1st floor of Barcelona buildings (known also as the principal, or even noble, floor) was the most important and comfortable. When Gaudí was commissioned to refashion this building, he went to town inside and out. The internal light patios shimmer with tiles of deep sea blue. Gaudí eschewed the straight line, and so the staircase wafts you up to the 1st floor, where the main salon looks on to Passeig de Gràcia. Everything swirls: the ceiling is twisted into a vortex around its sun-like lamp; the doors, window and skylights are dreamy waves of wood and coloured glass. The same themes continue in the other rooms and covered terrace. As you walk out onto the terrace, the floor on either side is obscurely transparent and shot with more curvaceous motifs. Twisting, tiled chimney pots add a surreal touch to the roof.

It is possible to visit just the main floor or the attic and roof (€11 each) but the best option is to do the lot.

CASA DE LES PUNXES Map pp294-5
Avinguda Diagonal 420; Ⓜ **Diagonal**
Puig i Cadafalch's Casa Terrades is better known as the Casa de les Punxes (House of the Spikes) because of its pointed turrets. This apartment block, built between 1903

and 1905, looks like a fairy-tale castle and has the singular attribute of being the only fully detached building in l'Eixample.

CASA LLEÓ MORERA Map pp294-5
Passeig de Gràcia 35; Ⓜ **Passeig de Gràcia**
Domènech i Montaner's contribution to the Manzana de la Discordia (built in 1905), with modernista carving outside and a bright, tiled lobby in which floral motifs predominate, is perhaps the least odd-looking of the three buildings that make up the block. If only you could get inside. The 1st floor is quite giddy with swirling sculptures, rich mosaics and whimsical décor.

FUNDACIÓ ANTONI TÀPIES Map pp294-5
☎ **93 487 03 15; www.fundaciotapies.org; Carrer d'Aragó 255; adult/student €4.20/2.10;** ☉ **10am-8pm Tue-Sun;** Ⓜ **Passeig de Gràcia;** ♿
The Fundació Antoni Tàpies is both a pioneering modernista building (completed in 1885) and the major collection of a leading 20th-century Catalan artist.

The building, designed by Domènech i Montaner for the publishing house Editorial Montaner i Simón (run by a cousin of the architect), combines a brick-covered iron frame with Islamic-inspired decoration. Tàpies saw fit to crown it with the meanderings of his own mind – to some it looks like a pile of coiled barbed wire, to others…well, it's difficult to say. He calls it *Núvol i Cadira* (Cloud and Chair).

Antoni Tàpies, whose experimental art has often carried (not always easily decipherable) political messages – he opposed Francoism in the 1960s and '70s – launched the Fundació in 1984 to promote contemporary art, donating a large part of his own work. The collection spans the arc of Tàpies' creations (with more than

Casa de les Punxes (left), Avinguda Diagonal

800 works) and contributions from other contemporary artists. In the main exhibition area (Level 1, upstairs) you can see an ever-changing selection of about a dozen of Tàpies' grander works, like *Armari* (Wardrobe; 1973) and *Tres Peus* (Three Feet; 1981). For a historical perspective on his work, head for the basement Level 3, where you'll find displays of his drawings and colourful canvases from the 1940s and 1950s, a far cry from his mixed-materials creations for which he later became better known.

FUNDACIÓN FRANCISCO
GODIA Map pp294-5
☎ 93 272 31 80; www.fundacionfgodia.org; Carrer de València 284; adult/under 5yr/student & senior €4.50/free/2.10; ⏰ 10am-8pm Wed-Mon; Ⓜ Passeig de Gràcia; ♿

Francisco Godia (1921–90), head of one of the great establishment families of Barcelona, liked fast cars (he came sixth in the 1956 Grand Prix season driving Maseratis) and fine art. An intriguing mix of medieval art, ceramics and modern paintings make up this eclectic private collection. Jaume Huguet is represented by *Santa Maria Magdalena,* a bright, Gothic representation of Mary Magdalene dressed in red ermine. Godia's interests ranged from the Neapolitan baroque painter Luca Giordano through to Catalan modernisme and Valencia's Joaquim Sorolla. Antoni Tàpies leads the way into the museum's modern pieces. Also on display is a ceramics collection, with some exquisite pieces from such classic Spanish pottery-production centres as Manises in Valencia, Toledo and Seville.

HOSPITAL DE LA SANTA CREU I DE
SANT PAU Map pp290-1
☎ 902 076621; www.santpau.es; Carrer de Cartagena; Ⓜ Hospital de Sant Pau; ♿

Domènech i Montaner excelled himself as architect and philanthropist with this modernista masterpiece, long one of the city's most important hospitals. He wanted to create a unique environment that would also cheer up patients. The whole complex, including 16 pavilions (together with the Palau de la Música Catalana a joint World Heritage site), is lavishly decorated and each pavilion is unique. Among the many artists who contributed statuary, ceramics and artwork was the prolific Eusebi Arnau.

MODERNISME UNPACKED

Aficionados of Barcelona's modernista heritage should consider the *Ruta del Modernisme* pack. For €12 you receive a guide to 115 modernista buildings great and small, a map and discounts of up to 50% on the main modernista sights in Barcelona, as well as some in other municipalities around Catalonia. The discounts are valid for a year. For €18 you get another guide and map, *Sortim,* which leads you to bars and restaurants located in modernista buildings around the city. The proceeds of these packs go to the maintenance and refurbishment of modernista buildings. The *Ruta del Modernisme* guide (in various languages) is available in bookstores. You can then take it to one of three Centres del Modernisme to obtain the discount cards, or you can buy the lot at those centres. They are located at the main tourist office at Plaça de Catalunya 17, the Hospital de la Santa Creu i Sant Pau and the Pavellons Güell in Pedralbes.

You can wander around the grounds at any time, and it is well worth the stroll up Avinguda de Gaudí from La Sagrada Família.

The hospital facilities are gradually being transferred from the modernista buildings to a new facility on the premises, freeing up the century-old structures for a variety of uses. Part of the site will become a museum dedicated to Montaner, medicine and the 600-year history of the hospital (which was first established in El Raval in the early 15th century; see p91), along with a Modernisme Centre, but not before 2009. You can join a guided tour for €5 (10.15am and 12.15pm in English, 11.15am in Catalan and 1.15pm in Spanish).

LA PEDRERA Map pp294-5
☎ 902 400973; www.fundaciocaixacatalunya.es; Carrer de Provença 261-265; adult/student & EU senior €8/4.50; ⏰ 10am-8pm; Ⓜ Diagonal

This hallucinatory, undulating beast is yet another madcap Gaudí masterpiece, built between 1905 and 1910 as a combined apartment and office block. Formally called Casa Milà, after the businessman who commissioned it, it's better known as La Pedrera (The Quarry) because of its uneven grey stone façade, which ripples around the corner of Carrer de Provença. In spite of appearances, the building is coated in a layer of stone rather than built of it. The wave effect is emphasised by elaborate wrought-iron balconies. Pere Milà had married the older and far richer Roser Guardiola and knew how to spend her money (he was one of the city's first car-owners and Gaudí built parking space into this building, itself a first). With this apartment building he wanted to top anything done in l'Eixample.

The Fundació Caixa Catalunya has opened the top-floor apartment, attic and roof, together called the **Espai Gaudí** (Gaudí Space), to visitors. The roof is the most extraordinary element, with its giant chimney pots looking like multicoloured medieval knights (they say the evil imperial soldiers in the movie series *Star Wars* were inspired by them). Gaudí wanted to put a tall statue of the Virgin up here too: when the Milà family said no, fearing it might make the building a target for anarchists, Gaudí resigned from the project in disgust. Mrs Milà was no fan of Gaudí and it is said that no sooner had the job been completed than she had all his personally designed furniture tossed out!

One floor below the roof, where you can appreciate Gaudí's taste for McDonald's-style parabolic arches, is a modest museum dedicated to his work. You can see models and videos dealing with each of his buildings.

On the next floor down you can inspect the apartment (El Pis de la Pedrera). It is fascinating to wander around this elegantly furnished home, done up in the style a well-to-do family might have enjoyed in the early 20th century. The sensuous curves and unexpected touches in everything from light fittings to bedsteads, from door handles to balconies, can hardly fail to induce a heartfelt desire to move in at once. All those curves might seem admirable to us today, but not everyone thought so at the time. The story goes that one tenant, a certain Mrs Comes i Abril, had complained that there was no obvious place to put her piano in these wavy rooms. Gaudí's response was simple: 'Madame, I suggest you take up the flute.'

Some of the lower floors of the building, especially the grand 1st floor, often host temporary expositions.

From mid-June to late July, La Pedrera opens on Friday and Saturday evenings (9.30pm to midnight). The roof is lit in an eerie fashion and, while you are taking in the night views, you can sip a flute of *cava* (the Catalan version of champagne) and listen to live music (€10). This has become such a popular event that you should come

by and book a day or two in advance. On winter Thursday evenings, film cycles are sometimes staged.

LA SAGRADA FAMÍLIA Map p107

☎ 93 207 30 31; www.sagradafamilia.org; Carrer de Mallorca 401; adult/student €8/5, combined with Casa-Museu Gaudí in Park Güell €9; ⊙ 9am-8pm Apr-Sep, 9am-6pm Oct-Mar; Ⓜ Sagrada Família; ♿

If you have time for only one sightseeing outing in Barcelona, this should be it. La Sagrada Família inspires awe by its sheer verticality and, in the true manner of the great medieval cathedrals it emulates, it's still under construction after more than 100 years. When completed, the topmost tower will be more than half as high again as those that stand today. Unfinished it may be, but it attracts more than two million visitors a year, more than double its nearest rival for tourists' interest, the Museu Picasso. Indeed, it is the most visited monument in all Spain.

The Temple Expiatori de la Sagrada Família (Expiatory Temple of the Holy Family), to give it its full name, was Antoni Gaudí's last great hurrah, an all-consuming obsession. Given the commission by a conservative society that wished to build a temple as atonement for all the city's sins of modernity, Gaudí would wind up seeing its completion as his holy mission. As funds dried up he contributed his own, and in the last years of his life was never shy of importuning anyone he thought a likely donor.

What you're visiting is a building site, but the completed sections and the museum can be explored at leisure. Up to four times daily, 50-minute guided tours are offered (€3.50). Alternatively, pick up one of the audio tours (€3.50), for which you need to leave some ID as security. You can enter from Carrer de Sardenya and Carrer de la

---

GOD'S ARCHITECT

Gaudí, virtually a pauper and doubtless ruminating on how to solve some architectural conundrum on his unfolding masterpiece, was run over by a tram in 1926. His story is far from over. The rector of La Sagrada Família, Lluís Bonet Armengol, is promoting Gaudí's beatification. In March 2000 the Vatican decided to proceed with the examination of the case for canonising him. Says Bonet Armengol, Gaudí's contemporaries 'knew he was God's architect'.

LA SAGRADA FAMÍLIA

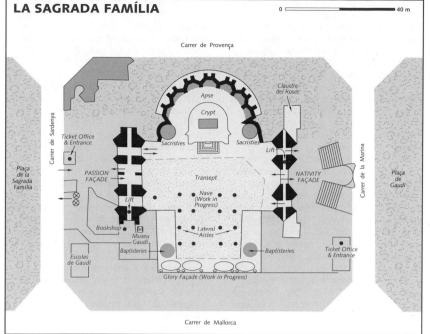

0 _____ 40 m

Carrer de Provença

Apse

Claustre del Roser

Crypt

Ticket Office & Entrance

Carrer de Sardenya

Sacristies

Sacristies

Lift

Plaça de la Sagrada Família

PASSION FAÇADE

Transept

NATIVITY FAÇADE

Carrer de la Marina

Plaça de Gaudí

Lift

Nave (Work in Progress)

Lateral Aisles

Bookshop

Museu Gaudí

Baptisteries

Baptisteries

Ticket Office & Entrance

Escoles de Gaudí

Glory Façade (Work in Progress)

Carrer de Mallorca

Marina. Once inside, you can spend a further €2 per ride on lifts that take you inside one of the towers in both the Nativity and Passion façades.

These two façades, each with four skyscraping towers, are the *sides* of the church. The main Glory Façade, on which work has now begun, closes off the southeast end on Carrer de Mallorca.

Gaudí devised a temple 95m long and 60m wide, able to seat 13,000 people, with a central tower 170m high above the transept (representing Christ) and another 17 of 100m or more. The 12 along the three façades represent the Apostles, while the remaining five represent the Virgin Mary and the four Evangelists. With his characteristic dislike for straight lines (there were none in nature, he said), Gaudí gave his towers swelling outlines inspired by the weird peaks of the holy mountain Montserrat outside Barcelona, and encrusted them with a tangle of sculpture that seems an outgrowth of the stone.

At Gaudí's death only the crypt, the apse walls, one portal and one tower had been finished. Three more towers were added

by 1930 – completing the northeast (Nativity) façade – but in 1936 anarchists burned and smashed everything they could in the church, including the workshops, plans and models. Work only began again in 1952.

The **Nativity Façade** is the artistic pinnacle of the building, mostly created under Gaudí's personal supervision and much of it by his own hands. You can climb high up inside some of the four towers by a combination of lifts and narrow spiral staircases – a vertiginous experience. Do not climb the stairs if you have cardiac or respiratory problems. The towers are destined to hold tubular bells capable of playing complicated music at great volume. Their upper parts are decorated with mosaics spelling out *'Sanctus, Sanctus, Sanctus, Hosanna in Excelsis, Amen, Alleluia'*. Asked why he lavished so much care on the tops of the spires, which no-one would see from close up, Gaudí answered: 'The angels will see them.'

Three sections of the portal represent, from left to right, Hope, Charity and Faith. Among the forest of sculpture on the Charity portal you can see, low down, the manger surrounded by an ox, an ass, the shepherds

107

and kings, and angel musicians. Some 30 different species of plant from around Catalonia are reproduced here, and the faces of the many figures are taken from plaster casts done of local people and the occasional one made from corpses in the local morgue!

Directly above the blue stained-glass window is the Archangel Gabriel's Annunciation to Mary. At the top is a green cypress tree, a refuge in a storm for the white doves of peace dotted over it. The mosaic work at the pinnacle of the towers is made from Murano glass, from Venice.

To the right of the façade is the curious **Claustre del Roser**, a Gothic style mini-cloister tacked on to the outside of the church (rather than the classic square enclosure of the great Gothic church monasteries). Once inside, look back to the intricately decorated entrance. On the lower right-hand side you'll notice the sculpture of a reptilian devil handing a terrorist a bomb. Barcelona was regularly rocked by political violence and bombings were frequent in the decades prior to the Civil War. The sculpture is one of several on the 'temptations of men and women'.

The southwest **Passion Façade**, on the theme of Christ's last days and death, was built between 1954 and 1978 based on surviving drawings by Gaudí, with four towers and a large, sculpture-bedecked portal. The sculptor, Josep Subirachs, continues to add to its decoration. He has not attempted to imitate Gaudí, producing angular, controversial images of his own. The main series of sculptures, on three levels, are in an S-shaped sequence starting with the Last Supper at the bottom left and ending with Christ's burial at the top right.

The main **Glory Façade** will, like the northeast and southwest façades, be crowned by

four towers (taller than the other eight) – the total of 12 representing the Twelve Apostles. Gaudí wanted it to be the most magnificent façade of the church. Inside will be the narthex, a kind of foyer made up of 16 'lanterns', a series of hyperboloid forms topped by cones.

The semicircular apse wall at the northwest end of the church was the first part to be finished (in 1894). The soaring interior of the church is progressing apace. The nave and transept have been roofed over and a forest of extraordinary angled pillars is in place. As the pillars soar towards the ceiling, they sprout a web of supporting branches that creates the effect of a forest canopy. The image of the tree is in no way fortuitous; Gaudí envisaged such an effect. Everything was thought through, including the shape and placement of windows to create the mottled lighting effect one would see with sunlight pouring through the branches of a thick forest. Unusually, the pillars are made of four different types of stone. They vary in colour and in load-bearing strength, from the soft Montjuïc stone pillars along the lateral aisles through granite, dark grey basalt and finally burgundy-tinged Iranian porphyry for the key columns at the intersection of the nave and transept. Tribunes built high above the aisles will be able to hold a choir of 1500!

The **Museu Gaudí** in the church's crypt includes material on Gaudí's life and work, including models, photos and other material on La Sagrada Família. You can see a good example of his plumb-line models that showed him the stresses and strains he could get away with in construction. A side hall towards the eastern end of the museum leads to a viewing point above the simple crypt in which the genius is buried. To the right, in front of the Passion Façade, the **Escoles de Gaudí** is one of his simpler gems. Gaudí built this as a children's school, creating an original, undulating roof of brick that continues to charm architects to this day. Inside is a re-creation of Gaudí's modest office as it was when he died, and explanations of the geometric patterns and plans at the heart of his building techniques.

At the present rate of construction, it is hoped the church will be completed in the 2020s. It is hoped the ceiling will be finished by 2008, which would allow the first services to be held.

A HIDDEN PORTRAIT

If you take a careful look at the central images of the Passion Façade, you will espy a special tribute from sculptor Josep Subirachs to architect Antoni Gaudí. The central sculptural group (below Christ crucified) shows, from right to left, Christ bearing his cross, Veronica displaying the cloth with Christ's bloody image after wiping his face, a pair of soldiers and, watching it all, a man called the Evangelist. Subirachs used a rare photo of Gaudí, taken a couple of years before his death, as the model for the Evangelist's face.

MUSEU DE CARROSSES FÚNEBRES Map pp290-1

☎ 902 076902; www.funerariabarcelona.com; Carrer de Sancho d'Àvila 2; admission free; ⏲ 10am-1pm & 4-6pm Mon-Fri, 10am-1pm Sat, Sun & holidays; Ⓜ Marina

If late-18th-century to mid-20th-century hearses (complete with period-dressed dummies) are your thing, then this museum, probably the city's weirdest sight, is where to contemplate the pomp and circumstance of people's last earthly ride. The hearses range from grand horse-drawn carriages to a few motorised options. The funeral company that runs the rather lugubrious basement museum claims it is the biggest of its kind in the world.

MUSEU DEL PERFUM Map pp294-5

☎ 93 216 01 21; www.museodelperfum.com; Passeig de Gràcia 39; adult/student & senior €5/3; ⏲ 10.30am-2pm & 4.30-8pm Mon-Fri, 11am-2pm Sat; Ⓜ Passeig de Gràcia

Housed in the back of the Regia perfume store, this museum contains everything from ancient Egyptian and Roman scent receptacles to classic Eau de Cologne bottles – all in all some 5000 bottles of infinite shapes, sizes and histories. Also on show are old catalogues and advertising posters.

MUSEU EGIPCI Map pp294-5

☎ 93 488 01 88; www.fundclos.com; Carrer de València 284; adult/child €6/5; ⏲ 10am-8pm Mon-Sat, 10am-2pm Sun; Ⓜ Passeig de Gràcia; ♿

Hotel magnate Jordi Clos has spent much of his life collecting ancient Egyptian artefacts, brought together in this private museum, with some 500 objects spread over an airy seven-floor exhibition space. It's divided into different thematic areas (the pharaoh, religion, daily life etc). In the basement is an exhibition area and library, in which volumes including original editions of works by Carter, the Egyptologist who led the Tutankhamen excavations, are on display.

MUSEU I CENTRE D'ESTUDIS DE L'ESPORT DR MELCHIOR COLET Map p292

☎ 93 419 22 32; Carrer de Buenos Aires 56-58; admission free; ⏲ 10am-2pm & 3-7pm Mon-Fri; 🚌 27, 32, 59, 66, 67 or 68

Puig i Cadafalch's 1911 modernista caprice, the Casa Company, looks like an odd Tyrolean country house, and is marvellously out of place. An eclectic collection of photos, documents and other sports memorabilia stretches over two floors – from a 1930s pair of skis and boots (how did they get down mountains on those things?) to the skull-decorated swimming costume of a champion Catalan water-polo player. A curio on the ground floor is the replica of a stone commemoration in Latin of Lucius Minicius Natal, a Barcelona boy who won a *quadriga* (four-horse chariot) race at the 227th Olympic Games…in AD 129.

MUSEU TAURÍ Map pp290-1

☎ 93 245 58 03; Gran Via de les Corts Catalanes 749; adult/child €4/3; ⏲ 10.30am-2pm & 4-7pm Mon-Sat, 10am-1pm Sun Apr-Sep; Ⓜ Monumental

Housed in the Plaça de Braus Monumental bullring, this bullfighting museum displays stuffed bulls' heads, old posters, *trajes de luces* (bullfighters' gear) and other memorabilia. You also get to wander around the ring and corrals.

PALAU DEL BARÓ QUADRAS Map pp294-5

☎ 93 238 73 37; Avinguda Diagonal 373; ⏲ 10am-8pm Mon-Sat, 10am-2pm Sun; Ⓜ Diagonal; ♿

A few blocks north of La Pedrera is Puig i Cadafalch's Palau del Baró Quadras, created between 1902 and 1906 for the baron in question in an exuberant Gothic-inspired style. The main façade is its most intriguing, with a soaring, glassed-in gallery. Take a closer look at the gargoyles and reliefs, among them a pair of toothy fish and a knight wielding a sword – clearly the same artistic signature of the architect behind the Casa Amatller (see p103). Décor inside is incredibly eclectic, but dominated by Middle Eastern and Oriental themes. Since 2003 it has housed the Casa Asia, a cultural centre celebrating the relationship between Spain and the Asia-Pacific region. Visiting the varied temporary exhibitions (mostly on the 2nd floor) allows you to get a peek inside this intriguing building. Take in the views from the roof terrace too.

PALAU MONTANER Map pp294-5

☎ 902 076621; Carrer de Mallorca 278; adult/child & senior €5/2.50; ⏲ guided visit only 10.30am in English, 11.30am in Catalan & 12.30pm in Spanish Sat, 10.30am in Catalan, 11.30am in Spanish & 12.30pm in Catalan Sun; Ⓜ Passeig de Gràcia

Interesting on the outside and made all the more enticing by its gardens, this creation by Domènech i Muntaner is spectacular on the inside. Completed in 1896, its central feature is a grand staircase beneath a broad, ornamental skylight. The interior is laden with sculptures (some by Eusebi Arnau), mosaics and fine woodwork. Both the inside and exterior feature decoration depicting themes related to the printing industry. It is advisable to call ahead if you want to be sure to visit, as the building is sometimes closed to the public on weekends too.

XALET GOLFERICHS Map pp296-7

☎ 93 323 77 90; www.golferichs.org; Gran Via de les Corts Catalanes 491; ⊗ 10am-2pm & 5-9pm Mon-Sat; Ⓜ Rocafort

This quirky country-style mansion could not look more out of place on one of the city's busiest boulevards. Its owner, businessman Macari Golferichs, wanted a modernista villa and he got one. Brick, ceramics and timber are the main building elements of the house, which displays a distinctly Gothic flavour. It came close to demolition in the 1970s but was saved by the Town Hall and converted into a cultural centre.

GRÀCIA & PARK GÜELL

Drinking & Nightlife p184; Eating p158; Shopping p210; Sleeping p222

Once a separate village north of l'Eixample, and then in the 19th century an industrial district famous for its Republican and liberal ideas, Gràcia was definitively incorporated into the city of Barcelona (the town had been 'annexed' and then won its 'freedom' several times down the century) in 1897, much to the disgust of the locals. In those days it had some catching up to do, as the town had poor roads, schools and clinics, and no street lighting or sewers. In the 1960s and '70s it became fashionable among radical and bohemian types, and today it retains some of that flavour – plenty of hip local luminaries make sure they are regularly seen around the bars and cafés of Gràcia. A little way north of the *barri* and within the municipal district of the same name lies another of Gaudí's extraordinary creations – the undulating Park Güell.

Orientation

You know you are out of l'Eixample and in Gràcia when you hit the maze of crowded narrow streets and lanes that characterise

TRANSPORT

FGC trains get you closest to the sights in Gràcia described following. Metro Línia 3 (Fontana stop) also gets you close, leaving you in Carrer Gran de Gràcia and close to the network of busy squares described on p135.

the *barri*. The official district of Gràcia extends quite a way beyond, taking in such areas as the residential valley of Vallcarca, which nuzzles up alongside Park Güell.

Gràcia itself is bounded by Carrer de Còrsega and Avinguda Diagonal in the south, Via Augusta and Avinguda del Príncep d'Astúries to the west, Carrer de Sardenya to the east and Travessera de Dalt to the north. Plunge into the atmosphere of its narrow streets and small plazas, and the bars and restaurants on and around them.

The liveliest plazas are Plaça del Sol, Plaça de Rius i Taulet and the tree-lined Plaça de la Virreina. On Plaça de Rovira i Trias, to the north of Gràcia, you can sit on a bench next to a statue of Antoni Rovira, Ildefons Cerdà's rival in the competition to design l'Eixample in the late 19th century. Rovira's design has been laid out in the pavement so you can see what you think of it.

CASA VICENÇ Map p292

Carrer de les Carolines 22; Ⓡ FGC Plaça Molina

The angular, turreted and vaguely Mudéjar-inspired 1888 Casa Vicenç was one of Gaudí's first commissions. Tucked away west of Gràcia's main drag, Carrer Gran de Gràcia, this private house (which cannot be visited) is awash with ceramic colour and shape. As was frequently the case, Gaudí sought inspiration in the past, in this case the rich heritage of building in brick so typical of the Mudéjar (architecture created by Spanish Arabs allowed to remain in Spain after the Christian conquests) style found in much of Spain reconquered from the Muslims.

MERCAT DE LA LLIBERTAT Map pp294-5

☎ 93 415 90 93; Plaça de la Llibertat; admission free; ⊗ 5-8pm Mon, 8am-2pm & 5-8pm Tue-Fri, 7am-3pm Sat; Ⓡ FGC Gràcia; ⑤

Built in the 1870s and covered over in 1893 in typically fizzy modernista style, employing generous whirls of wrought iron, this market is emblematic of the Gràcia district, full of life and all kinds of fresh produce. The man behind it was Francesc Berenguer i Mestres (1866–1914), Gaudí's longtime assistant.

PARK GÜELL Map pp290-1

☎ 93 413 24 00; Carrer d'Olot 7; admission free; ⏰ 10am-9pm Jun-Sep, 10am-8pm Apr, May & Oct, 10am-7pm Mar & Nov, 10am-6pm Dec-Feb; Ⓜ Lesseps or Vallcarca or 🚌 24

North of Gràcia and about 4km from Plaça de Catalunya, Park Güell is where Gaudí turned his hand to landscape gardening. It's a strange, enchanting place where his passion for natural forms really took flight – to the point where the artificial almost seems more natural than the natural.

Park Güell originated in 1900 when Count Eusebi Güell bought a tree-covered hillside (then outside Barcelona) and hired Gaudí to create a miniature city of houses for the wealthy, in landscaped grounds. The project was a commercial flop and abandoned in 1914 – but not before Gaudí had created 3km of roads and walks, steps, a plaza and two gatehouses in his inimitable manner. In 1922 the city bought the estate for use as a public park.

Just inside the main entrance on Carrer d'Olot, which is immediately recognisable by the two Hansel-and-Gretel gatehouses, visit the park's Centre d'Interpretació (☎ 93 285 68 99; adult/under 16yr/student €2/free/1.50; ⏰ 11am-3pm) in the Pavelló de Consergeria, the typically curvaceous, Gaudían former porter's home that hosts a display on Gaudí's building methods and the history of the park. There are nice views from the top floor. For €4 you get entry here and to the Museu d'Història de la Ciutat (p87) and the Museu-Monestir de Pedralbes (p113).

The steps up from the entrance, guarded by a mosaic dragon/lizard (a copy of which you can buy in many downtown souvenir shops), lead to the Sala Hipóstila, a forest of 84 stone columns (some of them leaning like mighty trees bent by the weight of time), intended as a market. To the left from here curves a gallery whose twisted stonework columns and roof give the effect of a cloister beneath tree roots – a motif repeated in several places in the park. On top of the Sala Hipóstila is a broad open space whose centrepiece is the Banc de Trencadís, a tiled bench curving sinuously around its

perimeter and designed by one of Gaudí's closest colleagues, architect Josep Maria Jujol (1879–1949).

The spired house to the right is the Casa-Museu Gaudí (☎ 93 219 38 11; admission €4; ⏰ 10am-8pm Apr-Sep, 10am-6pm Oct-Mar), where Gaudí lived for most of his last 20 years (1906–26). It contains furniture by him and other memorabilia. The house was built in 1904 by Francesc Berenguer i Mestres as a prototype for the 60 or so houses that were originally planned here.

Much of the park is still wooded, but it's full of pathways. The best views are from the cross-topped Turó del Calvari in the southwest corner.

The walk from Metro stop Lesseps is signposted. From Vallcarca stop it is marginally shorter and the uphill trek eased by escalators. Bus 24 drops you at an entrance near the top of the park.

The park is extremely popular (it gets an estimated four million visitors a year), and its quaint nooks and crannies are irresistible to photographers – who on busy days have trouble keeping out of each other's pictures. With so many visitors, the park is inevitably damaged by some. Treat this unique place with respect.

Casa-Museu Gaudí (above), Park Güell

LA ZONA ALTA

Drinking & Nightlife p184; Eating p160; Sleeping p222

Welcome to posh Barcelona. For some, the Quadrat d'Or in l'Eixample remains prime real estate, but most locals with healthy bank accounts opt for the spacious mansions with private gardens and garages that dot the 'High Zone', a loose name for the heights where Barcelona's topography climbs to the Collserola hills marking the city's inland limits. The highest point in this range is Tibidabo, with its amusement park, luxury hotel and bombastic church. Apart from expensive residential living, the other high points are the Parc de Collserola, the CosmoCaixa science museum and monuments of Pedralbes further southwest.

Orientation

Tibidabo (512m) is the highest hill in the wooded range that forms the backdrop to Barcelona. It's great for the fresh air and on a good day you can see inland as far as Montserrat. Tibidabo gets its name from the devil, who, trying to tempt Christ, took him to a high place and said, in Latin: *'Haec omnia tibi dabo si cadens adoraberis me'* ('All this I will give you if you fall down and worship me').

The leafy(ish) suburban heights of Sarrià attracts much of the serious money in Barce-

lona. Taken at its broadest, it covers the area arching between Avinguda de Tibidabo (and its cute blue tram) and Via Augusta. At the turn of the 20th century, when this was still largely untouched countryside, wealthy families built whimsical fantasy residences along Avinguda de Tibidabo. More recent are the gated, alarmed mansions further west.

The heart of Sarrià is Plaça de Sarrià and its busy main street, Carrer Major de Sarrià, is lined with shops, restaurants and local bars. A little down the hill is the equally residential *barri* of Sant Gervasi, between Gràcia, Avinguda Diagonal and the thundering Ronda del General Mitre freeway.

The better parts of Pedralbes, to the southwest, also attract money for their space and quiet but there is no shortage of apartment block clumps interspersed amid the greenery, and along Avinguda Diagonal. The same freeway has its high spots, such as the Palau Reial de Pedralbes and university campus.

LA ZONA ALTA TOP FIVE

- CosmoCaixa (opposite)
- Jardins del Laberint d'Horta (opposite)
- Museu-Monestir de Pedralbes (opposite)
- Palau Reial de Pedralbes (p114)
- Parc d'Atraccions (p115)

TRANSPORT

Transport options vary wildly depending on where you want to go. Metro Línia 3 will get you to the Jardins del Laberint d'Horta and Palau Reial de Pedralbes. From the latter you could walk to the Museu-Monestir de Pedralbes. Otherwise, take an FGC train to the monastery. FGC trains are generally the easiest way of getting close to most of the sights in and around Tibidabo and the Parc del Collserola.

Tibidabo Transport

Take an FGC train to Avinguda de Tibidabo from Catalunya station on Plaça de Catalunya (€1.20, 10 minutes). Outside Avinguda de Tibidabo station, hop on the *tramvia blau*, Barcelona's last surviving tram, which runs between fancy modernista mansions (note particularly Casa Roviralta at 31 Avinguda de Tibidabo) to Plaça del Doctor Andreu (one way/return €2.30/3.50, 15 minutes, every 15 or 30 minutes 10am to 8pm late June to early September, 10am to 6pm Saturdays, Sundays & holidays mid-September to late June) — it has been doing so since 1901. On days and at times when the tram does not operate, a bus serves the route (€1.20).

From Plaça del Doctor Andreu, the Tibidabo funicular railway climbs through the woods to Plaça de Tibidabo at the top of the hill (one way/return €2/3, five minutes). Departures start at 10.45am and continue until shortly after the Parc d'Atraccions closing time.

An alternative is bus T2, the 'Tibibús', from Plaça de Catalunya to Plaça de Tibidabo (€2.20, 30 minutes, every 30 to 50 minutes on Saturdays, Sundays & holidays year-round & hourly from 10.30am Monday to Friday late June to early September). Purchase tickets on the bus. The last bus down leaves Tibidabo 30 minutes after the Parc d'Atraccions closes. You can also buy a combined ticket that includes the bus and entry to the Parc d'Atraccions (€22).

COSMOCAIXA (MUSEU DE LA CIÈNCIA) Map pp290-1

☎ 93 212 60 50; www.fundacio.lacaixa.es; Carrer de Teodor Roviralta 47-51; adult/student €3/2; ⏰ 10am-8pm Tue-Sun; 🚌 60 or 🚇 FGC Avinguda de Tibidabo; ♿

This bright, modern science museum, reopened in 2005 after extensive remodelling, is housed in a modernista building (completed in 1909). Kids (and kids at heart) will be fascinated by some of the displays here. The single greatest highlight is the recreation over 1 sq km of a chunk of flooded Amazon rain forest (Bosc Inundat). More than 100 species of genuine Amazon flora and fauna (including anacondas and poisonous frogs) prosper in this unique, living diorama in which you can even experience a tropical downpour. In another original section, the Mur Geològic, seven great chunks of rock (90 tonnes in all) have been assembled to create a 'geological wall'. Check out the planetarium and a host of smaller-scale, frequently interactive sections. The Clik i Flash section is especially designed for younger children (to nine), with all sorts of gizmos. In 2006 CosmoCaixa received the European Museum of the Year award.

JARDINS DEL LABERINT D'HORTA

☎ 93 428 39 34; Carrer dels Germans Desvalls; adult/student €2/1.25, Wed & Sun free; ⏰ 10am-sunset; Ⓜ Mundet

Laid out in the twilight years of the 18th century by Antoni Desvalls, Marquès d'Alfarras i de Llupià, this carefully manicured park remained a private family idyll until the 1970s, when it was opened to the public. Many a fine party and theatrical performance was held here over the years, but it now serves as a kind of museumpark. The gardens take their name from a maze in their centre, but other paths take you past a pleasant artificial lake (estany), waterfalls, a neoclassical pavilion and a false cemetery. The latter is inspired by 19th-century romanticism, characterised by an obsession with a swooning, anaemic (some might say silly) vision of death.

The labyrinth itself, in the middle of these cool gardens (somehow odd in their environment, with modern apartments and ring roads nearby), can be surprisingly frustrating! Aim to reach the centre from the bottom end, and then exit towards the ponds and neoclassical pavilion. This is a good one for kids! At Mundet Metro, take the right exit upstairs, on emerging turn right and then left along the main road (with football fields on your left) and then the first left uphill to the gardens (about five minutes).

The team behind the mega-European adaptation of Patrick Süskind's novel *Perfume*, due out in 2006, filmed scenes in the garden.

MUSEU-MONESTIR DE PEDRALBES Map pp290-1

☎ 93 203 92 82; www.museuhistoria.bcn .es; Baixada del Monestir 9; admission €4 (incl Museu d'Història de la Ciutat & Park Güell Centre d'Interpretació); ⏰ 10am-5pm Tue-Sat, 10am-3pm Sun Jun-Sep, 10am-2pm Tue-Sat, 10am-3pm Sun Oct-May; 🚇 FGC Reina Elisenda or 🚌 22, 63, 64 or 75

This peaceful old convent, first opened to the public in 1983 and now a museum of monastic life (the nuns have moved into more modern neighbouring buildings), stands at the top of Avinguda de Pedralbes in a residential area that until the 20th century was countryside but which remains a divinely quiet corner of Barcelona.

The architectural highlight is the large, elegant, three-storey cloister, a jewel of Catalan Gothic, built in the early 14th century. Following its course to the right, stop at the first chapel, the **Capella de Sant Miquel**, whose murals were done in 1346 by Ferrer Bassá, one of Catalonia's earliest documented painters. A few steps on is the ornamental grave of Queen Elisenda, who founded the convent. It is curious, as it is divided in two. This side in the cloister shows her dressed as a penitent widow, while the other part, inside the adjacent church, shows her dressed as queen.

As you head around the ground floor of the cloister, you can peer into the restored refectory, kitchen, stables, stores and a reconstruction of the infirmary – all giving a good idea of convent life. Eating in the refectory must have been a whole lot of fun, judging by the exhortations to *Silentium* (Silence) and *Audi Tacens* (Listen and Keep Quiet) written around the walls. Harder still must have been spending one's days in the cells on the ground and 1st floors in a state of near perpetual prayer and devotional reading.

Upstairs is a grand hall that was once the **Dormidor** (sleeping quarters). It was lined by tiny night cells but they were long ago removed. Today a modest collection of the monastery's art, especially Gothic devotional

GAUDÍ OFF THE BEATEN TRACK

Gaudí, like any freelance, was busy all over town. While his main patron was Eusebi Güell and his big projects were bankrolled by the wealthy bourgeoisie, he took on smaller jobs too, especially earlier in his career. One example is the **Casa Vicenç** (p110) in Gràcia. Another example is the **Col.legi de les Teresianes** (Map pp290–1; ☎ 93 212 33 54; Carrer de Ganduxer 85-105; ⓡ FGC Tres Torres), to which he added some personal touches in 1889. Although you can see parts of the wing he designed (to the right through the entrance gate) from the outside, the most unique features are those hardest to see – the distinctive parabolic arches inside. Unfortunately it is no longer possible to visit the school. Gaudí fanatics might also want to reach **Bellesguard** (Map pp290–1; Carrer de Bellesguard; ⓡ FGC Avinguda Tibidabo or ⓑ 60), a private house he built in 1909 on the site of the ancient palace of the Catalan count king, Martí I. You can get a reasonable idea of the house peering in from the roadside. The castle-like appearance is reinforced by the heavy stone work, generous wrought iron and tall spire. Gaudí also worked in some characteristically playful mosaic and colourful tiles.

works, and furniture grace this space. Most is by largely unknown Catalan artists, with some 16th-century Flemish works, and was acquired thanks to the considerable wealth of the convent's mostly high-class nuns.

Next to the convent, the sober church is an excellent example of Catalan Gothic.

OBSERVATORI FABRA Map pp290-1
☎ 902 502220; Carretera del Observatori s/n; admission €8
Inaugurated in 1904, this modernista observatory is still a functioning scientific foundation. It can be visited on certain evenings to allow people to observe the stars through its grand old telescope. Visits (generally in Catalan or Spanish) have to be booked. The easiest way here is by taxi. Or take the funicular to Tibidabo and then bus 111 to the Torre de Collserola and walk about 15 minutes.

PALAU REIAL DE PEDRALBES Map pp290-1
☎ 93 280 50 24; Avinguda Diagonal 686; both museums & Museu Tèxtil i d'Indumentària adult/student €3.50/2, 1st Sun of month free; ⏰ 10am-6pm Tue-Sat, 10am-3pm Sun & holidays, park 10am-6pm daily; Ⓜ Palau Reial; ♿
Across Avinguda Diagonal from the main campus of the Universitat de Barcelona is the

entrance to the verdant **Parc del Palau Reial**. In the park is the Palau Reial de Pedralbes, an early-20th-century building that belonged to the family of Eusebi Güell (Gaudí's patron) until they handed it over to the city in 1926 to serve as a royal residence – among its guests have been King Alfonso XIII, the president of Catalonia and General Franco.

Today the palace houses two museums. The **Museu de Ceràmica** (www.museuceramica .bcn.es) has a good collection of Spanish ceramics from the 13th to 19th centuries, including work by Picasso and Miró. Spain inherited from the Muslims, and then further refined, a strong tradition in ceramics – here you can compare some exquisite work (tiles, porcelain tableware and the like) from some of the greatest centres of pottery production across Spain, including Talavera de la Reina in Castilla, Manises and Paterna in Valencia, and Teruel in Aragón. Upstairs is a display of fanciful modern ceramics from the 20th century – here they have ceased to be a tool with aesthetic value and are purely decorative.

Across the corridor, the **Museu de les Arts Decoratives** (www.museuartsdecoratives.bcn .es) brings together an eclectic assortment of furnishings, ornaments and knick-knacks dating as far back as the Romanesque period. The plush and somewhat stuffy elegance of Empire- and Isabelline-style divans can be neatly compared with some of the more tasteless ideas to emerge on the subject of seating in the 1970s. It is planned eventually to house these collections in a brand-new design museum at Plaça de les Glòries Catalanes. When this will happen is open to speculation. The city was supposed to hand the Palau de Pedralbes over to the Generalitat in 2005 in exchange for the latter's participation in the creation of the new museum. At the time of writing, no progress had been made on this.

Over by Avinguda de Pedralbes are the stables and porter's lodge designed by Gaudí for the Finca Güell, as the Güell estate here was called. Known also as the **Pavellons Güell** (☎ 902 076621; guided tour adult/child & senior €5/2.50; ⏰ 10.15am in English, 11.15am in Catalan, 12.15pm in English & 1.15pm in Spanish Fri-Mon), they were built in the mid-1880s, when Gaudí was strongly impressed by Islamic architecture. Outside of visiting hours, there is nothing to stop you admiring Gaudí's wrought-iron dragon gate from the outside.

PARC D'ATRACCIONS

☎ 93 211 79 42; www.tibidabo.es; Plaça de Tibidabo 3-4; admission for six attractions & Museu d'Autòmats €11, access to all rides adult/child shorter than 1.2m €22/9; ⊗ noon-10pm or 11pm Wed-Sun Jul–early Sep, other closing times vary (from 5pm to 9pm) Sat, Sun, holidays & some other days in warmer months

The reason most Barcelonins come up to Tibidabo is for some thrills (but hopefully no spills) in this funfair, close to the top funicular station. Among the top attractions are the seven minutes in Hotel Krueger, a *hospedaje* (hostelry) of horrors inhabited by actors portraying Dracula, Hannibal Lecter and other fantasies. The 1920s prop plane doing circuits is a classic for kids. A curious sideline is the Museu d'Autòmats, 35 automated puppets going as far back as 1880 and part of the original amusement park. You can still see some of these gizmos at work.

PARC DE COLLSEROLA

☎ 93 280 35 52; www.parccollserola.net; Carretera de l'Església 92; ℝ FGC Peu de Funicular then Funicular to Baixador de Vallvidrera

Barcelonins needing an escape from the city without heading too far into the countryside seek out this extensive (8000 hectares) park in the hills. It is a great place to hike and bike and bristles with eateries and snack bars.

Pick up a map from the Centre d'Informació (⊗ 9.30am-3pm). Aside from nature, the principal point of interest is the sprawling Museu-Casa Verdaguer (☎ 93 204 78 05; www.museuhistoria.bcn.es; Vil.la Joana, Carretera de l'Església 104; admission free; ⊗ 10am-2pm Sat, Sun & holidays), 100m from the information centre and a short walk from the train station. Catalonia's revered and reverend writer Jacint Verdaguer (see p30) lived in this late-18th-century country house before his death on 10 July 1902. On the ground floor is a typical 19th-century country kitchen, with coal-fired stove and hobs in the middle. Upstairs you can see a raft of Verdaguer memorabilia (from original published works through to photos and documents) as you wander through the rooms. The bed in which he died remains exactly where it was in 1902. Labels are in Catalan only.

Beyond, the park has various other minor highlights, including a smattering of country churches (some Romanesque), the ragged ruins of the 14th-century Castellciuro castle in the west, various lookout points and, to the north, the 15th-century Can Coll (a grand farmhouse open 9.30am to 3pm on Sundays and holidays and now used as an environmental education centre where you can see how richer farmers lived around the 17th to 19th centuries).

Bus 111 runs between Tibidabo and Vallvidrera (passing in front of the Torre de Collserola).

TEMPLE DEL SAGRAT COR

☎ 93 417 56 86; Plaça de Tibidabo; admission free; ⊗ 8am-7pm

The Church of the Sacred Heart, looming above the top funicular station, is meant to be Barcelona's answer to Paris' Sacré Coeur and was built to atone for the events of the Setmana Tràgica in 1909 (see p65), when mobs ransacked churches across Barcelona. The church is certainly as visible as its Parisian namesake, and even more vilified by aesthetes. It's actually two churches, one on top of the other. The top one is surmounted by a giant statue of Christ and has a lift (€2; ⊗ 10am-2pm & 3-6pm Mon-Sat, 10am-2pm & 3-7pm Sun) to take you to the roof for the panoramic (and often wind-chilled) views.

TORRE DE COLLSEROLA Map pp290-1

☎ 93 406 93 54; www.torredecollserola.com; Carretera de Vallvidrera al Tibidabo; adult/child/senior €5.20/3.60/4.20; ⊗ 11am-2.30pm & 3.30-6pm Wed-Sun; Funicular de Vallvidrera then 🚍 111

Sir Norman Foster designed the 288m-high Torre de Collserola telecommunications

Sights LA ZONA ALTA

PERPETUAL ADORATION

Since 1966 devout citizens of Barcelona have taken turns to maintain a permanent vigil of the Holy Sacrament on show in the Temple del Sagrat Cor. Adoradors Diurns (Day Adorers) and Adoradors Nocturns (Night Adorers) donate an hour of their time each month to praying. The idea is that there should be someone praying before the Holy Sacrament 24 hours a day. Night Adorers without a car spend the night in the church, picked up by bus at 10.30pm and taken back down at 6am the following day. When not praying, they stretch out in monastery-style cells or indulge in a chat with their fellow adorers.

Torre de Collserola (p115), Tibidabo

tower, which was built between 1990 and 1992. The external glass lift to the visitors' observation area, 115m up, is as hair-raising as anything at the nearby Parc d'Atraccions. People say you can see for 70km from the top on a clear day. If ever anyone wanted to knock out Barcelona's TV and radio sets, this would be the place to do it. All transmissions are sent from here, and repeater stations across Catalonia are also controlled from this tower.

SANTS & LES CORTS

Drinking & Nightlife p185; Eating p161; Shopping p210; Sleeping p223

Once a village in its own right, the working class *barri* of Sants was gradually swallowed up by Barcelona in the course of the late 19th century. Although there is little of specific interest in the area, a wander around Carrer de Sants and surrounding streets allows you to plunge into the daily life of your average urban Catalan far from the hue and cry of the tourist-saturated centre. Les Corts is a quieter, more spacious residential quarter whose epicentre is the Camp Nou football stadium.

TRANSPORT

The Metro is the easiest way to get around here. Línia 3 will take you from central Barcelona to Plaça d'Espanya and then another two stops north to Estació Sants, where you can change to Línia 5 and trundle west three stops for the Camp Nou stadium.

Orientation

Where the grid system of l'Eixample peters out listlessly at Carrer de Tarragona, Sants begins, marked by the city's main railway station. It spreads down to Gran Via de les Corts Catalanes, the boulevard shooting southwest out of the city from the grand roundabout of Plaça d'Espanya. Avinguda de Madrid divides Sants from Les Corts, itself cut in half by the thundering Gran Via de Carles III.

West of this expressway and wedged between Avinguda Diagonal and Carrer de Sants is a leafy but somehow quite odd corner of town. Dominated by Camp Nou, the temple to Barcelona's star football team, it is also home to much of the modern Universitat de Barcelona campus (the area is known as the Zona Universitària).

CAMP NOU Map pp290-1

☎ 93 496 36 08; www.fcbarcelona.es; Carrer d'Aristides Maillol; adult/child €6/4.50; ☒ 10am-6.30pm Mon-Sat, 10am-2.30pm Sun & holidays; Ⓜ Collblanc

Among Barcelona's most-visited museums – hard on the heels of the Museu Picasso – comes the **Museu del Futbol Club Barcelona** near the club's giant Camp Nou (aka Nou Camp) stadium. Barça is one of Europe's top football clubs, and its museum is a hit with football fans the world over.

Camp Nou, built in 1957 and enlarged for the 1982 World Cup, is one of the world's biggest stadiums, holding 100,000 people. The club has a world-record membership of 130,000 (and growing). Football fans who can't get to a game (see p195) should find a visit to the museum worthwhile. The best bits are the photo section, the goal videos and the views out over the stadium. Among the quirkier paraphernalia are old sports board games, a 19th-century leather football, the life-sized diorama of old-time dressing rooms, posters and magazines from way back and the *futbolín* (table soccer) collection. You can join a **guided tour** (adult/child

€10.50/8; ☺ 10am-5.30pm Mon-Sat, 10am-1.30pm Sun & holidays) of the stadium, starting in the team's dressing rooms and heading out through the tunnel, on to the pitch and winding up in the presidential box.

PLAÇA D'ESPANYA & AROUND Map pp296-7

Plaça d'Espanya; Ⓜ Espanya

The whirling roundabout of Plaça d'Espanya is flanked on its northern side by the façade of the former **Plaça de Braus Les Arenes** bullring. Built in 1900 and at one point one of three bullrings in the city, it is being converted into a shopping and leisure centre by Lord Richard Rogers. Behind the bullring is the **Parc Joan Miró**, created in the 1980s – worth a quick detour for Miró's phallic sculpture *Dona I Ocell* (Woman and Bird) in the western corner. Locals know the park (which apart from Miró is a dispiriting affair) as the Parc de l'Escorxador (Abattoir Park), as that's what once stood here – not surprising given the proximity to the bullring.

Just south of Estació Sants is the odd **Parc d'Espanya Industrial**. Looked at in the most favourable light possible, it is supposed to be an inventive public space, full of ingenious things. It is actually a fairly sad cement structure lined by sci-fi prison-camp searchlight towers. It does have a sports centre that comes in handy for locals.

MONTJUÏC & POBLE SEC

Drinking & Nightlife p186; Eating p161; Shopping p210

Montjuïc, overlooking the city centre from the southwest, may only be a hill in dimension, but it's a mountain of activity. Home to some of the city's finest art collections (including the Museu Nacional d'Art de Catalunya, CaixaForum and Fundació Joan Miró), it also hosts several lesser museums, curious sights like the Poble Espanyol (a pastiche of architectural remakes from

around the country), the sinister Castell de Montjuïc and a remake of Mies van der Rohe's 1920s German pavilion. The bulk of the Olympic installations of the 1992 Games are also here. Throw in various parks and gardens and you have the makings of an extremely full day (or two). It has its nocturnal side too, with the engaging La Font Màgica, several busy theatres and a couple of skeleton-shaking dance clubs.

The name Montjuïc (Jewish Mountain) suggests the presence of a one-time Jewish settlement here, or at least a Jewish cemetery. Some speculate the name also comes from the Latin Mons Jovis (Mt Jupiter), after the Roman God. Before Montjuïc was turned into parks in the 1890s, its woodlands had provided food-growing and breathing space for the people of the cramped Ciutat Vella below.

Montjuïc also has a darker history: its fort was used by the Madrid government to bombard the city after political disturbances in 1842, and as a political prison up until the Franco era. The first main burst of building on Montjuïc came in the 1920s when it was chosen as the stage for Barcelona's 1929 World Exhibition. The Estadi Olímpic, the Poble Espanyol and some museum buildings date from this time. Montjuïc got a thorough make-over for the 1992 Olympics, and it is home to the Olympic stadium and swimming complex.

Sloping down the north face of the hill is the tight warren of working-class Poble Sec ('Dry Village'), short on sights but hiding a couple of interesting little bars. The only reminders of its more industrial past are the three chimney stacks making up the Parc de les Tres Xemeneies (Three Chimneys Park) on Avinguda del Paral.lel. They belonged to La Canadenca, an enormous power station. The avenue itself was, until the 1960s, the centre of Barcelona nightlife, crammed with theatres and cabarets. A handful of theatres and cinemas survive, and one, the Sala Apolo, managed to convert itself successfully into a club.

Orientation

The swirling traffic roundabout of Plaça d'Espanya marks the boundary between the *barri* of Sants and Barcelona's seaside oasis hill, Montjuïc. From the roundabout unrolls the most majestic approach to the mountain, Avinguda de la Reina Maria

Sights MONTJUÏC & POBLE SEC

MONTJUÏC & POBLE SEC TOP FIVE

- CaixaForum (p118)
- Font Màgica (p120)
- Fundació Joan Miró (p120)
- Museu Nacional d'Art de Catalunya (p121)
- Poble Espanyol (p123)

TRANSPORT

Metro Línia 3 runs through Poble Sec. The closest stops to Montjuïc are Espanya, Poble Sec and Paral.lel. You *could* walk from Ciutat Vella (the foot of La Rambla is 700m from the eastern end of Montjuïc). A series of escalators runs up to the Palau Nacional from Avinguda de Rius i Taulet and Passeig de les Cascades. They continue as far as Avinguda de i'Estadi.

Bus

Bus 50 runs to Montjuïc along Gran Via de les Corts Catalanes via Plaça de l'Universitat and Plaça d'Espanya. Bus 61 runs (six times a day, Monday to Friday only) along Avinguda del Paral.lel to Montjuïc via Plaça d'Espanya. Bus 55 runs across town via Plaça de Catalunya and Carrer de Lleida past the Museu d'Arqueologia to terminate near the Fundació Joan Miró. The PM (Parc de Montjuïc) line does a circle trip from Plaça d'Espanya to the Castell de Montjuïc. It operates every 20 minutes or so from 8am to 8pm on weekends and holidays. The Bus Turístic (p251) also makes several stops on Montjuïc.

Metro & Funicular

Take the Metro (Línia 2 or 3) to the Paral.lel stop and pick up the **funicular railway** (Map pp304–5; 🕑 9am-10pm Apr-Oct, 9am-8pm Nov-Mar), part of the Metro fare system, from there to Estació Parc Montjuïc.

Transbordador Aeri

The quickest way to get to the mountain from the beach is this cable car that runs between Torre de Sant Sebastià in La Barceloneta (p101) and the Miramar stop on Montjuïc.

Telefèric de Montjuïc

From Estació Parc Montjuïc, this cable car normally carries you to the Castell de Montjuïc via the Mirador (a lookout point). It is out of action for long-term repairs.

Tren Turístic

This little road train runs every half-hour from Plaça d'Espanya and stops at all points of interest (adult/child under 11 years €3/2, 10am to 8.30pm late June to early September, 10am to 8.30pm weekends and holidays Easter to mid-June and mid-September to October).

Cristina, flanked by buildings of the Fira de Barcelona, the city's main fairgrounds.

Before you rises the monumental façade of the Palau Nacional (which houses the Museu Nacional d'Art de Catalunya). Approaching Montjuïc on foot this way has the advantage of allowing you to follow a series of escalators all the way up to Avinguda de l'Estadi.

For information on the park, head for the Centre Gestor del Parc de Montjuïc (Map pp304–5; Passeig de Santa Madrona 28; 🕑 10am-8pm Apr-Oct, 10am-6pm Nov-Mar) in the Font del Gat building (a nice late modernista job done in 1919 by Puig i Cadafalch), a short walk off Passeig de Santa Madrona, east of the Museu Etnològic. It also has a pleasant bar-restaurant. Another information office open the same hours operates in the Castell.

The south side of the hill is bounded by the container port to the southeast and, beyond the southwest cemeteries, the Zona Franca commercial zone, where further trade fairgrounds are located.

ANELLA OLÍMPICA Map pp304-5
Avinguda de l'Estadi; 🚌 50, 61 or PM
The Olympic Ring is the group of sports installations where the main events of the 1992 Olympics were held, on the ridge above the Museu Nacional d'Art de Catalunya. Westernmost is the Institut Nacional d'Educació Física de Catalunya (INEFC), a kind of sports university, designed by Ricard Bofill. Past a circular arena, the Plaça d'Europa, with the slender white Torre Calatrava communications tower behind it, is the Piscines Bernat Picornell building, where the swimming events were held (now open to the public; see p197). Separating the pool from the Estadi Olímpic is a pleasant garden, the Jardí d'Aclimatació.

CAIXAFORUM Map pp304-5
☎ 93 476 86 00; www.fundacio.lacaixa.es; Avinguda del Marquès de Comillas 6-8; admission free; 🕑 10am-8pm Tue-Sun; Ⓜ Espanya; ♿
The Caixa building society prides itself on its involvement in (and ownership of) the arts,

CaixaForum (opposite), Montjuïc

in particular all that is contemporary. Its premier art expo space in the city hosts part of the bank's extensive collection from around the globe. The setting is a completely renovated former factory, the Fàbrica Casaramona, an outstanding modernista brick structure designed by Puig i Cadafalch. From 1940 to 1993 it housed the First Squadron of the police cavalry unit – 120 horses in all. Now it houses selected items of the 800-strong collection, rotated on view every month or two, while much space is set aside for external temporary exhibitions (in 2006 anything from the photography of Diane Arbus to ancient Persian art). The permanent collection includes works by Antoni Tàpies and Miquel Barceló. In the courtyard where the police horses used to drink is a steel tree designed by the Japanese architect Arata Isozaki. It is possible to join one-hour tours (€12) of the building; call to find out on which days they will take place .

CASTELL DE MONTJUÏC & AROUND Map pp304-5

☎ 93 329 86 13; admission €2.50; ☉ 9.30am-5pm Tue-Sun Nov–mid-Mar, 9.30am-8pm mid-Mar–Oct; ▣ PM

The forbidding Castell (castle or fort) de Montjuïc dominates the southeast heights of Montjuïc and enjoys commanding views over the Mediterranean. It dates, in its present form, from the late 17th and 18th centuries, and for most of its dark history it has been used to watch over the city and as a political prison and killing ground. Anarchists were executed here around the end of the 19th century, fascists during the civil war and Republicans after it – most notoriously Lluís Companys in 1940. The castle is surrounded by a network of ditches and

walls (from which its strategic position over the city and port become clear).

It houses the **Museu Militar**, a time-warp bastion of the army in all probability destined for a short existence, if the Ministry of Defence and Barcelona Town Hall can ever agree on conditions for handing the castle over to the city. For now, you enter an artillery-lined courtyard, off which rooms are filled with a ragbag of weapons old and new, as well as uniforms, yellowing maps and fighting men's gewgaws. Stairs lead down to another series of halls lined with more of the same, along with castle models, a couple of portraits of General Franco and even an equestrian statue of him half hidden in a nondescript corner. If the Town Hall has its way, the museum will be turned into a peace museum in an attempt to exorcise some of the awful ghosts that waft around here. Perhaps the tombstones, some dating to the 11th century, from the one-time Jewish cemetery on Montjuïc will get a more imaginative exhibition space too.

Best of all are the excellent views from the castle area of the port and city below. You can eat amid the cannons at the museum café.

Around the seaward foot of the castle is an airy walking track, the **Camí del Mar**, which offers breezy views of city and sea. Towards the foot of this part of Montjuïc, above the thundering traffic of the main road to Tarragona, the **Jardins de Mossèn Costa i Llobera** (admission free; ☉ 10am-sunset) has a good collection of tropical and desert plants – including a veritable forest of cacti. Near the Estació Parc Montjuïc funicular/Telefèric station are the ornamental **Jardins de Mossèn Cinto Verdaguer**. From the **Jardins del Mirador** opposite the Mirador Transbordador Aeri station you have fine views over the port of Barcelona.

CEMENTIRI DEL SUD-OEST Map pp304-5

☎ 93 484 17 00; ☉ 8am-5.30pm; ▣ 38 or PM

On the hill south of the Anella Olímpica you can see the top of a huge cemetery, the Cementiri del Sud-Oest or Cementiri Nou, which extends down the southern side of the hill. Opened in 1883, it's an odd combination of elaborate architect-designed tombs for rich families and small niches for the rest. It includes the graves of numerous Catalan artists and politicians. Among the big names are Joan Miró, Carmen Amaya (the flamenco dance star from La Barceloneta),

Jacint Verdaguer (the 19th-century priest and poet to whom the rebirth of Catalan literature is attributed), Francesc Macià and Lluís Companys (both nationalist presidents of Catalonia, the latter executed by Franco's henchmen in the Castell de Montjuïc in 1940), Ildefons Cerdà (who designed l'Eixample) and Joan Gamper (the founder of the FC Barcelona football team, aka Hans Gamper). Many victims of Franco's postwar revenge were buried in unmarked graves here – the last of them in 1974. From the PM bus stop it's about an 800m walk southwest. Bus 38 from Plaça de Catalunya stops close to the cemetery entrance.

ESTADI OLÍMPIC Map pp304-5
Avinguda de l'Estadi; admission free; 10am-6pm Oct-Apr, 10am-8pm May-Sep; 50, 61 or PM
First opened in 1929, the 65,000-capacity stadium was given a complete overhaul for the 1992 Olympics. You enter from the northern end, in the shadow of the dish in which the Olympic flame burned. At the opening ceremony a long-range archer set it alight by spectacularly depositing a flaming arrow into it. Well, more or less. He actually missed, but the organisers had foreseen this possibility. The dish was alive with gas, so the arrow only had to pass within 2m of it to set the thing on fire. The stadium is used by the city's second football side, Espanyol, as they wait for a brand-new stadium to be built. It rocks to the rhythms of such world acts as the Rolling Stones when they come to town too.

At its southern end (enter from outside the stadium) is the Galería Olímpica (93 426 06 60; www.fundaciobarcelonaolimpica.es; Passeig Olímpic s/n; adult/senior & child/student €2.70/1.50/2.40; 10am-1pm & 4-6pm Mon-Fri), which has an exhibition, including videos, on the 1992 games. You will need to be quite a fan of all things Olympian to get much out of this. Favourite items are the models of the standard daily diet of cyclists and gymnasts – there's something vaguely nauseating about the plates of plastic pasta. Or you can behold the splendours of an athlete's bed made up with duvet and pillowcases sporting Barcelona's Olympic mascot, Cobi. Speaking of which, a whole display is dedicated to Cobi, dreamed up by the ubiquitous Valencian designer Javier Mariscal.

West of the stadium is the Palau Sant Jordi, a 17,000-capacity indoor sports, concert and exhibition hall opened in 1990 and designed by Isozaki.

FONT MÀGICA Map pp304-5
Avinguda de la Reina Maria Cristina; admission free; every ½hr 7-8.30pm Fri & Sat Oct–late Jun, 9.30-11.30pm Thu-Sun late Jun–Sep; Espanya
With a flourish, the Magic Fountain erupts into a feast of musical, backlit liquid life. It is extraordinary how an idea that was cooked up for the 1929 Exposition has, since the 1992 Olympics, again become a magnet. On hot summer evenings especially, this 15-minute spectacle (repeated several times through the evening) mesmerises onlookers. The main fountain of a series that sweeps up the hill from Avinguda de la Reina Maria Cristina to the grand façade of the Palau Nacional, La Font Màgica is a unique performance in which the water at times looks like seething fireworks or a mystical cauldron of colour. Depending on the music chosen (anything from Swan Lake through Sting to Beyonce), it can be quite moving. And it's free! On the last evening of the Festes de la Mercè in September there's a particularly spectacular display that includes fireworks.

FUNDACIÓ JOAN MIRÓ Map pp304-5
93 443 94 70; www.bcn.fjmiro.es; Plaça de Neptu; adult/senior & child €7.50/5, temporary exhibitions €4/3; 10am-7pm Tue, Wed, Fri & Sat, 10am-9.30pm Thu, 10am-2.30pm Sun & holidays; 50, 55, 61 or PM;
This shimmering white temple to the art of one of the stars of the 20th-century Spanish firmament seems to rest at ease amid the greenery of its privileged position on the mountain.

Joan Miró, the city's best-known 20th-century artistic progeny, left his home town this art foundation in 1971. Its light-filled buildings, designed by close friend and architect Josep Lluís Sert (who also built Miró's Mallorca studios), are crammed with seminal works, from Miró's earliest timid sketches to paintings from his last years.

This is in fact the greatest single collection of the artist's work, comprising around 300 of his paintings, 150 sculptures, some textiles and more than 7000 drawings spanning his entire life. Only a smallish portion is ever on display. The exhibits tend to concentrate on Miró's more settled last 20 years, but there are some important exceptions.

In some respects, his earlier work is the most intriguing because it's the least known.

The bulk of it is contained in the Sala Joan Prats and Sala Pilar Juncosa (named after his wife). The first shows the young Miró moving away, under surrealist influence, from his *relative* realism (for instance his 1917 painting of the *Ermita de Sant Joan d'Horta*), towards his own recognisable style. This section includes the 1939–44 Barcelona series of tortured lithographs – Miró's comment on the Spanish Civil War. The big 1st-floor galleries burst with the colour and light of his better-known work from the 1960s on. Here you can see grand-scale canvases and a sprinkling of sculpture.

Another interesting section is devoted to the 'Miró Papers', which include many preparatory drawings and sketches, some on bits of newspaper or cigarette packets. *A Joan Miró* is a collection of work by other contemporary artists, donated in tribute to Miró and held in a basement hall.

Outside on the east flank of the museum is the **Jardí de les Escultures** (admission free; 10am-dusk), a small garden with various odd bits of modern sculpture.

JARDÍ BOTÀNIC Map pp304-5

☎ 93 426 49 35; www.jardibotanic.bcn.es; Carrer del Doctor Font i Quer; adult/student €3/1.50, last Sun of month free; 10am-8pm Jul & Aug, 10am-5pm Mon-Fri & 10am-8pm Sat & Sun & holidays Apr-Jun & Sep, 10am-5pm Oct-Mar; 50, 61 or PM
Across the road to the south of the Estadi, this botanical garden was created atop what was an old municipal dump. The theme is 'Mediterranean' fauna and the collection includes some 2000 species that thrive in areas with a climate similar to that of the Med, including the Eastern Mediterranean, Spain (including the Balearic and Canary Islands), North Africa, Australia, California, Chile and South Africa.

MUSEU D'ARQUEOLOGIA DE CATALUNYA Map pp304-5

☎ 93 424 65 77; www.mac.es; Passeig de Santa Madrona 39-41; adult/child €2.40/1.70; 9.30am-7pm Tue-Sat, 10am-2.30pm Sun; 55 or PM;
The archaeology museum, housed in what was the Graphic Arts palace during the 1929 Exposition, covers Catalonia and related cultures elsewhere in Spain. Items range from copies of pre-Neanderthal skulls to lovely Carthaginian necklaces and jewel-studded Visigothic crosses. There's good material on the Balearic Islands (rooms X

to XIII) and Empúries (Emporion), the Greek and Roman city on the Costa Brava (rooms XIV and XVII). The Roman finds upstairs were mostly dug up in Barcelona.

MUSEU ETNOLÒGIC Map pp304-5

☎ 93 424 64 02; www.museuetnologic.bcn.es; Passeig de Santa Madrona 16-22; adult/child/senior & student €3/free/1.50, 1st Sun of month free; noon-8pm Tue-Sat, 11am-3pm Sun late Jun-late Sep, 10am-7pm Tue & Thu, 10am-2pm Wed, Fri & Sun late Sep-late Jun; 55
Barcelona's ethnology museum presents a curious permanent collection, Ètnic, in which several thousand wide-ranging items are on show in three themed sections, Orígens (Origins), Pobles (Peoples) and Mosaics. Along with lots of material from rural areas of Catalonia and parts of Spain, the museum's collections include items from as far afield as Australia, Ecuador, Ethiopia, Japan and Morocco, along with a handful of objects from other parts of Europe. The Spanish collections range from Andalucian ceramics to extraordinary traditional festive dress from the remote Pyrenean valley, Vall d'Ansó. From distant Australia comes a collection of 45 colourful Aboriginal bark paintings and weapons (including boomerangs). From Japan comes a broad selection of traditional furniture, clothes and household items.

MUSEU NACIONAL D'ART DE CATALUNYA Map pp304-5

☎ 93 622 03 76; www.mnac.es; Mirador del Palau Nacional; adult/senior & child/student €8.50/free/6; 10am-7pm Tue-Sat, 10am-2.30pm Sun & holidays; Espanya;
From vantage points across the city the bombastic neobaroque silhouette of the so-called Palau Nacional (National Palace) can be seen halfway up the slopes of Montjuïc. Built for the 1929 World Exhibition and restored in 2005, it houses a vast collection of mostly Catalan art spanning the early Middle Ages to the early 20th century. The high point is the collection of extraordinary Romanesque frescoes, but there is plenty of other material to keep you busy for hours.

Built under the centralist dictatorship of Miguel Primo de Rivera, there is a whiff of irony in the fact that it has come to be one of the city's prime symbols of the region's separate, Catalan identity.

Head first to the Romanesque art section, one of the most important concentrations of early medieval art in the world. It consists of frescoes, woodcarvings and painted altar frontals (low-relief wooden panels that were the forerunners of the elaborate altarpieces that adorned later churches) transferred from country churches across northern Catalonia early in the 20th century. The insides of several churches have been re-created and the frescoes – in some cases fragmentary, in others extraordinarily complete and alive with colour – have been placed as they were when *in situ*.

The two most striking fresco sets follow one after the other. The first, in Àmbit V, is a magnificent image of Christ in majesty done around 1123. Based on the text of the Apocalypse, we see Christ enthroned on a rainbow with the world at his feet. He holds a book open with the words *Ego Sum Lux Mundi* (I am the Light of the World) and is surrounded by the four Evangelists. The images were taken from the apse of the Església de Sant Climent de Taüll in northwest Catalonia. In Àmbit VII are frescoes done around the same time in the nearby Església de Santa Maria de Taüll. This time the central image taken from the apse is of the Virgin Mary and Christ child. These images were not mere decoration. Try to set yourself in the medieval mind of the average citizen: illiterate, ignorant, fearful and in most cases eking out a subsistence living. These images transmitted the basic personalities and tenets of the faith and were accepted at face value by most.

Opposite the Romanesque collection on the ground floor is the museum's Gothic art sections. In these halls you can see Catalan Gothic painting (look out especially for the work of Bernat Martorell in Àmbit XI and Jaume Huguet in Àmbit XII), and that of other Spanish and Mediterranean regions. Among Martorell's works figure images of the martyrdom of St Vincent and St Llúcia. Huguet's *Consagració de Sant Agustí*, in which St Augustine is depicted as a bishop, is dazzling in its detail.

As the Gothic collection draws to a close, you pass through two separate and equally eclectic private collections, the Cambò bequest and works from the Thyssen-Bornemisza collections that until 2005 hung in the Museu-Monestir de Pedralbes. Works by the Venetian Renaissance masters Veronese (1528–88), Titian (1490–1557) and

THE MADNESS OF MARTYRDOM

In Àmbit X of the museum's Romanesque section, have a look at item 116, an altar frontal in which the martyrdom of several saints is among the main themes. See the medieval mind at work, depicting holy individuals who contemplate their own slow deaths with supreme indifference – whether boiling in water, having nails slammed into the head, being sliced up by sword or, a personal favourite, being sawn in half from head to toe! The scary thing is that these kinds of torture and execution were not uncommon in medieval Europe!

Canaletto (1697–1768), along with Rubens (1577–1640) and even England's Gainsborough (1727–88) feature.

From here you pass into the great central hall, topped by a majestic dome. This area is sometimes used for concerts. Up on the next floor, after a series of rooms devoted to mostly minor works by a variety of classic 17th-century Spanish Old Masters, the collection turns to modern Catalan art. It is an uneven affair, but it is worth looking out for modernista painters Ramon Casas (Àmbit 71) and Santiago Rusiñol (Àmbit 72). Also on show are items of modernista furniture and decoration.

If you have any energy left, check out the photography section, which encompasses work from mostly Catalan snappers from the mid-19th century on. Coin collectors will enjoy the Gabinet Numismàtic de Catalunya, with coins from Roman Spain, medieval Catalonia and some engaging notes from the Civil War days. After all this, you can relax in the museum restaurant, which offers great views north towards Plaça d'Espanya. Finally, students can use the **Biblioteca General d'Història de l'Art** (9.30am-6.30pm Mon-Fri, 9.30am-2pm Sat), the city's main art reference library.

PAVELLÓ MIES VAN DER ROHE Map pp304–5

93 423 40 16; www.miesbcn.com; Avinguda del Marquès de Comillas s/n; adult/under 18yr/student €3.50/free/2; 10am-8pm; M Espanya;
Just to the west of La Font Màgica is a strange building. In 1929 Ludwig Mies van der Rohe erected the Pavelló Alemany (German Pavilion) for the World Exhibition. Now known by the name of its architect, it was

actually removed after the show. Decades later, a society was formed to rebuild what was in hindsight considered a key work in the trajectory of one of the world's most important modern architects. Reconstructed in the 1980s, it is a curious structure of interlocking planes – walls of marble or glass, ponds of water, ceilings and just plain nothing, a temple to the new urban environment. A graceful copy of a statue of *Alba* (Dawn) by Berlin sculptor Georg Kolbe (1877–1947) stands in one of the exterior areas.

POBLE ESPANYOL Map pp304-5

☎ 93 508 63 30; www.poble-espanyol.com; Avinguda del Marquès de Comillas; adult/child/senior & student €7.50/4/5.50; ☯ 9am-8pm Mon, 9am-2am Tue-Thu, 9am-4am Fri & Sat, 9am-midnight Sun; Ⓜ Espanya or 🚌 50, 61 or PM

Welcome to Spain! All of it! This Spanish Village is both a cheesy souvenir-hunters' haunt and an intriguing scrapbook of Spanish architecture built for the Spanish crafts section of the 1929 Exhibition. You can wander from Andalucía to the Balearic Islands in the space of a couple of hours' slow meandering, visiting surprisingly good copies of characteristic buildings from all the country's regions.

You enter from beneath a towered medieval gate from Ávila. Inside, to the right, is an information office with free maps. Straight ahead from the gate is the Plaza Mayor (town square), surrounded with mainly Castilian and Aragonese buildings. Elsewhere you'll find an Andalucian *barrio*, a Basque street, Galician and Catalan quarters and even a Dominican monastery (at the eastern end). The buildings house dozens of restaurants, cafés, bars, craft shops and workshops (such as glass-makers), and some souvenir stores. Spare some time for the Fundació Fran Daurel (☎ 93 423 41 72; admission free; ☯ 10am-7pm), an eclectic collection of 200 works of art including sculptures, prints, ceramics and tapestries by modern artists ranging from Picasso and Miró to more contemporary figures, including Miquel Barceló.

At night the restaurants, bars and especially the discos become a lively corner of Barcelona's nightlife.

THE OUTSKIRTS

Two key architectural sights lie on the edge of town. Gaudí's crypt in the Colònia Güell provides eye-catching insights into his theories of architecture, while the grand cloisters of the monastery at Sant Cugat del Vallès take us travelling back centuries.

Orientation

Sant Cugat del Vallès lies about 15km north of central Barcelona, over the Serra de Collserola hills. The Colònia Güell is in Santa Coloma de Cervelló, about 15km west of Barcelona on the west bank of the Riu Llobregat.

TRANSPORT

For the Colònia Güell, take an FGC train (the S4, S7, S8 or S33) from Plaça d'Espanya and get off at the Colònia Güell station (€1.20, 21 minutes). To reach Sant Cugat del Vallès, take the FGC train from Catalunya station (S1, S2, S5 or S55) to Sant Cugat del Vallès (€1.60, 25 minutes). From the train station, head left out of the station along Avinguda d'Alfonso Sala Conde de Egara and turn right down Carrer de Ruis i Taulet, followed by a left into Carrer de Santiago Rusiñol, which leads to the monastery.

Poble Espanyol (above), Montjuïc

COLÒNIA GÜELL

☎ 93 630 58 07; www.coloniaguellbarcelona.com; Santa Coloma de Cervelló; crypt €4; ☒ crypt 9am-2pm & 3-7pm Mon-Sat, 10am-3pm Sun Apr-Oct, 10am-3pm Nov-Mar, info centre 9am-7pm Mon-Sat; ☒ FGC lines S4, S7, S8 or S33

Apart from La Sagrada Família, Gaudí's last big project was the creation of a Utopian textile workers' complex for his magnate patron Eusebi Güell outside Barcelona at Santa Coloma de Cervelló. Gaudí's main role was to erect the colony's church. Work began in 1908 but the idea fizzled eight years later and Gaudí only finished the crypt, which still serves as a working church.

This structure is a key to understanding what the master had in mind for his *magnum opus*, La Sagrada Família. The mostly brick-clad columns that support the ribbed vaults in the ceiling are inclined at all angles in much the way you might expect trees in a forest to lean. That effect was deliberate, but also grounded in physics. Gaudí worked out the angles so that their load would be transmitted from the ceiling to the earth without the help of extra buttressing. Similar thinking lay behind his plans for La Sagrada Família, whose Gothic-inspired structure would tower above any Middle Ages building, without requiring a single buttress. Gaudí's hand is visible down to the wavy design of the pews. The primary colours in the curvaceous plant-shaped stained-glass windows are another reminder of the era in which the crypt was built.

Near the church spread the cute brick houses designed for the factory workers and still inhabited today. A short stroll away, the 23 factory buildings of a modernista industrial complex, idle since the 1970s, have been brought back to life in a €60 million project under the direction of local building star Òscar Tusquets. Shops and businesses have moved in (or are being encouraged to do so) to the renovated complex. You can pick up a map at the information centre and wander around or join guided visits of the crypt alone (€5) or the crypt and former factory complex (€8) at noon on weekends. Several languages theoretically are catered for.

SANT CUGAT DEL VALLÈS

☎ 93 675 99 51; www.museu.santcugat.org; Plaça Octavià; adult/under 16yr €3/free; ☒ 10am-1.30pm & 3-7pm Tue-Sat, 10am-2.30pm Sun & holidays; ☒ FGC lines S1, S2, S5 or S55

Marauding Muslims razed the one-time Roman encampment–turned–Visigothic monastery of Sant Cugat del Vallès to the ground in the 8th century. These things happen, so after the Christians got back in the saddle, work on a new, fortified Benedictine monastic complex was stoically begun. What you see today is a combination of Romanesque and Gothic buildings. The lower floor of the cloister is a fine demonstration of Romanesque design and it's the principal reason for making the effort to come. In particular, the decoration of the 72 pairs of columns, with scenes ranging from pious scriptural events to completely medieval fantasy, is captivating. The former monastery holds occasional temporary exhibitions.

Walking Tours

Walking Tours

Those shoes are meant for walking and they are by far the best means of transport for getting a feel for Barcelona, although judicious use of the city's excellent Metro system can save on sweat, especially when on the modernisme trail. The following walks offer quite different visions of the city, from the ancient to the artistic. The time you spend exploring each trail will depend greatly on whether you stop to visit sights or have a coffee along the way. Times given are for nonstop but unhurried strolls.

OLD BARCELONA

Plaça de Sant Jaume 1 (p88) is at the core of Barcelona in the Barri Gòtic. This is where the Romans built their outpost, upon which medieval Barcelona slowly grew – it remains the secular and religious centre of the city to this day. The northwest and southeast sides of the square are lined respectively by the Palau de la Generalitat 2 (p88) and Ajuntament 3 (Town Hall; p88), the seats of regional and city governments. Just north of the medieval square, and probably incorporating much of it, lay Roman Barcino's forum. Together these features formed the centre of civic life in the Roman town. The two main roads crossed through the forum. From north to south ran the *decumanus* (roughly Carrer del Bisbe Irurita), intersected by the *cardo* – the standard Roman town plan.

From Plaça de Sant Jaume, head southwest along Carrer del Call, which was the main street in medieval Barcelona's Call (Jewish quarter), then dogleg up to Carrer de Marlet. At No 5 are the remains of the Sinagoga Major 4 (p90). A few steps further on, at No 1, is a Hebrew inscription in the wall, one of the few overt reminders of the area's former identity. According to the Spanish (Castilian) translation underneath (1820), a rabbi, Samuel Hasareri, must have lived or died here. What is truly intriguing is the apparent date of his death (AD 692). The plaque in Hebrew is, apparently, not an original.

The next major junction is with Carrer dels Banys Nous, where the Jewish community was permitted to build new public baths just beyond the then city walls (before Jaume I raised new walls along La Rambla). From here the street changes name to Carrer de la Boqueria. Take the next right and follow it into Plaça de Sant Josep Oriol (a nice spot for a drink). The Gothic church is Església de Santa Maria del Pi 5 (entrance in the adjoining square; p89). Opposite it, at No 4, stands the Palau de Fiveller 6, a one-time private mansion dating from 1571.

Palau de la Generalitat (p88), Plaça de Sant Jaume

Wend your way back east down Carrer de l'Ave Maria, dogleg left up Carrer dels Banys Nous and take the first right up Baixada de Santa Eulàlia (back into the Call). Where the street name changes to Carrer de Sant Sever, you'll see a tiny lane to your left. Head down this into a quiet, leafy square, which boasts the rather obscure **Museu del Calçat** (7; Footwear Museum; ☎ 93 301 45 33; Plaça de Sant Felip Neri 5; admission €2.50; 🕙11am-2pm Tue-Sun), with everything from Egyptian sandals to dainty ladies' shoes of the 18th century on display. The museum and cobblers' guild, with roots in the city's medieval past, were moved here shortly after the civil war.

The church before you is the baroque **Església de Sant Felip Neri 8**, completed in 1752. The façade is shattered by the impact of machine-gun fire. One story says that pro-Franco troops carried out summary executions here shortly after they marched into the city in 1939. Another story claims much of the damage to the wall came from a bomb dropped by a Fascist plane. Judging by the kind of damage done, the latter seems an unlikely option. A kind of haunted silence hangs over the square, with its peacefully bubbling fountain. The church adjoins the **Palau Episcopal 9** (also known as Palau del Bisbat, p85).

Follow Carrer de Montjuïc del Bisbe, surely one of the narrowest lanes in Barcelona, into Carrer del Bisbe Irurita. You are now facing the entrance to the shady cloister of **La Catedral 10** (p84). The narrow lanes around La Catedral are traffic free and dotted with sometimes quite accomplished buskers. You *could* turn right and head back to Plaça de Sant Jaume, passing first the modest **Església de Sant Sever 11** and then the main Gothic façade of the Palau de la Generalitat. But continuing on with the walk, you should turn left (northwest) and head out through the old city gates (parts of the Roman originals are still in existence) where Carrer del Bisbe Irurita leads into Plaça Nova. (For the record, the southwest gates stood on Carrer del Call. To the southeast, the entrance to Barcino was on what is now Carrer de Regomir, while the northeast exit was about where Carrer de la Llibreteria runs into Baixada de la Llibreteria.)

Proceed up Carrer dels Arcs and a short way along Avinguda del Portal de l'Àngel before hanging a left into Carrer de la Canuda. It is speculated this was part of the Roman branch road off the Via Augusta (which linked Rome to Cádiz) into Barcelona. Proceed until you come to Plaça de la Vila de Madrid, marked by a series of road-side **Roman Tombs 12**.

Take Carrer de Bertrellans north a block to Carrer de Santa Anna. Turn right and you'll find almost immediately to your left a lane that leads into a surprisingly tranquil square backed by the unassuming **Església de Santa Anna 13**. It dates from the 12th century, but little remains of the original Romanesque structure. The Gothic cloister is a shady haven – if you can get in.

Back on Carrer de Santa Anna, cross Avinguda del Portal de l'Àngel and continue down Carrer Comtal. Taking a right down Carrer de N'Amargos is interesting if only to see the plaque at No 8. It claims the **palace garden walls 14** of the first Comte (Count) of Barcelona, Guifré el Pelós (Wilfred the Hairy, see p60) stood here. Carrer de N'Amargos was also the first street in the city to get gas lighting.

Turn right at Carrer de Montsió and left at Avinguda del Portal de l'Àngel to retrace your steps to Plaça Nova.

Re-enter the Roman gates (note on your left the remnants of the aqueducts that supplied Roman Barcino with water) and take the first left. You are on Carrer de Santa Llúcia. On your right is the Romanesque **Capella de Santa Llúcia 15** (p85), wedged onto La Catedral and dedicated to the saint of the same name. On your left is **Casa de l'Ardiaca 16** (p85). Further ahead on your right is the main entrance to La Catedral. The building directly ahead of you is the **Casa de la Pia Almoina 17** (p83).

ALONG THE WAY

Depending on when you get started, you might want to stop in for one of Barcelona's great *entrepans* (filled rolls) in **Can Conesa** (p142). Otherwise, Plaça del Pi offers some shady terraces for drinks and snacks. You might call in for a bagel at the **Bagel Shop** (p142) or stop for a big lunch in the former haunt of the modernista crowd, **Els Quatre Gats** (p143). The leafy café in the Museu Frederic Marès is another handy pause point. You could pop into **Bodega La Palma** (p142) for a cosy glass of wine or a light meal, or the über-stylish **Cometacinc** (p143). Across in La Ribera the choice of eateries and bars is endless. **La Vinya del Senyor** (p170) is a fine wine bar in front of the Església de Santa Maria del Mar.

The lane heading southeast down the eastern flank of La Catedral, Carrer dels Comtes de Barcelona, will lead you to the complex of buildings making up the former Palau Reial Major. Before entering the complex you pass the **Museu Frederic Marès 18** (p88). Further down the street, turn left into the courtyard known as **Plaça del Rei 19** (p88). Access to the complex (which includes an underground tour of this sector of Roman Barcino) is through the **Museu d'Història de la Ciutat 20** (p87), where you can learn more about Barcino's military camp background. When you're through, leave Plaça del Rei via the street you entered it from, cross over Carrer dels Comtes de Barcelona and take the next left to dogleg your way down Carrer del Paradis, including a quick look at what's left of the **Temple Romà d'Augusti 21** (p90), Barcino's Roman temple, which stood on a slight rise known as Mont Taber. This brings you back to Plaça de Sant Jaume.

From here head southeast down Carrer de la Ciutat along the only remaining Gothic façade of the Ajuntament. Turn right around the building and you end up in the

WALK FACTS

Start Plaça de Sant Jaume
Finish Museu Picasso
Distance 3.4km
Duration Two hours
Transport Ⓜ Jaume I

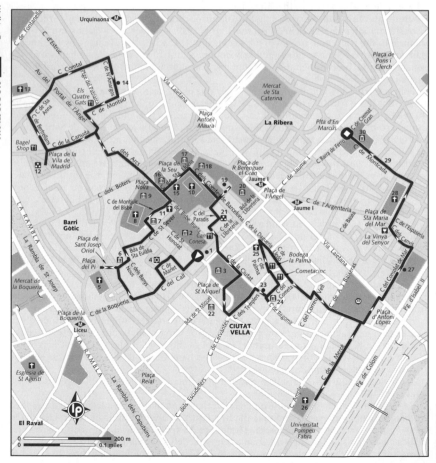

rather nondescript Plaça de Sant Miquel. The one-time Roman baths here have long since been covered up. Still in one piece, however, is the charming 15th-century **Casa Centelles 22**, on the corner of Baixada de Sant Miquel. You can wander into the fine Gothic-Renaissance courtyard if the gates are open, but that's as far as you'll get.

Head northeast again along Carrer dels Templers and make a right down Carrer de la Ciutat. Where it becomes Carrer de Regomir you will notice the site of Roman Barcino's southernmost city gate and parts of the 3rd- and 4th-century city wall. To get a closer look, walk up a side passage and enter the **Centre Cívic Pati Llimona** (23; ☎ 93 268 47 00; admission free; ☙9am-2pm & 4.30-8.30pm). Just beyond the gate at No 13 is another 15th-century mansion, **Casa Gualbes 24**. Backtrack a little and turn into Carrer del Cometa and then left into Carrer de Palma. Follow this street into the charming little Plaça de Sant Just, flanked by the Gothic **Església de Sants Just i Pastor 25** (p83).

From the square you can now take another street, Carrer de Lledó, back down towards the waterfront. It's a run-down old lane, but once was a fine medieval residential street. Follow it (don't mind the changes of name en route) all the way down to Carrer de la Mercè. The baroque church of the same name, **Església de la Mercè 26** (home to Barcelona's most celebrated patron saint), lies three blocks southwest. Raised in the 1760s on the site of its Gothic predecessor, the church was badly damaged during the Civil War, when all its ornamentation was destroyed. What remains is however quite a curiosity. The baroque façade facing the square contrasts with the Renaissance flank along Carrer Ample. The latter was actually moved here from another nearby church that was subsequently destroyed in the 1870s.

To finish, cross traffic-choked Via Laietana into La Ribera, and stroll along Carrer del Consolat de Mar past **La Llotja 27**, the city's medieval stock exchange. The centrepiece is the fine Gothic Saló de Contractacions, built in the 14th century. Pablo Picasso and Joan Miró attended the art school that from 1849 was housed in the Saló dels Cònsols. These and five other halls were encased in a neoclassical shell in the 18th century. The stock exchange was in action until well into the 20th century and the building remains in the hands of the city's chamber of commerce. In 2002 restoration work was completed and the various rooms and halls are rented out for meetings and banquets. Two or three times a year they open their doors to the public (☎ 902 448448).

Turn left on Carrer dels Canvis and take this to reach Plaça de Santa Maria del Mar. The area is sprinkled with appealing little bars and places to eat, and dominated by the Gothic **Església de Santa Maria del Mar 28** (p95). Wander along the church's eastern flank and around the apse, and you'll find yourself in **Carrer de Montcada 29** (p94), a medieval Bond St bursting with mansions, museums, shops and a couple of choice watering holes. The major sight here is the **Museu Picasso 30** (p96).

EL RAVAL

Start at Barcelona's own phoenix risen from the flames, the **Gran Teatre del Liceu 1** (p83) opera house. As you wander down La Rambla, duck to the right into Carrer Nou de la Rambla (carved through El Raval at the end of the 18th century to give quicker access to Montjuïc from the city centre) to see Gaudí's **Palau Güell 2** (p93) or to the left for **Plaça Reial 3** (p89). Further down La Rambla on the left is the **Museu de Cera 4** (Wax Museum; p87) and at the end on the waterfront roundabout rises the 19th-century **Monument a Colom 5** (p86), where you can take a lift to the top for excellent views. West of the monument are the great Gothic shipyards, the Drassanes, which house the **Museu Marítim 6** (p92).

From here each sight requires a bit of legwork. Head west along Avinguda de les

ALONG THE WAY

There is no shortage of watering holes and eateries along La Rambla, although they fall under the loose heading of tourist traps. The restaurant-café in the Museu Marítim makes for a pleasant rest stop. Rambla del Raval is teeming with choices, from kebab stops to the occasional surviving old-time restaurant. There's no shortage of bars around here either. One of the unchanged classics is **Bar Marsella** (p167). A great vegetarian location is **Biocenter** (p144), or you could wait until you get into the **Mercat de la Boqueria** (see the boxed text, p141), which hosts several fun eateries within the market and a few others nearby.

Drassanes and left onto Carrer de Sant Pau. A few blocks towards Avinguda del Paral.lel is the Romanesque **Església de Sant Pau del Camp 7** (p92). Head north most of the way along Carrer de Sant Pau towards La Rambla, and then turn left up Carrer de l'Arc de Sant Agustí. **Església de Sant Agustí 8** is where the city's main Good Friday procession begins. At Carrer de l'Hospital head west for the **Antic Hospital de la Santa Creu 9** (p91).

For a change of scene and a departure from the medieval side of Barcelona's life, you can wander from the hospital across Plaça de la Gardunya into the back end of the bustling **Mercat de la Boqueria 10** (p86) before re-emerging on La Rambla. To the left (heading towards Plaça de Catalunya) are, first, the 18th-century **Palau de la Virreina 11** (p85) and then, across Carrer del Carme, the baroque **Església de Betlem 12** (p85). Cross La Rambla to No 118 and the **Llibreria & Informació Cultural de la Generalitat de Catalunya 13** (p203), housed in a former mansion, the Casa de Comillas, which was built in 1774. It was one of many such houses of the well-to-do that went up along La Rambla during the late 18th and early 19th centuries.

WALK FACTS

Start Gran Teatre del Liceu
Finish Casa de Comillas
Distance 2.8km
Duration 1½ hours
Transport Ⓜ Liceu

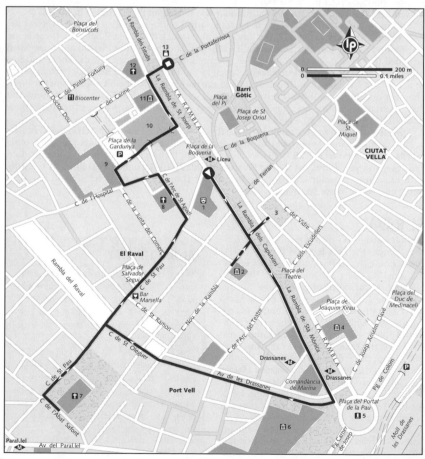

MODERNISME IN L'EIXAMPLE

Although examples of modernisme can be found across the old town and in other parts of Barcelona, it was in l'Eixample that architects could really go to town, either modifying relatively new, existing buildings or starting from scratch on newly zoned residential land. The filling of l'Eixample from the late 19th century and into the 1920s was one of Barcelona's great building booms.

If you wanted to see every vaguely modernista building or façade in l'Eixample, you'd probably need a week. This itinerary is far from exhaustive but aims to take in the highlights and some lesser-known gems.

We start at one of the great emblems of modernisme, Domènech i Montaner's **Palau de la Música Catalana 1** (p97), which will have you enthralled before you even walk inside

ALONG THE WAY

As it happens, some of the modernista stops along the way now house restaurants, among them Casa Calvet, and **La Dama** (p156) in Casa Sayrach. They are not the kind of place you stop in at for a snack, however. You will pass plenty of bars and the occasional restaurant along this route but you can often find more appealing options by making a brief detour. Try the busy **Cerveseria Catalana** (p153) or Basque country gem **Taktika Berri** (p154) for tapas. Another excellent tapas stop is **De Tapa Madre** (p153), in among some of the minor modernista jewels. The pickings are slimmer around La Sagrada Família, but you could pop into **Michael Collins Pub** (p182) for a soothing ale.

to join a tour. From Carrer de Sant Pere més alt, turn right into Carrer de Francesc de Paula and walk past the Palau's outdoor café, then dogleg to the left (you have no choice in the matter) along the little lane called Carrer de Ramon Mas, which leads you into the roaring Via Laietana. Pause to admire the **Caixa de Pensions 2** at Via Laietana 56. This largely neo-Gothic fantasy was headquarters to the bank of the same name from 1914 to 1917.

Cruise north along Carrer de les Jonqueres and cross Plaça d'Urquinaona. As you head up Carrer de Roger de Llúria you will pass the **Cases Cabot 3** (1905) at Nos 8-14, designed by Josep Vilaseca. The first doorway has fine decoration. Around the corner is Gaudí's **Casa Calvet 4** (1900) at Carrer de Casp 48. Inspired by the baroque, the main attraction is the internal staircase, which you can admire on your way into the swank restaurant inside (see p156).

Continue up to Gran Via de les Corts Catalanes where, at No 654, you pass Enric Sagnier's **Casa Mulleras 5** (1904), the best feature of which is the gallery on the façade. Further west, Josep Vilaseca's **Casa Pia Batlló 6** (1906), at Rambla de Catalunya 17, is interesting in its use of ironwork.

Cross Gran Via and then head northwest a couple of blocks along Rambla de Catalunya, turn right into Carrer del Consell de Cent and go on a block to the corner of Passeig de Gràcia. Here is **Casa Lleó Morera 7** (p104), first of the Manzana de la Discòrdia buildings. The other two, **Casa Amatller 8** (p103) and **Casa Batlló 9** (p103), are around the corner to your left. The next left into Carrer d'Aragó takes you to the **Fundació Antoni Tàpies 10** (p104).

Heading up Passeig de Gràcia (notice its modernista street lamps) you pass **Casa Enric Batlló 11**, at No 75, another apartment building by Vilaseca and now part of the Comtes de Barcelona hotel (see p221). Across the road on the corner of Carrer de Provença is Gaudí's masterpiece, **La Pedrera 12** (p105). One block up, turn left a block and then head northwest along Rambla de Catalunya to pass Puig i Cadafalch's **Casa Serra 13** (1903). Make the detour two blocks west along Avinguda Diagonal to admire Manuel Sayrach's **Casa Sayrach 14** (1918), one of the last modernista buildings and

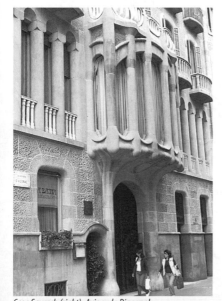
Casa Sayrach (right), Avinguda Diagonal

vaguely resembling La Pedrera (it is home to a chic restaurant). Cross the boulevard and head back east past Sagnier's **Església de Pompeia 15** (1915). You could pop up Passeig de Gràcia to drool before Domènech i Montaner's **Casa Fuster 16** (1910), long a bank and now restored as a luxury hotel (see p222).

Back on Avinguda Diagonal, turn east. On your left is the **Casa Comalat 17** (1911) by Salvador Valeri. The Gaudí influence on this modernista latecomer is obvious. Head around the back to Carrer de Còrsega to see a lighter, more playful façade. If you can sneak in, you can admire the fine mosaics and stained glass inside. Across the road on the corner of Carrer de Pau Claris is Puig i Cadafalch's **Palau del Baró Quadras 18** (p109). Shortly thereafter, you reach the hard-to-miss pointy-turreted **Casa de les Punxes 19** (p104).

Yet more minor modernista creations are sprinkled south of Avinguda Diagonal between Carrer de Roger de Llúria and Passeig de Sant Joan. From Casa de les Punxes drop down Carrer del Bruc to Carrer de Mallorca. Turn right for your first port of

WALK FACTS

Start Palau Güell
Finish Hospital de la Santa Creu i Sant Pau
Distance 5km
Duration Two hours
Transport Ⓜ Urquinaona

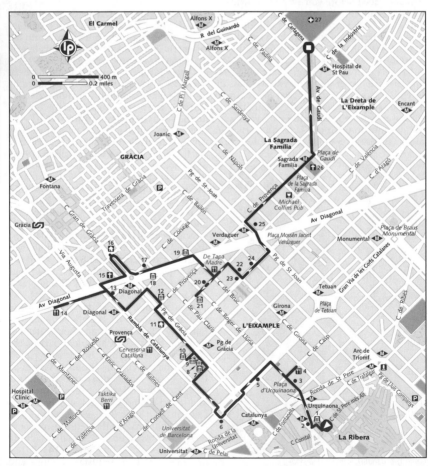

Walking Tours

MODERNISME IN L'EIXAMPLE

call, **Casa Thomas 20** (1898), at No 291, built by Domènech i Montaner. It is one of his earlier efforts – the ceramic details are a trademark. Less than a block away, **Palau Montaner 21** (p109) was finished off by the same architect in 1893–96. Backtrack northeast on Carrer de Mallorca, continue on and turn right at Carrer de Girona. At No 122 you'll find Jeroni Granell's colourful creation **Casa Granell 22** (1903). Virtually across the road at No 113 is Domènech i Montaner's **Casa Lamadrid 23** (1902). Northeast on Carrer de València at No 339 is **Casa Llopis i Bofill 24** (1902), an interesting block of flats by Antoni Gallissà – the façade is particularly striking. A left turn on Passeig de Sant Joan, across Avinguda Diagonal, takes you to Puig i Cadafalch's **Casa Macaya 25** (1901), which has a wonderful courtyard.

Head to the Verdaguer Metro station and whisk yourself one stop on line 5 to **La Sagrada Família 26** (p106), the city's most extravagant and popular monument. You could end the walk here with a visit or jump back on line 5 another stop to reach the **Hospital de la Santa Creu i de Sant Pau 27** (p105). Diehard walkers can skip the Metro and follow the route from Casa Macaya along Carrer de Provença to La Sagrada Família and then left onto Avinguda de Gaudí, which sports some fine modernista street lamps (designed by Pere Falqués and originally located around Plaça de Joan Carles I), up to the hospital.

MODERNISTA WINING & DINING

On and around La Rambla are scattered a series of spots where you can literally drink in a little modernisme or sit down for a meal surrounded by a century of history. At the time the modernista architects were doing their thing, La Rambla was still a fairly upmarket boulevard. The lower end of El Raval was a mix of respectable shopping and residential streets and lanes lined with downright dodgy dives, the kind of places where Picasso and his Bohemian pals would hang out carousing late into the night. A taste of this has come down to us today.

You could start the evening with a meal at was **Els Quatre Gats 1** (p143), which started life as Casa Martí (1896), one of Puig i Cadafalch's first creations. From 1897 to 1903, it was *the* hang-out for modernista artists and other hip souls. Ramon Casas, one of the leading lights of the small coterie of modernista painters (his closest pals were fellow painters Santiago Rusiñol, Miguel Utrillo and Pere Romeu), bought the house in 1897 and entrusted its management to Romeu. It became a restaurant, bar and meeting place for the luminaries of modernisme that came to be known as Els Quatre Gats (The Four Cats). In Catalan the expression also means 'a handful of people'. That handful consisted of the four friends, who proceeded to organise all sorts of get-togethers, from art exhibitions to concerts by emerging composers such as Isaac Albéniz and Enric Granados. The young Picasso, in whom the Cats saw great potential, had his first exhibition here in 1900. Nowadays it dines out on its history, but the food is not bad at all and the atmosphere in the galleried restaurant infectious. Either way, you could skip the meal and just drop in to the bar for the evening's first tipple.

From here, dogleg along Avinguda del Portal de l'Àngel and then west down Carrer de Santa Anna to La Rambla, which you cross directly into Carrer de Elisabets. Along here on the right drop in for a quiet modernista beer in **Casa Almirall 2** (p168). Long run by the Almirall family that opened it in the mid-19th century, this corner tavern preserves much of its modernista décor, especially in the picture windows opening on to the street and the counter and display cabinet. You'll recognise similarly sinuous curves as you enter **Bar Muy Buenas 3** (p167), a short stroll south via Carrena de Joaquim Costa on Carrer del Carme. Opened as a milk bar in the late 19th century, it too retains much of its original decoration. It's a welcoming, cosy spot, but it's too early to get settled in. Head down narrow Carrer d'en Roig

ALONG THE WAY

From a drinking point of view, you should have little need of adding too many more places to your list on this walk. In keeping with the historical flavour of this crawl, you may want to sidestep into **Bar Marsella** (p167), which is right on the route and not to be missed, no matter how many *guiris* (foreigners) crowd in there. Food could be another matter, although most of the places on this walk can offer you sustenance. An excellent minor detour, however, is **Biblioteca** (p146) in El Raval.

and swing round into the broad, busy Rambla del Raval. This part of town has undergone enormous change in the past 10 years. The boulevard lies at the heart of the city's Pakistani community. They must like Turkish food too, judging by the number of döner kebab joints that have sprung up here!

At Carrer de Sant Pau swing right and head right to the end of the street, where it runs into Ronda de Sant Pau. **La Confitería 4** (p168), once a barbershop and then long a confectioner's, was lovingly restored for its reconversion into a classy little bar in 1998. Most of the elements, including façade, bar counter and cabinets, are the real McCoy.

Backtracking northeast along Carrer de Sant Pau, you will pass numerous other tempting bars and eateries in what can be a slightly dodgy street. Before emerging on La Rambla you will see, on the right, the **Hotel España 5** (p216), a marvellous modernista jewel known above all for its two dining rooms, part of the 1903 design by Domènech i Montaner. To the left of the reception is the Sala Arnau (Arnau Room),

WALK FACTS

Start Els Quatre Gats
Finish London Bar
Distance 3.2km
Duration 1½ hours (unless you're drinking!)
Transport Ⓜ Urquinaona or Catalunya

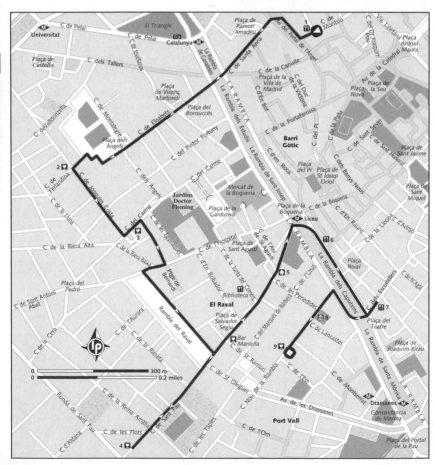

featuring a magnificent alabaster fireplace designed by sculptor Eusebi Arnau. You can have a fairly simple and moderately priced traditional Catalan meal here. The hotel was long popular with visiting bullfighters in Barcelona.

Should you wish to do so, save your post-prandial coffee for the next stop. Having passed the Gran Teatre del Liceu on your right, cross La Rambla and head right for a few metres and you arrive at another city classic, the Cafè de l'Òpera 6 (p143). Here you step into yet another time warp. Since 1929 it has been the traditional café stop before and after a night at the opera across the road at the Liceu, and it still fulfils that role today. In addition, curious passers-by of every possible description also pop in during the course of the day and evening. Prior to the Civil War it was a haunt of Catalan nationalist politicians and a favourite with members of the International Brigades during the war. The décor is much as it was when Antoni Dòria turned what had been a chocolate bar into a café-restaurant.

About 200m further along La Rambla, turn into Carrer dels Escudellers and at No 8 you will strike another Barcelona institution that has, unfortunately in some respects, been overwhelmed by tourists. The Grill Room 7 was originally opened in the 18th-century building as the Petit Torino, a café run by Flaminio Mezzalana, an Italian from Turin who, among other things, was a rep for Martini e Rossi and introduced Italian vermouth to Barcelona. In the 1920s it changed hands and the ground-floor restaurant that to this today specialises in grills became a sizzling dinner-time beacon for locals. Elements from the turn-of-the-century establishment include the cast iron pillars, some cabinets and the two bars, not to mention the typically and elaborately curvaceous timber entrance. The food is actually not bad, but there's not a Catalan in sight.

Whether you have just popped in for a tipple or tucked into some beef at the Grill Room, it's time to head on for what could easily be the last stop of a long night out. Back on La Rambla, cross over and head north one block and then dive down Carrer Nou de la Rambla. Just as you start down this street you pass, on the left, one of Gaudí's earlier big commissions, Palau Güell 8 (p93), a remarkable building. At this time of night one can only make out the restrained oddness of the façade. Make a mental note (or better, scribble it down, because it could be a late night) and come back to visit another day.

A mere 100m stumble further down the street on the right is a classic of Barcelona nightlife for over a century and still going strong. Open until 5am, the London Bar 9 (p168) is a fitting place to end your modernista drinking tour. The bar, with a simple but unmistakeable modernista décor, is still in the same family of the waiter who founded it in 1910. The first bar as you enter retains the original marble counter. It's opening hours are pretty generous as it is, but in its heyday it opened 24 hours a day, which attracted the likes of Picasso and Miró for countless swifties.

THE SQUARES OF GRÀCIA

Gràcia, a separate town until 1897, when it was absorbed into the Barcelona metropolitan area against the wishes of the bulk of its inhabitants, has until this day maintained an atmosphere quite separate from that of central Barcelona. Its long and uneven narrow streets, crowded by dense housing, are interrupted on occasion by a series of pleasant squares. Tracing a path between them is an excellent way to dive into a vibrant part of the city, without the 'distraction' of major sights.

Start on the busy roundabout that is Plaça de Joan Carles I 1, surprisingly named after the Spanish king in this city that is none too enamoured of anything related to Spanish rule, and still less the Bourbon descendent of King Felipe V, who crushed Barcelona at the tail end of the War of the Spanish Succession

ALONG THE WAY

Since this is more of an atmospheric stroll than a sightseeing hunt, this walk lends itself to frequent coffee and drinking stops. Take note of Maria (p184), a great little bar for some rock 'n' roll, pool and a tipple. For food, drop in at El Roure (p158) for a few tapas and a beer, or the timeless Envalira (p159) on Plaça del Sol for rice and seafood specialities. Any of the cafés on this square with their al fresco seating are good for taking a load off. You might want to catch a film in the original language at the nearby Verdi (p192) and Verdi Park (p192) cinemas.

in 1714. The obelisk monument in honour of the present king went up after he effectively stifled the attempted coup d'état of February 1981, just six years after the death of Franco and the birth of a fragile democracy in Spain. The king ordered the army back into the barracks and assured his backing for the Spanish parliament.

Avinguda Diagonal, one of the city's three main arteries, ploughs through the roundabout and only got this official name in 1979. This boulevard has had more than its fair share of name changes, the most lasting official one was Avenida de Francisco Franco. Few Barcelonins could bring themselves to utter the dictator's name and so most folk simply referred to the road as 'la Diagonal'. The name stuck.

Heading northwest along the top end of Passeig de Gràcia, occasionally the scene of boisterous local fairs, you reach Carrer Gran de Gràcia, the showcase boulevard of what was until the 19th century a separate town. Where the street begins, a grand modernista edifice now turned hotel, **Casa Fuster 2** (p222), rises up in all its glory.

WALK FACTS

Start Plaça de Joan Carles I
Finish Plaça del Diamant
Distance 2.3km
Duration One hour
Transport [M] Diagonal

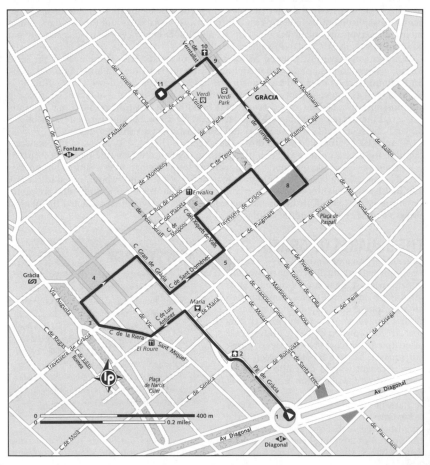

Hotel Casa Fuster (p222), Passeig de Gràcia

Past some of the grand houses lining Carrer Gran de Gràcia, turn left into Carrer de Luis Antúnez and then right along Carrer de la Riera Sant Miquel. A river once ran along here, flanked by a country trail linking Barcelona and Gràcia in the 18th century. The street leads into **Plaça de Gal.la Placídia 3**, notable only for its name, which recalls the brief sojourn of the Roman empress–to-be here as captive and wife of the Visigothic chief Athaulf in the 5th century AD. An about-face east down Carrer de Milton brings us into **Plaça de la Llibertat 4** (Liberty Sq), site of a bustling modernista produce market designed by one of Gaudí's colleagues, Francesc Berenguer (see p110).

Back on Carrer Gran de Gràcia, head south a little way and then east along Carrer de Sant Domènec to **Plaça de Rius i Taulet 5**, one of the most popular of the *barri's* squares. Named after the mayor under whom Gràcia was absorbed by Barcelona, Francesc Rius i Taulet, it is fronted by what is still the local town hall (designed by Berenguer). At the heart of the square stands the Torre del Rellotge (Clock Tower), which in the late 19th century was a symbol of republican and left-wing agitation. In March 1870, during a week-long workers' revolt over attempts to draft cannon-fodder for Spain's colonial tussles in northern Morocco, the bells here tolled constantly to keep the revolutionary spirit fired up.

Two blocks northwest along Carrer dels Xiquets de Valls is possibly the rowdiest of Gràcia's squares. **Plaça del Sol 6** is lined with bars and eateries and especially comes to life on long summer nights. After the disturbances of March 1870, the square was the scene of summary executions. During the 1936–39 Civil War an air-raid shelter was installed. Two blocks northeast you wind up in another busy little square, **Plaça de la Revolució de Setembre de 1868 7**. The name of the square commemorates the toppling of Queen Isabel II, a cause of much celebration in this working-class stronghold. Another produce market, the **Mercat de l'Abaceria Central 8**, opens out one block away. After snooping around here, head northwest along Carrer to Torrijos to the prettiest of the area's squares, **Plaça de la Virreina 9**. Pleasant terraces spill out on to this pedestrianised square, which is also notable for its shady trees, a rarity in this greenery-starved part of Barcelona. The 17th century **Església de Sant Joan 10**, which caps its north end, was largely destroyed by anarchists during the unrest that rocked the city in the Setmana Tràgica (Tragic Week) of July 1909. Rebuilt by Berenguer, who was indeed busy in this part of town, although he was never awarded a diploma as an architect, the church was damaged again during the Civil War.

Two blocks southwest is the rather down-at-heel **Plaça del Diamant 11**, which lays at the heart of one of the best known works of 20th-century Catalan literature, Mercè Rodoreda's eponymous novel. In the course of 2006 the square will be spruced up, along with its Civil War air-raid shelter, which at some point will be opened for visits.

Eating ▮

Eating

You could come to Barcelona for the food alone. The options seem limitless, from a rusting grill in a centuries-old farmhouse in the outer suburbs to great pots of fish stew near the waterfront. Barcelona, long considered one of the two main gourmet bastions in Spain (along with the Basque Country), is cooking more than ever. Treat yourself to avant-garde super-chic dining in some of the city's most exclusive hotel restaurants, or opt

TOP FIVE TAPAS

- Bar Celta (p142)
- Cal Pep (p149)
- Cerveseria Catalana (p153)
- Taktika Berri (p154)
- Vaso de Oro (p150)

for towering views at a swish eatery by the sea. Search out lively old taverns for traditional old fare or join the hippest of the hip in the designer haunts of El Born and l'Eixample. And mix it up with a rapidly growing choice of foreign cuisines, just to keep the palate lean and keen.

The innards of Ciutat Vella, from El Raval across the Barri Gòtic to La Ribera (especially in the humming El Born area), are teeming with places, from classics of Spanish and Catalan cuisine with jacketed waiters, tiled walls and creaking timber-beam roofs to the latest in avant-garde chic eating. For a shoal of seafood possibilities, explore La Barceloneta (although there are some great fish finds elsewhere in town too). As a general rule, skip La Rambla.

In l'Eixample the variety is unlimited. Forget the barnlike tapas joints along Passeig de Gràcia and head inland, especially southwest. Stacks of locales, from Mexican to moneyed, are scattered like confetti in the area between Passeig de Gràcia and Carrer d'Aribau. The latter street is particularly blessed with eateries (and bars). Although quieter, you'll find a handful of options in the streets immediately northeast of Passeig de Gràcia too. All sorts of goodies lie in wait up along the narrow lanes of Gràcia too.

There is no shortage of classier options, often catering to a high-end business market, along and around the west end of Avinguda Diagonal. Here and scattered across La Zona Alta are some of the most exclusive A-list joints in town.

Opening Hours & Meal Times

Most restaurants and other types of eatery open from 1pm to 4pm and from 8pm to midnight. Few locals would sit down to lunch before 2pm or to dinner before 9pm. Bars and cafés that offer *tapes*/tapas generally adhere to similar hours as far as food goes, although you can often purchase snacks from the bar outside these times. A few places open through the day, typically from 1pm to 1.30am. Restaurants listed in this chapter are open for lunch and dinner, unless stated otherwise. No specific times are given unless they vary considerably from the norm.

Many restaurants take a day off during the week and most are shut on Christmas Eve and on New Year's Eve (or Christmas Day and New Year's Day). Some close over Easter, and a good deal also shut for most or all of the month of August. Beware that Sunday and Monday evenings can be frustrating, as this is when most places take time off.

Meal times are important events in the daily life of the average Barcelonin. People take the time to enjoy their food, and where possible they still have a full sit-down meal at lunch time. Lunch can easily go on for a couple of hours. Dinner frequently is a lighter affair.

How Much?

Barcelona is not the cheap night out it once was, but lunch can be an economical affair if you opt for the set *menú del día* (meal of the day).

In this chapter a 'meal' is understood to mean a starter, main course and dessert, including a little modestly priced wine. Listings come with estimated meal prices and € symbol categorising each entry as a budget, midrange or top-end location (see the boxed text El Compte, Sisplau, opposite). You are rarely likely to spend much more than €100 for a top quality meal. In the course of this chapter, restaurants are listed in each district by price, from budget to top end.

Cafes, tearooms and the like appear separately at the end of each district division.

The *menú del día*, a full set meal (usually with several options), water and wine, is a great way to cap prices at lunch time. They start from around €8 or €10. Many restaurants listed here offer this cost-saving option, where you might otherwise pay much more *a la carta*, so you can sample some pricier spots by day, even if you're on a budget.

At higher-end restaurants you can occasionally opt for a *menú de degustación*, a tasting menu involving samples of several different dishes. This can be a great way to get a broader view of what the restaurant does and has the advantage of coming at a fixed price.

EL COMPTE, SISPLAU (THE BILL, PLEASE)

The price ranges used here indicate the cost per person of a full meal (starter, main and dessert), including a bottle of modest wine:

€	up to €15
€€	€16 to €50
€€€	€51 and above

Booking Tables

At many of the midrange restaurants and simpler taverns with *menjadors/comedores* (dining rooms) you can usually turn up and find a spot without booking ahead. At better restaurants, and for dinner especially, it is safer to make a booking.

Tipping

Many eating establishments have a cover charge, usually up to a few euros per head. A service charge is usually included in the bill (but take a look at it if you are unsure) so any further tipping becomes strictly a personal choice. Catalans (and other Spaniards) are not overwhelming tippers. If you are particularly happy, 5% to 10% on top would be fine.

Self-Catering

Shopping in the big produce markets such as Mercat de la Boqueria and complementing your purchases with a quick run around the many *supermercats/supermercados* (supermarkets) around town will provide you with all the cheese, sausages, fruit and drink you could need. Supermarkets close to the city centre include **Champion** (Map pp298–9; La Rambla dels Estudis 113; 9am-10pm Mon-Sat; Catalunya), near the northern end of La Rambla, and **Superservis** (Map pp298–9; Carrer d'Avinyó 13; 8am-2pm & 4-8pm Mon-Sat; Liceu), in the heart of Barri Gòtic. For more market tips, see the boxed text, below. For freshly baked bread, head for a *forn* or *panadería* (bakery). For a gourmet touch, the food section of **El Corte Inglés** (Map pp298–9; 93 306 38 00; Plaça de Catalunya 14; Catalunya) has some tempting local and imported goodies. The branch at **Avinguda Diagonal 617** (Map pp290–1; 93 366 71 00; Maria Cristina) also has a food section. Specialist food shops abound too; see the Shopping chapter.

Eating

TO MARKET, TO MARKET

One of the greatest sound, smell and colour sensations in Europe is Barcelona's most central produce market, the **Mercat de la Boqueria** (Map pp298–9; La Rambla). It spills over with all the rich and varied colour of plentiful fruit and vegetable stands, seemingly limitless varieties of sea critters, sausages and cheeses, meat (including the finest Jabugo ham) and sweets. It is also sprinkled with half a dozen or so unassuming places to eat, and eat well, with stallholders at lunch time. According to some chronicles there has been a market on this spot since 1217! Mind you, nowadays it's no easy task getting past the gawping tourists to indicate the slippery slab of sole you're after, or the tempting piece of Asturian *queso de cabra* (goat's cheese).

La Boqueria is not the only market in Barcelona. The city is bursting with bustling markets, which for the most part are tourist-free. Try **Mercat de Sant Antoni** (Map pp296–7; Carrer de Mallorca 157; Hospital Clínic); **Mercat de Santa Caterina** (Map pp302–3; Avinguda de Francesc Cambó; Jaume I); **Mercat del Ninot** (Map pp296–7; Carrer de Mallorca 157; Hospital Clínic); **Mercat de la Llibertat** (Map pp294–5; Plaça de la Llibertat; FGC Gràcia); **Mercat de l'Abaceria Central** (Map pp294–5; Travessera de Gràcia 186; Fontana) and **Mercat de la Concepció** (Map pp294–5; Carrer de València 332; Girona). Markets generally open from Monday to Saturday from around 8am to 8pm. Some close around 2pm on Saturday. They are all at their animated best in the morning.

BARRI GÒTIC & LA RAMBLA

First things first. Skip the strip. La Rambla is great for people-watching but no great shakes for the palate. Head off into the streets on either side and your tum will be eternally grateful. Inside the medieval labyrinth choices abound. If you had to pinpoint any one area it would be the half of the *barri* (neighbourhood) between Plaça de Sant Jaume and the waterfront, especially towards Via Laietana. On and around Carrer de la Mercè a huddle of old-time tapas bars survives, as if caught in a time warp in postwar Spain, down-dirty and simple. Some are simply dirty, others are wonderful, immutable finds. All are laden with dollops of atmosphere.

CAN CONESA Map pp298-9 — Snacks €

☎ 93 310 57 95; Carrer de la Llibreteria 1; rolls & toasted sandwiches €2.50-4.50; ☾ Mon-Sat; Ⓜ Jaume I

Locals (especially workers from the Ajuntament and Generalitat at lunch time) have been lining up here for the succulent *entrepans* (filled rolls), toasted sandwiches and other snacks since the 1950s.

MAOZ Map pp298-9 — Middle Eastern €

Carrer de Ferran 13; falafels €2.90-4; ☾ noon-2am; Ⓜ Liceu

There's a lot of goodness packed into a tiny space here. You can stuff yourself with a filling Israeli-style falafel, helping yourself to the fillings. Basically a takeaway, many punters hang about to gobble up their falafel on the spot.

BAGEL SHOP Map pp298-9 — Bagels €

☎ 93 302 41 61; Carrer de la Canuda 25; meal €8-10; ☾ 9.30am-9.30pm Mon-Sat, 11am-4pm Sun; Ⓜ Liceu; ☒

Searching for a smoked salmon and cream cheese bagel? You've found the spot for this and a whole army of savoury and sweet bagels using different types of bread. You can take a seat in the long, narrow eatery out back or simply order to go in this Canadian-run touch of North America.

BODEGA LA PALMA Map pp302-3 — Tapas €

☎ 93 315 06 56; Carrer de la Palma de Sant Just 7; meal €10-15; ☾ Mon-Fri, lunch Sat; Ⓜ Jaume I

Time warp out of contemporary designer-conscious Barcelona to the hearty medieval Catalonia of yore. Below the low timber beams perch at a wine barrel and rustle up some rough-and-ready platters of Manchego cheese and cured ham, sluiced down with a little throaty house red.

BAR CELTA Map pp302-3 — Galician €€

☎ 93 315 00 06; Carrer de la Mercè 16; meal €20; ☾ noon-midnight; Ⓜ Drassanes

This bright, straightforward bar-cum-restaurant specialises in *pulpo* (octopus). It does a good job: even the most demanding of Gallegos gives this spot the thumbs up. Sit at the zinc bar, order a bottle of Ribeiro and the traditional Galician *tazas* (little white cups) to drink it from and tuck into your *raciones* (large portions of tapas). A serving of 12 *navajas* (razor clams) costs just €6.20!

EL PARAGUAYO Map pp298-9 — South American €€

☎ 93 302 14 41; Carrer del Parc 1; meal €25-30; ☾ Tue-Sun; Ⓜ Drassanes

This place sizzles. Vegetarians stay well clear: this is a den of carnivores, a superb hideaway for succulent slabs of meat bigger than your head. Try the *entraña;* the word means 'entrails', but the meal is actually a juicy slice of prime beef folded over onto itself and accompanied by a herb sauce.

AGUT Map pp302-3 — Catalan €€

☎ 93 315 17 09; Carrer d'En Gignàs 16; meal €25-30; ☾ Tue-Sat, lunch Sun; Ⓜ Jaume I; ☒

Deep in the Gothic labyrinth lies this classic eatery. A series of cosy dining areas are connected by broad arches. High up, the walls are tightly lined by artworks, and there's some art in what the kitchen serves up too, from a succulent *suquet de rap* (monkfish stew, €18.30) to a healthy slab of *solomillo de buey con salsa de trufa y trompetas de la muerte* (sirloin beef in a truffle sauce with 'trumpets of death', €16.80). No, these latter items are not some bedevilled musical accompaniment, but a prized mushroom!

BARRI GÒTIC & LA RAMBLA TOP FIVE

- Agut (right)
- Cafè de l'Acadèmia (opposite)
- El Paraguayo (right)
- Pla (opposite)
- Restaurant Pitarra (opposite)

CAFÈ DE L'ACADÈMIA Map pp298-9 Catalan €€
☎ 93 319 82 53; Carrer de Lledó 1; meal €30;
🕑 Mon-Fri; Ⓜ Jaume I; ⊠

This 'café' offers a mix of traditional dishes with the occasional creative twist. At lunch time, local Ajuntament office workers pounce on the *menús del día* (€11.50). In the evening it is rather more romantic, as soft lighting emphasises the intimacy of the timber ceiling and wooden décor. You might start with a bitter-sweet *amanida d'herbes amb encenalls de parmesà, pera i vinagreta de rúcula* (herb salad with Parmesan shavings, pear and rocket vinaigrette), followed perhaps by a mushroom lasagne.

COMETACINC Map pp302-3 Fusion €€
☎ 93 310 15 58; Carrer del Cometa 5; meal €30-35;
🕑 dinner Wed-Mon; Ⓜ Jaume I; ⊠

In this grand medieval space, the kitchen churns out a forever-changing menu that crisscrosses all boundaries. The candlelit tables over two floors set the mood for, say, some *tonyina vermella a la brasa amb confitura agre-dolça de albercoc* (charcoal grilled red tuna with chutney, €16).

LOS CARACOLES Map pp298-9 Spanish €€
☎ 93 302 31 85; Carrer dels Escudellers 14; meal €30-35; 🕑 1pm-midnight; Ⓜ Drassanes; ⊠

'The Snails' started life as a tavern in 1835 and is one of Barcelona's best-known, if extremely touristy, restaurants. Several interlocking rooms, with centuries of his-

Los Caracoles (above), Barri Gòtic

tory seemingly greased into the tables and garlic-clad walls, may well distract you from the rotisserie chicken (you'll see them rotating on your way in) and snails that are the house specialities.

PLA Map pp298-9 Fusion €€
☎ 93 412 65 52; Carrer de Bellafila 5; meal €30-35;
🕑 dinner; Ⓜ Liceu; ⊠

You could be forgiven for thinking you have waltzed into a dark designer cocktail bar. Actually it's a medieval den (with a huge stone arch) of devious culinary mischief, where the cooks churn out anything from *bacallà amb salsa de pomes verdes* (salted cod in a green-apple sauce) to grilled kangaroo.

ELS QUATRE GATS Map pp298-9 Catalan €€
☎ 93 302 41 40; Carrer de Montsió 3bis; meal €30-40; 🕑 1pm-1am; Ⓜ Urquinaona; ⊠

Once the lair of Barcelona's *modernista* artists, Els Quatre Gats exudes charm with its colourful tile and timberwork (and some reproductions of its former customers' portraits). To sample the atmosphere, a drink in the bar will suffice. Otherwise head out to the grand rear dining courtyard. The veranda around the 1st floor is the choice spot to enjoy standard Catalan fare.

RESTAURANT PITARRA
Map pp302-3 Catalan €€
☎ 93 301 16 47; Carrer d'Avinyó 56; meal €35-40;
🕑 Mon-Sat, closed Aug; Ⓜ Drassanes; ⊠

Once the house of clockmaker and founder of Catalan theatre Frederic Soler (aka Serafí Pitarra), this place is stuffed with clocks and paintings (many autographed by appreciative diners). Local politicians (check out the autographed photos) of every political persuasion have at some point been treated to some *suquet de rap* or *peus de porc* (pig's trotters meat, in this case turned into a kind of carpaccio).

CAFÉS

CAFÈ DE L'ÒPERA Map pp298-9 Café
☎ 93 302 41 80; La Rambla 74; 🕑 9am-3am;
Ⓜ Liceu; ⊠

Opposite the Gran Teatre del Liceu is La Rambla's most intriguing café. Founded in 1876 and operating as a café since 1929, it is pleasant for an early evening tipple or coffee and croissants. Head upstairs for an

MUNCHING IN MUSEUMS

A growing number of museums and other sights host great restaurants and cafés. Keep in mind the following.

In the medieval courtyard of the **Museu Tèxtil i d'Indumentària** (p97) sits the charming **Tèxtil Cafè** (Map pp302–3; ☎ 93 268 25 98; ☼ 10am-midnight Tue-Sun), where you can enjoy light meals, cake and coffee in between visits to the surrounding museums. In the Barri Gòtic the most attractive museum snack stop is the **Cafè d'Estiu** (Map pp298–9; ☼ 10am-10pm Apr-Sep) in the leafy courtyard of the **Museu Frederic Marès** (p88). At the **Museu Marítim** (p92), a fine **café-restaurant** (☎ 93 317 52 56; ☼ café as for museum, restaurant lunch Mon-Sat, dinner Wed-Sat) is housed beneath the vaults of the shipyards. The restaurant sprawls outside in the gardens. In summer come for dinner and chill-out music.

The **Museu d'Història de Catalunya** (p100) offers a great rooftop terrace café and restaurant, **La Miranda del Museu** (Map pp302–3; ☎ 93 225 50 07; ☼ café as for museum, restaurant Tue-Sat).

On Montjuïc you have a couple of options: the café in the **Fundació Joan Miró** (p120), and **Oleum** (Map pp304–5; ☼ as for museum), a restaurant with good views in the **Museu Nacional d'Art de Catalunya** (p121).

elevated seat above the busy boulevard. Can you be tempted by the *cafè de l'Òpera* (coffee with chocolate mousse in it)?

CAFÈ ZURICH Map pp298-9 _Café_
☎ 93 317 91 53; Carrer de Pelai 39; coffee & pastry €3-4; ☼ 8am-midnight; Ⓜ Catalunya; ☒
It doesn't quite exude the atmosphere of the café of the same name that once occupied this prime spot, but not even the hardest of hearts can deny the location is impeccable. Pull up a ringside outdoor pew for the human circus that is Plaça de Catalunya. Or huddle up on the mezzanine inside over a paper on a winter's day.

XOCOLATERIA LA XICRA
Map pp298-9 _Café & Pastries_
☎ 93 318 07 86; Plaça de Sant Josep Oriol 2; pastries €3, coffee €1.50; ☼ 9.30am-9pm; Ⓜ Liceu
The *xocolata calenta* (hot chocolate) is so thick here it's listed on the menu under desserts. You could go one further and accompany it with a pastry. Or perhaps steady on a little and settle for coffee or tea.

SALTERIO Map pp298-9 _Tearoom_
Carrer de Sant Domènec del Call 4; ☼ 6pm-1am; Ⓜ Jaume I
If it got any mellower here you'd nod off to the gentle Middle Eastern music and low whispering. How long can it take to prepare a mint tea? Wait for it, because it's filled with real mint, almost as good as in Morocco.

CAJ CHAI Map pp298-9 _Tearoom_
Sant Domènec del Call 12; ☼ 3-10pm; Ⓜ Jaume I
A completely different atmosphere reigns up the lane from Salterio. Open and bright, this

is a tea and tea infusion connoisseur's paradise. Make your choice, order a bit of pastry and settle in for a nice cuppa and chat.

EL RAVAL

For contrast, this is possibly the most interesting part of the old town. Timeless classics of Barcelona dining are scattered across this, long the city's poorest *barri*. And since the late 1990s, battalions of hip new eateries and artsy restaurants have sprung up, especially in the area around the Museu d'Art Contemporani de Barcelona. From Carrer de Sant Pau north towards Carrer de Pelai, the university and Ronda de Sant Antoni is where you'll find most places of interest.

BIOCENTER Map pp298-9 _Vegetarian €_
☎ 93 301 45 83; Carrer del Pintor Fortuny 25; meal €7.50-10; ☼ 1-5pm Mon-Sat; Ⓜ Catalunya; ☒
Head past the coffee bar through the dining area, with its warm exposed brickwork and dark timber tables, to the kitchen at the back to order your *menú del día* (€8.45) or *plat combinat* (€7.25, a huge plate heaped with your choice of hot food). Augment these with as much salad as you can stand at the open salad buffet.

EL RAVAL TOP FIVE
- Bar Central (opposite)
- Biblioteca (p146)
- Ca L'Isidre (p146)
- Casa Leopoldo (p146)
- Organic (opposite)

ORGANIC Map pp298-9 Vegetarian €
☎ 93 301 09 02; Carrer de la Junta de Comerç 11; meal €8-12; ⏰ 1pm-midnight; Ⓜ Liceu; ✕

On the left as you wander into this sprawling vegetarian spot is the open kitchen, where you place your order. Choose from a limited range of options that change from day to day. The place has an easy cafeteria feel and the dishes are plentiful and imaginative. The salad buffet is copious and desserts good.

CEBAR Map pp298-9 Mediterranean €
☎ 93 301 33 15; Plaça de Joan Coromines; meal €10-15; ⏰ 8am-2am; Ⓜ Universitat

A cross-section of students from the nearby communications faculty and contemporary art lovers exploring the Macba converge on this laid-back restaurant-bar for breakfast, light meals and a drink. The best time is the afternoon, from lunch time on, as the sun bathes the outdoor terrace while you nibble at your *verdures al wok* (wok-fried vegetables and rice, €6). At night, DJs turn the place into a chilled bar.

RESTAURANTE POLLO RICO
Map pp298-9 Spanish €
☎ 93 441 31 84; Carrer de Sant Pau 31; meal €15; ⏰ Thu-Tue; Ⓜ Liceu; ✕

The 'Tasty Chicken' is true to its name with fast, cheap, abundant grub. Head upstairs and carve out a space amid the noise of garrulous punters, then rattle off your order to a high-speed waiter. Chicken (a whole one costs €11), meat and various other options can be put together to help you fill to bursting. Skip the paella, though.

MESÓN DAVID Map pp298-9 Spanish €
☎ 93 441 59 34; Carrer de les Carretes 63; meal €15; ⏰ Thu-Tue; Ⓜ Paral.lel

With its smoky timber ceiling, excitable waiting staff and generally chaotic feel, this is a tavern the likes of which they don't make any more, a slice of old Spain. Plonk yourself down on a bench for gregarious dining. House specialities include *caldo gallego*, a sausage broth for €2, and the main course of *lechazo asado*, a great clump of roast suckling lamb (€6).

BAR CENTRAL Map pp298-9 Catalan & Tapas €€
☎ 93 301 10 98; Mercat de la Boqueria; meal €15-20; ⏰ lunch Mon-Sat; Ⓜ Liceu

Hiding out towards the back of Barcelona's best-known market is this fabulously chaotic

PYJAMA PARTY

If a waiter proposes '*pijama*', it is not an invitation to head home for bed and jammies. It is rather a suggestion to try one of the country's most lurid desserts. It consists of tinned peach (and maybe pineapple) slices, a clump of flan, two balls of ice cream (say strawberry and vanilla) and covered in whipped cream with chocolate topping! After that you may well want to have a lie down.

lunch-time bar. Marketeers, local workers and the occasional curious tourist jostle for a stool – get there early or be prepared to wait around. Order a few generous *raciones*, and make one of them the grilled fish of the day.

BAR PINOTXO Map pp298-9 Tapas & Snacks €€
☎ 93 317 17 31; Mercat de la Boqueria; meal €15-20; ⏰ 6am-5pm Mon-Sat, closed Aug; Ⓜ Liceu

Of the half-dozen or so tapas bars and informal eateries within the market, this one near the La Rambla entrance is about the most popular. Roll up to the bar and enjoy the people-watching as you munch on tapas assembled from the products on sale in the stalls around you.

BAR KASPARO Map pp298-9 International €€
☎ 93 302 20 72; Plaça de Vicenç Martorell 4; meal €20; ⏰ 9am-10pm; Ⓜ Catalunya

Sit down in the shade of the arcade or opt for some sun on this tranquil pedestrian square for great mixed salads and other healthy, light food. Various mild curries frequently appear on the ever-changing menu.

ELISABETS Map pp298-9 Catalan €€
☎ 93 317 58 26; Carrer de Elisabets 2-4; meal €20; ⏰ Mon-Sat, closed Aug; Ⓜ Catalunya

A crumbling office until the 1950s, this unassuming restaurant is popular for no-nonsense local fare. The walls are lined with old radio sets and the *menú del día* (€7.50) varies daily. *A la carta*, try the *ragú de jabalí* (wild boar stew) and finish with *mel i mató* (honey and fresh cream cheese).

ÁNIMA Map pp298-9 Fusion €€
☎ 93 342 49 12; Carrer dels Ángels 6; meal €25; ⏰ Mon-Sat (dinner only Aug); Ⓜ Liceu; ✕

This boho fusion eatery is also the scene of occasional art expos. From the ceiling

Eating

EL RAVAL

hangs a marvellous mirror that allows you to see the reflected goings-on in the kitchen. What is going on can seem strange indeed, with such creations as *sopa de meló i espècies amb cigales i gambes* (melon and spice soup with crayfish and prawns).

RESTAURANT EL CAFETÍ

Map pp298-9   Catalan €€

☎ 93 329 24 19; Passatge de Bernardí; meal €25-30; 🕑 Tue-Sat, lunch Sun; Ⓜ Liceu; ✖
Down a narrow arcade off Carrer de Sant Rafael 18, this diminutive upstairs eatery is crammed with antique furniture and offers traditional local cooking, with one or two unorthodox variations. Paella and other rice dishes dominate, but you might prefer the chicken grilled in cream of *cava*.

EL RINCÓN DE ARAGÓN

Map pp298-9   Aragonese €€

☎ 93 302 67 89; Carrer del Carme 28; meal €25-30; 🕑 Tue-Sun, closed Aug; Ⓜ Liceu; ✖
Carnivores stand up and be counted. Leave Catalonia and head for the big country of Aragón, land of *cochinillo* (suckling pig), *cabrito* (kid meat) and above all the Teruel speciality of *ternasco* (young suckling lamb). You can hear it sizzle…no *nueva cocina* here! The dining room, which has an authentic, deep Spanish feel, is out the back.

ÉS Map pp298-9   Mediterranean €€

☎ 93 301 00 68; Carrer del Doctor Dou 14; meal €30; Ⓜ Catalunya; ✖
The setting is a fusion of old and new. The broad Catalan brick vaults of what was once a warehouse for the nearby Boqueria market have been painstakingly revealed. Dangling from the ceiling and around the pillars floats an assortment of strangely shaped light shades. Flop onto a white lounge for mixed Mediterranean cooking, including vegetarian dishes like the *bunyols d'alberginia amb mel i curry* (aubergine fritters with honey and curry).

BIBLIOTECA

Map pp298-9   Navarran-Mediterranean €€

☎ 93 412 62 21; Carrer de la Junta del Comerç 28; meal €35; 🕑 Tue-Sat; Ⓜ Liceu
No, it's not the district library, but a pleasing study in original and inventive cooking. Taking Navarran and Mediterranean cuisine as a base, the chef produces such items

as *bacallà confitat amb suc d'escamarlans i llegums de temporada* (pickled salt cod with crayfish juice and seasonal legumes). The long, narrow restaurant with its high ceilings is light and airy. The *menú del día* (€9) is worth a detour.

CA L'ISIDRE Map pp298-9   Catalan €€

☎ 93 441 11 39; Carrer de les Flors 12; meal €45; 🕑 Mon-Sat; Ⓜ Paral.lel
Lurking in an unappealing backstreet off El Raval, Ca L'Isidre is an old-world gem. Once inside, immaculately kept dining areas stretch away from the entrance, dominated by warm timber and tiles. Quietly efficient waiters waft about the place, which is frequently full. King Juan Carlos and superchef Ferran Adrià love it. The chefs search out their ingredients each morning at the Mercat de la Boqueria.

CASA LEOPOLDO Map pp298-9   Catalan €€€

☎ 93 441 30 14; Carrer de Sant Rafael 24; meal €50; 🕑 Tue-Sat, lunch Sun, closed Easter & Aug; Ⓜ Liceu; ✖
Long hidden in the slum alleys of El Raval, this was writer Manuel Vázquez Montalbán's favourite restaurant; it figures constantly in the urban wanderings of his best-loved character, detective Pepe Carvalho (see p30). Several rambling dining areas, sporting magnificent tiled walls and exposed timber-beam ceilings, make this a fine option. The mostly seafood menu is extensive and the wine list is strong.

CAFÉS

GRANJA VIADER

Map pp298-9   Chocolate & Pastries

☎ 93 318 34 86; Carrer d'En Xuclà 4; pastries €2-3; 🕑 9am-1.45pm & 5-8.45pm Tue-Sat, 5-8.45pm Mon; Ⓜ Liceu
For more than a century people have flocked down this alley to get to the cups of homemade hot chocolate and whipped cream (ask for a *suís*, €3) ladled out here. Accompanied by one of the many pastries on display, it makes the sweet tooth's ideal breakfast.

BARAKA Map pp298-9   Tearoom

☎ 93 304 10 61; Carrer de Valldonzella 25; 🕑 11am-11pm Mon-Fri, 1-11pm Sat; Ⓜ Universitat; ✖
With its multicoloured tile floors, soft autumn paint scheme and chilled background music, this tearoom and organic goods

shop carved out of a meandering old store is a good spot for a tranquil tea, coffee or beer. Head for the antique sofa out the back and take a weight off. Or book yourself into the Friday massage (1pm to 4.30pm).

LA RIBERA

If you'd mentioned El Born (El Borne in Spanish) in the early 1990s you wouldn't have raised much interest. But now...on the gentrification fast track, the area is peppered with bars, dance dives, groovy designer stores and restaurants. El Born is where Barcelona is truly cooking. Avantgarde chefs and fusion masters have zeroed in on this southern corner of La Ribera to conduct their culinary experiments. If you don't want to play such wild games, there's plenty of the traditional stuff to choose from too. One or two ethnic locales add some delightful taste spin.

EL XAMPANYET Map pp302-3   Tapas €
☎ 93 319 70 03; Carrer de Montcada 22; meal €15; ☾ Tue-Sat, lunch Sun; Ⓜ Jaume I
Nothing much has changed in this, one of the city's best-known *cava* bars. Plant yourself at the bar or seek out a table jammed up against the old-style decoratively tiled walls for a glass or three of *cava* and an assortment of tapas, such as the tangy *boquerons en vinagre* (white anchovies in vinegar). It's the atmosphere that makes this place.

CASA DELFIN Map pp302-3   Spanish €
☎ 93 319 50 88; Passeig del Born 36; meal €15, menú del día €9; ☾ 6am-7pm Mon-Sat; Ⓜ Barceloneta
While surrounding restaurants may serve up exquisitely designed *nouvelle* Sino-Moroccan-Venezuelan creations, the bustling waiters at the 'Dolphin House' content themselves with serving bountiful Spanish classics. And they are right to do so, for finding a free lunch time table at their sprawling terrace requires a modest portion of luck. Choose from more than 30 tried-and-true dishes.

ORÍGEN 99.9% Map pp302-3   Catalan €-€€
☎ 93 310 75 31; Carrer de la Vidrieria 6-8; meal €15-20; ☾ 12.30pm-1am; Ⓜ Jaume I; ✂
First and foremost, this is a treasure chest of Catalan regional products, with shelves groaning under the weight of bottles and packets of goodies. Better still, it has a long menu of bite-sized dishes (mostly around €5), like *ànec amb naps* (duck and turnip) or *civet de senglar* (jugged boar), that you mix

Eating   **LA RIBERA**

El Xampanyet (above), La Ribera

BARCELONA'S GOURMET GAUDÍ

He presents his latest culinary inventions like a child who has just made a fabulous mud pie. Indeed, if Ferran Adrià came up with a mud dish, it wouldn't come as much of a surprise. Born in 1963, this self-taught chef has rocketed to the forefront of international *haute cuisine* with his fearless experimentation. The Gaudí of gourmets, he has been dubbed by his three-star Michelin colleague from the Basque Country, Juan Maria Arzak, 'the most imaginative cook in all history'.

Adrià worked his way up in the 1980s to head chef at a good if unspectacular Franco-Catalan restaurant, **El Bulli** (see p238), in a splendidly wild spot on the Costa Brava. By the early 1990s he was co-owner of the business and had begun to let rip, converting El Bulli into one of the country's most exclusive restaurants, where anything from essence of carrot to solidified edible coffee might appear on the multicourse menu.

Aided by brother Albert and a staff of 30, Adrià runs El Bulli for six months of the year – dinner only. What the lucky guests get to eat is entirely a matter of chance. He spends the rest of the year like a mad scientist in El Bulli Taller, his kitchen workshop in Carrer de la Portaferrissa, virtually across the road from the Mercat de la Boqueria in central Barcelona. He has also branched out, opening quality fast-food eateries in Madrid, a hotel in Seville and even lending his name to bags of crisps (which are nothing remarkable, it has to be said).

Adrià (voted world's best chef by a committee of 60 gastronomy journalists in 2006) is not alone. One of his disciples, fellow Catalan Sergi Arola, named chef of the year in Spain in 2003 and known for his avant-garde redoubt in Madrid, La Broche, couldn't resist the call of a spot in Hotel Arts Barcelona, where he runs Arola. Another El Bulli alumnus, Carles Abellán, has received acclaim in his dramatic **Comerç 24** (opposite), a focus of special kitchen effects in El Born.

and match over wine by the glass. At the branch in **l'Eixample** (Map pp296–7; ☎ 93 453 11 20; Carrer d'Enric Granados 9; ☽ 1pm-1am; ⓜ Universitat) you can dine outside.

HABANA VIEJA Map pp302-3   Cuban €€
☎ 93 268 25 04; Carrer dels Banys Vells 2; meal €20; ☽ Mon-Sat; ⓜ Jaume I

Since the early 1990s this Cuban hideaway, the first of its kind in Barcelona and still one of the best, has offered old island faves such as the stringy meat dish *ropa vieja* (literally 'old clothes', €13) and rice dishes. With its antique light fittings and predilection for timber furnishings, this Ribera house could easily be an Old Havana eatery.

LA FLAUTA MÀGICA
Map pp302-3   Vegetarian & Mediterranean €€
☎ 93 268 46 94; Carrer dels Banys Vells 18; meal €20-25; ☽ dinner; ⓜ Jaume I; ✗

It is hard to resist entering this happy, pastel-coloured salon, which caters to vegetarians and carnivores alike. How about rice 'n' curry *del país de la eternal sonrisa* (from the land of the eternal smile)? The 'magic flute' itself is an ingenious cheese and carrot roll.

PLA DE LA GARSA Map pp302-3   Catalan €€
☎ 93 315 24 13; Carrer dels Assaonadors 13; meal €25; ☽ dinner; ⓜ Jaume I; ✗

This 17th-century house is the ideal location for a romantic candlelit dinner.

Timber beams, anarchically scattered tables and soft ambient music combine to make an enchanting setting for traditional, hearty Catalan cooking, with dishes like *bacallà amb cigronets del Pla de Llerona* (salted cod with chick peas, €9.50). For the best the house has to offer, opt for a *tast selecte* (tasting menu, €23.90).

TANTARANTANA Map pp302-3   Mediterranean €€
☎ 93 268 24 10; Carrer de Tantarantana 24; meal €25-30; ☽ dinner Mon-Sat; ⓜ Jaume I or Arc de Triomf

Surrounded as it is by furiously fashionable, designer-driven front-line nuclei of *nueva cocina,* this spot is a refreshing mix. There is something comforting about the old-style marble-top tables, upon which you can sample simple but well-prepared dishes such as risotto or grilled tuna served with vegetables and ginger. It attracts an early-30-something crowd who also enjoy the outdoor seating in summer.

CENTRE CULTURAL EUSKAL ETXEA Map pp302-3   Basque €€
☎ 93 310 21 85; Placeta de Montcada 1; tapas €15-20, meal €30; ☽ Tue-Sat, lunch Sun; ⓜ Jaume I

Barcelona is awash with a *txacolí*-flavoured wave of Basque eateries, but few have a genuine feel. This one started off as a cultural centre and captures the essence of San Sebastián. Choose your *pintxos* (snacks), sip *txacolí* wine and keep the toothpicks so the staff can count them up and work out your bill. A full sit-down meal out the back might include *llom de bacallà confitat a la biscaïna* (strips of salted cod prepared in a tomato-paprika sauce, €17.25).

SANTA MARIA Map pp302-3   Creative Tapas €€
☎ 93 315 12 27; Carrer de Comerç 17; meal €30-40;
◔ Tue-Sat; Ⓜ Barceloneta
Welcome to the designer *tapa*. Forget your standard olives and whitebait tapas. In this small converted warehouse you're more likely to be offered *mejillones picantes con plátano macho frito* (spicy mussels with fried male plantain). The tasting menu (€33) is recommended.

COMERÇ 24 Map pp302-3   International €€
☎ 93 319 21 02; Carrer del Comerç 24; meal €35-45; ◔ Tue-Sat; Ⓜ Barceloneta; ⊠
The black-red-grey décor in the rear dining area lends this cauldron of culinary creativity an edgy New York feel. The red chairs look like strange sea shells. Chef Carles Abellán whips up a series of eccentric dishes, inspired by everything from sushi to crostini. Plump for the tasting menu (€48) and leave it all up to Abellán.

CAL PEP Map pp302-3   Tapas €€
☎ 93 310 79 61; Plaça de les Olles 8; meal €45; ◔ Tue-Sat, dinner Mon, closed Aug; Ⓜ Barceloneta; ⊠
It's getting a foot in the door here that's the problem. And if you want one of the five tables out the back, you'll need to call *way* ahead. Most people are happy elbowing their way to the bar for some of the tastiest gourmet seafood tapas in town. Pep recommends *cloïsses amb pernil* (clams and ham – seriously! – at €11.70) or the *trifàsic* (combo of calamari, whitebait and prawns, 11.10).

I'VE GOT THE MUNCHIES!

Stumbling out into the early morning light after a night pushing the boat out can unleash sudden desires for grub. Surprisingly, there aren't too many options. A useful place in l'Eixample is **Granja O'Vall Douro** (Map pp294–5; ☎ 93 237 10 40; Carrer de París 198; meal €15; ◔ 6am-3am; Ⓜ Diagonal). Down in the Via Laietana area, a possibility is **Tablao Nervión** (see p194). Try the mushrooms!

HOFMANN Map pp302-3   Mediterranean €€€
☎ 93 319 58 89; Carrer de l'Argenteria 74; meal €50-60; ◔ Mon-Fri; Ⓜ Jaume I; ⊠
Discretely tucked upstairs in the plant-filled annexe of a renowned cuisine school is this refined restaurant. Some of the nation's great chefs learned the trade here and you will not be disappointed with the present students' efforts. An imaginative and changing menu keeps everyone on their toes. Especial care is put into the desserts and there is a lunch *menú del día* for around €30.

EL PASSADÍS DEL PEP
Map pp302-3   Seafood €€€
☎ 93 310 10 21; Plaça del Palau 2; meal €70-80; ◔ Tue-Sat, dinner Mon, closed Aug; Ⓜ Barceloneta; ⊠
There's no sign, but locals know where to head for a seafood feast. They say the restaurant's raw materials are delivered daily from fishing ports up and down the Catalan coast. There is no menu – what's on offer depends on what the sea has surrendered on the day. Just head down the long, ill-lit corridor and entrust yourself to their care.

ÀBAC Map pp302-3   Gourmet Mediterranean €€€
☎ 93 319 66 00; Carrer del Rec 79-89; meal €90-100; ◔ Tue-Sat, dinner Mon, closed Easter & Aug; Ⓜ Barceloneta
Minimalist designer décor dominated by neutral, light colouring provides an austere setting to allow the diner to concentrate on the food. Perhaps they could relax a little in that respect, but the effort is repaid. And who'd have thought that a combination like *calamars amb pèsols* (squid and peas, €24) could be so enticing?

PORT VELL & LA BARCELONETA

In the Maremàgnum complex on the Moll d'Espanya you can eat close to the water's edge at a handful of fun if fairly slapdash joints. For good grub and atmosphere, head around to La Barceloneta, traditional haven of simple seafood cooking and, in spite of rampant gentrification and publicity, still laden with everything from good-naturedly noisy, beer-swigging tapas bars to upmarket seafood restaurants. Almost everything here shuts on a Sunday and Monday evening.

CAN PAIXANO Map pp302-3   Tapas €

☎ 93 310 08 39; Carrer de la Reina Cristina 7; meal €10-15; ☽ 9am-10.30pm; Ⓜ Barceloneta; ☒
Tucked away amid the bright tacky lights of cheap electronics stores in what could almost be a backstreet in Southeast Asia, this lofty old champagne bar has long run on a simple, winning formula. The standard tipple is bubbly rosé in elegant little glasses, combined with bite-sized *bocadillos* (filled rolls, €1.85). Sound old-world refined? Uh-uh. The place is jammed to the rafters, and elbowing your way through to the bar to ask harried staff for the above-mentioned items can be a titanic struggle.

CAN MAÑO Map pp302-3   Spanish €

☎ 93 319 30 82; Carrer del Baluard 12; meal €15; ☽ Mon-Sat; Ⓜ Barceloneta
The owners have been dealing with an onslaught of punters for decades and swear they are going to retire soon (but they never do). You'll need to be prepared to wait before being squeezed in at a packed table for a raucous night (or lunch) of *raciones* (posted on a board at the back) over a bottle of *turbio,* a cloudy white plonk.

VASO DE ORO Map pp302-3   Tapas €

☎ 93 319 30 98; Carrer de Balboa 6; meal €15; Ⓜ Barceloneta; ☒
Enter by one of three doors and that's as far as you'll get in what must be one of the world's narrowest bars. At either end, the space balloons a little to allow for a handful of tables. Squeeze in and enjoy the show. Fast-talking, white-jacketed waiters will serve up a few quick quips with your tapas of grilled *gambes* or *solomillo* (sirloin) chunks.

CAN RAMONET Map pp302-3   Seafood €€

☎ 93 319 30 64; Carrer de la Maquinista 17; meal €25-30; ☽ Mon-Sat; Ⓜ Barceloneta; ☒
Perching at one of the little tables set up across the lane is the perfect way to pass a warm summer evening over some *escamarlans a la graella* (grilled crayfish, €25). Or step inside and hunker down for tapas around a barrel-cum-table. Slip down a serving of glistening *ostres* (oysters, €15) as a starter.

CAN ROS Map pp302-3   Seafood €€

☎ 93 221 45 79; Carrer del Almirall Aixada 7; meal €25-30; ☽ Thu-Tue; Ⓜ Barceloneta or ☒ 45, 57, 59, 64 or 157; ☒
The fifth generation is now at the controls in this immutable seafood favourite. In a restaurant where the décor is a reminder of simpler times, there's a simple guiding rule – give the punters succulent fresh fish cooked with a light touch. They also do a chunky *fideuá amb cloïsses i gambes* (noodles with clams and prawns, €10.50).

RESTAURANT SET (7) PORTES

Map pp302-3   Catalan & Seafood €€
☎ 93 319 30 33; Passeig d'Isabel II 14; meal €25-30; ☽ 1pm-1am Ⓜ Barceloneta; ☒
Founded in 1836 as a café and converted into a restaurant in 1929, this is a classic. In the hands of the Parellada clan, which runs several quality restaurants in and beyond Barcelona, it exudes an old-world atmosphere with its wood panelling, tiles, mirrors and plaques naming some of the famous – such as Orson Welles – who have passed through. Paella (€16.80) is the speciality. Or go for the surfeit of seafood in the *gran plat de marisc* ('big plate of seafood') at €47 for two. We dare you to finish it!

CAN MAJÓ Map pp302-3   Seafood €€

☎ 93 221 58 18; Carrer del Almirall Aixada 23; meal €30-40; ☽ Tue-Sat, lunch Sun; Ⓜ Barceloneta or ☒ 45, 57, 59, 64 or 157
Virtually on the beach (with tables outside in summer), Can Majó has a long and steady reputation for fine seafood, particularly its rice dishes (around €18 to €20) and cornucopian *suquets* (stews, around €25). Simpler options include various oven-cooked fish.

SUQUET DE L'ALMIRALL

Map pp302-3   Seafood €€
☎ 93 221 62 33; Passeig de Joan de Borbó 65; meal €45-50; ☽ Tue-Sat, lunch Sun, closed 2 weeks in Aug; Ⓜ Barceloneta or ☒ 17, 39, 57 or 64; ☒
A family business run by one of the acolytes of Ferran Adrià's El Bulli, the order of

---

PORT VELL & LA BARCELONETA TOP FIVE

- Can Majó (right)
- Can Ros (right)
- Suquet de l'Almirall (right)
- Torre de l'Alta Mar (opposite)
- Vaso de Oro (above)

the day is top-class seafood. A starter of *ventresca de tonyina* (the prized and tastiest tuna meat), followed perhaps by a house speciality such as *arròs a la barca* (rice laden with various types of fish, squid and to mato) or *suquet* makes for a delicious feast. Grab one of the few outdoor tables.

TORRE D'ALTA MAR Map pp290-1 Seafood €€€
☎ 93 221 00 07; Torre de Sant Sebastià, Passeig de Joan de Borbó 88; meal €70-80; ⏱ Tue-Sat, lunch Mon; Ⓜ Barceloneta or 🚌 17, 39, 57 or 64; ✗
Head to the top of the Torre de Sant Sebastià and instead of the Transbordador Aeri, take a ringside seat for the best views of the city and fine seafood (a few meaty alternatives are thrown in). The setting alone, high up above the city and port, makes this a unique dining experience, perfect for a romantic couple. Those feeling particularly capricious might go for the *crema de patata amb ou escalfat i caviar irani* (€45), a creamy potato dish laced with poached egg and Iranian caviar.

PORT OLÍMPIC, EL POBLENOU & EL FÒRUM

This yachties' pleasure port is lined on two sides by dozens of restaurants and tapas bars, popular in spring and summer but mostly lacking in interest. A more upmarket series of places huddles at the northeast end of Platja de la Barceloneta. It's hard to beat the sand, sea and palm tree backdrop. Otherwise, the search for culinary curios will take you behind the scenes, as it were, into the depths of El Poblenou, where a few gems glitter.

EL CHIRINGUITO DE MONCHO'S
Map pp290-1 Seafood €
☎ 93 221 14 01; Avinguda Litoral 36; meal €15; ⏱ noon-1am; Ⓜ Ciutadella Vila Olímpica; ✗
The Moncho's seafood chain is cheap and cheerful. There are no designer frills in this good-natured, noisy barnyard of a place, where you can feast on fish and seafood by the sea without blowing your budget. It's a Saturday afternoon at the beach kind of place, although the kitchen is fired up all day long, so you can pop in any time.

AGUA Map pp302-3 Mediterranean €€
☎ 93 225 12 72; Passeig Marítim de la Barceloneta 30; meal €30; Ⓜ Ciutadella Vila Olímpica; ✗
You enter by what looks vaguely like an elevator shaft on the waterfront and wander downstairs into a brightly lit dining area at beach level, gaily decorated with marine motifs. By day you almost feel you are on the beach itself. Food is bright, with some original options such as *arroz con alcachofas, gambas y setas* (rice with artichokes, prawns and mushrooms).

OVEN Map pp290-1 Fusion €€
☎ 93 221 06 02; Carrer de Ramon Turró 126; meal €40, menú del día €10; ⏱ Tue-Sat, dinner Sun; Ⓜ Bogatell; ✗
In the middle of the former industrial district of El Poblenou, Oven opens back from a courtyard like a cross between a hangar and a film studio. Low tables spread out beneath theatre stage lighting, which comes in handy when dining gives way to dancing (until about 2.30am). The ever-changing menu is a kaleidoscope of mix-and-match international flavours. You can eat in the garden, chill in the lounge.

EL CANGREJO LOCO
Map pp302-3 Seafood €€-€€€
☎ 93 221 05 33; Moll de Gregal 29-30, Port Olímpic; meal €45-60; Ⓜ Ciutadella Vila Olímpica; ✗
Of all the hive of eating activity along the docks of Port Olímpic, the 'Mad Crab' is the best. Inevitably it has a thoroughfare feel, attracting swarms of tourists like everything here. The difference is that the food is generally of a reasonable standard. The *gambes de Palamós* (€42), richly flavoursome king prawns from the Costa Brava, are a delicacy. Otherwise, such fish standards as *bacallà* and *rap* are served in various guises and melt in the mouth.

L'EIXAMPLE

This huge grid area can seem a little daunting but the first thing to remember is that most of the many varied and enticing restaurants are concentrated in the Quadrat d'Or between Carrer de Pau Claris and Carrer de Muntaner east to west and Avinguda Diagonal and Gran Via de les Corts Catalanes north to south. There is no shortage of perfectly acceptable bar-restaurants, often with tables set up on the street, that offer reasonable menús del día and stock-standard dishes *a la carta*. In among these places are sprinkled real finds, with local and foreign cuisine.

L'ATZAVARA Map pp296-7 Vegetarian €
☎ 93 454 59 25; Carrer de Muntaner 109; meal €10-12; ⏰ lunch Mon-Sat; Ⓜ Hospital Clínic; ☒
A hushed air reigns in this brightly lit place – it could almost be grandma's tearooms. A limited and varying *menú del día* (€9.10) is offered, and while servings are hardly gargantuan, the grub is tasty. The menu changes regularly but you might encounter a scrumptious *paella d'arròs integral amb verdures* (whole rice vegetable paella).

LA FLAUTA II Map pp294-5 Tapas €
☎ 93 323 70 38; Carrer de Balmes 164-166; meal €10-15; ⏰ Mon-Sat; Ⓜ Diagonal; ☒
Sidle up to the long bar and admire the long stretch of tapas. All the classics are here, from *ensalada rusa* (Russian salad, a potato and vegetable mix in mayo) through to seafood critters such as the all-time favourite *pop a la gallega* (chunks of octopus with slices of boiled potato in an oily paprika sauce). Or opt for the *flautes* (thin baguettes with a variety of fillings, €4 to €6.45). The place is perfect for a meal on the run.

AMALTEA Map pp296-7 Vegetarian €
☎ 93 454 86 13; Carrer de la Diputació 164; meal €10-15; ⏰ Mon-Sat; Ⓜ Urgell
The ceiling fresco of blue skies sets the scene in this popular vegetarian eatery. The weekday set lunch (€9) offers a series of dishes that change frequently with the seasons. Get in early for dinner Monday to Thursday (when they close at 10pm) and savour an *escalopa de seitan* (seitan escalope) and *empanadillas* (pastry pocket) stuffed with spinach or hiziki algae and tofu. The place is something of an alternative lifestyle centre, with yoga tai chi and belly-dancing classes.

L'EIXAMPLE TOP FIVE

- Casa Darío (p156)
- Cata 1.81 (p155)
- L'Hostal de Rita (right)
- Restaurant de L'Escola de Restauració i Hostalatge (opposite)
- Speakeasy (p156)

CAMPECHANO MERENDERO
Map pp294-5 Catalan €€
☎ 93 215 62 33; Carrer de València 286; meal €20; Ⓜ Passeig de Gràcia; ☒
Follow the noise down the arcade next door to the Fundación Francisco Godia and you'll push open the doors to this riotous, barn-like eatery. The 'pally snack joint' offers its boisterous customers all sorts of grilled meats, such as a beef entrecôte at €14.

L'HOSTAL DE RITA
Map pp294-5 Mediterranean €€
☎ 93 487 23 76; Carrer d'Aragó 279; meal €20; Ⓜ Passeig de Gràcia; ☒
Barcelonins have a reputation for being fickle, with restaurants heading in and out of favour faster than you can print guidebooks, but this place falls into another category. It still attracts queues of locals for its lunch-time *menú del día* (€7.90) and wideranging menu at dinner. There's plenty of fish on offer, or you could tuck in to a juicy *entrecot de vedella amb pebrots verds* (veal entrecôte with green peppers for €8.85).

EL RINCÓN MAYA Map pp296-7 Mexican €€
☎ 93 451 39 46; Carrer de València 183; meal €20; ⏰ Tue-Sun; Ⓜ Passeig de Gràcia
Getting a seat in this Mexican eatery can be a real trial. The setting is warm, modest and thankfully devoid of the excesses of kitsch, pseudo-Mexican décor. The nachos, guacamole and fajitas all burst with flavour. You'll also discover lesser-known items like *tacos de pibil* (pork tacos, four for €8.50) and *tinga,* little pasta pockets of chicken. The owner-chef spent much of his life in the restaurant business in Mexico City. On quieter nights, he'll emerge from the kitchen to chat animatedly with his guests.

BALTHAZAR Map pp294-5 Mediterranean €€
☎ 93 217 82 50; Carrer de Rosselló 189; meal €20; Ⓜ Diagonal; ☒
Balthazar offers a spacious and buzzy dining atmosphere with several main areas and a lot of black in the décor. The extensive menu of Catalan and Mediterranean dishes is good without being spectacular, but locals converge here for stylish but economical dining. After all, where else might you encounter a *carpaccio de bou amb encenalls de parmesà* (beef carpaccio with Parmesan cheese shavings) for €6.25?

RELAIS DE VENISE Map pp294-5 French €€

☎ 93 467 21 62; Carrer de Pau Claris 142; meal €20; ☯ closed Aug; Ⓜ Passeig de Gràcia; ⊠

You can eat anything you want here, so long as it's meat. Indeed, there's just one dish, a succulent beef entrecôte with their secret 'sauce Porte-Maillot' (named after the location of the original restaurant in Paris), chips and salad. It is served in slices and in two waves so that it doesn't go cold. The setting does not lack elegance although it is a little barnlike. Any variation in price depends on the wine you select.

CERVESERIA CATALANA

Map pp294-5 Tapas €€

☎ 93 216 03 68; Carrer de Mallorca 236; meal €20-25; Ⓜ Passeig de Gràcia; ⊠

This 'Catalan Brewery' is good for breakfast, lunch and tea. Come in for your morning coffee and croissant, or wait until lunch to enjoy choosing from the cornucopia of tapas (€3 to €4.50) and montaditos (canapés, €1.50 to €2.50). You can sit at the bar, on the pavement terrace or in the restaurant at the back. The variety of hot tapas, mouth-watering salads and other snacks draws a well-dressed crowd from all over the barri. The same people run an equally good place not far off, Ciudad Condal (Map pp298–9; ☎ 93 318 19 97; La Rambla de Catalunya 18; meal €20-25; Ⓜ Catalunya).

KOYUKI Map pp294-5 Japanese €€

☎ 93 237 84 90; Carrer de Còrsega 242; meal €20-30; ☯ Tue-Sat, dinner Sun Ⓜ Diagonal

This unassuming basement Japanese diner is one of those rough-edged diamonds that repays a visit. Take a seat at one of the long tables and order from the cheesy menu with pictures from the sometimes gruff Japanese owner. You won't be disappointed. The mix of sashimi moriawase is varied, generous and fresh. The tempura udon (€7.80) is a hearty thick noodle option. Splash down with Sapporo beer.

INOPIA Gourmet Tapas €€

☎ 93 424 52 31; Carrer de Tamarit 104; meal €25-30; ☯ dinner Tue-Fri, lunch & dinner Sat; Ⓜ Rocafort

Albert Adrià, brother of star chef Ferran and something of a kitchen celebrity himself, runs this popular corner tapas temple. If you can't grab one of the handful of tables, don't worry; grab a standing spot inside or out

and select a pincho moruno de pollo (chicken bites on a skewer), the lightly fried, tempura-style vegetables (fresh from La Boqueria market), wash down with house red or Moritz beer and finish with the 4 bombones con vino dulce de Castaño (four pralines with a heavenly sweet red dessert wine).

EL RACÓ D'EN BALTÀ

Map pp294-5 Mediterranean €€

☎ 93 453 10 44; Carrer d'Aribau 125; meal €25-30; ☯ Tue-Fri, dinner Sat, lunch Mon; Ⓡ FGC Provença; ⊠

With artworks, an almost hippy decorative touch, cool colours and dining over three floors, this corner restaurant is a welcoming place. The menu changes frequently, according to season and whim, and has a vaguely international flavour. Offerings include hearty meat mains and dreamy desserts. The suprema de pollastre farcida de bacó amb salsa de coco (chicken supreme stuffed with bacon in a coconut sauce, €11.50) is an aromatic treat.

RESTAURANT DE L'ESCOLA DE RESTAURACIÓ I HOSTALATGE

Map pp296-7 Catalan €€

☎ 93 453 29 03; Carrer de Muntaner 70-72; meal €30-35; ☯ Mon-Fri, closed Aug; Ⓜ Universitat; ⊠

Greenery hangs from the ceiling, bright contemporary paintings hang from the beige walls and diners hang at elegantly set tables to await the trainee cooks' latest creations. These guys are at the top of their class, offering a combination of local fish of the day and tangy meat dishes like fricandó de vedella amb moixernons (veal fricandeau with St George mushrooms).

DE TAPA MADRE Map pp294-5 Catalan €€

☎ 93 459 31 34; Carrer de Mallorca 301; meal €30-35; Ⓜ Verdaguer; ⊠

A lively, chatty atmosphere greets you from the bar as you swing open the door. A few tiny tables line the window, but head upstairs for more space in the gallery that hovers above the array of tapas on the bar below, or deeper inside past the bench with the ham legs. Choose from a range of tapas (€3 to €5.50), or opt for a full meal. The arròs caldós amb llagostins (a hearty rice dish with king prawns) is delicious. The fish of the day (€20) can also be a good choice.

THAI GARDENS Map pp294-5   Thai €€

☎ 93 487 98 98; Carrer de la Diputació 273; meal €35; ☾ Mon-Sat; Ⓜ Passeig de Gràcia; ⊠
One of the first and still one of the best for Thai food in Barcelona. Tables for two set in quiet corners contrast with great round-party sittings amid a veritable forest of tropical greenery reaching for the high ceiling. The set meal (€29) allows you to try a broad range of dishes and can be a good idea for larger groups.

CHICOA Map pp296-7   Catalan €€

☎ 93 453 11 23; Carrer d'Aribau 73; meal €35; ☾ Tue-Sat, lunch Sun; Ⓜ Hospital Clínic; ⊠
It looks as rustic on the inside as out, with ceramic plates decorating the walls, stone arches and dark timber all over. For traditional Catalan cooking, this is an address that loyal locals come back to time and again. Indeed, time seems to have stood still here since they opened back in the deep dark 1970s. A speciality of the house is anything to do with *bacallà* (salted cod).

REÑÉ Map pp294-5   Fusion €€

☎ 93 488 27 71; Carrer del Consell de Cent 362-364; meal €35; ☾ Tue-Sat, lunch Sun Ⓜ Girona; ⊠
In what was once a modernista pastry shop, whose furniture and décor have been scrupulously respected (the bar is spectacular), a young team of chefs has created a fashion fusion locale. Sup on *sopa japonesa de gambes i verdures* (clear soup with vegetables and prawns, €10), followed by a *saltat d'arròs Basmati i integral amb gambes, poma i mango* (fried Basmati and whole rice with prawns, apple and mango), to light background jazz music.

PARCO Map pp294-5   Sushi & Cocktails €€

☎ 93 238 78 22; Passeig de Gràcia 119; meal €30-40; ☾ Tue-Sun; Ⓜ Diagonal
The Italian love affair with Barcelona manifests itself here with this Barcelona branch of the stylish Milan sushi restaurant–cum–cocktail bar. With a little Eastern fusion music in the background, start the evening with a round of bulbous cocktails before ordering plates of sushi and sashimi. Lighting is low, reds and black dominate the décor and those unlucky enough to miss out on a lounge may find themselves uncomfortably perched on backless chairs.

YAMADORY Map pp296-7   Japanese €€

☎ 93 453 92 64; Carrer d'Aribau 68; meal €30-40; ☾ Mon-Sat; Ⓡ FGC Provença
Yamadory remains one of the steadiest ambassadors of Japanese cooking in the city. As the door slips closed behind you, the first thing you notice is the hushed atmosphere of the place. Divided into several different dining areas with a contemporary Japanese décor, it is notable for its gliding efficiency. Head upstairs to sit on a ground-level tatami. The sushi, sashimi, udon and tempura are all good.

TAKTIKA BERRI Map pp296–7   Basque €€

☎ 93 453 47 59; Carrer de València 169; tapas €25, meal €35-40; ☾ Mon-Fri, lunch Sat; Ⓜ Hospital Clínic
Get in early here as the tapas bar teems with punters from far and wide anxious to wrap their mandibles around some of the best Basque tapas in town. The hot ones are all snapped up as soon as they arrive from the kitchen, so keep your eyes peeled. The seated dining area out the back is also good. Note in the evening it's all over by about 10.30pm.

FERNÁNDEZ Map pp294-5   International €€

☎ 93 238 48 46; Passeig de Gràcia 116; meal €35-45; Ⓜ Diagonal; ⊠
A broad, clean-lined restaurant with black and white chessboard décor and widescreen window view of the kitchen at the rear, Fernández offers a broad mix of Catalan, Spanish (*estofado de rabo de toro,* bull's tail stew, €11) and international dishes. The hamburger entree, for instance, is no ordinary hamburger. You are served four dainty *hamburguesitas* (four little minced meat balls deftly prepared one each with a cheese sauce, mushroom sauce, onion topping and crystallised onion topping) at €10.50.

JOSÉ LUIS Map pp294-5   Spanish €€

☎ 93 200 83 12; Avinguda Diagonal 520; meal €35-45; Ⓜ Diagonal
Welcome to Madrid! Long established in the Spanish capital, the Barcelona branch occupies a privileged spot. It is said this place introduced the *montadito* (delicious little canapés) to Barcelona. Pick and choose from these and a long list of *pinchos* (tapas) and *raciones,* including the all-time Madrid favourite, *callos* (tripe). Or sit down in this

elliptical basement for a classy meal served by brisk waiters in black jackets and bow ties. The *confit de pato* (duck confit, €16) is a leg of tender meat in a caramelised pear sauce. It's perfect for a business lunch.

PATAGONIA Map pp294-5 Argentine €€
☎ 93 304 37 35; Gran Via de les Corts Catalanes 660; meal €40-45; ⊙ Mon-Sat; Ⓜ Passeig de Gràcia; ⊠

An elegant Argentinean beef fest awaits in this stylish new arrival. Start with empanadas (tiny meat-crammed pies, €3 to €4.50). You might want to skip past the *achuras* (offal) and head for a hearty meat main, such as a juicy beef *medallón con salsa de colmenillas* (a medallion in a morel sauce). You choose from one of five side dishes to accompany your pound of flesh.

TRAGALUZ Map pp294-5 Mediterranean €€
☎ 93 487 01 96; Passatge de la Concepció 5; meal €40-45; Ⓜ Passeig de Gràcia; ⊠

Inventive Mediterranean cuisine (with an Italian leaning) is the name of the game in this 1980s designer relic by Javier Mariscal. Sit under the sloping glass roof on one side of this town house, which allows streams of daylight to flood in. A delicate starter is the seasonal *assortiment de tomàquets del país amb virutes de mahó* (assortment of country tomatoes with cheese shavings, €11). Some of the seafood mains are tempting, such as the feather-soft *rodaball, suquet de romesco* (turbot with a romesco-sauce based stew, €21).

ALKÍMIA Map pp294-5 Creative Catalan €€
☎ 93 207 61 15; Carrer de l'Indústria 79; meal €40-50; ⊙ Mon-Fri, dinner Sat; Ⓜ Verdaguer

Jordi Vila, a culinary alchemist, serves up refined Catalan dishes with a twist in this elegant, white-walled locale well off the tourist trail. Dishes like his *arròs amb nyora i escarmalans* (a rice dish with crayfish and a sweetish chilli) have earned Vila his first Michelin star.

CINC SENTITS Map pp296-7 International €€
☎ 93 323 94 90; Carrer d'Aribau 58; meal €40-50; ⊙ Tue-Sat, lunch Sun, closed Easter & Aug; Ⓜ Passeig de Gràcia

Enter this somewhat overlit realm of the 'Five Senses' to indulge in a tasting menu (from €26 to €50) of a series of small, experimental dishes. What's on offer changes from one day to the next, but think wine reduction sauces, *pols de cansalada* (bacon fat powder), cuttlefish noodles and other hitherto never-dreamed-up elements in a brief menu that includes a balance of fish and meat. You'll either love it or be somewhat puzzled by it!

CATA 1.81 Map pp296-7 Creative Tapas €€
☎ 93 323 68 18; Carrer de València 181; meal €45-50; ⊙ dinner only Mon-Sat, closed Aug; Ⓜ Passeig de Gràcia

If you like an Al Capone–style conspiratorial feel, call ahead to book the little room out the back past the busy, compact kitchen. Surrounded by shelves of fine wines packed to the rafters, you will be treated to a series of dainty gourmet dishes, such as *raviolis amb bacallà* (salt cod dumplings) or *truita amb tòfona* (a thick potato tortilla with a delicate trace of truffle). Since wines feature so high here, let rip with the list of fine Spanish tipples.

PRINCIPAL
Map pp294-5 Modern Mediterranean €€-€€€
☎ 93 272 08 45; Carrer de Provença 286-288; meal €45-55; Ⓡ FGC Provença; ⊠

You want to be well dressed to get in for the at-times microscopic servings of fine delicacies at dark timber tables. Out the back spreads a magnificent garden. You can tiptoe through a starter of *arròs cremòs de gambes* (creamy prawn rice, €18) and follow with *tatin de quatlla i foie gras* (quail tatin with foie gras, €17).

NOTI Map pp294-5 Mediterranean €€€
☎ 93 342 66 73; Carrer de Roger de Llúria 35; meal €50-60; ⊙ Mon-Sat; Ⓜ Passeig de Gràcia; ⊠

Hard to believe that this was once home to a newspaper, the *Noticiero Universal*. The news now is that Noti is a serious culinary player with muted club sounds, under siege by the city's glitterati. The ample, square dining room is plastered with mirrors that seem to multiply the steely design tables, some of them huge round affairs for groups. Try a dreamy *risotto cremoso de rúcula y rape* (creamy monkfish and rocket risotto, €19.20) or perhaps a meat dish, anything from beef tartar to chicken curry. Afterwards, pick at a French cheese platter.

CASA DARÍO Map pp296-7 · Seafood €€€
☎ 93 453 31 35; Carrer del Consell de Cent 256; meal €50-60; ⏰ Mon-Sat, closed Aug; Ⓜ Passeig de Gràcia
Step into the timeless world of old-time silver service and ample helpings of the gifts of the sea. White-jacketed waiters worry around tables with hushed efficiency to serve up a seafood feast as only the folks from the northwest Atlantic region of Galicia know how. Opt for one of the set menus (around €45) and you will be served endless rounds of seafood wonders, many of which are flown in daily from Galicia.

CASA CALVET Map pp294-5 · Catalan €€€
☎ 93 412 40 12; Carrer de Casp 48; meal €60; ⏰ Mon-Sat; Ⓜ Urquinaona; ☒
An early Gaudí masterpiece loaded with the curvy features that were his trademark now houses a swish restaurant (just to the right of the building's main entrance). Dress up and try for an intimate *taula cabina* (wooden booth). You could opt for a tangy *llom de cervol amb salsa de groselles i crema de castanyes* (deer with red currant sauce and chestnut cream, €24.30) or *vieires saltades amb perfum de gingebre i espàrrecs* (sautéed scallops with ginger aroma and asparagus, €26.65).

SPEAKEASY Map pp294-5 · International €€€
☎ 93 217 50 80; Carrer d'Aribau 162-166; meal €60; ⏰ Mon-Fri, dinner Sat; Ⓜ Diagonal
This 'clandestine' restaurant lurks behind the Dry Martini bar. You will be shown a door through the open kitchen area to the 'storeroom', which is lined with hundreds of bottles of backlit, quality tipples. Dark tones in the décor, a few works of art, low lighting, light jazz music and smooth service complete the setting. What's on the menu depends in part on the markets, in part on the cook's whim. The *rellom argentí* (€23) is a melt-in-the-mouth cut of sirloin. Or you might opt for a healthier route with the *wok d'espaguettis amb verdures, vedella i foie* (stir-fried spaghetti with vegetables, beef strips and foie gras, €17.50).

LA DAMA Map pp294-5 · Catalan-French €€€
☎ 93 202 06 86; Avinguda Diagonal 423; meal €60; Ⓜ Diagonal
At home in the stunning modernista Casa Sayrach, this place will satiate your eyes

---

before you even get inside the restaurant. The interior is less exuberant and the *haute cuisine* carefully elegant. It is the perfect spot to take your loved one for an anniversary or similar worthy occasion. Select a tasting menu (€62 or €85) or choose *a la carta* from such options as *perdiu amb foie i tòfones* (partridge with foie gras and truffles, €32.25).

SAÜC Map p292 · Catalan €€€
☎ 93 321 01 89; Passatge de Lluís Pellicer 12; meal €60-70; ⏰ Tue-Sat; Ⓜ Hospital Clínic; ☒
Pop down into this basement place on a little Eixample lane and you enter a soothing sanctuary. Sober designer décor, dominated by ochres, creams and buttercup yellows, allows you to concentrate on what emerges from the kitchen, such as *garrí confitat i rostit amb patates i xalotes saltades* (marinated and roast suckling pig with sautéed potatoes and shallots, €25.95). The €56 tasting menu comprises an appetiser, five courses, followed by a cheese selection and two desserts!

CAFÉS

ORXATERIA SIRVENT Map pp298-9 · Orxata
☎ 93 441 76 16; Ronda de Sant Pau 3; glass of orxata €2; ⏰ Mon-Sat; Ⓜ Sant Antoni
A haven of *orxata/horchata* (tiger-nut drink), this busy locale serves up the best you'll try without having to catch the Euromed train down to this drink's spiritual home, Valencia. You can get it by the glass

or take it away by the bottle. This place also purveys ice cream, *granissat* (iced fruit crush) and *turrón* (nougat).

CREMERIA TOSCANA Map pp294-5 · Gelato
☎ 93 539 38 25; Carrer de Muntaner 161; gelato from €2; ☺ 1-9pm Tue-Sun; M Hospital Clínic

Yes, you can stumble across quite reasonable ice-cream in Barcelona, but close your eyes and think yourself across the Med to the real ice-cream wizards. This corner *gelateria* is a slice of Italy in central Barcelona. Creamy *stracciatella* and wavy *nocciola*… and myriad other flavours await in this, the most authentic gelato outlet in town. Buy a cone, or a tub!

CACAO SAMPAKA
Map pp298-9 · Café & Chocolate
☎ 93 272 08 33; Carrer del Consell de Cent 292; hot chocolate €2.50; ☺ 9am-8.30pm Mon-Sat, 5-8.30pm Sun; M Passeig de Gràcia; ✗

Chocoholics will be convinced they have died and passed on to a better place. Load up in the shop or head for the bar in the back where you can have a classic *xocolata calenta* and munch on exquisite chocolate cakes, tarts, ice cream, endless sweets and even sandwiches!

MAURI Map pp294-5 · Pastries & Café
☎ 93 215 10 20; La Rambla de Catalunya 102; ☺ 8am-9pm Mon-Sat, 8am-3pm Sun; M Diagonal; ✗

Since 1929 this grand old pastry shop has had its regular customers salivating over the endless range of sweet things, melt-in-the-mouth chocolate-filled croissants and gourmet delicatessen items. You can take away your plunder or sit in the tearoom to the right of the bar and have a coffee and juice with your morning brioche.

ESCRIBÀ Map pp296-7 · Pastries
☎ 93 454 75 35; Gran Via de les Corts Catalanes 546; pastries €2-3, hot chocolate €2; ☺ 8am-9pm; M Urgell; ✗

Antoni Escribà carries forward a family tradition (since 1906) of melting Barcelonins' hearts with remarkable pastries and criminal chocolate creations. When not building models of La Sagrada Família out of dark chocolate, the Escribà clan bakes slightly more down-to-earth delicacies, such as its Easter *bunyols de xocolata* (little round pastry balls filled with chocolate cream). Sit down for a cake and coffee. Escribà has another branch at La Rambla de Sant Joseph 83 (p202).

Eating

L'EIXAMPLE

Escribà (above), La Rambla

GRÀCIA & PARK GÜELL

Gràcia is loaded, for some inexplicable reason, with Middle Eastern and, to a lesser extent, Greek restaurants, which are chirpy and good value, if no great culinary adventure. Spread right across this busy *barri* are all sorts of other enticing options, from simple tapas bars to classy Italian, and a few of Barcelona's top joints, discreetly tucked away along tiny lanes. There's little of interest, however, around Park Güell.

EL ROURE   Map pp294-5   Tapas €
☎ 93 218 73 87; Carrer de la Riera Sant Miquel 51; meal €10-15; Mon-Sat; M Fontana
This old-time locals' bar is what Hemingway meant by a 'clean, well-lighted place'. Sidle up to the bar or pull up a little wooden chair and tuck into a choice of good-value tapas from the bar, washed down by a few cold Estrellas. The choice is abundant. The *bunyols de bacallà* are delightful battered balls of cod that demand to be gobbled up. The place is full to bursting most of the time.

NOU CANDANCHÚ
Map pp294-5   Tapas, Bocadillos & Grills €
☎ 93 237 73 62; Plaça de Rius i Taulet 9; meal €12-20; Wed-Mon; M Fontana
The liveliest locale on the square, Nou Candanchú is a long-time favourite for myriad reasons. Many flock to its sunny terrace just for a few drinks. You could accompany the liquid refreshment with one of the giant *entrepans* for which it is justly known (€3 to €4.50). Otherwise, it offers a limited range of tapas and does some reasonable grilled meat dishes. What more could you ask for than a carafe of wine and the *menú del día* (€8 to €10) outside on the square?

KRAMPUS   Map p292   Crepes €
☎ 93 200 85 97; Carrer de Saragossa 89; meal €15; Mon-Sat, dinner Sun; M Lesseps
A little out of the way on a narrow, car-choked street at the outer limits of Gràcia is this young, dynamic little haven of crepes. You may have to queue on weekends in order to sample this Breton-inspired dish. Choose your own ingredients or select from the speciality range, anything from Thai to French (blue cheese and walnuts). For dessert…well, you can probably guess.

GRÀCIA & PARK GÜELL TOP FIVE
- Botafumeiro (opposite)
- Restaurant Jean Luc Figueras (p160)
- Restaurant Roig Robí (opposite)
- Specchio Magico (opposite)
- Taverna La Llesca (below)

HIMALI   Map pp294-5   Nepalese & Vegetarian €
☎ 93 285 15 68; Carrer de Milài Fontanals 60; meal €15; Tue-Sun; M Joanic
Spacious and simple, with gruff service and paper place mats, this is a great spot for Nepalese chow and vegetarian dishes. You can pick up a filling lentil-based *dal bhat* menu or a *sabji tarkari* (mixed vegetable curry). Carnivores can opt for mixed grills with rice and naan, or *kukhurako fila* (roast chicken in walnut sauce). Mains come in at €7.50 to €8.50.

TAVERNA LA LLESCA   Map pp294-5   Catalan €
☎ 93 285 02 46; Carrer de Terol 6; meal €15; Mon-Sat; M Fontana
Head out to the back of this wonderfully boisterous eatery where the name of the game is hearty servings of meat (which you can temper with a little salad if you want), washed down with throaty house red. A good option is *entrecot de vedella* (beef entrecôte), best done with pepper, which arrives in generous portions. Other options include roast rabbit or *pincho moruno* (skewers of grilled pork).

LAC MAJÙR   Map pp294-5   North Italian €€
☎ 93 192 36 78; Carrer de Tordera 33; meal €15-25; Mon-Sat; M Fontana or Verdaguer
You could easily stride past this cosy little slice of northwest Italy as you step out along this quiet and unusually leafy lane. Stop! Inside, all sorts of home-cooking delights await, and you will be tempted to do things the Italian away: have a pasta first course and follow with a main. Gnocchi and *trofie* are the house specials. The latter are little twists of pasta, usually served with pesto sauce in Liguria. Try the pesto and gorgonzola cheese variant (€7.40) followed by, say, a *saltimbocca alla romana* (a veal slice cooked with ham, sage and sweet marsala wine) for €8.90.

CANTINA MACHITO Map pp294-5 Mexican €€

☎ 93 217 34 14; Carrer de Torrijos 47; meal €20-25; Ⓜ Fontana or Joanic; ✗

¡Andale! Gringos (which can mean just about anyone not from Mexico) can't wait to get into this cheerful Mexican hideout, for lashings of tacos, enchiladas and other classics. Less well-known dishes, like the sopa malpeña (a chicken, chickpea and tomato soup), beg to be tried. For dessert, the tequila and lime mousse is refreshing. The place is generally full to bursting and the dinner-time atmosphere warms up nicely to the tune of tequila and margaritas as the night progresses.

ENVALIRA Map pp294-5 Catalan €€

☎ 93 218 58 13; Plaça del Sol 13; meal €25; ✓ Tue-Sat, lunch Sun; Ⓜ Fontana

Surrounded by cool hangouts, Lebanese eateries and grunge bars, you'd barely notice the modest entrance to this delicious relic from another era. Past the handful of tables by the bar you head into the tiny dining room out the back, where the décor seems to have stood still since the 1950s. Serious jacketed waiters deliver all sorts of seafood and rice dishes to your table, from arròs a la milanesa (a savoury rice dish with chicken, pork and a light cheese gratin, €10) to a bullit de lluç (a slice of white hake boiled with herb-laced rice and a handful of clams, €11). You could start with a sopa ¼ hora ('quarter hour soup', a fish and rice broth, €5.60).

KIBUKA Map pp294-5 Japanese €€

☎ 93 415 92 17; Carrer de Goya 9; meal €20-30; ✓ Mon-Fri, dinner Sat & Sun; Ⓜ Diagonal

It is easy to imagine that this corner restaurant was once an old-time vermouth bar. The dark timber tables and doors have been retained, as has the old chessboard tile floor. But behind the bar nowadays are Japanese cooks busily rolling up sushi and other goodies for you. Eight pieces of maki, the house speciality, cost €10. What most strikes one here is the complete absence of any feigned Japanese décor or 'ambience'. A nice transcultural change.

LA ROSA DEL DESIERTO

Map pp294-5 Moroccan €€

☎ 93 237 45 90; Plaça de Narcís Oller 7; meal €35; ✓ Tue-Sat, lunch Sun; Ⓜ Diagonal

The horseshoe-arched doorway clues you in to the North African flavour of this long-standing favourite in the city for couscous. Indeed, it offers nine varieties of the stuff, ranging from curry couscous (€16.50) to lobster couscous (€42.50), along with other Moroccan dishes. Take your place amid piles of cushions and don't forget to finish with a refreshing mint tea.

SPECCHIO MAGICO Map pp294-5 Italian €€

☎ 93 415 33 71; Carrer de Luis Antúnez 3; meal €35-50; Ⓜ Fontana

This remains one of the finest Italian eateries in town. As soon as you push through the doors you feel you have walked out of Spain and into Italy. Get off to a cheesy start with gnocchi al gorgonzola (€16.90). If you're really hungry, make like the Italians and proceed to a main course of, say, filetto all'aceto balsamico (a delicate steak fillet prepared in balsamic vinegar) for €24.90.

RESTAURANT ROIG ROBÍ

Map pp294-5 Catalan €€€

☎ 93 218 92 22; Carrer de Seneca 20; meal €60; ✓ Mon-Fri, dinner Sat; Ⓜ Diagonal; ✗

Grab a rattan seat at a quiet table by the windows or, in summer, in the little internal courtyard. The mandonguilles de lluç amb bolets i sipia (salt cod meatballs with mushrooms and cuttlefish, €26) are delicious. This is an altar to traditional cooking, but with an unusual delicacy. Even the simplest items, like croquetes de pollastre (chicken croquettes) are prepared to perfection.

BOTAFUMEIRO Map pp294-5 Seafood €€€

☎ 93 218 42 30; Carrer Gran de Gràcia 81; meal €60-70; ✓ 1pm-1am; Ⓜ Fontana; ✗

It is hard not to mention this classic temple of Galician shellfish and other briny delights but, perhaps overconfident after years as one of Barcelona's premier eateries with a constant stream of BMWs parked outside, it runs the danger of pricing itself out of the market. Share a few medias raciones (small dishes) to avoid financial hari-kiri and still taste a range of the bounteous marine offerings. This is one place where you can try percebes (€20.50 for a media ración), the strangely twisted goose barnacles harvested along Galicia's north Atlantic coast.

RESTAURANT JEAN LUC FIGUERAS

Map pp294-5   Franco-Catalan €€€

☎ 93 415 28 77; Carrer de Santa Teresa 10; meal €80-90; ⌚ Mon-Sat, closed Easter & Aug; Ⓜ Diagonal; ✕

Soft lights, white-draped tables, barely audible music and faultless service are just some of the hallmarks of one of the greats of Barcelona's cuisine scene. The menu depends in part on the season. You may need to book several days in advance before slipping down the narrow lane towards meals that could include *tartar de bou amb caviar* (beef tartar with caviar, €30), followed by a white-chocolate brownie drenched in rhubarb and orange sauce!

LA ZONA ALTA

Some of the grandest kitchens of the city, those with a history of excellence if not always adventurousness (if you want adventure, head for El Born), are scattered across La Zona Alta, from Tibidabo across Sant Gervasi (as far down as Avinguda Diagonal west of Gràcia) to Pedralbes.

BAR TOMÀS Map pp290-1   Tapas €

☎ 93 203 10 77; Carrer Major de Sarrià 49; meal €10-15; ⌚ Thu-Tue; Ⓡ FGC Sarrià

Forever and a day Barcelonins have claimed that Bar Tomàs is the best place in the city for *patates braves*, prepared here with a special variation on the classic spicy tomato and mayonnaise sauce, whose secret they are not about to reveal to anyone.

CAN CORTADA   Catalan €€

☎ 93 427 23 15; Avinguda de l'Estatut de Catalunya s/n; meal €30-35; Ⓜ Montbau; ✕

More than anything else, it is the setting and the hearty welcome that makes this 11th-century *masia* (Catalan country farmhouse; this one is a lordly country estate complete with the remains of a defensive tower) worth the excursion. Try to get a table in the former cellars. Healthy portions of simple dishes such as *truita* (tortilla), *bacalao* (salted cod) and Catalan classics such as *escalivada* (grilled red pepper and aubergine) are the order of the day.

ORANGE Map pp290-1   International €€

☎ 93 418 10 85; Carrer del Rosari 52; meal €35; ⌚ Mon-Sat; Ⓡ FGC Tres Torres

Set in a fine house where timber window frames, indoor plants and warm colours create a tranquil and cosy atmosphere, this restaurant offers a curious international mix, including Argentine Angus steaks and Italian pasta dishes. There are several dining areas and terraces (one with just a single table).

CAN TRAVI NOU   Catalan €€

☎ 93 428 04 34; Carrer de Jorge Manrique s/n, Parc de la Vall d'Hebron; meal €40-45; ⌚ Mon-Sat, lunch Sun; Ⓜ Montbau; ✕

Yes, it has been discovered by tourists. But who can blame them? This expansive 18th-century *masia*, with warm colours, a grandfather clock and a wholesome, bucolic air, is a magical setting for a Catalan splurge. Several dining areas stretch out across two floors. The *risotto de formatge* (cheese risotto, €10) makes a hearty starter but the generous mains will please you more. The *arròs caldós amb llamàntol i cloïsses* (a rice stew with lobster and clams, €22) is irresistible.

LA BALSA Map pp290-1   Mediterranean €€€

☎ 93 211 50 48; Carrer de la Infanta Isabel 4; meal €50-60; ⌚ Tue-Sat, lunch Sun, dinner Mon; Ⓡ FGC Avinguda del Tibidabo; ✕

With its grand timber ceiling and scented gardens surrounding the main open terrace dining area, La Balsa is one of the city's top dining experiences. The menu changes frequently and is a mix of traditional Catalan and carefully off-centre inventiveness. Lounge over a cocktail at the bar before being ushered over to your table. The place is famous for its August all-in dinner buffet (€25).

VIA VENETO Map p292   Catalan €€€

☎ 93 200 72 44; Carrer de Ganduxer 10; meal €80-100; ⌚ Mon-Fri, dinner Sat; Ⓡ FGC La Bonanova; ✕

Dalí used to regularly waltz into this high-society eatery after it opened in 1967. The vaguely Art Deco setting (note the oval mirrors), orange-rose tablecloths, leather upholstered chairs and fine cutlery must cater perhaps to more conservative souls, but the painter was here for the kitchen exploits. Catalan dishes predominate and the mouth fairly waters at the mere mention of, say, *llebre a la royal amb pomes saltades al Calvados* (hare with apples sautéed in Calvados, €42). You barely notice the presence of the waiters, their service is so good.

SANTS & LES CORTS

About the only time visitors venture into these *barris* is when arriving or leaving by train, or to get to Camp Nou. While there is not an awful lot going on in these areas, a handful of restaurants are worth sniffing out – you'll certainly be far away from the tourist trail!

ZARAUTZ Map pp296-7 Catalan-Basque €€
☎ 93 325 28 13; Carrer de l'Elisi 13; meal €25; ⏲ 8am-11.30pm Mon-Sat, closed Aug; Ⓜ Sants Estació or Tarragona; ⊠
A short hop away from the train station, you can take in some quality Basque tapas at the bar any time of the day here, or retire to the restaurant for a full meal, such as *carpaccio de bou amb formatge Idiazábal* (Argentine beef *carpaccio* with a tangy Basque cheese). The owner is a dessert specialist, so save some room.

EL PEIXEROT Map pp296-7 Seafood €€
☎ 93 424 69 69; Carrer de Tarragona 177; meal €40-50; Ⓜ Sants Estació; ⊠
Twinned with the restaurant of the same name in the seaside town of Vilanova, southwest of the city, El Peixerot has sea-blue décor and has long been famous for fresh seafood (sold by weight) and rice dishes. It's big and boisterous, but service is rapid and the food is always good.

MONTJUÏC & POBLE SEC

Montjuïc, for the obvious reason that it is mostly parks and gardens, is largely bereft of notable eating options. In gruff old Poble Sec, however, you'll turn up all sorts of priceless nuggets, and we're not talking chicken either.

QUIMET I QUIMET Map pp304-5 Tapas €€
☎ 93 442 31 42; Carrer del Poeta Cabanyes 25; tapas €2-3; ⏲ Tue-Sat, lunch Sun; Ⓜ Paral.lel; ⊠
A tapas bar *de toda la vida* (which has been around forever), Quimet i Quimet is a

family-run business that has been passed down from generation to generation. Stepping into this gourmet telephone box (there's barely space to swing a calamari in this bottle-lined, standing-room-only spot) is a treat for the palate. Just look at all those gourmet tapas waiting for you. Let the folk behind the bar advise you, and order a drop of fine wine to accompany. Or opt for their behind the counter malt beer, especially bottled for them in Belgium!

LA BELLA NAPOLI Map pp304-5 Pizza €
☎ 93 442 50 56; Carrer de Margarit 12; pizza €8-10; ⏲ Wed-Sun, lunch Tue; Ⓜ Paral.lel
There are pizza joints all over Barcelona. And then there's the real thing, the way they make it in Naples. This place even feels like Naples. The waiters are mostly from across the Med and have that cheeky southern Italian approach to food, customers, everything. The pizzas are second to none and the atmosphere nice and sunny southern.

RESTAURANT KASBAH
Map pp304-5 French-Moroccan €€
☎ 93 329 83 84; Carrer de Vila i Vilà 82; meal €20; ⏲ Tue-Sun, closed Aug; Ⓜ Paral.lel
A modest shopfront belies the North African aromas and setting inside. Sit down over a low round table amid cushions and Oriental music for an array of Moroccan and other North African dishes. The *tajines* (try the lamb one at €9.25), cooked in a strange-looking ceramic bowl and funnel, are tempting. Or try the limited French menu. The mint tea here is good, made the Moroccan way with lots of leaves and sugar.

RESTAURANT ELCHE
Map pp304-5 Paella, Fideuá & Rice €€
☎ 93 441 30 89; Carrer de Vila i Vilà 71; meal €25; Ⓜ Paral.lel
With tables spreading over two floors and old-world service and settings, this spot has been doing some of Barcelona's best paella (of various types) and *fideuá* (similar to paella, but using vermicelli noodles as the base) since the 1960s. Other places come and go, but this classic never seems to wilt.

EL ABREVADERO

Map pp304-5   Catalan & Mediterranean €€

☎ 93 441 38 93; Carrer de Vila i Vilà 77; meal €25-35; ⏱ Wed-Sat, lunch Mon & Tue; Ⓜ Paral.lel; ⊠

Still a beacon of creative kitchen antics in this otherwise fairly traditional corner of town, El Abrevadero has taken some of the edge off its weirder dishes and is offering some nice spins on local cooking done with a delicate touch. A tempting dish is *mar i muntanya de peus de porc amb escamarlans* (surf and turf with pig's trotters and crayfish, €15). To get a taster of the gourmet talents at a fraction of the regular *a la carta* price, drop in for their *menú del día* (€14).

TAPIOLES 53 Map pp304-5   Mediterranean €€

☎ 93 329 22 38; www.tapioles53.com; Carrer de Tapioles 53; meal €35-45; ⏱ dinner Tue-Sat; Ⓜ Paral.lel; ⊠

A stylish place in a former umbrella factory, this is a little gem. The Australian-born chef, Sarah, has been cooking around the world for years and it shows in her limited, constantly changing international menu. She searches out her ingredients daily in the city's markets and creates something different every day. Asian touches are sometimes present but you might just as easily find yourself with a Moroccan-style *tajine*. Start the evening at the little bar and then proceed to one of the simple, intimate timber tables and let Sarah guide you. Book ahead.

Drinking & Nightlife

Drinking & Nightlife

As the hordes of stag- and hen-night partiers demonstrate, there is no shortage of places to get a tipple or six in Barcelona. Indeed, there is more drinking, bar-hopping and carousing to be done here than most average mortals can bear. The trick is finding the right zone for you and on the right nights.

Most visitors converge on Ciutat Vella (Old City) and as a result you can be sure of plenty of activity seven nights a week. The lower end of the Barri Gòtic, especially on and around Plaça Reial and Carrer dels Escudellers, is chockers, from the series of tourist-infested pseudo-Irish boozers on Carrer de Ferran to cool dance locals and quieter (everything is relative) bars hidden away in side lanes. In La Ribera the place to be is Passeig del Born and the lanes that branch off it. In El Raval the action is more spread out – from the student faves of Carrer de Joaquín Costa to the mixed set on and around La Rambla del Raval, Carrer Nou de la Rambla and Carrer de Santa Mònica. Some of the city's classic old bars are scattered about in here.

In l'Eixample, Carrer d'Aribau (on both sides of Avinguda Diagonal) is charged (so is Carrer de Balmes, but it's mostly more teenage), but only really gets going from Thursday to Saturday nights. The bars of Gaixample (gay l'Eixample) are clustered around the Carrer del Consell de Cent end of Carrer d'Aribau.

The squares and some streets of Gràcia are laced with bars, as sleepless local residents are constantly reminded. A handful of options sparkle in Poble Sec, while some clubs are spread across the city, from La Barceloneta to Montjuïc and the Zona Alta.

Guía del Ocio (€1; www.guiadelociobcn.es), the city's weekly entertainment mag, is a good starting point available from newsstands. Look for the free mags and booklets distributed around some bars. They include *Micro, Go Mag* and *Salir* (all are in Spanish). There is a growing number of websites also loaded with information. Take a look at Barceloca (www.barceloca.com) and BCN-Nightlife (www.bcn-nightlife.com).

Bars

You could write a book on Barcelona's bars (but it might not be good for your health), which run the gamut from wood-panelled wine cellars to bright waterfront places and trendy design haunts. Some are very local; some are full of foreigners. Some are favoured by students, others by the well-dressed middle classes.

You can pay anything from €2 to €4 for a 330mL bottle of Estrella beer (draught costs a little less) – it all depends on where and when you order it. Mixed drinks *(combinats)* cost between €5 and €8, as do most cocktails.

Most bars are at their liveliest from around 11pm and close between 2am (Sunday to Thursday) and 3am (Friday and Saturday). A handful of places, bless 'em, keep their doors open as late as 5am. That there are not more is largely the result of irate neighbours and the increasingly rigorous application of noise regulations.

Clubs

Barcelona's clubs *(discotecas)* come alive from about 2am until 5am or 6am, and are best Thursday to Saturday. Indeed, many open only on these nights.

In the old-town labyrinth lurks a surprising variety of spots, ranging from plush former old-time dance halls to grungy subterranean venues that fill to the gills.

Along the waterfront it's another ball game. At Port Olímpic a sun-scorched crowd of visiting yachties mixes it up with tourists and a few locals at noisy, back-to-back dance bars right on the waterfront.

Class, they will tell you, is reserved for l'Eixample and La Zona Alta. A sprinkling of well-known clubs is spread over these parts of town. As a rule of thumb they attract a beautiful crowd, although that is in the eye of the beholder.

Some places stage live music before converting into clubs (see p188). Cover charges range from nothing to €18. If you go early, you'll often pay less. In almost all cases the admission price includes your first drink. Bouncers have last say on the dress code and your eligibility to enter.

BARRI GÒTIC & LA RAMBLA

La Rambla holds little interest, so leave it to those settling for expensive pints and plunge into the narrow streets and back alleys of the lower end of the Barri Gòtic.

BARCELONA PIPA CLUB Map pp298-9
☎ 93 302 47 32; Plaça Reial 3; ✆ 6pm-2am;
Ⓜ Liceu
This pipe-smokers' club is like an apartment, with all sorts of interconnecting rooms and knick-knacks – notably the pipes after which the place is named. You buzz at the door and head two floors up. Generally it is for members only until 11pm. It is under constant threat of closure due to neighbours' complaints but has so far survived.

CAFÉ ROYALE Map pp298-9
☎ 93 412 14 33; Carrer Nou de Zurbano 3;
✆ 6pm-2.30am; Ⓜ Liceu or Drassanes
This popular spot lurks in what must be one of the foulest streets in central Barcelona. An improbably high, blue fabric bench lines the wall opposite the bar, but if you get in early enough you can trip down a few stairs to the spacious hardwood back

TOP FIVE DRINKING ESTABLISHMENTS
- Bar Marsella (p167) Absinthe and noisy nostalgia.
- Barcelona Pipa Club (above) That gin-in-private-club feeling.
- Café Royale (above) Where drinking and dancing come naturally together.
- Dry Martini (p181) Make mine a…Martini bar.
- Vaixell Luz de Gas (p179) Wine on the water.

area and grab a lounge. Later on everyone gets in the mood for dancing.

CLUB FELLINI Map pp298-9   Club
☎ 687 969825; La Rambla 27; ✆ midnight-5.30am Mon & Thu-Sat; Ⓜ Drassanes
Although you can drop in here for anything from house to '90s hits on the weekend, this place comes into its own on those slow Monday nights when there's nothing happening elsewhere. Pop along for rock 'n' roll and indie rock at the Nasty Mondays session. Resurrected in 2005, the club has three spaces (the Bad Room, the Red Room and the Mirror Hall) dedicated to anything from house to disco.

DOT LIGHT CLUB Map pp298-9
☎ 93 302 70 26; Carrer Nou de Sant Francesc 7;
✆ 10pm-2.30am Sun-Thu, 10pm-3am Fri & Sat;
Ⓜ Drassanes
Since the late 1990s this has been one of the hippest hang-outs in this part of town. Each night the DJs change the musical theme, ranging from deep funk to deeper house.

GINGER Map pp298-9
☎ 93 310 53 09; Carrer de Lledó 2; ✆ 7pm-2am Tue-Sat; Ⓜ Jaume I
This cosy wine bar also offers beer by the tall glass and cheapish cocktails. It is above all a place to sink into a comfy lounge chair over a quiet tipple, chat and maybe order some light food.

GLACIAR Map pp298-9
☎ 93 302 11 63; Plaça Reial 3; ✆ 4pm-2.30am;
Ⓜ Liceu
This classic, with marble bar and timber seating inside, and aluminium tables and chairs outside beneath the porch, remains a favourite for warm-up tipples and watching the free street theatre of Plaça Reial.

JAMBOREE Map pp298-9   Club

☎ 93 319 17 89; Plaça Reial 17; ⏰ 10.30pm-5am; Ⓜ Liceu

After all the live stuff (see p189) finishes, Jamboree takes on a little different hue as a club from about 1.30am. Sounds under the low arches range fairly inevitably from hip-hop through funk to R&B.

KARMA Map pp298-9   Club

☎ 93 302 56 80; Plaça Reial 10; admission €8; ⏰ midnight-5am Tue-Sun; Ⓜ Liceu

Sick of the metallic sounds of the new century? What about some good, mainstream indie music (during the week)? At weekends it all becomes a little unpredictable, with anything from rock to 1980s disco fever. The odd Madonna track even pops up.

LA CLANDESTINA Map pp302-3

☎ 93 319 05 33; Baixada de Viladecols 2bis; ⏰ 10am-10pm Sun-Thu, 9am-midnight Fri & Sat; Ⓜ Jaume I

Berets and goatees go down well in this right-on teashop, where you can also opt for a beer, relax over a Middle Eastern narghile (the most elaborate way to smoke), get a head massage or eat cake.

LA MACARENA Map pp298-9   Club

Carrer Nou de Sant Francesc 5; admission up to €5; ⏰ 11.30pm-4.30am; Ⓜ Drassanes

You simply won't believe that this was once a tile-lined Andalucian flamenco musos' bar. Now it is a very dark dance space, of the kind where it is possible to sit at the bar, meet people around you and then stand up for a bit of a shake to the DJs' electro and house offerings, all within a couple of square metres.

NEW YORK Map pp298-9   Club

☎ 93 318 87 30; Carrer dels Escudellers 5; admission €10; ⏰ midnight-5am Thu-Sat; Ⓜ Drassanes

This onetime dive (Carrer dels Escudellers was lined by them) has converted itself into a grunge club with a big following. Friday night is best, with anything from reggae and Latin rhythms through to rocksteady and even ska. Remember ska?

SCHILLING Map pp298-9

☎ 93 317 67 87; Carrer de Ferran 23; ⏰ 9.30am-2.30am Mon-Sat, noon-2.30am Sun; Ⓜ Liceu

A gay-friendly favourite with a classy low-lit feel. Perch at the bar, take a little table or

---

RETURN OF THE HOLE IN THE WALL

For decades from 1912, the **Kiosco La Cazalla** (Map pp298–9; Carrer de l'Arc del Teatre) served up passing punters a beer, a wine or a glass of morello cherry–based firewater known as *cazalla*. This little-known Andalucian beverage, often served with a few raisins floating in it, is an acquired taste. After years closed up, the little hole in the wall just off La Rambla has been brought back to life by the owner of Bar Pastís and now attracts an ever-changing clientele through the day and night. It is a snippet of Barcelona history rescued from the steamroller of relentless and frequently tasteless change.

---

slink out the back to the lounges. Whatever you choose, it's a congenial place for a drink and some knowing eye contact.

SINATRA Map pp298-9

☎ 93 412 52 79; Carrer de les Heures 4-10; ⏰ 9pm-2.30am; Ⓜ Liceu

Lurking back a block from boisterous Plaça Reial is this no less raucous relative newcomer to the local bar scene. The fauna is largely comprised of foreigners (even finding a Spanish-speaking staff member is no easy task) who flop into splotchy cowhide pattern lounges, perch on long stools beneath the mirror ball and sip Desperados beer while listening to '80s tracks.

SÍNCOPA Map pp302-3

Carrer d'Avinyó 35; ⏰ 6pm-2.30am; Ⓜ Liceu

Lovers of self-conscious grunge will want to pop in here for the mellow music and conversation. It's just a short saunter from Plaça de George Orwell (or Plaça del Trippy to those who hang around here taking drugs).

EL RAVAL

What happened in the El Born area in the mid-1990s may be happening here now – new bars and clubs are opening up along the long, slummy alleys. Beside them, some great old harbour-style taverns still thrive – dark, wood panelled and bare except for the odd mirror and vast arrays of bottles behind the bar. The area around Carrer de Sant Pau retains its edgy feel, with drug dealers, pickpockets and rough-and-ready prostitutes mingling in a strange mix with streams of nocturnal hedonists.

ÁMBAR Map pp298-9
Carrer de Sant Pau 77; ⏱ 6pm-3am Tue-Sun;
Ⓜ Liceu

The high, grey walls are hung with strange 'works of art', such as framed frilly dresses, and a brightly coloured array of bubble lampshades that emit greens, reds and oranges. Street lighting does the rest. Sounds of the '70s and '80s lend a pleasing retro touch, which can be accompanied by such strange mixes as brownies and absinthe.

BAR LA CONCHA Map pp298-9
☎ 93 302 41 18; Carrer de la Guàrdia 14; ⏱ 5pm-3am; Ⓜ Drassanes

If it were a theme bar, the theme would be actress Sara Montiel: there are more than 250 photos of her here. This kitsch fetish unites a largely gay and transvestite crowd. The music ranges from paso dobles to modern Spanish.

BAR MARSELLA Map pp298-9
Carrer de Sant Pau 65; ⏱ 10pm-2am Mon-Thu, 10pm-3am Fri & Sat; Ⓜ Liceu

Hemingway used to slump over an absinthe in this bar, which has been in business since 1820. It still specialises in *absenta* (absinthe), a drink to be treated with some respect. Your glass comes with a lump of sugar, a fork and a little bottle of mineral water. Hold the sugar on the fork, over your glass, and drip the water onto the sugar so

Absinthe at Bar Marsella (above), El Raval

that it dissolves into the absinthe, which turns yellow. The result should give you a warm glow.

BAR MUY BUENAS Map pp298-9
☎ 93 442 50 53; Carrer del Carme 63; ⏱ 7.30am-2.30am; Ⓜ Liceu

What started life as a late-19th-century milk bar is now lacking the milk (well, you can have some in your coffee). The modernista décor and relaxed company make this a great spot for a quiet *mojito*. You may catch a little live music or even a poetry reading, and can nibble on a limited menu of Middle Eastern tidbits.

BAR PASTÍS Map pp298-9
☎ 93 318 79 80; Carrer de Santa Mònica 4;
⏱ 7.30pm-3am Tue-Sun; Ⓜ Drassanes

A French cabaret theme (lots of Piaf in the background) dominates this tiny, cluttered classic. It's been going, on and off, since the end of WWII. You'll need to be in here before 9pm to have a hope of sitting, getting near the bar or anything much else. On some nights it features live acts, usually performing French *chansons* (songs). Tuesday is tango night and Sunday you are likely to hear Brazilian or Portuguese sounds.

BOADAS Map pp298-9
☎ 93 318 88 26; Carrer dels Tallers 1; ⏱ noon-2am Mon-Thu, noon-3am Fri & Sat; Ⓜ Catalunya

Inside the unprepossessing entrance is one of the city's oldest cocktail bars (famed for its daiquiris). The bow-tied waiters have been serving up the creations since Miguel Boadas opened it in 1933. Joan Miró and Hemingway, among many others, tippled here. Miguel, the son of parents from Lloret de Mar, was born in Havana, where he was the first barman at the immortal La Floridita bar. He passed on in 1967, but the bar remains in the family.

CAFÉ DE LES DELÍCIES Map pp298-9
La Rambla del Raval 47; ⏱ 6pm-2am; Ⓜ Liceu

The oddest thing about this chatty locale is that it incorporates a house within its walls – look up at the internal window shutters and the little rooms they veil. With exposed brick walls and bright lighting, it is an attractive spot for a drink and a yarn. The music is kept nice and low.

Drinking & Nightlife   EL RAVAL

CAFÉ QUE PONE MUEBLES NAVARRO Map pp298-9
Carrer de la Riera Alta 4-6; ☾ 6pm-midnight Tue-Thu & Sun, 6pm-2am Fri & Sat; Ⓜ Sant Antoni
This place is a combined art gallery, lounge and bar where you can get great cheesecake! The café attracts an arty, chilled, studenty kind of crowd into its sprawling innards.

CANGREJO Map pp298-9
☎ 93 301 29 78; Carrer de Montserrat 9; ☾ 9.30pm-1am Sun, Wed & Thu, 9.30pm-3am Fri & Sat; Ⓜ Drassanes
This altar to kitsch, a dingy dance hall that has transgressed since the 1920s, is run by the tumescent underground cabaret figure of Carmen Mairena and exudes a gorgeously tacky feel, especially with the transvestite shows at midnight on Friday and Saturday. It has become so well known to tourists, however, that getting in is all but impossible unless you turn up early.

CASA ALMIRALL Map pp298-9
☎ 93 318 99 17; Carrer de Joaquín Costa 33; ☾ 7pm-2.30am; Ⓜ Universitat
In business since the 1860s, this unchanged corner bar is dark and intriguing, with modernista décor and a mixed clientele. There are some great original pieces in here, like the marble counter and the cast-iron statue of the muse of the Universal Exhibition held in Barcelona in 1888.

CORTO CLUB Map pp298-9
☎ 93 302 27 95; Carrer dels Tallers 68; admission sometimes €5; ☾ 10pm-5am; Ⓜ Universitat
This is one of those rare animals, a late-night bar you can stumble into without the trouble of lining up to enter a club and competing with a stampede of beautiful people. When propping up the long, sociable bar on your right as you enter, you can even hear yourself slur. Music, sometimes live, ranges from funk to bossa nova.

KENTUCKY Map pp298-9
☎ 93 318 28 78; Carrer de l'Arc del Teatre 11; ☾ 10pm-3am Tue-Sat; Ⓜ Liceu
A haunt of visiting US Navy boys, this exercise in smoke-filled Americana kitsch is the perfect way to finish an evening if you can squeeze in. All sorts of odd bods from the *barri* (neighbourhood) and beyond gather. An institution in the wee hours, this place often stays open as late as 5am.

LA CONFITERÍA Map pp298-9
☎ 93 443 04 58; Carrer de Sant Pau 128; ☾ 7am-2am; Ⓜ Paral.lel
This is a trip into the 19th century. Until the 1980s it was a confectioner's shop, and the look of the place has barely changed in its conversion into a laid-back bar. The original cabinets are now lined with booze. A quiet enough spot for a cuppa and chat during the day, it fills with theatre-goers and local partiers later at night.

LA PALOMA Map pp298-9   Club
☎ 93 301 68 97; www.lapaloma-bcn.com; Carrer del Tigre 27; admission €6-10; ☾ midnight-6am Thu-Sat; Ⓜ Sant Antoni
Draped in voluptuous red, this former theatre and still-functioning old-time ballroom (wander by on some afternoons at 6pm and you'll see an impressive queue of older Barcelona folk lining up for a knees-up) metamorphoses into a club later in the night. On Fridays and Saturdays from 2am things heat up with So Rebel Club, which whizzes you from acid through funk and punk to house.

LONDON BAR Map pp298-9
☎ 93 318 52 61; Carrer Nou de la Rambla 34-36; ☾ 7.30pm-5am Tue-Sun; Ⓜ Liceu
This is your best bet if you still need a drink after 3am. Open since 1909, the bar started as a hang-out for circus hands and was later frequented by the likes of Picasso, Miró and Hemingway (didn't he have any work to do?). They sometimes have off-the-wall music acts out the back.

MOOG Map pp298-9   Club
☎ 93 301 72 82; www.masimas.com/moog; Carrer de l'Arc del Teatre 3; admission €9; ☾ midnight-5am; Ⓜ Drassanes
This fun and minuscule club is a standing favourite with the downtown crowd. In the

---

TURNTABLE KINGS
Barcelona is crawling with DJs, some of them local and others passing through. Among the former, David Mas is one of the stars of the moment, regularly spinning his mixes at places like CDLC, Shôko and Sugar Club earlier in the evening and then as often as not winding up at headlining locations such as Discothèque later on. Right up there with him are DJs Jekey, Kefren and Toni Bass, among many others.

London Bar (opposite), El Raval

main downstairs dance area DJs dish out house, techno and electro, while upstairs (our favourite) you can groove to a nice blend of indie and occasional classic pop throwbacks. Very occasionally it gets in a live act too.

RESOLÍS Map pp298-9
☎ 93 441 29 48; Carrer de la Riera Baixa 22; ⏲ 10am-1am Mon-Sat; Ⓜ Liceu
Long a drab old neighbourhood dive, the bar has been resurrected as a tasteful image of its former self. The timber panelling, mirror-back bar and teeny tables all hark back to other times, but without the grime and vein-slitting depression. Drop by for a drink, a couple of limited tapas and occasional live music.

ZENTRAUS Map pp298-9   Club
☎ 93 443 80 78; www.zentraus.com; La Rambla del Raval 41; ⏲ noon-2.30am Tue-Sun; Ⓜ Liceu
After a wee while shut down for want of the right licences, Zentraus is now back in business as a bump-and-grind, semi-subterranean dance club. Light is provided by flickering black-and-white videos and the minimal lamps around the bar required to see what is being served to punters. Drum 'n' bass earlier in the week rises to a deep house crescendo on Saturdays, and drops back into a mellow mix on Sundays.

LA RIBERA

Along and near Passeig del Born, which links Església de Santa Maria del Mar and the former El Born market, you'll find stacks of possibilities. Since the early 1990s, when you could find little more than a couple of sad old bars for sad old punters, the place has been completely transformed.

BODEGA LA TINAJA Map pp302-3
☎ 93 310 22 50; Carrer de l'Esparteria 9; ⏲ 5pm-2am; Ⓜ Barceloneta
Once an old warehouse, this place has been opened up to reveal a towering stone ceiling and arches, filled with atmospheric amphorae. A small candlelit table beneath the brick vaults is a pleasurable place to sip wine and indulge in a few snacks.

FLOW Map pp302-3
☎ 93 310 06 67; Carrer de Fusina 6; ⏲ 8pm-3am Tue-Sun; Ⓜ Jaume I
A touched-up old-time bar, with a mirror ball and a little-used pool table, this is a curious spot for a mixed drink, where you may witness anything from experimental classical music to amateur theatre.

GIMLET Map pp302-3
☎ 93 310 10 27; Carrer del Rec 24; ⏲ 7pm-3am; Ⓜ Jaume I
Transport yourself to a Humphrey Bogart movie. White-jacketed bar staff with all the

appropriate aplomb will whip you up a gimlet or any other classic cocktail (around €6) your heart desires.

LA FIANNA Map pp302-3
☎ 93 315 18 10; Carrer dels Banys Vells 15; ☿ 7-11pm Sun, 7pm-2am Mon-Wed, 7pm-3am Thu-Sat; Ⓜ Jaume I
There is something medieval-Oriental about this bar, with its bare stone walls, forged iron candelabras and cushion-covered lounges. La Fianna has another big selling point – it is one of the only places in Barcelona that does Sunday brunch (from 2pm to 7pm).

LA VINYA DEL SENYOR Map pp302-3
☎ 93 310 33 79; Plaça de Santa Maria del Mar 5; ☿ noon-1am Tue-Sun; Ⓜ Jaume I
Relax on the *terrassa* (terrace), which lies in the shadow of Santa Maria del Mar, or crowd inside at the tiny bar. The wine list is as long as *War and Peace* and there is one table upstairs for those who opt to sample by the bottle rather than the glass.

MAGIC Map pp302-3   Club
☎ 93 310 72 67; Passeig de Picasso 40; ☿ 11pm-5am Wed-Sun; Ⓜ Barceloneta
Although it sometimes has live acts in this sweaty, smoky basement joint, it's basically a straightforward, subterranean dance club offering rock, mainstream dance faves and Spanish pop.

Va de Vi (right), La Ribera

MIRAMELINDO Map pp302-3
☎ 93 319 53 76; Passeig del Born 15; ☿ 8pm-2.30am; Ⓜ Jaume I
A spacious tavern in a Gothic building, this is a classic for mixed drinks; it fills to the brim. Soft jazz and soul sounds float overhead. Try for a comfy seat at a table towards the back.

MUDANZAS Map pp302-3
☎ 93 319 11 37; Carrer de la Vidrieria 15; ☿ 10am-2.30am; Ⓜ Jaume I
This was one of the first bars to get things into gear in El Born and it still attracts a faithful crowd today. It's a straightforward place for a beer, a chat and perhaps a sandwich.

OVER THE CLUB Map pp302-3
☎ 93 268 10 80; Carrer de Fusina 7; ☿ 11pm-3am Thu-Sat; Ⓜ Jaume I
Black lounges and poufs, a separate area with tables for intimate chats, Internet access and a small dance area make up the eclectic presentation of this former games arcade.

VA DE VI Map pp302-3
☎ 93 319 29 00; Carrer dels Banys Vells 16; ☿ 6pm-2am; Ⓜ Jaume I
The wonderful Gothic setting of Va de Vi, all heavy stone arches, is perfect for tasting a broad selection of Spanish wines. You can also order nibbles. •

PORT VELL & LA BARCELONETA
A bevy of bars and clubs are open until the wee hours in the Maremàgnum complex. In July and August the place is particularly popular. Possibilities range from Irish pubs to salsa spots…otherwise a couple of notable targets await in or around La Barceloneta.

DAGUIRI Map pp302-3
☎ 93 221 51 09; Carrer de Grau i Torras 59; ☿ 11am-1am Thu-Mon; Ⓜ Barceloneta, ᰡ 45, 57, 59 & 157
Guiri (foreigner) by name, *guiri* by clientele. Foreigners who have found seaside nirvana in Barcelona hang out in this chilled bar back from the beach. A curious crowd of

(Continued on page 179)

1 *The monumental* cascada *in Parc de la Ciutadella (p97)* 2 *The gardens of Castell de Montjuïc (p119)* 3 *The leafy cloister of La Catedral (p84)*

1 *The classic Café de l'Òpera (p143), La Rambla* 2 *Pintxos at Centre Cultural Euskal Etxea (p148), La Ribera* 3 *Mercat de la Boqueria (p141) is home to countless varieties of meat, seafood, vegetables and sweets* 4 *Seafood on sale at the bustling Mercat de la Boqueria (p141)* 5 *J Murrià (p208) has been supplying speciality food goods for over a century* 6 *Sweet temptations at Xocoa (p204), Barri Gòtic* 7 *És (p146) specialises in Mediterranean cuisine*

1 *Els Quatre Gats (p143), the former hang-out of the luminaries of modernisme*
2 *The gay-friendly Schilling bar (p166), Barri Gòtic* **3** *El Raval's classic Bar Marsella (p167) specialises in absinthe*

1 *A salsa band performs at La Paloma (p168), El Raval* **2** *The rhythms of traditional flamenco at Tablao Cordobés (p194), La Rambla* **3** *Jazz and blues feature at Jamboree (p189), Barri Gòtic*

1 *Designer homewares on display at Vinçon (p209), l'Eixample* **2** *Women's fashion at world-renowned Mango (p209), l'Eixample* **3** *Window display at cosmopolitan Custo Barcelona (p205), La Ribera* **4** *Shoppers rummage for treasure at Els Encants Vells market (p208), l'Eixample*

1 *Supporters of premier side FC Barcelona (p16) can show their true colours* **2** *Riding the Ferris wheel, l'arc d'Atraccions (p115), Tibidabo* **3** *Barcelona's grand old opera house, Gran Teatre del Liceu (p83), La Rambla*

1 *The mountain peaks of Montserrat (p234), home to the Black Madonna* **2** *Dalí's bedroom, Teatre-Museu Dalí (p232), Figueres* **3** *The magical seaside town of Cadaqués (p238) was an old stomping ground of Dalí* **4** *The well-preserved Amfiteatre Romà (p243), Tarragona*

(Continued from page 170)

TOP FIVE CLUBS

- La Paloma (p168)
- Otto Zutz (p184)
- Space (p185)
- Sutton the Club (p184)
- Terrrazza (p186)

crusties and switched-on dudes chat over light meals and a beer at black-white-red *trencadís*-style tables or relaxing outside over a late breakfast.

LE KASBAH Map pp302-3
☎ 626 561309; Plaça de Pau Vila s/n; ☽ 11pm-3am Wed-Sun; Ⓜ Barceloneta
From the narghiles to the Moroccan furniture, everything here is designed to induce a chilled feel, aided by the slow music. On warmer nights you may prefer the *terrassa*.

SUGAR CLUB Map pp290-1
☎ 93 508 83 25; Moll de Barcelona; ☽ 11pm-3am Wed-Sat; Ⓜ Drassanes
Set inside the World Trade Center, this is a dapper restaurant-club with DJ sounds and a snappily dressed crowd. The food is fusion funky and skipped without remorse, but the music served up can be top class, with such local DJs at the turntables as David Mas.

VAIXELL LUZ DE GAS Map pp302-3
☎ 93 209 77 11; moored on Moll del Dipósit; ☽ noon-3am May-Oct; Ⓜ Barceloneta
Sit on the top deck of this boat and let go of the day's cares. Sip wine or beer, nibble tapas and admire the yachts. On shore they play some good dance music at night.

PORT OLÍMPIC, EL POBLENOU & EL FÒRUM

All the beaches have at least one *chiringuito*, a beach bar that in summer can stay open until 1am. The Port Olímpic yacht harbour is lined with brassy bars and clubs, all a bit touristy and tacky but can be fun in their own rough way. In summer 2006 a series of seasonal bars and clubs (some closing at

5am), the Carpes del Fòrum, set up in the Fòrum area just back from the waterfront, adding a whole new nightlife dimension to the city. If the experiment works, they could become a permanent feature of Barcelona's summer scene.

Inland, the old industrial district of El Poblenou is grittier, with a handful of places worth experiencing, including one of the city's music and dance meccas, Razzmatazz.

BAJA BEACH CLUB Map pp302-3   Club
☎ 93 225 91 00; www.bajabeach.com; Passeig Marítim de la Barceloneta 34; ☽ 1pm-5am Thu-Sun; Ⓜ Ciutadella Villa Olímpica
Unashamedly tacky, big and boisterous, this is the all-drinking, all-dancing seaside dance club where you can be beautiful or not. It doesn't really matter. The surf theme, with gogo boys and girls, a rush of mainstream rock and pop and streams of locals and out-of-towners make this mad meat market a fun, if not overly classy, night out.

CATWALK Map pp302-3   Club
☎ 93 221 61 61; Carrer de Ramon Trias Fargas s/n; admission €15; ☽ midnight-6am Thu-Sun; Ⓜ Ciutadella Villa Olímpica
A well-dressed crowd piles in here for good, danceable house, occasionally mellowed down with more body-hugging electro and funk. Alternatively, you can sink into a fat lounge for a quiet tipple and whisper. Sunday nights is house night with Silicon.

CDLC Map pp302-3
☎ 93 224 04 70; Passeig Marítim de la Barceloneta 32; ☽ noon-3am; Ⓜ Ciutadella Villa Olímpica
Seize the night by the scruff at the Carpe Diem Lounge Club, where you can lounge

NOT QUITE AS CHEAP AS CHIPS

The Baja Beach Club has brought clubbing and the 21st century into harmony, offering punters the €125 option of having a tiny chip implanted under the skin for use as ID and payment. So long as you have charged the chip with dosh, no need to take your purse to the Baja Beach Club. A doctor implants the chip with a simple injection, and it can be easily removed too. Something of a club gimmick, plenty of punters have opted for it. As the promoters say, nowadays everyone has piercings and tattoos, so why not a little chip too?

in semi-Oriental surrounds. Ideal for a slow warm-up before heading to the nearby clubs, if you can be bothered lifting yourself back up onto your feet, that is.

RAZZMATAZZ Map pp290-1   Club

☎ 93 272 09 10; Carrer dels Almogàvers 122 or Carrer de Pamplona 88; admission €15; ☽ 1-6am Fri & Sat; Ⓜ Marina or Bogatell

No fewer than five different clubs in one huge space make this one of the most popular dance destinations in town. The main space, the Razz Club, is a haven for timeless rock and indie music. The Loft does house and electronic dance music, while the Pop Bar offers anything from garage to soul. The Lolita room is the land of techno pop and deep house, while upstairs in the Rex Room guys and gals sweat it out to high rhythm electro-rock.

SHÔKO Map pp302-3

☎ 93 225 92 03; www.shoko.biz; Passeig Marítim de la Barceloneta 36; ☽ midnight-3am Wed-Sun; Ⓜ Ciutadella Villa Olímpica

Too cool for anything really, let alone school, this chilled restaurant and bar is all far-out concepts. Wafting over your mixed Asian-Med food is an opiate mix of Shinto music and Japanese electro. As the food is cleared away, the place turns into a funky beat kinda place, into which you may or may not penetrate without dinner depending on the bouncers' mood.

L'EIXAMPLE

Much of middle-class l'Eixample is dead at night, but several streets are exceptions. Noisy Carrer de Balmes is lined with a rowdy adolescent set. Much more interesting is the phalanx of locales lining Carrer d'Aribau between Avinguda Diagonal and Carrer de Mallorca. They range from quiet cocktail bars to '60s retro. Lower down, on and around Carrer del Consell de Cent and Carrer de la Diputació, is where the heart of Gaixample beats, with several gay bars and clubs (see the boxed text, right).

AIRE Map pp294-5   Club

☎ 93 487 83 42; Carrer de València 236; ☽ 11.30pm-3am Thu-Sat, 6-10pm Sun; Ⓜ Passeig de Gràcia

A popular dance locale for lesbians, also known as Sala Diana. The dance floor is

spacious and there is usually a DJ in command of the tunes. Some gay men sneak in to this club too, along with a growing trickle of heteros, except on Sundays, when it's strictly gals only.

ANTILLA BCN Map pp296-7   Club

☎ 93 451 45 64; www.antillasalsa.com; Carrer d'Aragó; ☽ 11pm-5am; Ⓜ Urgell

The salsateca in town, this is the place to come for Cuban *son*, merengue, salsa and a whole lot more. If you don't know how to dance any of this, you may feel a little silly (as a bloke) but will probably get free lessons (if you're a lass). The blokes can come back at another time and pay for lessons (see p257).

ARENA Map pp298-9   Club

☎ 93 487 83 42; Carrer de Balmes 32; admission €5-10; ☽ midnight-5am; Ⓜ Passeig de Gràcia

Popular with a young gay crowd, Arena is one of the top clubs in town for boys seeking boys. Keep an eye out for drag shows on Wednesdays and handbag nights on Thursdays.

ARENA CLASIC Map pp298-9   Club

☎ 93 487 83 42; Carrer de la Diputació 233; admission €5-10; ☽ 12.30-5am Fri & Sat; Ⓜ Passeig de Gràcia

Around the corner from Arena, this place is a little more sedate than its partner, and tends to get more of a mixed crowd.

ASTORIA Map pp294-5   Club

☎ 93 414 47 99; Carrer de París 193-197; ☽ 10pm-3am Mon-Sat; Ⓜ Diagonal

Reds and black dominate the colour scheme in this wonderful former cinema. Beautiful people gather here to drink, dance a little and eye one another up. Some come a little earlier for a bite to eat. What is odd about this club is the early closing time.

ÁTAME Map pp296-7 Club

☎ 93 454 92 73; Carrer del Consell de Cent 257;
🕒 8pm-2.30am; Ⓜ Universitat

Cool for a coffee in the early evening, Átame (Tie Me Up) heats up later in the night as the gay crowd comes out to play. There is usually a raunchy show on Friday night.

BACON BEAR Map pp296-7

Carrer de Casanova 64; 🕒 6pm-2.30am; Ⓜ Urgell

Every bear needs a cave to go to, and this is a rather friendly one. It's really just a big bar for burly gay folk. Thursday night from 7pm to 10pm is happy hour and on weekends the music cranks up enough for a bit of bear-hugging twirl.

BERLIN Map p292

☎ 93 200 65 42; Carrer de Muntaner 240;
🕒 10am-1.30am Mon-Wed, 10am-3am Thu-Sat;
Ⓜ Diagonal or Hospital Clínic

This elegant corner chill-out space offers views over Avinguda Diagonal. There is a cluster of tables outside on the 1st floor, and designer lounges downstairs. Punters tend to be beautiful (or at least think they are), but there's a relaxed feel about the place and all ages snuggle in well. Many kick on to Luz de Gas, virtually next door, afterwards.

BIKINI Map pp296-7 Club

☎ 93 322 00 05; www.bikinibcn.com; Carrer de Déu i Mata 105; admission €14; 🕒 midnight-5am Wed-Sun; Ⓜ Entença or 🚌 6, 7, 33, 34, 63, 67 or 68

Three main spaces define this, one of the grand old stars of the Barcelona nightlife scene. Every possible kind of music gets a run here, depending on the space you choose and the night. From Latin and Brazilian hip-jigglers to 1980s disco, from funk to hip-hop, it all happens here.

BÚCARO Map p292 Club

☎ 93 209 65 62; Carrer d'Aribau 195; admission Fri & Sat €10; 🕒 11pm-3.30am Sun-Wed, 11pm-5am Thu-Sat; Ⓜ Diagonal

You can take a 'quiet' drink while sitting on the lounges and tables scattered in front of the long, low-lit bar, but you might still find it hard to hear yourself over the music pounding out of the dance areas out the back and upstairs. The great thing about this place is there's no cover charge during the week and a relaxed attitude to letting people in.

CITY HALL Map pp298-9 Club

☎ 93 238 07 22; La Rambla de Catalunya 2-4; admission €12; 🕒 midnight-5.30am Wed-Sun; Ⓜ Catalunya

A corridor leads to the dance floor of this place, which has had uneven fortunes. House and other electric sounds dominate, including a rather forward-sounding session of 'electro clash' called *Fucked!* on Wednesdays. Look forward to deep house on Saturdays and the more chilled Zen Club, an electronic session on Sundays.

DIETRICH GAY TEATRO CAFÉ Map pp296-7

☎ 93 451 77 07; Carrer del Consell de Cent 255;
🕒 10.30pm-3am; Ⓜ Universitat

It's show time at 1am, with at least one drag-queen gala a night in this cabaret-style locale dedicated to Marlene Dietrich. Soft house is the main musical motif and the place has an interior garden.

DISTRITO DIAGONAL Map pp294-5 Club

Avinguda Diagonal 442; admission after 4am €15;
🕒 10pm-4am Wed & Thu, 10pm-8am Fri & Sat;
Ⓜ Diagonal

Slip into the red, the dominating hue here. A huddle of tables offers quiet time at the front of this club. To move your booty, slide past the long bar to the raised dance area out the back. On weekends all sorts of strange nocturnal beasts wind up in this, one of the precious few locations available to all-nighter drinkers. After all, it's open even after most clubs have turfed out their punters!

DRY MARTINI Map pp294-5

☎ 93 217 50 72; Carrer d'Aribau 162-166; 🕒 1pm-2am Sun-Thu, 1pm-3am Fri & Sat; 🚈 FGC Provença

White-jacketed waiters with a whisper of a discreetly knowing smile will attend to your cocktail needs here. The house tipple, taken at the timber-lined bar or in one of the plush green leather lounges, is a safe bet. The gin and tonic comes in an enormous mug-sized glass – a couple of these and you're well on the way! Out the back is the Speakeasy restaurant (p156).

GALERÍA GASTRONÓMICA Map pp294-5

☎ 93 298 87 30: Passatge de la Concepció 7;
🕒 9pm-3am; Ⓜ Passeig de Gràcia

To some it's a rather pricey Italian restaurant, to others a place to sip on a drink and admire the art on the walls. It is all of these things, but comes into its own as a cocktail stop on a busy night's bar hopping. On the menu, a selection of Italian and Spanish wines and generous, colourful cocktails. Downstairs is a modest dance space and the whole place is laced with sculptures by Lorenzo Quinn, son of the actor Anthony.

LA BASE Map p292 — Club

Carrer de Casanova 201; 11pm-3am Mon-Thu, midnight-5am Fri & Sat, 8pm-3am Sun; **M** Hospital Clínic

This heavy, heated gay bar and club has something for just about everyone: nude nights, rude nights, leather cruising evenings and dark rooms. There's even music!

LA CAMA 54 Map pp296-7

93 325 91 20; **Carrer de Sepúlveda 178;** 6pm-3am Tue-Sat, 5.45-11am Sat & Sun; **M** Urgell

Welcome to the city's cheerful, gay karaoke bar, a curious place that attracts a very mixed crowd in terms of age and sexual orientation. The biggest attraction is its dawn sessions on Saturday and Sunday mornings, perfect if you want to kick on after the clubs.

CHILLIN' ON THE BEACH

Summer lounging on the beaches of Barcelona is not just about towels on the sand. Scattered along Barcelona's beaches is a series of hip little beach bars bringing chilled club sounds to the seaside. Sip on your favourite cocktail as you take in the last rays of the day. And there's no need to head straight home at sundown, as these places keep humming until 1am (Easter to October). On Platja de Sant Miquel there is a good one, the **Chiringuito de Barceloneta** (Map pp302–3; www.chiringuito-barceloneta.com). Northeast of Port Olímpic on Platja de Bogatell are three spots, among them the magnetic Chiringuito del Escribà and gay-oriented El Deseo de Lorenzo. One of the most popular is **Mochima** (Map pp290–1; 679 888836; www.mochimabar.com). By far the best beach booty experience takes place outside Barcelona, a train ride to the northeast in Mataró. There, head for **Lasal** (www.lasal.com; May-Sep) on Platja Sant Simó, with top local DJs, food and a great party atmosphere.

LA FIRA Map pp294-5 — Club

Carrer de Provença 171; admission €8-12; 11pm-5am; **FGC** Provença

A designer bar with a difference. You wander in past distorting mirrors and ancient fairground attractions from Germany. Put in coins and listen to hens squawk. Speaking of squawking, the music swings wildly from '90s hits to Spanish pop classics.

LES GENS QUE J'AIME Map pp294-5

93 215 68 79; **Carrer de València 286;** 6pm-2.30am; **M** Passeig de Gràcia

This intimate relic of the 1960s follows a deceptively simple formula: chilled jazz music in the background, minimal lighting from an assortment of flea-market lamps and a cosy, cramped scattering of red velvet-backed lounges around tiny dark tables.

LUZ DE GAS Map p292 — Club

93 209 77 11; www.luzdegas.com; **Carrer de Muntaner 244-246; admission up to €15;** midnight-5am; **M** Diagonal then 6, 7, 15, 27, 32, 33, 34, 58 or 64

Set in a grand theatre that is frequently the scene of live acts (see p189), this club attracts a crowd of well-dressed beautiful people whose tastes in music vary according to the night: soul on Thursday, rock on Friday, and '60s on Saturday, to name a few. It gets a little sweatier in the dedicated club room Sala B, which opens on Friday and Saturday nights only.

METRO Map pp298-9 — Club

93 323 52 27; www.metrodiscobcn.com; **Carrer de Sepúlveda 185;** midnight-5am; **M** Universitat

Metro attracts a casual gay crowd with its two dance floors, three bars and very dark room. Check out the porn on the toilet walls, and watch for shows and parties, which can range from parades of models to bingo nights (with interesting prizes).

MICHAEL COLLINS PUB Map pp294-5

93 459 19 64; **Plaça de la Sagrada Família 4;** noon-3am; **M** Sagrada Família

Locals and expats alike patronise this place, one of the city's best-loved Irish pubs. To be sure of a little Catalan-Irish *craic,* this barn-sized and storming pub's the ticket.

NEW CHAPS Map pp294-5   Club
☎ 93 215 53 65; Avinguda Diagonal 395; ☾ 9pm-3am; Ⓜ Diagonal

Leather lovers get in some close-quarters inspection on the dance floor and more, especially in the dark room, downstairs past the fairly dark loos in the vaulted cellars.

PREMIER Map pp294-5
☎ 93 532 16 50; Carrer de Provença 236; ☾ 9am-2.30am; Ⓡ FGC Provença

A little cross-pollination has happened in this funky little French-run cocktail bar. The wine list is almost exclusively French, but you can opt for that resurrected Barcelona brew, Moritz or a *mojito*. Hug the bar, sink into a lounge or hide up on the mezzanine. Or pop by for breakfast!

QUILOMBO Map pp294-5
☎ 93 439 54 06; Carrer d'Aribau 149; ☾ 7pm-2.30am daily Jun-Sep, Wed-Sun Oct-May; Ⓡ FGC Provença

Some formulas just work, and this place has been working since the 1970s. Set up a few guitars in the back room, which you jam with tables and chairs, add some cheapish pre-prepared *mojitos* (€5) and plastic tubs of nuts, and let the punters do the rest. They pour in, creating plenty of *quilombo* (fuss).

SALVATION Map pp298-9   Club
☎ 93 318 06 86; Ronda de Sant Pere 19-21; ☾ midnight-5am Fri-Sun; Ⓜ Urquinaona

Beautiful boys and fluttering fag hags crowd in here, where the sexy barmen will warm the hearts of some, and the occasional naughty show will do the rest. House hammers in one area, while DJs spin a broader mix in the other.

SWEET CAFÉ Map pp296-7
Carrer de Casanova 75; ☾ 8pm-2.30am Tue-Thu & Sun, 8pm-3am Fri & Sat; Ⓜ Urgell

It's like the lining inside a long illuminated stick of fluorescent lipstick-red candy in this tunnel of a bar. Gay-friendly in the Gaixample, but open to all and sundry, it occasionally hosts a little live music, expositions and other events. On Thursday nights you can catch some electropop fun with Sweet Popcorn.

TIPPLES WITHIN ELEVATOR DISTANCE OF YOUR ROOM

Hotel bars traditionally made for a rather sad night out but some establishments are changing all that. So much so that locals like to hang out in some of them too! Among those well worth seeking out are the ground-floor lounge bar in **Hotel Omm** (p221), the East 47 bar and rooftop terrace bar-restaurant at the **Hotel Claris** (p222), the too-cool-for-school gay-leaning options (the Chillout cocktail bar and the summer rooftop skybar) at **Hotel Axel** (p222) and the poolside rooftop cocktail bar at **Hotel Majèstic** (p222). Hotel Omm also hosts the **Ommsession Club** (☎ 93 445 40 00; ☾ 11.30pm-3am), a smallish but *fashion* dance venue.

TOSCANO ANTICO Map pp294-5
☎ 93 225 50 91; Carrer d'Aribau 167; cocktails €6-8; ☾ 8pm-2am Tue-Sat; Ⓜ Diagonal

Bored with running the family Tuscan restaurant in Milan, the young Italian owners of Toscano have transported the classy Milanese *aperitivo* (apéritif) to Barcelona, mixing it with local energy. On the bar are snacks *alla Milanese,* to be taken (free) with generous cocktails. Let the barmen fix you a special, unlisted concoction.

VELVET Map pp294-5   Club
☎ 93 217 67 14; Carrer de Balmes 161; ☾ 10.30pm-5am; Ⓜ Diagonal

A smallish, designer bar and club inspired by the film *Blue Velvet,* with a mix of music from the 1960s to the 1980s. Try not to slip on the shiny arched walkway from the door into the heart of the club (is this a drink test?). The back end is one long curving bar. It is busy with a mostly straight crowd in the lurid, bluish lighting.

ZSA ZSA Map pp294-5
☎ 93 454 72 59; Carrer de Rosselló 156; ☾ 8pm-3.30am Tue-Sat; Ⓜ Hospital Clínic

A designer classic of the late 1980s, this place has made a comeback. Behind the bar is an impressive line-up of back-lit brews. Scattered about are high tables and stools. This is the kind of place you might easily strike up a conversation, although they need to turn the Depeche Mode and other '80s hits down a tad.

GRÀCIA & PARK GÜELL

Gràcia is a quirky place. In many ways it's its own world, with rowdy beer-swillers and trendy music bars, places where time stands still and a couple of the city's big clubs. A sprinkling of gay bars also lurks up here.

ALFA Map pp294-5
☎ 93 415 18 24; Carrer Gran de Gràcia 36; ⏳ 11pm-3.30am Thu-Sat; Ⓜ Diagonal
Aficionados of good old-fashioned rock with a mix of '90s hits love this unchanging bar-cum–miniature disco, a Gràcia classic. Take up a stool for a drink and chat or head for the no-frills dance area just beyond.

BAR CANIGÓ Map pp294-5
☎ 93 213 30 49; Carrer de Verdi 2; ⏳ 5pm-2am Mon-Thu, 5pm-3am Fri & Sat; Ⓜ Fontana
Especially welcoming in winter, this corner bar looking onto Plaça de la Revolució de Setembre de 1868 is an animated spot to simply sip on an Estrella beer around rickety old marble-top tables, much as people have done here for decades. There's also a pool table.

CAFÉ DEL SOL Map pp294-5
☎ 93 415 56 63; Plaça del Sol 16; ⏳ 1pm-2.30am; Ⓜ Fontana
This lively bar is on one of Gràcia's liveliest squares, with a boho and grunge set mixing freely over a beer inside or, especially on languid summer evenings, on the terrace. It has been here forever and seems likely to remain for as long.

MARIA Map pp294-5
Carrer de Maria 5; ⏳ 9pm-3am; Ⓜ Diagonal
Even the music hasn't changed since this place got going in the late 1970s. Those longing for rock 'n' roll crowd into this animated bar, listen to old hits and knock back beers.

MARTIN'S Map pp294-5 Club
☎ 93 218 71 67; Passeig de Gràcia 130; ⏳ midnight-5am; Ⓜ Diagonal
Martin's is for gay men only. It's not quite the daring place it once was – after all, how risqué can a gay bar get nowadays? But local gay folk of all ages feel comfortable here and there's plenty of opportunity for a grope in the dark room.

OTTO ZUTZ Map p292 Club
☎ 93 238 07 22; Carrer de Lincoln 15; admission €15; ⏳ midnight-5.30am Tue-Sat; Ⓡ FGC Gràcia
Beautiful people only need apply for entry to this three-floor dance den. Downstairs, shake it all up to house, or head upstairs for funk and soul. DJs come from the Ibiza rave mould and the top floor is for VIPs (although at some ill-defined point in the evening the barriers all seem to come down). Friday is hip-hop night.

RAÏM Map pp294-5
Carrer de Progrés 34; ⏳ 1pm-2am; Ⓜ Diagonal
The walls in Raïm are plastered with black-and-white photos of Cubans and Cuba. Tired old wooden chairs of another epoch huddle around marble tables. Grand old timber-lined mirrors hang from the walls. They just don't make old Spanish taverns like this anymore.

SABOR CUBANO Map pp294-5
☎ 600 262003; Carrer de Francisco Giner 32; ⏳ 10pm-2.30am Mon-Sat; Ⓜ Diagonal
Ruled since 1992 by the charismatic Havana-born Angelito is this home of *ron y son* (rum and sound). A mixed crowd of Cubans and fans of the Caribbean island come to drink *mojitos* and shake their stuff.

SUTTON THE CLUB Map pp294-5 Club
☎ 93 414 42 17; www.thesuttonclub.com; Carrer de Tuset 13; admission €12; ⏳ 11.30pm-6am Tue-Sat; Ⓜ Diagonal
A classic disco with mainstream sounds on the main floor, some hopping house in a side bar and a fair spread of beautiful folks, this place inevitably attracts just about everyone pouring in and out of the nearby bars at some stage of the evening. The main dance floor is akin to a writhing bear pit. Jump in!

LA ZONA ALTA

North of Avinguda Diagonal the *pijos* (cashed-up mamma's boys and papa's gals) are in charge. Whether you sample the bars of Carrer de Marià Cubí or try the clubs around Carrer d'Aribau or Tibidabo, expect to be confronted by beautiful people who drive Pajeros and Audis. What do you care? The eye candy often more than compensates for the snobbery. Late-night transport to some clubs (such as Mirablau and Rosebud) is easiest by taxi.

BOCAYMA Map p292

☎ 93 237 94 08; Carrer de l'Avenir 50; ☽ 11pm-2am Tue-Wed, 11pm-3am Thu-Sat; ☒ FGC Muntaner

One of the best meeting places in this chi-chi uptown bar zone, Bocayma starts in fairly quiet fashion with people gathered around its little tables. After midnight the music takes off and punters rev up for an outing to nearby clubs. It often opens beyond its official hours.

ELEPHANT Map pp290-1   Club

☎ 93 334 02 58; www.elephantbcn.com; Passeig dels Til.lers 1; admission Wed, Thu & Sun free, Fri & Sat €15; ☽ 11pm-3am Wed, 11pm-5am Thu-Sun; Ⓜ Palau Reial

Getting in here is like being invited to some Beverley Hills private party. Models and wannabes mix with immaculately groomed lads who most certainly didn't come by taxi. A big tent-like dance space is the main game here, but punters smooth their way around a series of garden bars in summer too.

MAS I MAS Map p292

☎ 93 209 45 02; www.masimas.com; Carrer de Marià Cubí 199; ☽ 7pm-2.30am; ☒ FGC Muntaner

This is one of the area's best-known drinkeries (this street is lined with bars that really happen on the weekend) and a refreshing change from the usual uptown beautiful-people scene. Punters of all descriptions squeeze in here to enjoy a bit of highly danceable soul, funk and light rock.

MIRABLAU Map pp290-1   Club

☎ 93 418 58 79; Plaça del Doctor Andreu; ☽ 11am-5am

Gaze out over the entire city below from this privileged balcony restaurant on the way up to Tibidabo. Wander downstairs to join the beautiful folk in the squeeze-me small dance space. In summer you can step out on to the even tinier terrace for a breather.

ROSEBUD Map pp290-1   Club

☎ 93 418 88 85; Carrer d'Adrià Margarit 27; ☽ 11pm-4am Wed-Thu, 11pm-5am Fri & Sat

Inspired in name only by the film *Citizen Kane*, Rosebud is an assault on the senses, with blaring music (mostly 1980s and 1990s) and flashing lights. Go-go dancers keep punters in rhythm and from Tibidabo it looks like an enormous glasshouse. Those under 30-something may find it a little, well, 'old'.

MAKING A SPLASH

Guys and gals board their metal steeds on hot summer nights to bear down on one of the top outdoor club scenes in town, or out of town, since it's in neighbouring L'Hospitalet de Llobregat. **Liquid** (☎ 670 221209; www.liquidbcn.com; Complex Esportiu Hospitalet Nord, Carrer de Manuel Azaña; ☽ Jun-Sep) says what it is. A palm-studded islet is surrounded by a bottom-lit azure moat that tempts surprisingly few folks to plunge in while dancing the night away in this mega-club. Local and foreign DJs keep the punters, a mixed crowd from all over town, in the groove in a series of different internal spaces, as well as poolside.

SANTS & LES CORTS

With the exception of one year-round venue and occasional temporary tent clubs set up in the area around Camp Nou in summer, this is largely a dead zone.

PACHÁ Map pp290-1   Club

☎ 93 334 32 33; www.clubpachabcn.com; Avinguda del Doctor Gregorio Marañón 17; admission €15; ☽ midnight-6am Thu-Sat, 10pm-2am Sun; Ⓜ Palau Reial

A huge metallic dance hall with raised sides (the better to observe the gyrating fauna from), a back bar and an Ibiza import on Sunday night with its Sun Down sessions make up the offerings of this Spain-wide club classic.

SPACE Map pp296-7   Club

☎ 93 426 84 44; www.spacebarcelona.com; Carrer de Tarragona 141; admission €15; ☽ midnight-5am Fri & Sat; Ⓜ Maria Cristina

Inspired by the eponymous mega-club in Ibiza, this is one of the big-hitters with the beautiful dancers. House is the main baseline in this sprawling designer club where the nights can get rather hot and scantily clad. Sunday night (from 8pm) is Gay Day.

UP & DOWN Map pp290-1   Club

☎ 93 205 51 94; Carrer de Numància 179; admission €15; ☽ 11pm-5am Tue-Sat; Ⓜ Maria Cristina

An uptown club that, as its name suggests, has its ups and downs. Upstairs is more for drinking and (if you can) talking over revival music while downstairs you can dance to a fairly mainstream mix of international music. Lighting effects are very passé but this place gets packed early in the week when other venues can be a bit limp.

MONTJUÏC & POBLE SEC

A couple of curious bars in Poble Sec (literally 'Dry Town'!) make a good prelude to the clubs that hold sway up in the wonderfully weird fantasy world of the Poble Espanyol. There are also a few clubs on the lower end of Avinguda del Paral.lel worth seeking out.

BARCELONA ROUGE Map pp304-5
☎ 93 442 49 85; Carrer del Poeta Cabanyes 21; ⏱ 11pm-3am Tue-Sat; Ⓜ Poble Sec
Decadence is the word that springs to mind in this bordello-red lounge–cocktail bar, with acid jazz, drum 'n' bass and other soothing sounds drifting along in the background.

MAUMAU UNDERGROUND Map pp304-5
☎ 93 441 80 15; www.maumaunderground.com; Carrer de la Fontrodona 33; ⏱ 11pm-2.30am Thu & Sun, 11pm-3am Fri & Sat; Ⓜ Paral.lel
Funk, soul, hip-hop, you never know what you might run into in this popular little Poble Sec music and dance haunt. Above the backlit bar a huge screen spews forth psychedelic images, which contribute to the relaxed, chilled lounge effect.

SALA APOLO Map pp304-5   Club
☎ 93 441 40 01; www.sala-apolo.com; Carrer Nou de la Rambla 113; admission €6-12; ⏱ 12.30am-5am Wed-Sat, 10.30pm-3.30am Sun; Ⓜ Paral.lel
A fine old theatre where red velvet dominates, and you feel you could be in a movie-set dance-hall scene starring Eliot Ness. The scene changes regularly. The Nitsa team provides house, techno and break-beat sounds on the weekend. On Thursday night it's the Powder Room, with funk and rare grooves.

TERRRAZZA Map pp304-5   Club
☎ 93 423 12 85; Avinguda del Marquès de Comillas s/n; admission €18; ⏱ midnight-7am Fri & Sat May-Oct; Ⓜ Espanya
This is one of the most popular summertime dance locations, inside the fantasy land of Poble Espanyol. This outdoor club attracts bright young things from around the city for Ibiza-style nights of pure hedonism. Wacky dress or undress rules and the main danger is indeed not passing bouncers' muster. If you're in, you're in for a wild night.

TINTA ROJA Map pp304-5
☎ 93 443 32 43; Carrer de la Creu dels Molers 17; ⏱ 8pm-1am Wed & Thu, 8pm-3am Fri & Sat, 7pm-midnight Sun; Ⓜ Poble Sec
A succession of nooks and crannies, dotted with what could be a flea market's collection of furnishings, dimly lit in violets, reds and yellows, makes the 'Red Ink' an intimate spot for a drink and the occasional show in the back – with anything from actors to acrobats.

Entertainment

Entertainment

There is never a shortage of things to do in Barcelona. Top international acts from rock bands to major orchestras visit the city, and there is plenty going on locally in between. Year-round you can catch anything from a jazz session to a lavish opera, from an underground rockabilly show to the Stones. The theatre scene is busy with local productions, and if you're lucky you'll be in town when local loonies La Fura dels Baus are in action. Spanish contemporary dance is at its best in Barcelona, and flamenco also has its place here. A surprising number of cinemas put on subtitled films in the original version.

Sport lovers are spoiled for choice. You can see some of the best football in the world with local champions FC Barcelona, or indulge in your own activities, from swimming and other water sports to a workout in the gym.

To keep up with what's on, start with the weekly listings magazine *Guía del Ocio* (€1) from newsstands. For the club and bar music scene, keep an eye out for free magazines like *Go, Metropolitan, Mondo Sonoro* and the rivers of fliers that flow through many bars. Online, check out www.lecool.com, www.salirenbarcelona.com, www.barcelonarocks.com, www.clubbingspain.com and www.festivales.com.

The daily papers are good for cinema listings and the **Palau de la Virreina arts information office** (Map pp298–9; ☎ 93 301 77 75; La Rambla de Sant Josep 99; ☻ 10am-8pm Mon-Sat, 11am-3pm Sun; Ⓜ Liceu) has oodles of information on theatre, opera, classical music and more.

Tickets & Reservations

The easiest way to get hold of tickets *(entradas)* for most venues throughout the city is through the Caixa de Catalunya's **Tel-Entrada** (☎ 902 101212; www.telentrada.com) service or **ServiCaixa** (☎ 902 332211; www.servicaixa.com in Catalan & Spanish). Another one to try for concerts is **Tick Tack Ticket** (☎ 902 105025; www.ticktackticket.com). There's a ticket office *(venta de localidades)* on the ground floor of the **El Corte Inglés** (☎ 902 400222; www.el corteingles.es/entradas in Spanish) on Plaça de Catalunya and at some of its other branches around town (you can also buy tickets through El Corte Inglés by phone and online), and at the FNAC store on the same square.

You can purchase some half-price tickets at the Caixa de Catalunya desk in the tourist office (Plaça de Catalunya). To qualify, you must purchase the tickets in person no more than three hours before the start of the show you wish to see. The system is known as Tiquet-3.

For cinema bookings, see p191.

LIVE MUSIC

Barely a night goes by without an orchestra, ensemble or band filling the night air with the sounds of anything from world music and jazz to Wagner. A circuit of well-established jazz clubs is always busy, several grand theatres host classical music concerts regularly and bands, local and international, turn up in clubs around the city.

Jazz fans are also in for a treat in November, when the city's annual jazz festival is staged in bars across the city (see p13).

Start time for bands is rarely before 10pm. Admission charges range from nothing to €20 – the higher prices often include a drink. Note that some of the clubs listed in the Drinking & Nightlife chapter, such as La Paloma, sometimes stage concerts. Quite a few bars also occasionally have live music, and some of these are noted in the Drinking & Nightlife chapter.

Institutions as diverse as CaixaForum (p118), the Fundació Joan Miró (p120), La Casa Elizalde (p81), the Centre de Cultura Contemporània de Barcelona (CCCB; p92), Museu d'Art Contemporani de Barcelona (Macba; p92) and La Pedrera (p105) stage concerts of varying types, from world music to blues, from classical to *klezmer* (Jewish music).

To see big-name acts, either Spanish or from abroad, you will pay more and probably wind up at venues such as the 17,000-capacity Palau Sant Jordi on Montjuïc, the Teatre Mercat de les Flors or the Fòrum. Truly big acts play in the Estadi Olímpic.

BIKINI Map pp296-7

☎ 93 322 08 00; www.bikinibcn.com; Carrer de Déu i Mata 105; admission €10-20; ⏰ midnight-5am Wed Sun; Ⓜ Entença or 🚌 6, 7, 33, 34, 63, 67 or 68

This multi-hall dance space frequently stages quality acts, local and foreign, ranging from funk guitar to rock most nights of the week. Performances generally start around 9pm or 10pm (the club doesn't happen until midnight). This place has been keeping the beat in Barcelona since the darkest days of Franco.

HARLEM JAZZ CLUB Map pp298-9

☎ 93 310 07 55; Carrer de la Comtessa de Sobradiel 8; admission up to €10; ⏰ 8pm-4am Tue-Thu & Sun, 8pm-5am Fri & Sat; Ⓜ Drassanes

This narrow, smoky, old-town dive is one of the best spots in town for jazz. Every now and then it mixes it up with a little rock, Latin or blues. It attracts a mixed crowd who keep respectfully quiet during the acts. Get in early if you want a seat in front of the stage.

JAMBOREE Map pp298-9

☎ 93 319 17 89; www.masimas.com/jamboree; Plaça Reial 17; admission up to €10; ⏰ 10.30pm-5am; Ⓜ Liceu

Concerts start at 11pm and proceed until about 2am at the latest, at which point punters convert themselves into clubbers heaving to hip-hop and flailing to funk. Since long before Franco said adiós to this world, Jamboree has been bringing joy to the jivers of Barcelona, with headline jazz and blues acts of the calibre of Chet Baker and Ella Fitzgerald. The tradition lives on.

JAZZ SÍ CLUB Map pp298-9

☎ 93 329 00 20; www.tallerdemusics.com; Carrer de Requesens 2; admission minimum €5; ⏰ 6-11pm; Ⓜ Sant Antoni

A cramped little bar run by the Taller de Músics (Musicians' Workshop) serves as

the stage for a varied programme of jazz through to some good flamenco (Friday nights). Thursday night is Cuban night, Sunday is rock and the rest are devoted to jazz and/or blues sessions. It makes a mellow start to a long night in El Raval. Concerts start around 9pm.

LA COVA DEL DRAC – JAZZROOM Map p292

☎ 93 319 17 89; www.masimas.com/jazzroom; Carrer de Vallmajor 33; admission €10-20; ⏰ 9pm-3am; 🚈 FGC Muntaner

Run by the Mas i Mas group that owns Jamboree, this is a good if awkwardly located spot for jazz sessions most nights of the week. In a rather cosy atmosphere you can stumble across anything from local solo vocalists to Dixieland, from Afro Blues to experimental sounds. Start times vary – often nothing happens before 11pm. On weekends it can stay open as late as 5am.

LUZ DE GAS Map p292

☎ 93 209 77 11; www.luzdegas.com; Carrer de Muntaner 244-246; admission up to €20; ⏰ 11.30pm-5am; Ⓜ Diagonal or 🚌 6, 7, 15, 27, 32, 33, 34, 58 or 64

Several nights a week this beautiful-people's club stages concerts, starting at 10pm, that range through soul, country, salsa, rock, jazz or pop. You hang back in the relative obscurity of the bars (one in from the entrance and another hiding off to the right) or plunge down into the pit and boogie away before the grand stage. It's like being at a rock concert of old. From about 2am the grand stage is abandoned and the place turns into a club (see p182).

RAZZMATAZZ Map pp290-1

☎ 93 272 09 10; www.salarazzmatazz.com; Carrer dels Almogàvers 122 or Carrer de Pamplona 88; admission €20-30; ⏰ 8pm-6am Fri & Sat; Ⓜ Marina or Bogatell

Bands from far and wide occasionally create scenes of near hysteria in this, one of the city's classic live music and clubbing venues. Punters pile into the long main dance hall of the Razz Club and along its side galleries to see mostly the latest in international acts. Smaller acts are sometimes hosted in The Pop Bar and Lolita too.

Entertainment

LIVE MUSIC

TOP FIVE LIVE MUSIC VENUES

- Bikini (above)
- Harlem Jazz Club (above)
- Jamboree (above)
- Razzmatazz (right)
- Sala Tarantos (p193)

SALA APOLO Map pp298-9

☎ 93 441 40 01; www.sala-apolo.com; Carrer Nou
de la Rambla 113; Ⓜ Paral.lel

This wonderful old-time dance hall with
its plush balconies and swirling décor is
a classic on the Barcelona entertainment
circuit, as a club (see p186), occasional
cinema and concert location. Tastes are as
eclectic as possible, from Catalan singer-
songwriters like Lluís Llach to imports like
the Saddle Tramps. Their new basement
space, Sala 2, is for smaller, more intimate
concerts.

SIDECAR FACTORY CLUB Map pp298-9

☎ 93 302 15 86; www.sidecarfactoryclub.com;
Plaça Reial 7; admission €8-15; ⊗ 10pm-5am
Tue-Sat; Ⓜ Liceu

With its entrance on Plaça Reial, you can
come here for a meal before midnight or
a few drinks at ground level (which closes
by 3am at the latest), or descend into the
red-tinged bowels for live music most
nights. Just about anything goes here, from
UK indie pop through to country punk
or psychobilly. Most shows start at 10pm
(Thursday to Saturday).

ZAC CLUB Map p292

☎ 93 321 09 22; www.zac-club.com; Avinguda
Diagonal 477; admission €12-15; ⊗ 10pm-5.30am;
Ⓜ Hospital Clínic

In what was the classic La Boîte has
emerged this live-music venue, with a
broad range of concerts most nights of the
week. The small stage is occupied from
9pm to about midnight, from which point
on the place converts to a small, rather
congenial club.

CLASSICAL MUSIC & OPERA

Barcelona is blessed with a fine line-up of
theatres for grand performances of classical
music, opera and more. The two historic
music houses are the Gran Teatre del Liceu
and the Palau de la Música Catalana. The
former is the city's opera house and the
latter puts on an infinitely more eclectic
programme, from choral to Portuguese
fado. Both have been given a 21st-century
remake, the Liceu because it was burned
to the ground and the Palau because it so

badly needed it! The modern Auditori is
home to the city's orchestra.

Guía del Ocio has ample listings, but the
monthly *Informatiu Musical* leaflet has the
best coverage of classical music (as well as
other 'highbrow' genres). You can pick it
up at tourist offices and the Palau de la
Virreina, which also sells tickets for many
events.

CONCERT DE CARILLÓ Map pp298-9

www.gencat.net/presidencia/carillo; Palau de la
Generalitat, Plaça de Sant Jaume; admission free;
⊗ noon 1st Sun of month; Ⓜ Jaume I

Some 5000kg of bronze in 49 bells (a
carillon) swings into action for monthly
'concerts' in the seat of the Catalan government, allowing spectators a rare chance to
get inside. From the pretty Pati dels Tarongers the audience is treated to a midday
performance of just about anything, from
classical to especially cooked up pieces for
the Carilló, all with bells on. There are no
reservations – just turn up.

GRAN TEATRE DEL LICEU Map pp298-9

☎ 93 485 99 00; www.liceubarcelona.com; La
Rambla dels Caputxins 51-59; ⊗ box office 2-
8.30pm Mon-Fri & 1hr before show Sat & Sun;
Ⓜ Liceu

Barcelona's grand old opera house, restored after a fire in 1994, is one of the
most technologically advanced theatres in
the world (see p83). As well as opera, you
can see world-class dance companies strut
their stuff or attend classical-music concerts and recitals. Tickets can cost anything
from €7.50 for a cheap seat behind a pillar
to €150 for a well-positioned night at the
opera. You will need to book well in advance for the big shows.

Gran Teatre del Liceu (above), Barri Gòtic

L'AUDITORI Map pp290-1

☎ 93 247 93 00; www.auditori.org; Carrer de Lepant 150; admission €10-45; ⏰ box office noon-9pm Mon-Sat; Ⓜ Monumental

Barcelona's impressive modern home for serious music-lovers, L'Auditori (designed by Rafael Moneo) puts on plenty of orchestral, chamber, religious and other music throughout the year. L'Auditori is home to the Orquestra Simfònica de Barcelona i Nacional de Catalunya.

PALAU DE LA MÚSICA CATALANA Map pp298-9

☎ 93 295 72 00; www.palaumusica.org; Carrer de Sant Francesc de Paula 2; ⏰ box office 10am-9pm Mon-Sat; Ⓜ Urquinaona

A feast for the eyes, this modernista pudding is also the city's traditional venue for classical and choral music. It has a busy and wide-ranging programme that includes many groups and orchestras from abroad. You could pay €6 for a cheap seat in a middling concert and up to €160 or more for prestigious international performances.

PALAU ROBERT Map pp294-5

☎ 93 238 40 00; Passeig de Gràcia 107; admission €3; Ⓜ Diagonal

Once a month concerts are held in the peaceful gardens at the back of this fine building or its main hall. Concerts are usually held around 8pm. You need to pick up a pass the afternoon before (between 5pm and 7pm) or on the morning of the performance (from 10am to noon), as places are limited.

CINEMAS

Spain is proud of its dubbing industry, which could sound warning bells. The other great Mediterranean centre of dubbing, Italy, offers those not so enthusiastic about it few opportunities to avoid it. In Barcelona, fortunately, there is no shortage of cinemas showing foreign films with subtitles and original soundtracks. They are marked 'vo' (*versión original*) in movie listings and are extremely popular with locals.

The best movie listings are in the daily *El País* newspaper. A ticket usually costs €5.80 to €6.40, but most cinemas have a weekly *día del espectador* (viewer's day), often Monday or Wednesday, when they charge around €4.50. In some cinemas you can book by phone or online. Otherwise, you'll need to join the queue. In addition to the following mainstream cinemas, classic movies are sometimes shown in such diverse locations as La Pedrera (p105), Sala Apolo (opposite), FNAC record and book stores in the El Triangle shopping centre on Plaça de Catalunya (Map pp298–9) and the L'Illa del Diagonal shopping mall (Map pp296–7), CaixaForum (p118), the CCCB (p92) and civic centres.

CASABLANCA Map pp294-5

☎ 93 218 43 45; Passeig de Gràcia 115; Ⓜ Diagonal

A smallish local cinema that always screens movies in the original language.

FILMOTECA Map pp296-7

☎ 93 410 75 90; Avinguda de Sarrià 31-33; admission €2.70; Ⓜ Hospital Clínic

Also known as Cine Aquitania, it specialises in film seasons that concentrate on particular directors, styles and eras of film.

ICÀRIA YELMO CINEPLEX Map pp290-1

☎ 93 221 75 85; www.yelmocineplex.es in Spanish; Carrer de Salvador Espriu 61; Ⓜ Ciutadella Vila Olímpica

A vast cinema complex that always screens movies in the original language – this place always has the biggest choice.

MÉLIÈS CINEMES Map pp296-7

☎ 93 451 00 51; Carrer de Villarroel 102; admission €4; Ⓜ Urgell

Cosy cinema with two screens that specialises in old classics from Hollywood and European cinema.

RENOIR FLORIDABLANCA Map pp296-7

☎ 93 426 33 37; www.cinesrenoir.com in Spanish, bookings www.cinentradas.com in Spanish; Carrer de Floridablanca 135; Ⓜ Sant Antoni

One of a small chain of art-house cinemas showing quality flicks.

RENOIR-LES CORTS Map pp290-1

☎ 93 490 55 10; www.cinesrenoir.com in Spanish, bookings www.cinentradas.com in Spanish; Carrer de Eugeni d'Ors 12; Ⓜ Maria Cristina or Les Corts

This is another in the Renoir chain of art-house cinemas.

VERDI Map pp294-5

☎ 93 238 79 90; www.cinemes-verdi.com in Spanish; Carrer de Verdi 32; Ⓜ Fontana

A popular original-language movie house in the heart of Gràcia, handy to lots of local eateries and bars for pre- and post-film enjoyment.

VERDI PARK Map pp294-5

☎ 93 238 79 90; www.cines-verdi.com in Spanish; Carrer de Torrijos 49; Ⓜ Fontana

Sister to the Verdi, the Verdi Park is a block away and follows the same art-house philosophy.

THEATRE

Most local theatre is performed in Catalan or Spanish, although foreign companies, especially of a more avant-garde hue, are occasionally welcomed too. Some well-established Barcelona companies (see p36) provide a broad palette of drama, comedy and even musicals. Smaller, experimental theatre groups also have an enthusiastic local following. They try their hand at anything from Shakespeare revisited to new, home-grown drama. The monthly guide *Teatre BCN* has the latest listings and can be picked up at the Palau de la Virreina.

SALA BECKETT Map pp290-1

☎ 93 284 53 12; Carrer de Ca l'Alegre de Dalt 55bis; ⌚ box office 10am-2pm & 4-9pm Mon-Fri & 1hr before start of show; Ⓜ Joanic

One of the city's principal alternative theatres, the Sala Beckett is a smallish

---

THE FURIOUS FURA DELS BAUS

Keep your eyes peeled for any of the eccentric (if not downright crazed) performances of Barcelona's La Fura dels Baus theatre group. It has won worldwide acclaim for its brand of startling, often acrobatic, theatre in which the audience is frequently dragged into the chaos. The company grew out of Barcelona's street-theatre culture in the late 1970s and, although it has grown in technical prowess, it has not abandoned the rough-and-ready edge of street performances. In 2006 the company took its latest production, Metamorfosis, on tour. It is a disturbing exploration of the dissatisfaction and fearful aimlessness that seems to be a hallmark of modern Western life.

---

space that does not shy away from challenging theatre, contemporary or otherwise and usually in Catalan.

TEATRE LLANTIOL Map pp298-9

☎ 93 329 90 09; www.llantiol.com; Carrer de la Riereta 7; Ⓜ Sant Antoni

In this curious place on a dark alley in El Raval all sorts of odd stuff, from concerts and ballads to magic shows, is staged. This unlikely backstreet happens to be host to a nest of artists' studios. The box office opens 15 minutes before shows start.

TEATRE LLIURE Map pp304-5

☎ 93 289 27 70; www.teatrelliure.com; Passeig de Santa Madrona 3; ⌚ box office 5-8pm; Ⓜ Espanya

Housed in the former Palau de l'Agricultura building on Montjuïc (opposite the Museu d'Arqueologia) and consisting of two main theatre spaces (Espai Lliure and Sala Fabià Puigserver), the 'Free Theatre' puts on a variety of serious, quality drama, pretty much exclusively in Catalan. A restaurant and bar on the premises makes a night out here easy.

TEATRE MERCAT DE LES FLORS Map pp304-5

☎ 93 426 18 75; Carrer de Lleida 59; ⌚ box office 1hr before show; Ⓜ Espanya

Next door to the Teatre Lliure and together with it known as the Ciutat de Teatre (Theatre City), this is a key venue for music, dance and drama. Not afraid of diversity, the theatre has been known to welcome foreign theatre groups, regardless of the language they perform in.

TEATRE NACIONAL DE CATALUNYA Map pp290-1

☎ 93 306 57 00; www.tnc.es in Catalan & Spanish; Plaça de les Arts 1; ⌚ box office 3-8pm Tue-Sat & 1hr before show; Plaça de les Arts 1; Ⓜ Glòries or Monumental

Ricard Bofill's ultra-neoclassical theatre hosts a wide range of performances, principally drama (frequently worthies of the ilk of Ibsen or Catalonia's own Àngel Guimerà) but occasionally dance and other performances. The Sala Gran is reserved for big productions and the Sala Tallers for smaller-scale and more intimate plays and dance.

TEATRE NOU TANTARANTANA Map pp298-9

☎ 93 441 70 22; www.tantarantana.com in Catalan & Spanish; Carrer de les Flors 22; ⏰ box office ½hr before show; Ⓜ Paral.lel

Apart from staging all sorts of contemporary and experimental drama, this cosy theatre also often puts on kids' shows, including pantomime, puppets and so on. These shows tend to start at 6pm.

TEATRE NOVEDADES Map pp298-9

☎ 93 412 11 75; Carrer de Casp 1; ⏰ box office 4.30-8pm Tue-Sun; Ⓜ Catalunya

Anything goes, so long as it's a spectacle. The big musical hit in 2006 was *Mamá, Quiero Ser Famoso!* (Mum, I Want to be Famous!).

TEATRE PRINCIPAL Map pp298-9

☎ 93 301 47 50; La Rambla 27; ⏰ box office 5-8pm Tue-Sun; Ⓜ Liceu

There has been a theatre on this spot since the 16th century. Renovated and modernised in the 1990s, the theatre tends to concentrate on local productions of West End musicals. Renovated again in 2006, it has become a live concert stage too.

TEATRE ROMEA Map pp298-9

☎ 93 301 55 04; www.focus.es in Catalan & Spanish; Carrer de l'Hospital 51; ⏰ box office 4.30-8pm Tue-Sun; Ⓜ Liceu

Deep in El Raval, this theatre was resurrected at the end of the 1990s and has quickly become a reference point for quality drama in Barcelona. It stages a range of interesting plays, generally classics with a contemporary flavour, in Catalan and Spanish.

TEATRE TÍVOLI Map pp298-9

☎ 93 412 20 63; Carrer de Casp 8-12; ⏰ box office 1hr before show; Ⓜ Catalunya

This theatre has a fairly rapid turnover of drama, with pieces often not staying on for more than a couple of weeks. In 2006 it presented a Catalan version of *1001 Nights* by the Comedians.

TEATRE VICTÒRIA Map pp298-9

☎ 93 443 29 29; www.teatrevictoria.com in Spanish; Avinguda del Paral.lel 67-69; ⏰ box office 5-8pm & 1hr before show; Ⓜ Paral.lel

This theatre often stages ballet and contemporary dance, but otherwise the stage is used by well-known companies such as Tricicle. This trio of comic mimes has been doing the rounds with their version of 'intelligent humour' for 20 years.

TEATRENEU Map pp294-5

☎ 93 285 37 12; Carrer de Terol 26; ⏰ box office ½hr before show; Ⓜ Fontana or Joanic

This lively theatre (with a pleasant, rambling downstairs bar) dares to fool around with all sorts of material, from monologues to social comedy. Occasionally it changes the pace and opts for world music, but either way it has a busy programme.

DANCE

The dance scene can be a little patchy in Barcelona. Some fine local contemporary dance companies (see p33) perform occasionally, abetted by international visiting companies from time to time. For ballet and other big spectacles, you need to wait for acts to arrive from abroad.

Local contemporary dance companies perform in civic centres or across the gamut of the city's theatres, depending on the importance of the performance. Look for leaflets at Palau de la Virreina and watch theatre listings.

You can see traditional dance, whether the local *sardanes* (the national dance of Catalonia) in the streets or often saccharine versions of flamenco in *tablaos* (see below) throughout the year. For information on ticket booking services, see p188.

FLAMENCO

Although quite a few important flamenco artists grew up in Barcelona's *gitano* (Roma) neighbourhoods, seeing good performances of this essentially Andalucian dance and music is not always so easy. A few *tablaos*, where punters see flamenco while eating dinner, are scattered about. They are touristy but occasionally host good acts, but you need to keep a keen eye out for the names. Otherwise, watch Sala Tarantos in the Barri Gòtic, which is more likely to offer the genuine article.

SALA TARANTOS Map pp298-9

☎ 93 318 30 67; http://masimas.com/tarantos; Plaça Reial 17; admission from €5; ⏰ 10pm-5am Mon-Sat; Ⓜ Liceu

Since time immemorial, this basement locale has been the stage for some of the best flamenco to pass through or come out of Barcelona. You have to keep your eye on the place because top-class acts are not a daily diet. For lower-grade stuff, a *tablao* is put on most nights between around 8.30pm and 11pm. On an altogether unflamenco note, Tuesday nights is WTF (What the Fuck) Vocal Jams night, where some daring souls try their luck singing in a live virtual-reality show. It converts into a club later in the night and connects with neighbouring Jamboree.

TABLAO CORDOBÉS Map pp298-9
☎ 93 317 66 53; www.tablaocordobes.com; La Rambla 35; show only €30, with dinner €60; ⏰ shows 8.15pm, 10pm & 11.30pm; Ⓜ Liceu
This *tablao* is typical of its touristy genre and has been in business since 1970. Generally people book for the dinner and show, although you can skip the food and just come along for the performance (about 1¼ hours). You need to arrive about 1½ hours before the show for dinner, which is an indifferent assortment of paella, other hot dishes and salads. Some great names have come through here, so it is not always cheese.

TABLAO DE CARMEN Map pp304-5
☎ 93 325 68 95; www.tablaodecarmen.com; Carrer dels Arcs 9, Poble Espanyol; show only €31, with dinner €59; ⏰ shows 9.30pm & 11.30pm Tue-Sun; Ⓜ Espanya
Named after the great Barcelona *bailaora* (flamenco dancer) Carmen Amaya, the setup here is similar to that at the Tablao Cordobés. While it is true the shows do not excite connoisseurs, the quality can at times be quite high. Not a few up-and-coming flamenco stars tread the boards here on their way up.

TABLAO NERVIÓN Map pp302-3
☎ 93 315 21 03; www.restaurantenervion.com in Spanish; Carrer de la Princesa 2; show & set dinner €35; ⏰ shows 10pm & midnight Fri; Ⓜ Jaume I
For a little cheesy flamenco, this place has some near unbeatable offers. Come along to the second show from midnight and the only obligation is to have a drink (say a beer for €3). If you come at 10pm, you pay €12 for the show and a drink. Or you can do the whole dinner and show thing.

VENTA FLAMENCO BARCELONA Map pp298-9
☎ 670 437577; www.flamencobarcelona.com; Carrer del Marquès de Barberà 6; admission €10; ⏰ 8pm Tue-Sat
This modest flamenco club restores some of the feeling of a *peña*, where musicians and aficionados join to enjoy this temperamental music. The same place organises workshops and courses in guitar, dance and flamenco singing.

SARDANA
In Barcelona the best chance you have of seeing people dancing the *sardana* is at noon on Sunday in front of La Catedral. Other possibilities are at 6.30pm on Saturday and 7pm on Wednesday. You can also see the dance during some of the city's festivals. For more on this traditional dance, see p34.

CASINO
The city's casino, **Casino de Barcelona** (Map pp302–3; ☎ 93 225 78 78; www.casino-barcelona.com in Spanish; Carrer de la Marina 19-21; ⏰ 11am-5am; Ⓜ Ciutadella Vila Olímpica) in Port Olímpic, is the place for those who are feeling lucky or unfairly endowed fiscally. As well as the usual one-armed bandits and more sophisticated games, there are restaurants, bars and a club. If you can't be bothered moving from your home or hotel room, you can play on its online casino.

ACTIVITIES
Barcelona offers those with a hangover every chance to eliminate toxins by getting out and flexing other muscles besides your elbow. Options abound, from swimming and sailing to marathon running. There are plenty of gyms, and for those whose feelings of guilt over the previous night's excesses don't extend to physical exertions, the city's football and basketball teams provide class-A excitement when they play at home.

For information on where you can practise sports in Barcelona, try the **Servei d'Informació Esportiva** (Map pp304–5; ☎ 93 402 30 00; Avinguda de l'Estadi 30-40, Montjuïc; ⏰ 8am-2pm & 4-6pm Mon-Thu, 8am-2pm Fri), located in the same complex as the Piscines Bernat Picornell on Montjuïc.

WATCHING SPORT
Basketball
FC Barcelona's Winterthur-FCB Barcelona basketball team is almost as successful as its glamorous football outfit, last winning the league in 2004 and always close to the top of the table. The team plays (generally on Saturday afternoons) in the **Palau Blaugrana** (Map pp290–1; ☎ 902 189900; www .fcbarcelona.com; Carrer d'Aristides Maillol; Ⓜ Collblanc), next door to the Camp Nou football stadium in Les Corts. Tickets can be purchased direct in the Palau Blaugrana, on the phone and by Internet. You can also purchase them through the ServiCaixa ticketing service. In order to purchase tickets by phone or online, non-club members must do so at least 15 days before the match. Experience shows, however, that the online services do not always work for nonmembers. You can generally buy tickets without trouble just prior to the match. Ticket prices depend on the match but typically oscillate between €13 and €40, depending on position and match.

Bullfighting
Bullfighting takes place on Sunday in spring and summer at the **Plaça de Braus Monumental** (Map pp290–1; ☎ 93 245 58 02; cnr Gran Via de les Corts Catalanes & Carrer de la Marina; Ⓨ ticket office 11am-2pm & 4-8pm Mon-Sat, 10am-6pm Sun; Ⓜ Monumental). The 'fun' starts at around 6pm. Tickets are available at the arena or through ServiCaixa. You can also pick up tickets at **Toros Taquilla Oficial** (Map pp296–7; Carrer de Muntaner 26; Ⓜ Universitat). Prices range from €19 to €120. The higher-priced tickets are for the front row in the shade – any closer and you'd be fighting the bulls yourself.

Football
FC Barcelona (Barça for aficionados) has one of the best stadiums in Europe – the 100,000-capacity **Camp Nou** (Map pp290–1; ☎ 902 189900; www.fcbarcelona.com; Carrer d'Aristides Maillol; Ⓨ 9am-1.30pm & 3.30-6pm Mon-Fri; Ⓜ Collblanc) in the west of the city. The team is one of the world's best and has been on cracking form since 2005. Tickets are available direct at Camp Nou, by phone and theoretically online. You can also purchase them through the ServiCaixa ticketing service. To purchase tickets by phone or online, non-club members must do so at least 15 days before the match. As with the basketball, the Internet service seems to play up for nonmembers. They can cost on average anything from €30 to €120, depending

FC Barcelona fans at Camp Nou stadium (above)

CASTLES IN THE AIR

It's difficult to know how to classify making human castles, but to many a Catalan, the *castellers* (castle builders) are as serious in their sport as any footballer.

The 'building' of *castells* (castles) is particularly popular in central and southern Catalonia. *Colles* (teams) from all over the region compete in the summer and you are most likely to see *castellers* in town festivals. The amateur sport began in the 1880s, and although Barcelona's home teams are not among the best, it is always fun to watch. When teams from other towns come to compete, it can be quite exciting.

Without going into the complexities, the teams aim to erect human 'castles' of up to 10 storeys. These usually involve levels of three to five people standing on each others' shoulders. A crowd of team-mates and supporters forms a supporting scrum around the thickset lads at the base. To successfully complete the castle, a young (light!) child called the *anxaneta* must reach the top and signal with his/her hand. Sometimes the castle then falls in a heap (if it has not already done so) but successful completion also implies bringing the levels back down to earth in an orderly fashion.

Home and away teams sometimes converge on Plaça de Catalunya, Plaça de Sant Jaume and other city squares for friendly competitions during the various festivals. Ask the tourist office (p264) for more details. Beyond Barcelona, competition events can be seen in many towns, including Vilafranca del Penedès (p240) and Tarragona (p242).

on the seat and match. The ticket windows open again on Saturday morning and in the afternoon until the game starts. If the match is on Sunday, it opens Saturday morning only and then on Sunday until the match starts. You will almost definitely find scalpers lurking near the ticket windows. They are often club members and can sometimes get you in at a significant reduction. Don't pay your man until you are safely seated. Usually tickets are *not* available for matches with Real Madrid, the club's arch rivals.

The city's other club, Espanyol, based at the Estadi Olímpic (Map pp304–5; Avinguda de l'Estadi; 🚌 50, 61 or PM), traditionally plays a quiet second fiddle to Barça.

Formula One

Since 1991 the dashing knights in shining motorised armour have come to the Montmeló track, about a 30-minute drive north of Barcelona, every April. A seat for the Grand Prix race at the Circuit de Catalunya (☎ 93 571 97 71; www.circuitcat.com) can cost anything from €110 to €428. If you purchase before mid-March, tickets are slightly cheaper. Purchase tickets by phone, at the track, online with ServiCaixa or at advance ticket sales desks in El Corte Inglés department stores. You can get a regular *rodalies* train to Montmeló (€1.30, 30 minutes) but will need to walk about 3km or find a local taxi (about €8 to €10) to reach the track. On race days the Sagalés bus company (☎ 902 130014) often puts on buses from Passeig de Sant Joan, between Carrer de la Diputació and Carrer del Consell de Cent.

Sailing

The annual Trofeo Conde de Godó (www.trofeo godo.rcnb.com in Spanish) is Barcelona's prestige yachting competition, held off the city's coast over three days at the end of May and drawing crews from around the country.

OUTDOOR ACTIVITIES

Cycling

For suggestions on bicycle hire, see p251. Although cycle lanes have been laid out along many main arteries across the city, it is not the most relaxing place for a bike ride. Hillier but less stressful is Montjuïc, or you could head up into the Parc de Collserola (p115) with a mountain bike.

Golf

CLUB DE GOLF SANT CUGAT

☎ 93 674 39 08; www.golfsantcugat.com; Carrer de la Villa s/n, Sant Cugat del Vallès; green fees Mon-Thu €65, Fri, Sun & holidays €150; ⏰ 7.30am-dusk Mon-Fri, 7am-dusk Sat & Sun; 🚉 FGC Sant Cugat

Head out of town if you enjoy belting small round objects around the greenery. This 18-hole course was created in 1917 when a firm of British and American engineers working on electricity projects in Catalonia, realising the 'need' for such an amenity for its foreign employees, bought land at Sant Cugat and had the course designed by Scottish experts.

Hiking

Head to the Parc de Collserola for some decent hiking – not every city has such an expansive country zone within such easy reach.

Jogging

With all the traffic and crowds, Barcelona is hardly ideal for joggers. If you need to get your pins in motion, the most pleasant option is to head for Montjuïc, up above the traffic and smog. Better still is the aforementioned Parc de Collserola. A run along the beach in the cooler months can bring a little Zen relief, but in summer you'll find it hard not to stumble over all the oily bodies.

Marathon

Thousands of runners converge on Barcelona each year to participate in the city's marathon (www.maratobarcelona.es), in 2006 held in March on a new course. It starts and finishes at Plaça d'Espanya, passing Camp Nou, La Pedrera, La Sagrada Família, the Torre Agbar, Fòrum, Parc de la Ciutadella, Plaça de Catalunya and La Rambla.

Rollerblading

The most popular parts of town for a gentle Rollerblade are the esplanade along La Barceloneta beach and around Port Olímpic.

Sailing

Have you come to Barcelona to become a seadog? Head to **Base Nautica Municipal** (Map pp290–1; ☎ 93 221 04 32; www.basenautica .org; Avinguda Litoral s/n; Ⓜ Poblenou), just back from Platja de la Mar Bella, and enrol in a course in pleasure-boat handling, kayaking or windsurfing (€163 for 10 hours' tuition).

Skiing

In the ski season, several bus companies put on services departing from Ronda de l'Universitat 5 and Estació d'Autobusos de Sants to various ski resorts in the Catalan Pyrenees and Andorra. You can get day and weekend return tickets including lift pass; the price can range from around €40 for a day to €150 for a weekend with hotel room included. Ask at the **Palau Robert regional tourist office** (Map pp294–5; ☎ 93 238 40 00; Passeig de Gràcia 107; Ⓨ 10am-7pm Mon-Sat, 10am-2pm Sun; Ⓜ Diagonal).

Swimming

Swimmers are spoiled for choice in Barcelona. You can head down to the beach, either to one of the popular beaches in the city itself or to those up and down the coast beyond the city limits. Those who want to get in some more serious lap swimming have several good options.

CLUB NATACIÓ ATLÈTIC-BARCELONA Map pp290-1

☎ 93 221 00 10; www.cnab.org; Plaça de Mar s/n; adult/under 10yr €9.50/5.70; Ⓨ 6.30am-11pm Mon-Fri, 7am-11pm Sat year-round, 8am-5pm Sun & holidays Oct–mid-May, 8am-8pm Sun & holidays mid-May–Sep; Ⓜ Barceloneta or 🚌 17, 39, 57 or 64 Down near La Barceloneta beach, this athletic club has one indoor and two outdoor pools. Of the latter, one is heated for lap swimming in winter. Admission includes use of the gym and private beach access. Membership costs €31 a month plus €64 joining fee.

PISCINES BERNAT PICORNELL Map pp304-5

☎ 93 423 40 41; www.picornell.com in Catalan; Avinguda de l'Estadi 30-40; adult/15-25yr/senior & under 15yr €8.50/5.60/4.50, outdoor pool only Jun-Sep adult/6-14yr & senior €4.50/3.20; Ⓨ 7am-midnight Mon-Fri, 7am-9pm Sat, 7.30am-4pm Sun, outdoor pool 10am-7pm Mon-Sat, 10am-4pm Sun Oct-May, 9am-9pm Mon-Sat, 9am-8pm Sun Jun-Sep; 🚌 50, 61 or PM
Included in the standard entry price to Barcelona's official Olympic pool on Montjuïc is use of the gym, saunas and spa bath. Membership costs €33 to join and €30 a month.

WATERWORKS IN THE ALTOGETHER

There are a couple of options open to skinny-dippers in Barcelona. In addition to the ill-defined nudists' strip at the southwest end of Platja de la Mar Bella, which provides good opportunities for sunbathing, you can also get it all off year-round at the Piscines Bernat Picornell, the Olympic pool on Montjuïc. On Saturday nights, between 9pm and 11pm, the pool (with access to sauna and steam bath) is open only to nudists (adult/child & senior €4.50/3.20). On Sundays between October and May the indoor pool also opens to nudists only from 4.15pm to 6pm.

Entertainment

ACTIVITIES

POLIESPORTIU MARÍTIM Map pp302-3

☎ 93 224 04 40; www.claror.org/maritim.htm in Catalan; Passeig Marítim de la Barceloneta 33-35; Mon-Fri €13.50, Sat, Sun & holidays €16; ⊗ 7am-midnight Mon-Fri, 8am-9pm Sat, 8am-4pm Sun & holidays; Ⓜ Ciutadella Vila Olímpica

Water babies will squeal with delight in this thalassotherapeutic (sea-water therapy) sports centre. In addition to the smallish pool, there is a labyrinth of hot, warm and freezing-cold spa pools, along with thundering waterfalls for massage relief.

Tennis

Tennis players can serve it up near the Olympic precinct at Montjuïc, at the pleasant and relatively convenient **Tennis Pompeia** (Map pp304-5; ☎ 93 325 13 48; Carrer de Foixarda s/n; court hire per hr €12; ⊗ 8am-1pm Mon-Fri, 8am-2pm Sat; 🚌 50).

HEALTH & FITNESS
Gym

Barcelona is crawling with places for a workout, but most cater to long-term members. Some swimming pools, like the Piscines Bernat Picornell on Montjuïc, have gym facilities.

UBAE FRONTÓN Map pp298-9

☎ 93 302 32 95; La Rambla de Santa Mònica 18; admission €12; ⊗ 7.30am-2pm & 3-8pm Mon-Fri, 9am-7.30pm Sat, 9am-2pm Sun & holidays; Ⓜ Drassanes

Smack in the heart of the old city, this gym offers a fitness room with all manner of exercise equipment, a section with bicycles, step and other cardio machines, and a small swimming pool. If you want to come often, consider membership, which costs €32 a month plus a €47 joining fee.

Massage

All stressed out by sightseeing in the nearby modernista gems on Passeig de Gràcia? Pop by **Masajes a 1000** (Map pp294-5; ☎ 93 215 85 85; www.masajesa1000.com; Carrer de Mallorca 233; massages from €4; ⊗ 7am-1am; Ⓜ Passeig de Gràcia) for a quick, invigorating massage.

Pilates

Need to loosen up a bit? You could try **El Centre Pilates de Barcelona** (Map pp294-5; ☎ 93 301 08 46; www.barcelona-pilates.com in Catalan & Spanish; Carrer de Girona 15; 55min session €45; ⊗ 8am-8pm Mon-Fri, 10am-2pm Sat; Ⓜ Urquinaona), a high-class luxury setup where your particular requirements and physical condition will be assessed and the treatment will be tailored to your needs.

Shopping

Shopping

If your doctor has prescribed an intense round of shopping therapy to deal with the blues, then Barcelona is the place. Across Ciutat Vella (Barri Gòtic, El Raval and La Ribera), l'Eixample and Gràcia is spread a thick mantle of countless boutiques, historic shops, original one-off stores, gourmet corners, wine dens and more designer labels than you can shake your gold card at. The shopoholic could spend weeks just trawling around. You name it, you'll find it here, anything from chocolate to Mango. Decades-, and in some cases centuries-old gems purvey everything from hats and berets to old lace and nuts.

Barcelona is a style city and this shows in its flagship design stores – whether you are looking for homewares, gifts or decoration. Even the souvenirs fulminate with flair. Fashion, in the broadest possible sense, occupies a sizable wedge of the city's retail space. Local names such as Mango, Custo Barcelona, Antonio Miró and Purificación García jostle side by side with big Spanish names in *haute couture* and *prêt-à-porter* (such as Zara and Adolfo Domínguez). There is no shortage of French, Italian and international fashion either, with most of the major brands on show. Every taste is catered to, with loads of youthful designers, club-clothing purveyors, grunge dealers and secondhand operators spread across town. Not far north of Barcelona lies Roca Village, a huge fashion outlet village with countless name stores.

Stylish department stores, local and imported, are scattered about the centre of town. The biggest name is El Corte Inglés. Barcelona has also followed inevitable trends, installing mega-malls and hypermarkets around its periphery and in several key locations closer to the city centre.

As a rule, bargaining is not an option, although a discreetly posed question in name-fashion stores along the lines of 'Is that the best price you can do?' may meet with a surprising response. It is not a bad idea to look around and compare prices. They are generally inflated in high-fashion boutiques and shops on or around Passeig de Gràcia, although you may still find them better than for the same items in your home city.

In short, Barcelona is a Pandora's box of retail ruction. Leave space in your budget and bags to haul back the loot.

Shopping Areas

For high fashion, design, jewellery and several department stores, the principal shopping axis starts on Plaça de Catalunya, proceeds up Passeig de Gràcia and turns left (west) into Avinguda Diagonal, along which it proceeds as far as Plaça de la Reina Maria Cristina. The densely packed section between Plaça de Francesc Macià and Plaça de la Reina Maria Cristina is especially good hunting ground. The T1 Tombbús, a circular bus service, covers precisely this route for the ardent shopper (see p251).

TOP FIVE SHOPPING STRIPS

- Avinguda del Portal de l'Àngel (Map pp298–9) With El Corte Inglés leading the way, this broad pedestrian avenue is lined with everything from shoe shops to patisseries, and feeds into Carrer dels Boters and Carrer de la Portaferrissa, characterised more by stores offering light-hearted costume jewellery and fun young streetwear.
- Avinguda Diagonal (Map pp294–5) Another boulevard loaded up with international fashion names, department stores and design boutiques, suitably interspersed with eateries to allow weary shoppers to take a load off.
- Carrer d'Avinyó (Map pp298–9) Once a fairly squalid old-town road (Picasso and his friends used to frequent houses of ill repute along here), Carrer d'Avinyó has morphed into a delightfully dynamic young fashion street.
- Carrer del Rec (Map pp302–3) A raft of eager young fashion shops has sprouted along this street in the wake of El Born's gentrification. You'll find bright, sometimes quirky clothes in boutiques along and around here.
- Passeig de Gràcia (Map pp294–5) This is the premier shopping boulevard in central Barcelona, chic with a capital 'C' and leaning heavily towards high-street fashion with international names.

The heart of l'Eixample, bisected by chic Passeig de Gràcia, is known as the Quadrat d'Or (Golden Sq; the boulevard itself is known as the Milla d'Or, or Golden Mile) and is jammed with all sorts of glittering shops. You may find something that takes your fancy in one of the art galleries clustered on Carrer del Consell de Cent between Rambla de Catalunya and Carrer de Balmes. Some of the city's big-name designer stores, such as Vinçon and Favorita, are located here. Speciality delicatessen and wine boutiques abound, along with interesting poster and gift stores. Fashion names from Armani to Zara are at home here.

> ## BARCELONA'S BEST-KEPT SECRETS
>
> - Cafè de la Princesa (p203) A Pandora's box of disparate goodies down a hidden medieval lane.
> - Escribà (p202) One of the city's greatest chocolate makers.
> - Herboristeria del Rei (p203) Ancient herbs and traditional remedies.
> - La Portorriqueña (p205) Timeless coffee merchant in El Raval.
> - Sala Parés (p204) An historic private art gallery.

The old town offers all sorts of little wonders. The heart of the Barri Gòtic was always busy with small-scale merchants, but the area has come crackling to life since the mid-1990s, and local shopkeepers like to think of the whole area as 'Barnacentre'. Some of the most curious old stores, whether purveyors of hats or of candles, lurk in the narrow lanes around Plaça de Sant Jaume. The once-seedy Carrer d'Avinyó has become a minor young-fashion boulevard. Antique stores abound on and around Carrer de la Palla and Carrer dels Banys Nous.

Over in La Ribera there are two categories of shops to look out for: some fine old traditional stores dealing in speciality foodstuffs, and a new crop of fashion and design stores (particularly along the stretch of Carrer del Rec between Passeig del Born and Avinguda del Marquès de l'Argentera) catering to the yuppies who have moved into the *barri* (neighbourhood).

Over in El Raval you'll discover old-time stores that are irresistible to browse, and a colourful array of affordable, mostly secondhand clothes boutiques; the central axis is Carrer de la Riera Baixa, which hosts everything from '70s threads to military cast-offs. Art galleries, designer outlets and quality bookstores huddle together in the streets running east of the Museu d'Art Contemporani de Barcelona (Macba) towards La Rambla.

There's no shortage of shopping malls in Barcelona. One of the first to arrive was **L'Illa del Diagonal** (Map pp296–7; ☎ 93 444 00 00; www.lilla.com; Avinguda Diagonal 549; Ⓜ Maria Cristina), designed by star Spanish architect Rafael Moneo. The **Centre Comercial Diagonal Mar** (Map pp290–1; ☎ 902 530300; www.diagonalmar.com; Avinguda Diagonal 3; Ⓜ El Maresme Fòrum) by the sea is one of the latest additions. Other emporia include: **Centre Comercial de les Glòries** (Map pp290–1; ☎ 93 486 04 04; www.lesglories.com; Gran Via de les Corts Catalanes; Ⓜ Glòries), in the former Olivetti factory; **Heron City** (☎ 902 401144; www.heroncitybarcelona.com; Passeig de Rio de Janeiro 42; Ⓜ Fabra i Puig), just off Avinguda de la Meridiana about 4km north of Plaça de les Glòries Catalanes; and the **Centre Comercial Gran Via 2** (Map pp290–1; ☎ 902 301444; www.granvia2.com; Gran Via de les Corts Catalanes 75; Ⓡ FGC Ildefons Cerdà) in l'Hospitalet.

Opening Hours

In general, shops are open from 9am or 10am to 1.30pm or 2pm and from about 4pm to 8pm Monday to Friday. Many keep the same hours on Saturday, although some don't bother with the evening session.

> ## TAXES & REFUNDS
>
> Value-added tax (VAT) is known as IVA in Spain and is 16% on retail goods. Non-EU residents can claim these taxes back on purchases if they take the goods out of the EU within three months of purchase. See p262 for more details.

Big supermarkets and department stores such as El Corte Inglés stay open all day Monday to Saturday, from about 10am to 10pm. The same goes for shopping centres and malls. Many fashion boutiques, design stores and the like open from about 10am to 8pm Monday to Saturday.

A handful of shops opens on Sunday and holidays, and their number increases in the run up to key consumer holiday periods (eg for several weeks leading up to Christmas and Reis).

Shopping

BARRI GÒTIC & LA RAMBLA

A handful of interesting shops dot La Rambla, but the real fun starts inside the labyrinth. Young fashion on Carrer d'Avinyó, a mixed bag on Avinguda del Portal del Ángel, some cute old shops on Carrer de la Dagueria and lots of exploring in tight old lanes awaits.

ANTINOUS Map pp298-9 — Gay Books
☎ 93 301 90 70; Carrer de Josep Anselm Clavé 6; Ⓜ Drassanes

Gay and lesbian travellers may want to browse in this spacious and relaxed gay bookshop, which also has a modest café out the back. This is the place for porn mags, postcards of muscle-bound fellows and an awful lot of high-brow lit on homosexual issues mixed in with rather lower-brow lit to groan to.

BAGUÉS Map pp298-9 — Jewellery
☎ 93 318 38 42; La Rambla de Sant Josep 105; Ⓜ Liceu

This jewellery store, in business since the 19th century, is in thematic harmony with the city, being a repository of fanciful modernista creations and one of the most established names in local glister.

CAELUM Map pp298-9 — Food Specialities
☎ 93 302 69 93; Carrer de la Palla 8; ⏰ 10.30am-8pm Tue-Fri, 11.30am-9pm Sat & Sun, 5-8pm Mon; Ⓜ Liceu

In an exquisite medieval space in the heart of Barcelona is gathered centuries of heavenly gastronomic tradition from across Spain. Sweets (such as the irresistible marzipan from Toledo) made by nuns in convents across the country make their way to this den of delicacies.

CASA BEETHOVEN Map pp298-9 — Music
☎ 93 301 48 26; La Rambla de Sant Josep 97; Ⓜ Liceu

This isn't any old sheet-music shop. In business since 1880 and with an air more of a museum than of a store, Casa Beethoven's customers include Montserrat Caballé, Josep Carreras and Plácido Domingo. Keeping up with the times, you're as likely to find music by Metallica as by Mozart. On Saturdays small concerts are sometimes held.

CERERIA SUBIRÀ Map pp298-9 — Candles
☎ 93 315 26 06; Baixada de la Llibreteria 7; Ⓜ Jaume I

Even if you're not interested in myriad mounds of colourful wax, pop in just so you've been to the oldest shop in Barcelona. Open since 1761, and at this address since the 19th century, it has a voluptuous, baroque feel about it.

EL INGENIO Map pp298-9 — Masks & Costumes
☎ 93 317 71 38; Carrer d'En Rauric 6; Ⓜ Liceu

In this whimsical fantasy store you will discover giant Carnaval masks, costumes, theatrical accessories and other fun things. You can pick up some 'devil's batons' to do a little fiery juggling, a monocycle or clown make-up.

ESCRIBÀ Map pp298-9 — Pastries
☎ 93 301 60 27; La Rambla de Sant Josep 83; ⏰ 5-9pm Mon-Fri, 8am-9pm Sat & Sun; Ⓜ Liceu

Housed in the shimmering modernista Antiga Casa Figueras, this is one of the city's best-loved and possibly most devilish pastry purveyors. Escribà has another branch at Gran Via de les Corts Catalanes 546 (Map pp296–7; ☎ 93 454 75 37; Ⓜ Urgell), which has been in business since 1906. The Escribà clan is

El Ingenio (above), Barri Gòtic

known for its fantastical chocolate models, some of which can occasionally be seen in the **Museu de la Xocolata** (p96).

ESTAMPERIA D'ART Map pp298-9 Prints

☎ 93 318 68 30; Plaça del Pi 1; Ⓜ Liceu
As long ago as 1789 a shop was installed here in front of the Església de Santa Maria del Pi, in a building that had belonged to a religious brotherhood. It has regaled locals with art prints for generations, and been in the same family since the 1920s. It's a curious spot to drop by for postcards and prints.

GOTHAM Map pp298-9 Design

☎ 93 412 46 47; Carrer de Cervantes 7; Ⓜ Jaume I
Look back in fondness at the furniture and lights here, which date back to at least the 1960s, and in some cases the '30s. Much of it is restored and given a bright, decorative once-over. Retro design freaks will fall in love with this place.

HERBORISTERIA DEL REI

Map pp298-9 Herbs & Medicinal Plants
☎ 93 318 05 12; www.herboristeriadelrei.com; Carrer del Vidre 1; Ⓜ Liceu
Once patronised by Queen Isabel II, this timeless corner store flogs all sorts of weird and wonderful herbs, spices and medicinal plants. It's been doing so since 1823 and the décor has barely changed since the 1860s.

LA CONDONERIA Map pp298-9 Condoms

☎ 93 302 77 21; Plaça de Sant Josep Oriol 3; Ⓜ Liceu
Run out of kinky coloured condoms? Need a fresh batch of lubricant? Pick up these vital items and a host of bedside novelties and naughty bits here.

LA MANUAL ALPARGATERA

Map pp298-9 Shoes
☎ 93 301 01 72; Carrer d'Avinyó 7; Ⓜ Drassanes
The bright white shopfront is a local landmark. Everyone from the Pope to Michael Douglas has ordered a pair of espadrilles (rope-soled, canvas shoes or sandals) from a store that holds its own against Nike and co.

LE BOUDOIR Map pp298-9 Lingerie & Erotica

☎ 93 302 52 81; www.leboudoir.net; Carrer de la Canuda 21; Ⓜ Catalunya
Need to spice up the bedroom situation? Take a stroll around this sensual shop,

www.lonelyplanet.com

TAKING HOME PICASSO

A big Miró print or a Picasso poster can make the perfect gift. Some of the city's top museums have excellent thematic shops, where you can find prints, posters, books, bookends and other memorabilia related to the collections on show. Among them are the **Fundació Joan Miró** (p120), **Museu Picasso** (p96), **Museu Nacional d'Art de Catalunya** (p121), **Museu d'Art Contemporani de Barcelona** (p92) and **La Pedrera** (p105). There are also limited offerings in the **Oficina d'Informació de Turisme de Barcelona** (p264) and **Palau de la Virreina** (p264).

where anything from lacy, racy underwear to exuberant sex toys are available. Transparent handcuffs might be fun, or perhaps a bit of slap and tickle with a whip and mask?

LLIBRERIA & INFORMACIÓ CULTURAL DE LA GENERALITAT DE CATALUNYA

Map pp298-9 Books
☎ 93 302 64 62; La Rambla dels Estudis 118; Ⓜ Liceu
This is a good first stop for books and pamphlets on all things Catalan, ranging from huge coffee-table tomes on all facets of Catalan art and architecture through to turgid tracts on Catalan law. You can skip the latter, but the former are exquisite. The shop stocks very little in English (and even less in Spanish).

LOFT Map pp298-9 Fashion

☎ 93 301 24 20; Carrer d'Avinyó 22; Ⓜ Jaume I
Of the numerous hip fashion stores that have converted this once-slummy alley into a threads mecca for young men and women about town, Loft is one of the longest-established and biggest. It carries labels such as Diesel Style Lab and other cutting-edge names.

OBACH Map pp298-9 Millinery

☎ 93 318 40 94; Carrer del Call 2; Ⓜ Liceu
Since 1924 this store in the heart of the Call (Jewish quarter) has been purveying all manner of headgear for men. Time seems to have stood still here, and one assumes the bulk of the clientele belongs to a senior generation. Hats off to a remarkably long-lived institution.

Shopping

BARRI GÒTIC & LA RAMBLA

PAPABUBBLE Map pp302-3   Candied Sweets
☎ 93 268 86 25; www.papabubble.com; Carrer Ample 28; Ⓜ Liceu
It feels like a step into another era in this candy store, where they make up pots of rainbow-coloured boiled lollies, just like some of us remember them from corner store days as kids. Watch the sticky sweets being made before your eyes. For all its apparent timelessness, this is a relatively new venture. Started by Australians in Barcelona, this sweet reminiscence has spread, with shops in Amsterdam and Tokyo.

QUERA Map pp298-9   Books
☎ 93 318 07 43; Carrer de Petritxol 2; Ⓜ Liceu
Crammed into a tiny bookshop is a treasure-trove of travel material, mostly on Catalonia and the Pyrenees. It specialises in maps and guides, including a host of stuff for walking, and has been in business since 1916.

SALA PARÉS Map pp298-9   Art Gallery
☎ 93 318 70 20; www.salapares.com; Carrer del Petritxol 5; Ⓜ Liceu
Picasso had works on sale here a century ago in what is one of the city's most venerable and still dynamic private galleries. In business since 1877, the gallery has managed to evolve constantly and maintain its position as one of the city's leading art purveyors, with a strong stable of Catalan artists spanning the 20th century to promising young talents.

IT'S SALE TIME

The winter sales start shortly after Reis (6 January) and, depending on the store, can go on well into February. The summer sales start in July, with stores trying to entice locals to part with one last wad of euros before they flood out of the city on holiday in August. Some shops prolong their sales to the end of August, hoping above all to cash in on the presence of foreigners in town. The whole sales phenomenon comes complete with tricks attached. Some big-name fashion stores don't bother with sales, simply relying on consumer momentum to attract their usual customers in for a browse. Others wait it out a little to test the waters. If they don't move merchandise as they'd like, they might embark on a brief period of sales later in January.

SFERA Map pp298-9   Fashion
☎ 93 342 57 45; Plaça de Catalunya 23; Ⓜ Catalunya
Pop into this subsidiary of El Corte Inglés for relaxed, bright, middle-of-the-road fashion for him, her and the kids. Big, woolly winter knits alternate with primary-coloured men's shirts and frilly jeans for her. They have accessories and a line in sports clothes too.

VILLEGAS CERÀMICA Map pp298-9   Ceramics
☎ 93 317 53 30; Carrer Comtal 31; Ⓜ Urquinaona
For some curious ceramics that have nothing to do with traditional wares, poke your head in here. Arresting items include cat's head clocks in which the eyes move back and forth, or pottery statues of stretched human figures. More down to earth are the vases and other decorative items.

XOCOA Map pp298-9   Chocolate & Pastries
☎ 93 318 89 91; Carrer del Petritxol 11; Ⓜ Liceu
Shield your eyes from the ultra-bright rose-and-white décor and prepare yourself for a different kind of choc. Carefully arranged inside this den of dental devilry are ranks and ranks of original chocolate bars, chocolates stuffed with sweet stuff, gooey pastries and more.

EL RAVAL

The area boasts a handful of art galleries around the Macba, along with a burgeoning secondhand and vintage clothes scene on Carrer de la Riera Baixa. Carrer dels Tallers is one of the city's main music strips.

B-HUNO Map pp298-9   Fashion
☎ 93 412 63 05; Carrer de Elisabets 18; Ⓜ Catalunya
For bright, fun, handmade dresses, ranging from long burgundy numbers to sunny, flowery patterns, this is a great stop for gals. The original designs and cuts will have your heart aflutter as you prepare the coming season's wardrobe in early spring.

CASTELLÓ Map pp298-9   Music
☎ 93 318 20 41; Carrer dels Tallers 3, 7 & 79; Ⓜ Catalunya
These three stores are part of a large family business that has been going since 1935 and which is said to account for a fifth of the retail record business in Catalonia.

TOP FIVE WHIMSICAL SHOPS

- Caelum (p202) Traditional sweets from Spanish convents.
- El Ingenio (p202) Masks and costumes.
- Le Boudoir (p203) Naughty bedroom fun.
- Norma Comics (p209) An amazing collection of comics & super-hero models.
- Papabubble (opposite) Boiled sweeties, just like in Grandpa's day.

GI JOE Map pp298-9 — Fashion

☎ 93 329 96 52; Carrer de l'Hospital 82; Ⓜ Liceu

On the corner of Carrer de la Riera Baixa, which is lined with secondhand clothes shops, is this army-surplus warehouse. Get your khakis here, along with urban army fashion T-shirts. Throw in a holster, gas mask or sky-blue UN helmet for a kinkier effect.

LA PORTORRIQUEÑA Map pp298-9 — Coffee

☎ 93 317 34 38; Carrer d'En Xuclà 25; Ⓜ Catalunya

Coffee beans from around the world, freshly ground before your eyes, has been the winning formula in this store since 1902. It also offers all sorts of chocolate goodies. The street is good for little old-fashioned food boutiques.

LEFTIES Map pp298-9 — Fashion

☎ 93 317 50 70; Carrer de Pelai 2; Ⓜ Universitat

Don't mind being seen in last year's Zara fashions? Lefties (ie leftovers) could be the browsing spot for you, with men's, women's and kids' cast-offs from the previous year at silly prices. You could fill a wardrobe and your bank manager would be none the wiser.

TERANYINA Map pp298-9 — Textiles

☎ 93 317 94 36; Carrer del Notariat 10; Ⓜ Catalunya

Artist Teresa Rosa Aguayo runs this textile workshop in the heart of the artsy bit of El Raval. You can join courses at the loom, admire some of the rugs and other works that Teresa has created and, of course, buy them.

LA RIBERA

The onetime commercial heart of medieval Barcelona is today still home to a cornucopia of old-style specialist food and drink shops, a veritable feast of aroma and atmosphere. The late 1990s injected a flood of hip little fashion stores.

CAFÉ DE LA PRINCESA

Map pp302-3 — Bric-a-Brac

☎ 93 268 15 18; Carrer dels Flassaders 21; Ⓜ Jaume I

In a dark lane named after the blanket-makers that once worked here is this odd combination of cooperative store, art gallery and restaurant (entry to the latter is from Carrer de Sabateret). Its members make many of the oddities on sale, but others are objects imported from such disparate locations as Prague and Colombia. Leather bags, toys and clothes make up just part of the offerings.

CASA GISPERT Map pp302-3 — Nuts

☎ 93 319 75 35; Carrer dels Sombrerers 23; Ⓜ Jaume I

Nuts to you at the wood-fronted Casa Gispert, where they've been toasting nuts and selling all manner of dried fruit since 1851. Pots and jars piled high on the shelves contain an unending variety of crunchy titbits, some roasted, some honeyed, all of them moreish.

CASA MAURI Map pp302-3 — Chocolate

☎ 93 310 04 58; Carrer dels Flassaders 32; Ⓜ Jaume I

You couldn't have located this chocolate vendor, in business since 1840, any deeper in the labyrinth off Passeig del Born. It is hard to go past the window, glittering with the wrappers of sundry handmade and fiendishly enticing chunks of choc. Once lured inside, you will almost certainly take a seat and try a cup of hot chocolate.

CUSTO BARCELONA Map pp302-3 — Fashion

☎ 93 268 78 93; www.custo-barcelona.com; Plaça de les Olles 7; Ⓜ Jaume I

The psychedelic décor and casual atmosphere lend this avant-garde Barcelona fashion store a youthful edge. Custo presents new women's and men's collections each year on the New York catwalks and is having runaway international success.

EL MAGNÍFICO Map pp302-3 — Coffee

☎ 93 319 60 81; Carrer de l'Argenteria 64; Ⓜ Jaume I

These guys have been roasting all sorts of coffee since the early 20th century. The variety of coffee (and tea) available is remarkable – and the aromas hit you as you walk in. Across the road, the same people run the exquisite and much newer tea shop, **Sans i Sans** (☎ 93 319 60 81; Carrer de l'Argenteria 59).

EL REY DE LA MAGIA Map pp302-3   Magic
☎ 93 319 39 20; www.elreydelamagia.com; Carrer de la Princesa 11; Ⓜ Jaume I
For more than 100 years, the people behind this box of tricks have been keeping locals astounded and amused. Should you decide to stay in Barcelona and make a living as a magician, this is the place to buy levitation brooms, glasses of disappearing milk and decks of magic cards.

GALERIA MAEGHT Map pp302-3   Art Gallery
☎ 93 310 42 45; Carrer de Montcada 25; Ⓜ Jaume I
This high-end gallery, housed in one of the fine medieval mansions for which this street is known, specialises in 20th-century masters. It is as enticing for the building as the art.

MONTIEL Map pp302-3   Food & Drink
☎ 93 268 37 29; Carrer dels Flassaders 19; Ⓜ Jaume I
Run your eyes across the feast of goodies in this rustically arranged shop-cum-eatery. In this aroma-filled cornucopia are stacked Spanish cheeses, regional liquors, honeys, sausages. You name it. Initial intentions to shop could quickly be converted into a yen to sit down and enjoy a meal made of some of these products.

TOT FORMATGE Map pp302-3   Cheese
☎ 93 319 53 75; Passeig del Born 13; Ⓜ Jaume I
On entering, the aromas of an international assembly of fine cheeses waft towards you. Little platters are scattered about with samples of a handful of the store's products, which together form a bright display of the best of local and European cheeses.

VILA VINITECA Map pp302-3   Wine
☎ 93 268 32 27; www.vilaviniteca.es; Carrer dels Agullers 7; Ⓜ Jaume I
One of the best wine stores in Barcelona (and Lord knows, there are a few), this place has been searching out the best in local and imported wines since 1932. On a couple of November evenings they organise what has by now become an almost riotous wine-tasting event in Carrer dels Agullers and surrounding lanes, at which cellars

from around Spain present their young new wines. At No 9 they have another store devoted to gourmet food products.

PORT VELL & LA BARCELONETA
MAREMÀGNUM
Map pp302-3   Shopping Centre
☎ 93 225 81 00; www.maremagnum.es; Moll d'Espanya; Ⓜ Drassanes
Created out of largely abandoned docks, this chirpy shopping centre, with its bars, restaurants and cinemas, is pleasant enough for a stroll virtually in the middle of the old harbour, although the shops are largely on the tacky side. Football fans will be drawn to the paraphernalia at **FC Barcelona** (☎ 93 225 80 45).

L'EIXAMPLE
Most of the city's classy shopping spreads across the heart of l'Eixample, in particular along Passeig de Gràcia, La Rambla de Catalunya and adjacent streets.

ADOLFO DOMÍNGUEZ
Map pp294-5   Fashion
☎ 93 487 41 70; www.adolfo-dominguez.com; Passeig de Gràcia 32; Ⓜ Passeig de Gràcia
One of the stars of the Spanish fashion firmament from Galicia (in Spain's far north-

AN OUTLET OUTING
For the ultimate discount fashion overdose, head out of town for some outlet shopping at **La Roca Village** (☎ 93 842 39 00; www.larocavillage.com; La Roca del Vallès; ☼ 11am-8.30pm Mon-Fri, 10am-10pm Sat). Here, a village has been given over to consumer madness. At a long line of Spanish and international fashion boutiques you'll find clothes, shoes, accessories and designer homewares at (they claim) up to 60% off normal retail prices. To get here, follow the AP-7 tollway north from Barcelona, take exit 12 (marked Cardedeu) and follow the signs for La Roca. The **Sagalés bus company** (☎ 93 870 78 60; www.sagales.com) organises shuttles from Monday to Friday (at 9am, noon and 4pm; €2.60 each way) from outside the Fabra i Puig Metro station. Alternatively, take a *rodalies* train to Granollers and pick up a shuttle bus (Monday to Friday only) or taxi there.

west), this well-established label produces classic men's and women's garments from quality materials. They have branches all over town.

ALTAÏR Map pp298-9 — Books

☎ 93 342 71 71; www.altair.es; Gran Via de les Corts Catalanes 616; Ⓜ Universitat

Enter the world of travel in this extensive bookshop, mecca for guidebooks, maps, travel literature and all sorts of other books likely to induce a severe case of itchy feet. It has a travellers' notice board and travel agent out the back.

ANTONIO MIRÓ Map pp294-5 — Fashion

☎ 93 487 06 70; www.antoniomiro.es; Carrer del Consell de Cent 349; ☺ 10am-8pm Mon-Sat; Ⓜ Passeig de Gràcia

Antonio Miró is one of Barcelona's *haute couture* kings. He concentrates on light, natural fibres to produce smart, unpretentious men's and women's fashion – jackets are a strong point in his collections.

BSB ALFOMBRAS Map pp294-5 — Rugs & Carpets

☎ 93 410 74 41; Carrer de París 174; Ⓜ Hospital Clínic

Designer carpets and rugs are strung up like the modern works of art they are. Hand-knotted rugs maintain tradition in production and the use of fine Tibetan wool and Chinese silk, but designs are contemporary and challenging.

CAMPER Map pp294-5 — Shoes

☎ 93 215 63 90; www.camper.com; Carrer de València 249; Ⓜ Passeig de Gràcia

What started as a modest Mallorcan family business (the island has a long shoemaking tradition) has over the decades become the Clarks of Spain. Camper shoes, which range from the eminently sensible to the stylishly fashionable and are known for solid reliability, are sold all over the world.

CAN BACUS Map pp294-5 — Wine

☎ 93 453 43 58; Carrer d'Enric Granados 68; Ⓡ FGC Provença

Not only a fine wine store, this place has the added attraction of housing a gourmet snack stop. Call in to see what they proffer for tasting out back before contemplating a wine purchase.

CLOTHING SIZES

Measurements approximate only, try before you buy

Women's Clothing

Aus/UK	8	10	12	14	16	18
Europe	36	38	40	42	44	46
Japan	5	7	9	11	13	15
USA	6	8	10	12	14	16

Women's Shoes

Aus/USA	5	6	7	8	9	10
Europe	35	36	37	38	39	40
France only	35	36	38	39	40	42
Japan	22	23	24	25	26	27
UK	3½	4½	5½	6½	7½	8½

Men's Clothing

Aus	92	96	100	104	108	112
Europe	46	48	50	52	54	56
Japan	S		M	M		L
UK/USA	35	36	37	38	39	40

Men's Shirts (Collar Sizes)

Aus/Japan	38	39	40	41	42	43
Europe	38	39	40	41	42	43
UK/USA	15	15½	16	16½	17	17½

Men's Shoes

Aus/UK	7	8	9	10	11	12
Europe	41	42	43	44½	46	47
Japan	26	27	27½	28	29	30
USA	7½	8½	9½	10½	11½	12½

CASA DEL LLIBRE Map pp294-5 — Books

☎ 93 272 34 80; www.casadellibro.com; Passeig de Gràcia 62; ☺ 9.30am-9.30pm Mon-Sat; Ⓜ Passeig de Gràcia

With branches elsewhere in Spain, the 'Home of the Book' is a well-stocked general bookshop with reasonable sections devoted to literature in English, French and other languages. The website is a good place to look for Spanish literature if the shop is a walk too far.

EL BULEVARD DELS ANTIQUARIS

Map pp294-5 — Antiques

☎ 93 215 44 99; www.bulevarddelsantiquaris.com; Passeig de Gràcia 55-57; ☺ 10am-8pm Mon-Sat; Ⓜ Passeig de Gràcia

More than 70 stores are gathered under one roof (on the floor above the more general Bulevard Rosa arcade) to offer the most varied selection of collector's pieces, ranging from old porcelain dolls through to fine crystal, from Asian antique furniture to old French goods, from African and other ethnic art to jewellery.

EL CORTE INGLÉS

Map pp298-9   Department Store

☎ 93 306 38 00; Plaça de Catalunya 14;
Ⓜ Catalunya

The 'English Court' is Spain's flagship department store, with everything you'd expect, from computers to cushions, high fashion to homewares. The top floor is occupied by a restaurant with fabulous views over the city centre. El Corte Inglés has other branches, including at Avinguda Diagonal 617 (Map pp290–1) and Avinguda Diagonal 471–473 (Map p292) near Plaça de Francesc Macià.

ELS ENCANTS VELLS

Map pp290-1   Flea Market

☎ 93 246 30 30; Plaça de les Glòries Catalanes;
⏲ 7am-6.45pm Mon, Wed, Fri & Sat; Ⓜ Glòries

Also known as the Fira de Bellcaire, the 'Old Charms' flea market is the biggest of its kind in Barcelona. The markets moved here in 1928 from Avinguda Mistral, near Plaça d'Espanya. It's all here, from antique furniture through to secondhand clothes and old toys. A lot of the stuff is junk, but occasionally good things at *preus de ganga* (bargain-basement prices) come through – it depends on what falls off the back of the trucks.

FARRUTX Map pp294-5   Shoes

☎ 93 215 06 85; www.farrutx.es; Carrer de Rosselló 218; Ⓜ Diagonal

Another Mallorcan shoemaker, Farrutx specialises in exclusive upmarket footwear for uptown gals. You might fall for high-heeled summer sandals or elegant winter boots.

FAVORITA Map pp294-5   Design

☎ 93 476 57 21; Carrer de Mallorca 291;
Ⓜ Verdaguer

The store has changed hands and names but continues to be a key point in the interior-design scene in Barcelona. Some of the city's top designers contribute furniture and accessories of every imaginable type for the contemporary home, and taking a browse here is like wandering through a 3D *House and Garden* magazine (without the gardens). The store is in a modernista house built by Domènech i Montaner.

GRATACÒS Map pp294-5   Fashion

☎ 93 238 73 50; Passeig de Gràcia 108; Ⓜ Diagonal

In town for a wedding and left your dress behind? Perhaps you should pop by this luxury women's clothing store, a classic in Barcelona since 1940. Specialists in top-class materials, it produces lavish dresses for the most exclusive of cocktail gatherings. If nothing else, you can at least imagine yourself as Cinderella at the ball.

J MURRIÀ Map pp294-5   Delicatessen

☎ 93 215 57 89; Carrer de Roger de Llúria 85;
Ⓜ Passeig de Gràcia

Ramon Casas designed the century-old modernista shopfront advertisements fea-

---

THE URGE TO RUMMAGE

Lovers of old books, coins, stamps and general bric-a-brac can indulge their habits uninhibited at several markets around the centre of town. They generally get going from 9am and wind down around 8pm. The coin- and stamp-collectors market and the old-books peddlers around the Mercat de Sant Antoni usually pack up by around 2pm.

The Barri Gòtic is livened up by an **art and crafts market** (Plaça de Sant Josep Oriol; Ⓜ Liceu) on Saturday and Sunday, the antiques **Mercat Gòtic** (Plaça Nova; Ⓜ Liceu or Jaume I) on Thursday, and a **coin and stamp collectors' market** (Plaça Reial; Ⓜ Liceu) on Sunday morning (what a contrast to the previous night's revelry). Just beyond the western edge of El Raval, the punters at the **Mercat de Sant Antoni** (Map pp296–7; Ⓜ Sant Antoni) dedicate Sunday morning to old maps, stamps, books and cards.

Once a fortnight, gourmands can poke about the homemade honeys, sweets, cheeses and other edible delights at the **Fira Alimentació** (Plaça del Pi; Ⓜ Liceu) from Friday to Sunday. Ask at the **Oficina d'Informació de Turisme de Barcelona** (p264) for the dates of the market.

Some curious annual markets are also worth looking out for. In May stands set up in the Portal de l'Àngel (Avinguda del Portal de l'Àngel; Ⓜ Catalunya) for the **Fira del Llibre Antic** (Antique Book Fair). The same spot hosts the **Fira de Terrissa** (Pottery Fair; five days starting around 20 September) and the similar **Fira Ceramistes** (Ceramicists Fair; around 23 December to 5 January).

The **Fira de Santa Llúcia** on and around Avinguda de la Catedral (Ⓜ Liceu) is a kind of Christmas market held in December, where you can buy figurines, including many models of that infamous Catalan Christmas character, the *caganer* (crapper; see p14) to make your own Nativity scene.

tured at this culinary coven. For a century the gluttonous have trembled here at this altar of speciality food goods from around Catalonia and beyond.

LAIE Map pp298-9 — Books
☎ 93 318 17 39; www.laie.es; Carrer de Pau Claris 85; 🕐 10am-9pm Mon-Sat; Ⓜ Catalunya or Urquinaona
Laie has novels and books on architecture, art and film in English, French, Spanish (Castilian) and Catalan. Better still, it has a great café where you can examine your latest purchases or browse through the newspapers provided for customers in true Mitteleuropean style.

LOEWE Map pp294-5 — Fashion
☎ 93 216 04 00; www.loewe.es; Passeig de Gràcia 35; 🕐 10am-8.30pm Mon-Sat; Ⓜ Passeig de Gràcia
Loewe is one of Spain's leading and oldest fashion stores, founded in 1846. It specialises in luxury leather. This branch, which opened in 1943 in the modernista Casa Lleó Morera because the company altered the original façade. It has since attempted to undo some of the damage.

MANGO Map pp294-5 — Fashion
☎ 93 215 75 30; www.mango.com; Passeig de Gràcia 65; 🕐 10am-8pm Mon-Sat; Ⓜ Passeig de Gràcia
At home in the basement of a modest modernista town house (and in endless other locations around town), this busy hall of a store shines bright with the local fashion chain's flagship items – fun leather accessories to go with the breezy women's fashion.

MARC 3 Map pp298-9 — Posters & Paintings
☎ 93 318 19 53; Rambla de Catalunya 12; 🕐 10am-8.30pm Mon-Sat; Ⓜ Catalunya
A yawning cavern of posters, prints and original paintings awaits those who need to dress their walls. You can go for the tried and true Robert Doisneau kissing scenes or some wonderfully obscure reproduction adverts.

NORMA COMICS Map pp294-5 — Comics
☎ 93 244 84 23; www.normacomics.com; Passeig de Sant Joan 7-9; Ⓜ Arc de Triomf
With a huge range of comics, Spanish and international, this is Spain's biggest dealer – everything from Tintin to some of the weirdest sci-fi and sex comics can be found here. Also on show are armies of model super heroes and other characters produced by fevered imaginations. Kids from nine to 99 can be seen snapping up items to add to their collections.

PURIFICACIÓN GARCÍA
Map pp298-9 — Fashion
☎ 93 487 72 92; www.purificaciongarcia.es; Passeig de Gràcia 21; 🕐 10am-8.30pm Mon-Sat; Ⓜ Passeig de Gràcia
Ms García spreads out in this generous corner store, with light summer women's fashion and bright leather bags.

REGIA Map pp294-5 — Perfume
☎ 93 216 01 21; www.regia.es; Passeig de Gràcia 39; 🕐 9.30am-8.30pm Mon-Fri, 10.30am-8.30pm Sat; Ⓜ Passeig de Gràcia
Reputed to be one of the best perfume stores in the city and in business since 1928, Regia stocks all the name brands and also has a private **perfume museum** (p109) out the back.

VINÇON Map pp294-5 — Design
☎ 93 215 60 50; www.vincon.com; Passeig de Gràcia 96; 🕐 10am-8.30pm Mon-Sat; Ⓜ Diagonal
An icon of the Barcelona design scene, Vinçon has the slickest designs in furniture and household goods (particularly lighting), local and imported. Not surprising really, since the building, raised in 1899, belonged to the modernista artist Ramon Casas. Head upstairs to the furniture area – from the windows and terrace you get close side views of La Pedrera.

VIPS Map pp298-9 — Late-Night Store
☎ 93 317 48 05; Rambla de Catalunya 7-9; 🕐 9am-2am Mon-Tue, 9am-3am Wed-Sun; Ⓜ Catalunya
The concept of the 24-hour general store has yet to reach Barcelona, but an

Vinçon (above), Passeig de Gràcia

approximation is this central import from Madrid, where you can pick up snacks, magazines and books.

ZARA Map pp298-9 Fashion

☎ 93 318 76 75; www.zara.es; Passeig de Gràcia 16; Ⓜ Passeig de Gràcia

Started in Galicia, in Spain's far northwest, Zara is one of the great success stories of modern *prêt-à-porter*. Women's fashion is the name of the game, and this megastore on Barcelona's top shopping street is just the most obvious of its several outlets around the city.

GRÀCIA & PARK GÜELL

A wander along the narrow lanes of Gràcia turns up all sorts of surprises, mostly tiny enterprises producing anything from printed T-shirts to handmade table lamps. They tend to come and go, so you never quite know what you might turn up.

ÉRASE UNA VEZ Map pp294-5 Fashion

☎ 93 217 29 77; Carrer de Goya 7; Ⓜ Fontana

Once Upon a Time is the name of this fanciful little boutique, which proposes women's clothes by such emerging local designers as Juan Pedro López, Zazo & Brull,and Silvia Jordà.

RED MARKET Map pp294-5 Fashion

☎ 93 218 63 33; Carrer de Verdi 20; Ⓜ Fontana

Several funky fashion boutiques dot this street, best known to locals for the queues outside the art-house cinema. Here you run into bright, uninhibited urban wear and accessories. Red dominates the décor more than the threads, and various brands

of various things, from shoes to tops, are on offer.

SANTS & LES CORTS
LA BOTIGA DEL BARÇA
Map pp290-1 Football Souvenirs

☎ 93 492 31 11; http://shop.fcbarcelona.com; Carrer de Arístides Maillol s/n; Ⓜ Collblanc

For some, football is the meaning of life. If you fall into that category, your idea of shopping heaven may well be this store at the football museum next to Camp Nou stadium. Here you can get shirts, key rings, footballs – anything you can think of, all featuring the famous red and blue colours.

LA VINIA Map pp290-1 Wine

☎ 93 363 44 45; www.lavinia.es in Spanish; Avinguda Diagonal 605; ◷ 10am-9pm Mon-Sat; Ⓜ Maria Cristina

This huge wine store takes anything but a traditional approach to its products. In classy supermarket style, La Vinia (which originated in Madrid) presents a seemingly endless selection of wine from around Spain and the rest of the world.

MONTJUÏC & POBLE SEC
ELEPHANT Map pp304-5 Books

☎ 93 443 05 94; Carrer de la Creu dels Molers 12; ◷ 10am-8pm; Ⓜ Poble Sec

This bright little English bookshop is a bit off the main tourist track, but is a helpful haven of books in Her Majesty's tongue. They range from fiction to children's, with a smattering of reference works and a healthy secondhand section.

Sleeping

Sleeping

Barcelona's hotel building boom continues apace. This is good news for everyone. Some fine new, up-to-the-minute hotels in a broad price bracket have opened in historic buildings and key locations, the limited options near the sea have increased, and new high-end digs have popped up in various strategic spots to the joy of the business and convention crowd. As competition grows, many of the more established spots are being obliged to upgrade (at the upper

BOOK ACCOMMODATION ONLINE

For more accommodation reviews and recommendations by Lonely Planet authors, check out the online booking service at www.lonelyplanet.com. You'll find the true, insider lowdown on the best places to stay. Reviews are thorough and independent. Best of all, you can book online.

levels, this means more hotel pools, spas, designer bars, chic dining and sundry services) and in many cases rates have fallen considerably. At peak trade-fair time (which happens often) it can still be a trial finding a room, but otherwise hoteliers at mid- and upper levels sometimes scramble to fill beds. So look around, bargain, and remember that booking on the web is generally cheaper than simply turning up at the front door.

Accommodation Styles

The city has hundreds of hotels in all categories and a good range of alternatives, including numerous youth hostels.

If dorm living is not your thing but you are still looking for a budget deal, check around the many *pensiones* and *hostales*. These are family-run, small-scale hotels, often housed in what were once sprawling private apartments. Some are fleapits, while others are immaculately maintained gems. Many rooms do not have private bathrooms; instead there are shared bathrooms in the hall.

Hotels cover a broad range. At the bottom end there is often little to distinguish them from better *pensiones* and *hostales,* and from there they run the gamut up to five-star luxury (for which you often pay less than in other major European cities). Short-term apartment rental is another option.

Check-In & Check-Out Times

Always confirm your arrival, especially if it's going to be late in the afternoon or evening. Generally there is no problem if you have paid a deposit or left a credit-card number. While you can check in at any time of the morning, you may not get access to your room until after noon, when it has been vacated and cleaned. Most of the time you will be able to leave your luggage with the reception and go for a wander until the room is ready.

Check-out time is generally noon, although some places can be a little draconian and set a leaving time of 11am, or, in rare cases, even 10am! Technically, if you overstay you can be charged for another night.

Price Ranges

Even in the depths of the low season, you're unlikely to pay less than €18 to €20 for a dorm bed in a youth hostel. In small *pensiones* or *hostales* you are looking at a minimum of around €35/55 for basic single/double *(individual/doble)* rooms, mostly without a private bathroom (it is possible to find cheaper rooms, but they can be pretty unappetising). The top-end category in this guide starts at €250 for a double, but can easily rise to €400 to €500 in the best hotels. Prices can also drop as under-booked hotels flood the market with sometimes unbelievable offers.

Many places, especially those at the lower end, offer triples and quads as well as the standard single/double arrangement. If you are travelling in a group of three or four, these bigger rooms are generally the best value. If you want a double bed (as opposed to two singles), ask for a *llit/cama matrimonial*.

Single travellers are often penalised, frequently paying around two-thirds of the double-room rate (especially in those places that have no single rooms).

Some hotels, especially at the lower and mid levels, maintain the same prices year round. Others vary the rates for high season *(temporada alta)*, mid-season *(temporada media)* and low season *(temporada baja)*. Low season is roughly November to Easter, except the Christmas–New Year period. Whenever there is a major trade fair, high-season prices generally apply. Conversely, business-oriented hotels often consider weekends, holiday periods and other slow business times low season.

PRICE GUIDE

Prices for places to stay in this chapter are roughly divided into three categories and prices given are high-season maximums. Bear in mind that in many cases prices can fluctuate enormously, especially at the higher end. Rooms come with private bathrooms (which at lower-end places often means a shower and not a full bathtub) unless otherwise stated. These price categories are for doubles:

€€€	over €250 a night
€€	€70-250 a night
€	under €70 a night

Reservations

Booking ahead is recommended, especially in key periods such as Easter, around Christmas and New Year, during trade fairs and throughout much of summer (although August can be quite a slack month owing to the heat). You can book by phone and nearly always on hotel websites too. You may be asked for a credit-card number and be charged a night's accommodation in case of a no-show. If you prefer to check out rooms personally, you could book for the first night or two and then seek an alternative place once on the ground in Barcelona.

You can find out about and book accommodation by contacting the tourist office at Plaça de Catalunya (p264). If you prefer to wait until you arrive, you should generally be able to find something, although during trade fairs it can be truly tough.

Apartments

A cosier (and sometimes more cost-effective) alternative to hotels can be short-term apartment rental. A plethora of firms dedicated to short lets has sprung up in the past few years. Typical prices are around €80 to €100 for two people per night, but cheaper and more luxurious options are also available. Among these services (there are scores more) are: **Barcelona On Line** (Map pp294–5; ☎ 93 343 79 93/94; www.barcelona-on-line.es; Gran Via de les Corts Catalanes 662); **Barcelona Apartments** (Map p292; ☎ 93 414 55 28; www.barcelonapartments .com; Via Augusta 173); **Apartment Barcelona** (Map pp294–5; ☎ 93 215 79 34; www.apartment barcelona.com; Carrer de València 286); **Lodging Barcelona** (Map pp296–7; ☎ 93 467 78 00; www.lodgingbarcelona.com; Carrer de Balmes 62); **Rent a Flat in Barcelona** (Map pp298–9; ☎ 93 342 73 00; Carrer de Fontanella 18) and **Oh-Barcelona.Com** (Map pp298–9; ☎ 93 304 07 69; www.oh-barcelona.com; Avinguda del Portal de l'Àngel 42). If you're looking to do a short-term house swap, check out the ads on www.loquo.com.

Long-Term Rentals

The **Universitat de Barcelona** (Map pp298–9; ☎ 93 402 11 00; Gran Via de les Corts Catalanes 585; Ⓜ Universitat), the **British Council** (Map p292; ☎ 93 241 99 77; Carrer d'Amigó 83; Ⓡ FGC Muntaner) and **International House** (Map pp298–9; ☎ 93 268 45 11; Carrer de Trafalgar 14; Ⓜ Arc de Triomf) have notice boards with ads for flat shares. Another option for students coming to Barcelona to study is the private **Rent a Bedroom** (Map p292; ☎ 93 217 88 12; www.rentabedroom.com; Avinguda del Príncep d'Astúries 52). It can organise rooms in share houses for between €300 and €700 per month, inclusive of bills.

The free English-language monthly *Barcelona Metropolitan*, found in bars and some hotels, and occasionally at tourist offices, carries rental classifieds in English, as does another monthly freebie, *Catalunya Classified*. Check out the ads at www.loquo.com too. Otherwise,

Sleeping

get a hold of *Anuntis*, the weekly classifieds paper. The last few pages of the *Suplement Immobiliària* (Real-estate Supplement) carry ads for shared accommodation under the heading *lloguer/hostes i vivendes a compartir*. Count on rent of €300 a month or more. To this, you need to add your share of bills (gas, electricity, water, phone and *comunidad* – building maintenance charges).

Taxes

Virtually all accommodation is subject to IVA, the Spanish version of value-added tax, at 7%. This is often included in the quoted price at cheaper places, but less often at more expensive ones. Ask: *'¿Está incluido el IVA?'* ('Is IVA included?'). In some cases you will be charged IVA only if you ask for a receipt.

BARRI GÒTIC & LA RAMBLA

La Rambla is lined with hotels, *pensiones* and fleapits, and in the labyrinth of the Barri Gòtic are scattered countless others. Many of the smaller joints are nothing special, catering to an at-times rowdy party crowd. But there are some real gems too.

ALBERG HOSTEL ITACA Map pp298-9 Hostel €
☎ 93 301 97 51; www.itacahostel.com; Carrer de Ripoll 21; dm €17, d €48-60; Ⓜ Jaume I; ▣
This bright, quiet hostel option near La Catedral has spacious dorms (sleeping six, eight or 12 people), with pleasant spring colours and a couple of doubles with private bathroom. Breakfast costs €2, and you can make use of the upstairs kitchen and exchange books.

HOSTAL CAMPI Map pp298-9   Hostal €
☎ 93 301 35 45; hcampi@terra.es; Carrer de la Canuda 4; d €56, s/d without bathroom €25/46; Ⓜ Catalunya
This is an excellent budget deal that appeals mostly to younger backpackers. The

best rooms at this friendly, central *hostal* are doubtless the doubles with their own loos and showers. They are extremely roomy and bright. Located just off La Rambla, you are protected from much of the street noise.

HOSTAL LEVANTE Map pp298-9   Hostal €
☎ 93 317 95 65; www.hostallevante.com; Baixada de Sant Miquel 2; d €65, s/d without bathroom €33/56; Ⓜ Liceu or Jaume I
Off Plaça de Sant Miquel, this large, bright *hostal* has rooms of all shapes and sizes. Try for a double with a balcony. Sun streams in to warm the tiles of these simple but pleasing rooms. There is heating in winter.

HOTEL CONTINENTAL Map pp298-9 Hotel €€
☎ 93 301 25 70; www.hotelcontinental.com; La Rambla 138; s/d €75/95; Ⓜ Catalunya; ▨ ▣
Imagine being here in 1937, when George Orwell returned from the front line during the Spanish Civil War and Barcelona was tense with factional strife. Rooms at the Continental are a little spartan, but have romantic touches such as ceiling fans, brass bedsteads and frilly bedclothes. You will pay €10 more for a double with a balcony overlooking La Rambla. Take breakfast in bed.

HOTEL JARDÍ Map pp298-9   Hotel €€
☎ 93 301 59 00; www.hoteljardi-barcelona.com; Plaça de Sant Josep Oriol 1; s/d €70/96; Ⓜ Liceu; ▨
This fairly spartan option has a couple of attractive doubles with a balcony over one of the prettiest squares in the city. If you can snare one of them, it is worth putting up with the flappable staff and general mayhem. Otherwise, you're better off elsewhere.

TOP FIVE ROOMS WITH A VIEW

- Gran Hotel La Florida (p223) All of Barcelona spreads out before you.
- Grand Marina Hotel (p218) Low-level views back up La Rambla, across the port.
- Hotel Arts Barcelona (p219) Waterfront rooms with panoramic views up and down the coast.
- Hotel Barcelona Princess (p218) High-rise sea views or west across the city.
- Hotel Rey Juan Carlos I (p223) Bird's-eye views across the city from the west.

HOTEL ORIENTE Map pp298-9   Hotel €€

☎ 93 302 25 58; www.husa.es; La Rambla 45;
d €180; Ⓜ Liceu; 🌀

One of Barcelona's oldest hotels is built into
the shell of a former convent, among whose
most spectacular leftovers is the cloister
that is now a skylit restaurant. Rooms are a
trifle spare but elegant enough with parquet floors and dark timber furniture.

HOTEL NERI Map pp298-9   Hotel €€

☎ 93 304 06 55; www.hotelneri.com; Carrer de
Sant Sever 5; d from €248; Ⓜ Liceu; 🌀 💻

Occupying a beautifully adapted, centuries-
old building that backs on to the quiet Plaça
de Sant Felip Neri, this is a tranquil, luxury
stop. The light, sandy stone and timber
furnishings give the 22 rooms a rustic feel,
although they come with cutting-edge technology, including plasma-screen TVs and CD
player. Choose from a menu of sheets and
pillows. Sun yourself on the roof deck, where
you can also take a shower and order a drink.

HOTEL RACÓ DEL PI Map pp298-9   Hotel €€

☎ 93 342 61 90; www.h10.es; Carrer del Pi 7; s/d
€170/250; Ⓜ Liceu; 🌀 💻

Stylishly carved out of a historic Barri Gòtic
building, the hotel's 37 rooms have dark
wood beams, parquet floors, prettily tiled
en suite bathrooms and full soundproofing.
Décor mixes navy blue with light creamy
colours. Take breakfast in the interior patio.
The location is terrific, in the heart of the
more gentrified part of the Barri Gòtic. In
slow periods rates drop dramatically.

HOTEL COLÓN Map pp298-9   Hotel €€€

☎ 93 301 14 04; www.hotelcolon.es; Avinguda de
la Catedral 7; s/d €123/278; Ⓜ Jaume I; 🌀 💻

The privileged position opposite the cathedral lends this hotel a special grace. A range
of rooms, from modest singles to diapha-
nous doubles, offers quiet, elegant accommodation. Decoration varies considerably (eg
hardwood floors or carpet) and the top-
floor rooms with terrace are marvellous. The
likes of Hemingway, Somerset Maugham
and Jane Fonda have enjoyed these views.

HOTEL 1898 Map pp298-9   Hotel €€€

☎ 93 552 95 52; www.nnhotels.es; La Rambla 109;
d €267-396; Ⓜ Liceu; 🌀 💻 🖥 Ⓟ

The former Compañía de Tabacos Filipinas
(Philippines Tobacco Company), whose

Hotel 1898 (left), La Rambla

business was cut short when the islands
swapped Spanish for American masters
in 1898, has been resurrected as a luxury
hotel. Some of the rooms are smallish but
deluxe rooms and suites have their own
terraces and all combine modern comfort
and elegance, with parquet floors and
tasteful furniture.

EL RAVAL

A handful of good hotels and some youth
hostels lie scattered in or on the periphery of this, the mildly wild side of the old
town.

ALBERG CENTER RAMBLES

Map pp298-9   Hostel €

☎ 93 412 40 69; www.tujuca.com; Carrer de
l'Hospital 63; dm under 26yr or ISIC cardholders/
others incl breakfast up to €19/22.25;
Ⓜ Liceu; 🌀 💻

This Hostelling International (HI) hostel is
right in the thick of things, just off La Rambla. Beds are in single-sex dorms of four to
10 people, pretty much standard issue. The
place is open 24 hours and is secure. Safes
and laundry facilities are available.

HOSTAL GAT RAVAL Map pp298-9   Hostal €

☎ 93 481 66 70; www.gataccommodation.com; Carrer de Joaquín Costa 44; d €60, s/d without bathroom €38/54; Ⓜ Universitat; 🔀 🖵

There's pea-green and lemon-lime décor in this hip young *hostal* on the 2nd floor in one of the grittier lanes of El Raval. The individual rooms are pleasant and secure, but only some have private bathrooms. Some have views to the Macba art museum and its square, and safes are available. You are within spitting distance of a veritable beehive of buzzing bars.

HOTEL PENINSULAR Map pp298-9   Hotel €

☎ 93 302 31 38; www.hpeninsular.com; Carrer de Sant Pau 34; s/d €50/70, without bathroom €30/50; Ⓜ Liceu; 🔀

An oasis on the edge of the slightly louche Barri Xinès, this former convent (which was connected by tunnel to the Església de Sant Agustí) has a plant-draped atrium extending its height and most of its length. The 80 rooms are simple, clean and (mostly) spacious.

HOTEL ANETO Map pp298-9   Hotel €

☎ 93 301 99 89; www.hotelaneto.com; Carrer del Carme 38; s/d €50/70; Ⓜ Liceu; 🔀

Time stood still and the prices even dropped at this budget bargain, nestled in a lively street in one of the nicer parts of El Raval. The best rooms are the doubles with the shuttered little balconies looking onto the street. The singles are by and large characterless and small.

HOSTAL GAT XINO Map pp298-9   Hostal €€

☎ 93 324 88 33; www.gataccommodation.com; Carrer de l'Hospital 149-155; s/d €60/80; Ⓜ Liceu; 🔀 🖵

Better still than Gat Raval is this newer and, if possible, cooler version, deeper inside the *barri*. The lime-green décor theme continues here but rooms are more spacious and all have bathrooms. There is even a suite with its own terrace (€120), with views to Montjuïc.

HOTEL ESPAÑA Map pp298-9   Hotel €€

☎ 93 318 17 58; www.hotelespanya.com; Carrer de Sant Pau 9-11; s/d €80/112; Ⓜ Liceu; 🔀

The hotel is famous for its two marvellous dining rooms designed by the modernista architect Lluís Domènech i Montaner. One (used for private banquets) has big sea-life murals by Ramon Casas; the other has floral tiling and a wood-beamed roof. The rooms have seen better days, but have high ceilings and heating. They certainly exude the flavour of a past era.

ABBA RAMBLA HOTEL Map pp298-9   Hotel €€

☎ 93 505 54 00; www.abbaramblahotel.com; Rambla del Raval 4; s/d €96/112; Ⓜ Paral.lel; 🔀 🖵 🅿

Dominating the top end of El Raval's grand pedestrian strip, this modern hotel offers sunny rooms in light, neutral colours with functional furniture and dark parquet floors. Make a call from the bathroom phone, surf with wi-fi and enjoy satellite TV on plasma screens. Better still, get out into the theatre of the streets below.

HOTEL PRINCIPAL Map pp298-9   Hotel €€

☎ 93 318 89 70; www.hotelprincipal.es; Carrer de la Junta del Comerç 8; s/d €90/120; Ⓜ Liceu; 🔀 🖵 🅿

The hotel has clean-lined rooms with parquet floors, hairdryers and original art depicting Barcelona. All rooms have double-glazing and you can sunbathe on the roof. Prices vary considerably depending on season and how full they are.

HOTEL MESÓN DE CASTILLA
Map pp298-9   Hotel €€

☎ 93 318 21 82; www.husa.es; Carrer de Valldonzella 5; d €139; Ⓜ Catalunya; 🔀 🅿

Some modernista touches give character to the 1st floor of this elegant hotel. Heavy wooden furniture in several timeless sitting rooms contrasts with playful stained glass, murals and Gaudíesque window mouldings. Rooms have a classic charm and you can breakfast (included in the price) on the small terrace.

HOTEL SAN AGUSTÍN Map pp298-9   Hotel €€

☎ 93 318 16 58; www.hotelsa.com; Plaça de Sant Agustí 3; s/d €112/150; Ⓜ Liceu; 🔀 🖵

This one-time 18th-century monastery opened as a hotel in 1840, making it the city's oldest (it's undergone various refits since then!). The location is perfect, a quick stroll off La Rambla on a curious square. Rooms sparkle, are mostly spacious and light and have parquet floors. Consider an attic double (€165.85), with sloping ceiling and bird's-eye views.

HOTEL MILLENNI Map pp298-9   Hotel €€

☎ 93 441 41 77; www.hotel-millenni.com; Ronda de Sant Pau 14; s/d €95/160; Ⓜ Paral.lel; ⊠ 💻 Ⓟ

A comfortable modern hotel has been installed behind the beautiful corner façade of this early-20th-century building on the edge of El Raval. The rooms are crisp and warm, with parquet floors, bright colour scheme (soft sandy yellow and off white) and standard décor throughout. Geeks can get their wi-fi fix here.

CASA CAMPER Map pp298-9   Hotel €€€

☎ 93 342 62 80; www.camper.es; Carrer d'Elisabets 11; s/d €230.05/251.45; Ⓜ Liceu; ⊠ ⊠ 💻

An original designer digs in the middle of El Raval, Casa Camper belongs to the Mallorcan shoe company of the same name. The entire place is no-smoking (rare in Spain). The massive foyer looks more like a contemporary art museum entrance, but the rooms are the real surprise. Slip into your Camper slippers and contemplate the Vinçon furniture. Across the corridor from the room is a separate, private sitting room with balcony, TV and hammock.

Hotel Mesón de Castilla (opposite), El Raval

LA RIBERA

Hotels are noticeable by their absence in La Ribera. El Born is such a popular place, however, that several firms offer short-term apartment rentals here (see p213).

PENSIÓ 2000 Map pp298-9   Pension €€

☎ 93 310 74 66; www.pensio2000.com; Carrer de Sant Pere més Alt 6; s/d €51/73, without bathroom €41/51; Ⓜ Urquinaona

This simple, 1st-floor, family-run place is opposite the anything-but-simple Palau de la Música Catalana. Seven reasonably spacious doubles (which can be taken as singles) all have mosaic-tiled floors. Two have ensuite bathroom. Eat brekkie in the little courtyard.

CHIC & BASIC Map pp302-3   Hotel €€

☎ 93 295 46 52; www.chicandbasic.com; Carrer de la Princesa 50; d €90-150; Ⓜ Jaume I; ⊠ 💻

This new hotel 'concept' has landed in a part of town relatively starved of accommodation. In a completely renovated building with high vaults in the façade are 31 spotlessly white rooms. There are high ceilings, enormous beds (room types are classed as M, L and XL!) and lots of detailed touches (LED lighting, TFT TV screens and the retention of many beautiful old features of the original building). The philosophy of the promoters is avant-garde accommodation at an affordable price. Looking good.

HOTEL BANYS ORIENTALS

Map pp302-3   Boutique Hotel €€

☎ 93 268 84 60; www.hotelbanysorientals.com; Carrer de l'Argenteria 37; s/d €86/102; Ⓜ Jaume I; ⊠ 💻

Book well ahead to get into this magnetically popular designer haunt. Cool blue and aquamarines combine with dark-hued parquet floors to lend this clean-lined, inner-city, boutique hotel a quiet charm. All rooms, which admittedly are on the small side, look onto the street or back lanes. Next door they have some considerably bigger (duplex) and marginally more expensive suites (€133.75).

PARK HOTEL Map pp302-3   Hotel €€

☎ 93 319 60 00; www.parkhotelbarcelona.com; Avinguda del Marquès de l'Argentera 11; s/d €128/166; Ⓜ Barceloneta; ⊠ 💻 Ⓟ

Welcome to retro. This 1950s hotel, a short stroll from the waterfront and oozing details

TOP FIVE HOTEL POOLS

- Comtes de Barcelona (p221) Unbeatable rooftop indulgence.
- Grand Marina Hotel (right) Small but nicely placed for portside views.
- Hotel Arts Barcelona (opposite) Look down on the beach and do some short laps.
- Hotel Majèstic (p222) Panoramic views from the rooftop dipping pool.
- Hotel Rey Juan Carlos I (p223) Keep fit in the indoor and outdoor pools.

of that period, such as the sea-green tiles and angular spiral stairway, is a minor Barcelona landmark. Dark wood and fabrics dominate the rooms, some of which have terraces.

GRAND HOTEL CENTRAL

Map pp298-9   Hotel €€
☎ 93 295 79 00; www.grandhotelcentral.com; Via Laietana 30; d €189-294; Ⓜ Jaume I; ⊠ ▯ ▨
Enter a new designer digs on the edge of hotel-starved La Ribera. Set on one of the main arteries of the city with super-soundproofed rooms not smaller than 21 sq metres, with LCD-screen TVs, polished wood floors and subtle lighting. The top-class rooms and suite are more like studio apartments with king-size beds.

PORT VELL & LA BARCELONETA

There's just a handful of seaside options around Port Vell and La Barceloneta, ranging from a youth hostel to a grand five-star.

HOSTEL SEA POINT Map pp302-3   Hostel €
☎ 93 224 70 75; www.seapointhostel.com; Plaça del Mar 4; dm €23; Ⓜ Barceloneta or ▯ 17, 39, 57 or 64; ▯
Right on the beach in a rather ugly high-rise (but hey, you don't have to look at the high-rise) is this busy backpackers' hostel. Rooms are cramped and basic but you cannot get a room closer to the beach.

HOTEL DEL MAR Map pp302-3   Hotel €€
☎ 93 319 33 02; www.gargallohotels.es; Pla de Palau 19; s/d €120/152; Ⓜ Barceloneta; ⊠ ▯
For time immemorial Hotel del Mar was a flea-bitten doss-house. Hard to believe it

now as you step inside this nicely modernised option strategically placed between Port Vell and El Born. Some of the rooms in this classified building have balconies with waterfront views. You're in a fairly peaceful spot but no more than 10 minutes' walk from the beaches and seafood of La Barceloneta and the bars and mayhem of El Born.

GRAND MARINA HOTEL

Map pp290-1   Hotel €€€
☎ 93 603 90 00; www.grandmarinahotel.com; Moll de Barcelona s/n; r €289-332, ste €348-1284; Ⓜ Drassanes; ⊠ ▯ ▨ Ⓟ
Housed in the World Trade Center, the Grand Marina Hotel has a maritime flavour that continues into the rooms, with lots of polished timber touches and hydro-massage bathtubs. Some rooms on either side of the building offer splendid views of the city, port and open sea. The rooftop gym and outdoor pool have equally enticing views. Avoid the hotel's phones – they are among the most expensive in the universe!

PORT OLÍMPIC, EL POBLENOU & EL FÒRUM

For years the breathtakingly located Hotel Arts Barcelona has been *the* place to stay in Barcelona. It is getting some tower hotel competition in the Fòrum area, mostly aimed at a business crowd.

HOTEL BARCELONA PRINCESS

Map pp290-1   Hotel €€
☎ 93 356 10 00; www.hotelbarcelonaprincess .com; Avinguda Diagonal 1; s/d €150/172; Ⓜ El Maresme Fòrum; ⊠ ▯ ▨ Ⓟ
One of the new towering hotels to grace the northeast waterfront corner of the city offers light, smart rooms and a series of suites. Those oriented to the sea have fabulous views. The spa, pool and fitness centre are rather unspectacularly located on the 3rd floor. Hotel Barcelona Princess is directed at business folk in town for a conference at this end of town, which explains why prices are quite moderate at other times.

HOTEL ARTS BARCELONA

Map pp302-3   Hotel €€€

☎ 93 221 10 00; www.ritzcarlton.com; Carrer de la Marina 19-21; r €380-460; Ⓜ Ciutadella Vila Olímpica; 🅧 🖳 🕿 🅿

In one of the two sky-high towers that dominate Port Olímpic, this is Barcelona's most fashionable digs, frequented by VIPs from all over the planet. It has more than 450 rooms with unbeatable views, and prices vary greatly according to size and position. Luxury suites shoot into five-figure sums. Services range from personal bath butlers to the new spa facilities on the 43rd floor.

L'EIXAMPLE

It comes as little surprise that this extensive bourgeois bastion should also be home to the greatest range of hotels in most classes. The grid avenues house some of the city's classic hotels and a long list of decent midrange places.

HOSTAL CENTRAL Map pp298-9   Hostal €

☎ 93 302 24 20; info@al-hostalcentral.com; Ronda de la Universitat 11; s/d €52/65, without bathroom €33/45; Ⓜ Universitat; 🖳

Spread out over several renovated flats, some of the larger rooms have charming enclosed terraces looking onto the admittedly noisy street. Mosaic and parquet floors and some nice decorative touches make it an attractive option.

HOSTAL OLIVA Map pp294-5   Hostal €

☎ 93 488 01 62; www.lasguias.com/hostaloliva; Passeig de Gràcia 32; d €70, s/d without bathroom €35/58; Ⓜ Passeig de Gràcia; 🅧

A picturesque antique lift wheezes its way up to this 4th-floor hostal, a terrific cheapie

---

TOP FIVE STYLE HOTELS

- Casa Camper (p217) Original idea with Vinçon furniture, hammocks and foodballs.
- Hotel Banys Orientals (p217) Bite-sized boutique gem in the old town.
- Hotel Constanza (p220) A midrange jewel with bright colours and fresh flowers.
- Hotel Omm (p221) Fantasy-filled hotel with the 'peeling' façade.
- Hotel Prestige (p221) Chill in the hyper-modern ambience and the Zeroom.

---

in one of the city's dearest neighbourhoods. Some of the singles are barely big enough to fit a bed but the doubles are large, light and airy.

HOSTAL WINDSOR Map pp294-5   Hostal €€

☎ 93 215 11 98; Rambla de Catalunya 84; s/d €48/73; Ⓜ Passeig de Gràcia

An immaculately maintained, elegant hostal, with something of the fussy atmosphere you might expect at your grandmother's, the Hostal Windsor offers good value with its 15 rooms. Try to get one facing the street.

HOSTAL GOYA Map pp298-9   Hostal €€

☎ 93 302 25 65; www.hostalgoya.com; Carrer de Pau Claris 74; d €75-88, s/d without bathroom €37/67; Ⓜ Passeig de Gràcia; 🅧

This is a chichi address on the right side of l'Eixample and the hostal's renovated rooms are inviting, with parquet floors and a light colour scheme. The pricier doubles have nice balconies.

HOSTAL CÈNTRIC Map pp296-7   Hostal €€

☎ 93 426 75 73; www.hostalcentric.com; Carrer de Casanova 13; s/d up to €64/89; Ⓜ Urgell; 🅧 🖳

The hostal, in a good central location just beyond the old town, has a range of rooms, starting with some that have a shared bathroom in the corridor (€40/56 per single/double) and climbing up to renovated ones with private bathroom facilities.

HOTEL D'UXELLES Map pp294-5   Hotel €€

☎ 93 265 25 60; www.hoteluxelles.com; Gran Via de les Corts Catalanes 688; s/d €80/100; Ⓜ Tetuan; 🅧 🖳

A charming simplicity pervades the rooms here. Wrought-iron bedsteads are overshadowed by flowing drapes, room décor varies (from blues and whites to beige-and-cream combos) and some rooms have little terraces. Get a back room as Gran Via is incredibly noisy. It has similar rooms in another building across the road.

HOSTAL PALACIOS Map pp298-9   Hostal €€

☎ 93 301 37 92; www.hostalpalacios.com; Rambla de Catalunya 27; s €55-65, d €100; Ⓜ Passeig de Gràcia; 🅧 🖳

Housed in a classified building, this upmarket hostal offers lovely rooms with high ceilings, sun streaming through balcony doors and old-style furnishings. The 'suites' (€150), which can be taken as triples, are roomy and worth the extra fiscal effort.

HOTEL CONSTANZA

Map pp294-5   Boutique Hotel €€

☎ 93 270 19 10; www.hotelconstanza.com; Carrer del Bruc 33; s/d €107/128; Ⓜ Girona; 🖵 🎌

This boutique beauty has stolen the hearts of many a visitor to Barcelona. Even smaller singles are made to feel special with broad mirrors and strong colours (reds and yellows, with black furniture). Design touches abound, and little details like flowers in the bathroom add charm.

HOTEL CRAM Map pp296-7   Hotel €€

☎ 93 216 77 00; www.hotelcram.com; Carrer d'Aribau 54; s/d €145/163; Ⓜ Passeig de Gràcia; 🎌 🖵 🎌 Ⓟ

The standard rooms are indeed a little Cramped, but full of designer twirls and with a light, white and timber toned décor, all hidden behind an 1892 façade. Widescreen LCD TVs, comfortable Treca beds and high-pressure showers all make up for space shortages. Hang out on the roof terrace or dine downstairs in one the city's most exclusive restaurants.

HOTEL ONIX RAMBLA Map pp298-9 Hotel €€

☎ 93 342 79 80; www.hotelsonix.com; Rambla de Catalunya 24; s/d €158/169; Ⓜ Catalunya; 🎌 🖵 🎌 Ⓟ

Just steps away from Plaça de Catalunya, 40 modern rooms are spread through this former mansion. Rooms are simple and a little small but pleasant enough. Pluses include a small outdoor pool and a handful of exercise machines.

HOTEL CATALONIA BERNA

Map pp294-5   Hotel €€

☎ 93 272 00 50; www.hoteles-catalonia.com; Carrer de Roger de Llúria 60; d €184; Ⓜ Girona; 🎌 🖵 🎌 Ⓟ

It is difficult to miss the intriguing frescoes that grace the entire façade of this historic corner building, which was one of the first to go up in l'Eixample in the 1860s. The rooms are less surprising but perfectly comfortable and with marble bathrooms attached.

HOTEL ASTORIA Map pp294-5   Hotel €€

☎ 93 209 83 11; www.derbyhotels.es; Carrer de Paris 203; d €182-203; Ⓜ Diagonal; 🎌 🖵 🎌 Ⓟ

Nicely situated a short walk from Passeig de Gràcia, this classy three-star is equally well placed for long nights out in the restaurants, bars and clubs of adjacent Carrer d'Aribau. Room décor varies wildly – you might have black-and-white floor tiles or dark parquet. The hotel has its own mini gym and wi-fi connections and boasts paintings by Francesc Guitart.

HOTEL ADVANCE Map pp296-7   Hotel €€

☎ 93 289 28 92; www.hotenco.com; Carrer de Sepúlveda 180; s/d €178/193; Ⓜ Urgell

A modern hotel housed in an historic Eixample building, it's a quick walk from El Raval and the old-town heart. The hotel lives up to its name with plasma TVs and wi-fi Internet. Rooms are fairly standard in appearance but the location is great.

HOTEL DIAGONAL Map pp290-1   Hotel €€

☎ 93 489 53 00; www.hoteldiagonalbarcelona .com; Avinguda Diagonal 205; s/d €123/193; Ⓜ Glòries; 🖵 🎌 🎌 Ⓟ

Designed by local architect Juli Capella as an angular reply to its tubular neighbour, the Torre Agbar, the striking black-and-white exterior presages the designer interior, with purple lighted corridors leading to bright, light rooms, some of which enjoy stunning views of the tower next store and La Sagrada Família.

HOTEL BALMES Map pp294-5   Hotel €€

☎ 93 451 19 14; www.derbyhotels.es; Carrer de Mallorca 216; d €192-214; 🚃 FGC Provença; 🎌 🖵 🎌 Ⓟ

The décor varies greatly from one space to another in this tasteful designer hotel. Some of the more interesting rooms are duplexes and a few have private terraces. Hanging plants fill the internal garden and pool area with a cool green veil.

HOTEL HISPANOS SIETE SUIZA

Map pp294-5   Hotel €€

☎ 93 208 20 51; www.barcelona19apartments .com; Carrer de Sicilia 255; r (for up to 4 people) €193-257; Ⓜ Sagrada Família; 🎌 🖵 Ⓟ

Spitting distance from the towering madness of La Sagrada Família is this original lodging option. Wander in past seven vintage Hispano-Suiza cars to one of 19 apartments, which have two double rooms with separate bathrooms, a lounge, kitchen and terrace. There is also a suite (for up to six people).

COMTES DE BARCELONA

Map pp294-5   Hotel €€
☎ 93 445 00 00; www.condesdebarcelona.com; Passeig de Gràcia 73-75; d €193; Ⓜ Passeig de Gràcia; Ⓧ ▣ ☎ Ⓟ
Also known by its Castilian name, the Condes (Counts) de Barcelona, this premier hotel has a schizoid nature. Its most attractive half occupies the modernista Casa Enric Batlló, built in the 1890s, on one side of Carrer de Mallorca; there is a more modern extension across the road. Inside both, clean, designer lines dominate, with hardwood floors, some architectural touches reminiscent of the modernista exterior of No 75 and luxurious rooms. The vaguely figure-of-eight pool on the roof is a great place to relax after a hard day's sightseeing. Plop into a sun-lounger and take in some rays.

HOTEL PRESTIGE Map pp294-5 Design Hotel €€
☎ 93 272 41 80, 902 200414; www.prestigepaseo degracia.com; Passeig de Gràcia 62; d €173-229; Ⓜ Passeig de Gràcia; Ⓧ ▣ Ⓟ
Bowling up to the stark, steel-framed entrance to this place can be a little daunting. Once inside, you realise you are in a 21st-century designer set (housed in a well-preserved 1930s edifice). The design theme continues in the rooms, with Bang & Olufsen TVs and soft back-lighting above the expansive beds. Inside the block is a pretty garden and among the hotel's amenities is Zeroom, a library and music room to relax in.

HOTEL DUQUES DE BERGARA

Map pp298-9   Hotel €€
☎ 93 301 51 51; www.hoteles-catalonia.es; Carrer de Bergara 11; d €205; Ⓜ Catalunya; Ⓧ ▣ ☎ Ⓟ
This fine modernista hotel boasts an 18th-century intricate *artesonado* ceiling of Cuban mahogany and some nice Art Deco touches. The main building was designed by one of Gaudí's architecture teachers. Rooms have generous marble bathrooms, some with little Jacuzzis.

ST MORITZ HOTEL Map pp294-5   Hotel €€
☎ 93 412 15 00; www.hcchotels.com; Carrer de la Diputació 262bis; s/d €183/211; Ⓜ Passeig de Gràcia; Ⓧ ▣ Ⓟ
These upmarket digs have 91 fully equipped rooms and boast an elegant restaurant, terrace bar and small gym. Some of the bigger rooms, with marble bathrooms, even have their own exercise bikes. You can dine in the modest terrace garden.

HOTEL JAZZ Map pp298-9   Hotel €€
☎ 93 552 96 96; www.nnhotels.es; Carrer de Pelai 3; s/d €193/214; Ⓜ Universitat; Ⓧ ▣ ☎ Ⓟ
Jazz up your day in one of the 108 modern, soundproofed rooms at the edge of the boisterous old town. If you want to stay in, play on the hotel's plug and play or head up for a rooftop swim. Rooms are light and bright, but a bit samey.

HOTEL OMM Map pp294-5   Design Hotel €€€
☎ 93 445 40 00; www.hotelomm.es; Carrer de Rosselló 265; d €225-450; Ⓜ Diagonal; Ⓧ ☎
Design meets plain zane here, where the balconies look like strips of skin peeled back from the shiny hotel surface. The idea would have appealed to Dalí. In the foyer a sprawling, minimalist bar opens before you. Light, clear tones dominate in the ultra modern rooms, of which there are three categories.

The 'peeling' façade of Hotel Omm (above), l'Eixample

HOTEL MAJÈSTIC Map pp294–5   Hotel €€€

☎ 93 488 17 17; www.hotelmajestic.es; Passeig de Gràcia 68; d €254-391; Ⓜ Passeig de Gràcia; ✂ ▢ ♨ Ⓟ

This sprawling, award-winning hotel has the charm of one of the great European hotels. The rooftop pool is great for views and relaxing. The standard rooms (no singles) are smallish but the suites are stunning. You can get your newspaper of choice via satellite.

HOTEL PALACE Map pp294–5   Hotel €€€

☎ 93 510 51 30; www.hotelpalacebarcelona.com; Gran Via de les Corts Catalanes 668; d from €278; Ⓜ Passeig de Gràcia; ✂ ▢ Ⓟ

The Palace (formerly Ritz) has been going since 1919 and remains one of the city's top addresses, especially for those enjoying a little old-world pampering. Rooms are mostly spacious, with thick carpet, fireplaces, and the option of a king-size bed. Some suites (up to €2200) have a bedroom, salon and tiled step-down 'Roman bath'.

HOTEL CLARIS Map pp294–5   Hotel €€€

☎ 93 487 62 62; www.derbyhotels.es; Carrer de Pau Claris 150; d from €310; Ⓜ Passeig de Gràcia; ✂ ▢ ♨ Ⓟ

The designer upgrade of the 19th-century Palacio Verdura has resulted in one of the city's most stylish hotels. It houses plenty of art, from 19th-century Turkish kilims through two ancient Roman statues and on to a collection of Egyptian artefacts. The rooftop restaurant is divine.

GRÀCIA & PARK GÜELL

Staying up in Gràcia takes you out of the mainstream tourist areas and gives you a more 'real' feel for the town. All the touristy bits are never far away by Metro and the restaurant and bar life in Gràcia is great on its own.

APARTHOTEL SILVER Map p292   Hotel €€

☎ 93 218 91 00; www.hotelsilver.com; Carrer de Bretón de los Herreros 26; s/d up to €110/135; Ⓜ Fontana; ✂

There are no less than five types of rooms here, from chintzy, teensy basic rooms to the very spacious, parquet-floored 'superior

GAY STAYS

A couple of excellent gay options, one in the heart of the old town and fairly simple, the other a full design explosion in the heart of the Gaixample, cater nicely to the needs of gay visitors to Barcelona:

Hotel California (Map pp298–9; ☎ 93 317 77 66; www.hotelcaliforniabcn.com; Carrer d'En Rauric 14; s/d €65/95; Ⓜ Liceu; ✂) This friendly and central hotel has 31 straightforward but fastidiously clean rooms with light, neutral colours, satellite TV and good-sized beds. Meet new friends in the bustling breakfast room, and avail yourself of room service 24 hours a day. There is also a laundry service.

Hotel Axel (Map pp296–7; ☎ 93 323 93 93; www.hotelaxel.com; Carrer d'Aribau 33; s/d €133.75/197.95; Ⓜ Universitat; ✂ ▢ ♨) Favoured by a mixed fashion and gay set, Axel occupies a sleek, refurbished corner block and offers modern touches in its designer rooms. Plasma-screen TVs, a light colour scheme and (in the double rooms) king-sized beds are just some of the pluses. Take a break in the rooftop pool, the Finnish sauna or the spa bath. The rooftop skybar is open for chillin' and cocktails from May to September.

rooms'. The best policy is to aim for the better rooms. All come with a kitchenette and some have a terrace or balcony. There is a little garden too.

HOTEL CASA FUSTER Map pp294–5 Hotel €€€

☎ 93 255 30 00; www.hotelescenter.es; Passeig de Gràcia 132; d from €412; Ⓜ Diagonal; ✂ ▢ ♨ Ⓟ

This sumptuous modernista mansion at the top end of the city's showcase boulevard has been transformed into one of Barcelona's most luxurious hotels. Standard rooms are plush if smallish. Period features have been lovingly restored and complemented with hydro-massage tubs, plasma TVs and king-size beds.

LA ZONA ALTA

Except for a certain business clientele, this mostly residential area is a little too far from the action for most people. Several exceptional places are well worth considering if being in the centre of things is not a priority.

ALBERG MARE DE DÉU DE MONTSERRAT Map pp290-1 — Hostel €

☎ 93 210 51 51; www.tujuca.com; Passeig de la Mare de Déu del Coll 41-51; dm under 26yr or ISIC card-holders/others up to €19/22.25; Ⓜ Vallcarca then 🚌 28 or 92; 💻 🅿

This 220-bed hostel is 4km north of the city centre. The main building is a magnificent former mansion with a Mudéjar-style lobby set in a leafy location high up above the expanse of the city. Most rooms sleep six. The common areas are extensive and relaxed. The catch is the midnight curfew.

HOTEL TURÓ DE VILANA

Map pp290-1 — Hotel €€

☎ 93 434 03 63; www.turodevilana.com; Carrer de Vilana 7; s/d €144/182; 🚆 FGC Les Tres Torres or 🚌 64; ✂ 💻 🅿

This bright, designer hotel in residential Sarrià has hardwood floors, marble bathrooms and plenty of natural sunlight. There is not a lot to do in the immediate vicinity, but for those who like the idea of being able to dip in and out of central Barcelona at will, this is an attractive option.

RELAIS D'ORSÀ — Hotel €€

☎ 93 406 94 11; www.relaisdorsa.com; Carrer del Mont d'Orsà 35; d/ste €241/€385; 🚆 FGC Peu del Funicular then Funicular de Vallvidrera; ✂ 🅿

Hide away in this bucolic treat, a transformed neoclassical mansion near the edge of the Collserola woodlands. Every attention to detail has been paid here, with exquisite antique furniture in the five rooms and suite. Outside are verdant gardens and an enticing pool.

GRAN HOTEL LA FLORIDA — Hotel €€€

☎ 93 259 30 00; www.hotellaflorida.com; Carretera de Vallvidrera al Tibidabo 83-93; d from €428; Tibidabo Funicular or taxi; ✂ 💻 🅿

Spreading out 500m above the city and a short stroll from Parc d'Atraccions, the hotel was designed in 1923 and damaged during the civil war. The guest list has ranged from Himmler to Hemingway. Its rooms and suites are all quite different, and the labyrinthine building hosts a gourmet restaurant, jazz bar, disco, outdoor heated pools and a spa. Views across the entire city from various terraces are breathtaking. The main hassle is getting a cab out here at night.

TOP FIVE BUDGET OPTIONS

- Hostal Central (p219) Nicely restored and converted apartments with original mosaic floors.
- Hostal Gat Raval (p216) An original colour scheme and friendly, tuned in staff.
- Hostal Levante (p214) All sorts of rooms in the heart of the Barri Gòtic.
- Hostal Oliveta (p224) A simple getaway from the mainstream tourist spots.
- Pensió 2000 (p217) Family feeling next door to the Palau de la Música Catalana.

SANTS & LES CORTS

There's little incentive to sleep out in this part of town unless you need to be near Sants train station or the Montjuïc fairgrounds. You can, however, often get attractive weekend deals in the city's grand tower business hotels.

HOSTAL SOFIA Map pp296-7 — Hostal €

☎ 93 419 50 40; Avinguda de Roma 1-3; s/d €45/50, without bathroom €35/40; Ⓜ Sants Estació

Just across the square in front of Sants train station, this place has 12 sparkling-clean rooms. Although none too inspiring in terms of charm or location, it is handy if you need to make a quick getaway and/or hang around the fairgrounds of Montjuïc.

HOTEL REY JUAN CARLOS I

Map pp290-1 — Hotel €€€

☎ 93 364 40 40; www.hrjuancarlos.com; Avinguda Diagonal 661-671; d from €272; Ⓜ Zona Universitària; ✂ 💻 ✂ 🅿

Like an ultramodern lighthouse at this gateway to the city from the southwest, the glass towers of this luxury hotel hold spacious rooms, most with spectacular views. The hotel has extensive gardens that belonged to the farmhouse that stood here until well into the 20th century, along with pools and a gym.

MONTJUÏC & POBLE SEC

There's nothing on the mountain itself, but a few options are strung out along and near the Poble Sec side of Avinguda del Paral.lel.

HOSTAL OLIVETA Map pp290-1   Hotel €

☎ 93 329 23 16; Carrer del Poeta Cabanyes 18; s/d €35/55, without bathroom €30/45; Ⓜ Paral .lel; ✄

Six squeaky-clean little rooms huddle above a simple family eatery a short way off busy Avinguda del Paral.lel in Poble Sec. It's hard to argue with the prices and you get to live just beyond the tourist hubbub, although a short walk across the lower half of El Raval will have you on La Rambla.

Excursions

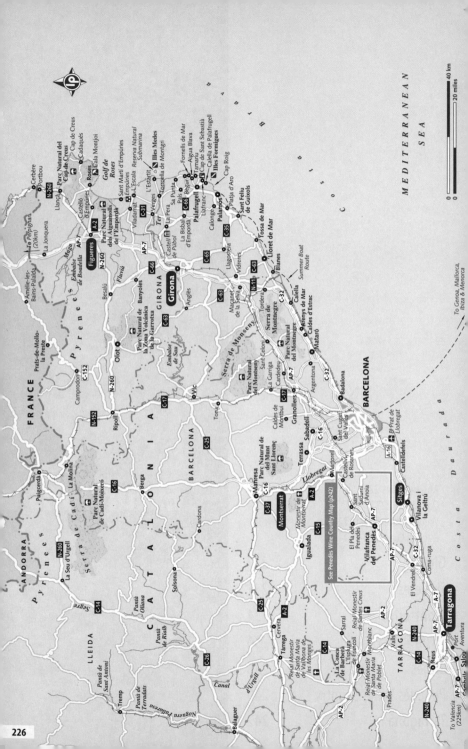

Excursions

Barcelona is just the beginning. Once you break through the choking ring of satellite suburbs and dormitory towns surrounding the capital, one of Spain's most diverse regions unfolds before you. Catalonia (Catalunya to the locals), a land with its own language and proud history setting it apart from the rest of Spain, offers everything from golden beaches to wicked ski runs, medieval monasteries to Roman ruins, top-quality wines to the art of Salvador Dalí. A weekender to Barcelona could easily be converted into a couple of weeks exploring the bustling city's hinterland.

The region, covering 31,932 sq km, is bounded by the mighty Pyrenees mountain range and the French frontier to the north, the Mediterranean Sea to the east and the inland region of Aragón to the west.

Barcelona is the big boy nowadays, but in the times of ancient Rome it was Tarragona that lorded it over this neck of the empire. Evidence today in this sunny port town of Roman grandeur includes the forum, amphitheatre and remains of the circus (chariot race track). To the northeast

ORGANISED TOURS

The Bus Turístic that takes people around Barcelona (see p251) has been such a success that the concept has been extended in the form of **Catalunya Bus Turístic** (Map pp298–9; ☎ 93 285 38 32), a series of day tours from Barcelona to various parts of the region. There are two routes: Girona and Figueres (€60, 8.30am to 8pm) and Colònia Güell, Sant Sadurní d'Anoia and Sitges (€40, 9am to 5.30pm). Both run daily (except Monday) from March to October. The tours leave from Plaça de Catalunya.

of Barcelona, the intensely Catalan town of Girona (you'll be lucky to hear Spanish spoken here) flourished during the Middle Ages. Its tightly packed medieval centre remains largely intact. To the north of Girona lies Figueres, stronghold of the hallucinatory genius of Salvador Dalí.

Catalonia is not all high culture. Myriad beaches, coves and seaside locales dot the breathtakingly rugged spectacle of the Costa Brava northeast of Barcelona. Another fine strand southwest of town is Sitges, loaded with bars and an obligatory stop on the gay partygoers' European circuit. Those who take their hedonism with more restraint can opt to trundle around the Penedès wine country west of Barcelona. And to uplift the soul, the jagged mountain range of Montserrat makes the perfect antidote to a seaside hangover.

ANCIENT CITIES

Tarragona (p242) is a busy port and beachside city with an unfair amount of sunshine! Southwest of Barcelona, it is *the* place in Catalonia for those wanting to know what the Romans ever did for any of us. Apart from the well-preserved vestiges of the city's amphitheatre, circus (where chariot races were held) and forum, Tarragona has an archaeological museum replete with ancient artefacts. Inland and to the northeast of Barcelona lies another Roman settlement, Girona (p228). With its closely cluttered medieval buildings in the crowded old town centre, Girona makes an enchanting counterpoint to the sprawl of the region's capital.

DALÍ MANIA

Zany Salvador Dalí, with his upturned handlebar moustache, outlandish dream paintings and outrageous lifestyle, is surely the most colourful character to emerge from 20th-century Catalonia. For all his globetrotting, he left the greater part of his artistic legacy on home turf. The core rests in his theatre-museum-mausoleum in Figueres (p231), a half-hour north of Girona by train. Enthusiasts can seek out more of his work in several nearby locations, including the magical coastal towns of Cadaqués (p238) and Port Lligat (p232).

BUBBLES AND MUD

For some, a day at the beach just isn't enough (and a little impractical in winter!). Never fear, for wellness is here. Indeed, it always was. Since Roman days, thermal baths have operated in various parts of Catalonia. Now there are 20 across the region, and several of them less than 40km from Barcelona.

In **La Garriga**, a pretty town 36km north of the city, are two fine historic installations that have been modernised. **Termes La Garriga** (☎ 93 871 70 86; www.termes.com; 🕑 9.30am-8pm Mon-Sat, 9.30am-1.30pm & 3.30-7pm Sun) sits atop waters that bubble out at temperatures as high as 60°. All sorts of treatments are possible, from mud baths to aroma massage. For €22 you can spend half a day wandering between a couple of pools, sauna and various showers. The other luxury option here is the five-star **Gran Hotel Blancafort** (☎ 93 860 56 00; www.blanearioblancafort.com).

In the pleasant seaside town of **Caldes d'Estrac**, 36km northeast of Barcelona, the Romans loved to slop around in the thermal waters. You can emulate them in the **Balneari de Caldes d'Estrac** (☎ 93 791 26 05; Carrer de la Riera 29; admission €5.70; 🕑 9am-1pm & 4-8pm Mon-Sat, 9am-3pm Sun). These public baths were built in the early 19th century, although people have been bathing in the waters for at least a couple of millennia. Come up on the train for a day and split your time between the baths (and other extra treatments if you wish), lunch and the beach. Or you could stay at the luxury **Hotel Colón** (☎ 93 791 04 00; www.hotel-colon.net; Plaça de les Barques s/n) and use its modern spa facilities. It offers all sorts of packages.

Caldes de Montbui, just 28km north of Barcelona, hosts three thermal bath hotels. You can use the facilities even if you don't stay in the hotels, although the price can mount depending on what you opt for. The Broquetas group (www .grupbroquetas.com) runs two of the hotels and thermal baths. The **Hotel Broquetas** (☎ 93 865 01 00; Plaça de la Font del Lleó 1) is the town's historic spa hotel, in front of the Roman baths and a public fountain from which water spouts forth at a scorching 76°. Founded in the 18th century and rebuilt several times, it is a predominantly modernista building. Inside it boasts an original Roman vaporarium, a 2nd-century AD steam bath. A session in the thermal pool and cervical showers costs €19. Installations are open to the public from 4.30pm to 8.30pm daily. You should book ahead. **Hotel Termes Victoria** (☎ 93 865 01 50; www.termesvictoria.com; 🕑 8am-1pm & 4-9pm Mon-Sat, 8am-2pm Sun) is a luxury spa hotel. You can use its facilities too, although it is more expensive.

Caldes d'Estrac and La Garriga are easily reached by *rodalies* trains from Barcelona. Caldes de Montbui is more easily reached by car.

WINE, PARTIES & PIETY

Barely 50km west of Barcelona stretch the vineyards of one of Spain's premier wine-making regions, the **Penedès** (p240). Most of the national production of *cava,* the local version of bubbly, pours out of this region. Alongside known names such as Freixenet and Codorníu, countless smaller wineries are in constant ferment.

Barely 20km south of Vilafranca del Penedès, **Sitges** (p238) was a modest fishing village a century ago. It is now a party animal's haven, with a notable gay leaning, and the scene of frenzied beachside Carnaval festivities in February.

On another plane altogether is Catalonia's most revered mountain and monastery, **Montserrat** (p234), northwest of Barcelona. People come here to venerate the Black Madonna, explore the monastery's art treasures and walk in the weirdly shaped mountains.

RUGGED COAST

Too often dismissed because of its tainted package-holiday image, the bulk of the Costa Brava (Rugged Coast, p236) is a joyous spectacle of nature. Blessed with high blustering cliffs, myriad inlets and minuscule coves alternating with long expanses of golden sand and thick stands of hardy pine, it begs to be explored.

GIRONA

Northern Catalonia's largest city, Girona (Gerona in Spanish) is draped in a valley 36km inland from the Costa Brava and 91km northeast of Barcelona. Its medieval centre, which seems to struggle uphill above the Riu Onyar, exudes a quiet, contemplative magnetism.

The Roman town of Gerunda lay on the Via Augusta, the highway from Rome to Cádiz (Carrer de la Força in Girona's old town follows part of its line). Wrested from the

Excursions

GIRONA

Muslims by the Franks in AD 797, Girona became capital of one of Catalonia's most important counties, only falling under the sway of Barcelona in the late 9th century. Its medieval wealth produced a plethora of fine Romanesque and Gothic buildings that survived repeated assaults and sieges to give us pleasure today.

TRANSPORT

Distance from Barcelona 91km
Direction Northeast
Travel time Up to 1½ hours
Car Take the AP-7 motorway via Granollers.
Train At least 17 trains daily from Barcelona Sants station (€5.45 to €6.25).

The narrow streets of the old town climb in a web above the east bank of the Riu Onyar. Commanding the northern half of the city with its majestic baroque façade placed high over a breezy square and stairway, the **Catedral** makes an obvious starting point for exploration. Most of the edifice, which has been altered repeatedly, is a great deal older than its exterior suggests. Wander inside to appreciate this. First you find yourself in Europe's widest Gothic nave (23m), but other treasures await in and beyond the cathedral **museum**. Head through the door marked 'Claustre Tresor'. The collection includes the masterly Romanesque *Tapís de la Creació* (Creation Tapestry) and a priceless Mozarabic illuminated *Beatus* manuscript from AD 975. Beyond the museum you emerge in the beautiful, if somewhat wonkily-shaped, 12th-century Romanesque **cloister**; the 112 stone columns display whimsical, albeit weathered, sculpture.

Next door to the cathedral, in the 12th- to 16th-century Palau Episcopal, the **Museu d'Art** boasts an extensive collection that ranges from occasionally delirious-looking Romanesque woodcarvings to rather more dour early-20th-century paintings.

Girona's second great church, the **Església de Sant Feliu**, is downhill from the cathedral. The 17th-century main façade, with its landmark single tower, is on Plaça de Sant Feliu, but the entrance is around the side. The nave has 13th-century Romanesque arches but 14th- to 16th-century Gothic upper levels. The northernmost of the chapels, at the far western end of the church, is graced by a masterly Catalan Gothic sculpture, Aloi de Montbrai's alabaster *Crist Jacent* (Recumbent Christ). It looks like it is made of perfectly moulded ice-cream.

The **Banys Àrabs** (Arab Baths), although modelled on Muslim and Roman bathhouses, is actually a 12th-century Christian affair in Romanesque style. It's the only public bathhouse discovered in medieval Christian Spain. Possibly in reaction to the Muslim obsession with water and cleanliness, in Christian Europe washing came to be regarded as ungodly (and water was feared as a source of germs and illness). Europe must have been the smelliest continent on earth! The bathhouse contains an *apodyterium* (changing room), followed by the *frigidarium* (cold water room) and *tepidarium* (hot water room), and the *caldarium*, a kind of sauna. Across the street from the Banys Àrabs, steps lead up into lovely gardens that follow the city walls in what is called the **Passeig Arqueològic** (Archaeological Walk) up to the 18th-century Portal de Sant Cristòfol gate, from which you can walk back down to the cathedral.

About 100m north of the Banys Àrabs across the bubbling Riu Galligants stands the 11th- and 12th-century Romanesque **Monestir de Sant Pere de Galligants**, a modest monastery with a lovely cloister. Get up close to the pillars that line the cloister; the closer you look the weirder the medieval imagination seems – all those bizarre animals and mythical monsters! The monastery also houses the **Museu Arqueològic**, with exhibits that range from prehistoric to medieval times, and include Roman mosaics and some medieval Jewish tombstones. Just opposite the monastery is the pretty Lombard-style 12th-century Romanesque **Església de Sant Nicolau**. It is unusual for its octagonal belltower, and it also has a triple apse in a trefoil plan.

South along Carrer de la Força, about 100m off the stairway leading up to Plaça de la Catedral, the **Museu d'Història de la Ciutat** (City History Museum) traces Girona's history from ancient times to the present. Dioramas, explanatory boards, videos and all sorts of objects ranging from Neolithic tools to the whining musical instruments used to accompany the *sardana* (traditional Catalan folk dance) help bring the town's story to life. Learn about the 18-month siege of the town by Napoleon's troops, which cost half Girona's population their lives.

Carrer de la Força lies at the heart of the Call (the Jewish quarter). Until 1492, when Jews had to convert to Catholicism or leave Spain, Girona was home to Catalonia's second most

Excursions

GIRONA

important Jewish community after Barcelona. For an idea of medieval Jewish life, visit the **Museu d'Història dels Jueus de Girona** (Jewish History Museum, aka the Centre Bonastruc Ça Porta). Named after Jewish Girona's most illustrious figure, a 13th-century Cabbalist philosopher and mystic, the centre hosts limited exhibitions and is a focal point for studies of Jewish Spain. It claims to have the biggest collection of Jewish funeral stones and sarcophagi in the country.

There is not a great deal to see in the modern half of Girona, on the west bank of the Riu Onyar. One outstanding exception is the **Museu del Cinema**, Spain's only cinema museum, housed in the Casa de les Aigües. Shadow puppets and magic lanterns introduce the Col.lecció Tomàs Mallol, a display that details the precursors to and story of the motion-picture

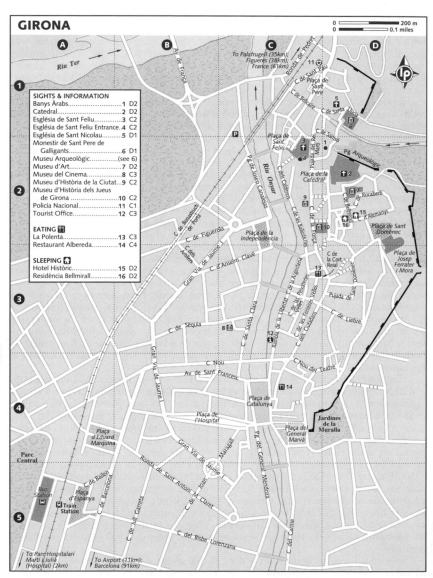

GIRONA

0 ——————— 200 m
0 ——————— 0.1 miles

SIGHTS & INFORMATION
Banys Àrabs......................................1 D2
Catedral...2 D2
Església de Sant Feliu.......................3 C2
Església de Sant Feliu Entrance...4 C2
Església de Sant Nicolau..................5 D1
Monestir de Sant Pere de
    Galligants.....................................6 D1
Museu Arqueològic...................(see 6)
Museu d'Art......................................7 D2
Museu del Cinema.............................8 C3
Museu d'Història de la Ciutat...9 C2
Museu d'Història dels Jueus
    de Girona 10 C2
Policía Nacional..............................11 C1
Tourist Office..................................12 C3

EATING
La Polenta......................................13 C3
Restaurant Albereda...................14 C4

SLEEPING
Hotel Històric.................................15 D2
Residència Bellmirall..................16 D2

business. Forms of screen entertainment include everything from the first still cameras and fairground moving-picture attractions of the late 19th century through to the earliest celluloid hits, a handful of which you can see. Take a closer look at some of the images for fairground magic lantern shows in the 18th century, like the devilish character working a bellows in someone's backside!

Sights

Banys Àrabs (☎ 972 21 32 62; Carrer de Ferran Catòlic; admission €1.50; ☺ 10am-8pm Tue-Sat Jul & Aug, 10am-7pm Tue-Sat Apr-Jun & Sep, 10am-2pm Tue-Sat Oct-Mar, 10am-2pm Sun & holidays)

Catedral (☎ 972 21 44 26; www.lacatedraldegirona.com; Plaça de la Catedral; museum admission €4, Sun free; ☺ 10am-2pm & 4-7pm Tue-Sat Mar-Jun, 10am-8pm Tue-Sat Jul-Sep, 10am-2pm & 4-6pm Tue-Sat Oct-Feb, 10am-2pm Sun & holidays)

Església de Sant Feliu (Plaça de Sant Feliu; ☺ 9.30am-2pm & 4-7pm Mon-Sat, 10am-noon & 4-7pm Sun)

Monestir de Sant Pere de Galligants/Museu Arqueològic (☎ 972 20 26 32; Carrer de Santa Llúcia; admission €1.80; ☺ 10.30am-1.30pm & 4-7pm Tue-Sat Jun-Sep, 10am-2pm & 4-6pm Tue-Sat Oct-May, 10am-2pm Sun & holidays)

Museu d'Art (☎ 972 20 38 34; www.museuart.com; Plaça de la Catedral 12; admission €2; ☺ 10am-7pm Tue-Sat Mar-Sep, 10am-6pm Tue-Sat Oct-Feb, 10am-2pm Sun & holidays)

Museu del Cinema (☎ 972 41 27 77; www.museudelcinema.org; Carrer de Sèquia 1; admission €3; ☺ 10am-8pm Tue-Sun May-Sep, 10am-6pm Tue-Fri, 10am-8pm Sat, 11am-3pm Sun Oct-Apr)

Museu d'Història de la Ciutat (☎ 972 22 22 29; Carrer de la Força 27; admission €2; ☺ 10am-2pm & 5-7pm Tue-Sat, 10am-2pm Sun & holidays)

Museu d'Història dels Jueus de Girona (☎ 972 21 67 61; Carrer de la Força 8; admission €2; ☺ 10am-8pm Mon-Sat Jun-Oct, 10am-6pm Mon-Sat Nov-May, 10am-3pm Sun & holidays)

Information

Parc Hospitalari (Hospital) Martí i Julià (☎ 972 18 25 00; Carrer del Doctor Castany s/n)

Policía Nacional (☎ 091; Carrer de Sant Pau 2)

Tourist office (☎ 972 22 65 75; www.ajuntament.gi/turisme; Rambla de la Llibertat 1; ☺ 8am-8pm Mon-Fri, 8am-2pm & 4-8pm Sat, 9am-2pm Sun)

Eating

La Polenta (☎ 972 20 93 74; Carrer de la Cort Reial 6; meals €15-20) For vegetarian goodies, this cheerful little place is a good option. Opening days vary.

Restaurant Albereda (☎ 972 22 60 02; Carrer de l'Albereda 9; meals €35-40; ☺ Tue-Sat, lunch Mon; ✗) The town's senior restaurant serves Catalan cuisine with interesting twists, such as frog's legs.

Sleeping

Hotel Històric (☎ 972 22 35 83; www.hotelhistoric.com; Carrer de Bellmirall 4/a; s/d €109/122; ✽ P) A bijou hotel in an historic building in the heart of old Girona. The eight pretty, spacious rooms are individually decorated. Also has apartments.

Residència Bellmirall (☎ 972 20 40 09; Carrer de Bellmirall 3; s/d €35/60; ☺ closed Jan-Mar; ✽) On the same lane, this is a simpler but engaging little spot in a medieval building.

FIGUERES

Just 12km inland from the Golf de Roses, Figueres (Figueras in Spanish) might generously be described as a humdrum town with a single serious attraction: Salvador Dalí. Born here in 1904, Dalí maintained ties with his home territory in all his long years of peregrination between Barcelona, Madrid, Paris and the US. Indeed, he lived over half his adult life at Port Lligat, a tiny settlement just north of Cadaqués, on the coast east of Figueres.

TRANSPORT

Distance from Barcelona 129km
Direction Northeast
Travel time 1½ to 2¼ hours
Car Take the AP-7 motorway via Granollers and Girona. From central Girona it should not take more than 30 minutes.
Train At least 16 trains daily from Barcelona Sants station via Girona (€7.90 to €9.10).

Towards the end of the Spanish Civil War in 1939, Figueres' theatre was largely destroyed by fire and in the following decades it was left to rot. In 1961 the by-now world-renowned eccentric Dalí had the money to buy the site and start work on one of his wackier projects, the **Teatre-Museu Dalí**, which he completed in 1974. It is at once art gallery, final testament and mausoleum. It was, and remains, the greatest act of self-promotion of a man who had made a supreme art form of such activities. But make no mistake, Dalí was a unique artistic talent, as the contents of his theatre-museum amply demonstrate. It is a multidimensional trip through one of the most fertile (or febrile) imaginations of the 20th century, full of surprises, tricks and illusions, and containing much of Dalí's life's work.

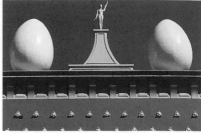

Dalí's trademark eggs on the roof of the Teatre-Museu Dalí (left), Figueres

The building aims to surprise even before you get inside. The fuchsia wall along Pujada del Castell is topped by a row of Dalí's trademark egg shapes and what appear to be female gymnasts ready to leap. Bizarre sculptures greet visitors outside the entrance on Plaça de Gala i Salvador Dalí. One can only imagine the parish priest at the adjacent centuries-old **Església de Sant Pere** looking with disapproval (Franco was still in charge in those days) upon this loopiness as it emerged from the theatre ruins.

Inside, the ground floor (level one) includes a semicircular garden area on the site of the original theatre stalls. In its centre is a classic piece of weirdness, *Taxi Plujós* (Rainy Taxi), composed of an early Cadillac – said to have belonged to Al Capone – and a pile of tractor tyres, both surmounted by statues, with a fishing boat balanced precariously above the tyres. Put a coin in the slot and water washes all over the inside of the car. The Sala de Peixateries (Fish Shop Room) off here holds a collection of Dalí oils including his *Autoretrat tou amb tall de bacon fregit* (Soft Self-Portrait with Fried Bacon) and *Retrat de Picasso* (Portrait of Picasso). Beneath the former stage of the theatre is the crypt, with Dalí's surprisingly plain tomb.

DALLYING WITH DALÍ DELIRIUM

Dalí left his mark in several locations around Catalonia, particularly at his seaside residence in Port Lligat and inland 'castle', Castell de Púbol.

Port Lligat, a 1.25km walk north of Cadaqués, is a tiny fishing settlement on a quiet, enchanting bay. God only knows what serious-minded fishermen thought of Dalí's seaside residence, antics and international jet-set pals. Dalí spent time (more than half his adult life) here from 1930 in what was at first a fisherman's hut, so no doubt the locals were well used to his unusual presence by the time he left for good in 1982. Dalí had not come by choice. His father had forbidden him to return to the family house in Cadaqués after Dalí presented what was for his father an intolerable painting in Paris. Across an image of the Sacred Heart Dalí had written: *Parfois je crache par plaisir sur le portrait de ma mère* (Sometimes I spit for fun on my mother's picture). His father never forgave him this insult to his deceased wife. By Dalí's standards the myriad white chimney pots and two egg-shaped towers on the house he 'grew' out of the original cabin are rather understated. The house was steadily altered and recreated according to the artist's own distorted vision down through the years. It is now a museum, **Casa Museu Dalí** (☎ 972 25 10 15; www.salvador-dali.org; adult/student & senior €8/5; ☷ 10.30am-9pm mid-Jun–mid-Sep, 10.30am-6pm Tue-Sun mid-Sep–mid-Jan & mid-Mar–mid-Jun, closed mid-Jan-mid-Mar, bookings essential).

The **Castell de Púbol** (☎ 972 48 86 55; www.salvador-dali.org; adult/student & senior €6/4; ☷ 10.30am-7.15pm mid-Jun–mid-Sep, 10.30am-5.15pm Tue-Sun mid-Sep–Oct & mid-Mar–mid-Jun, 10.30am-4.15pm Tue-Sat Nov-Dec), in the village of La Pera, just south of the C-66 road between Girona and Palafrugell, forms the southernmost point of the Dalí triangle. He bought the Gothic and Renaissance mansion – which includes a 14th-century church – in 1968 for his wife, Gala, who lived here without him (and apparently lusted after local young men to the end of her days) until her death at 88 in 1982. An inconsolable Dalí then moved in himself, but abandoned the place after a fire (which nearly burnt him to a crisp) in 1984 to live out his last years at Figueres. Dalí did the castle up in his own inimitable style, with lions' heads staring from the tops of cupboards, statues of elephants with giraffes' legs in the garden and a stuffed giraffe staring at Gala's tomb in the crypt.

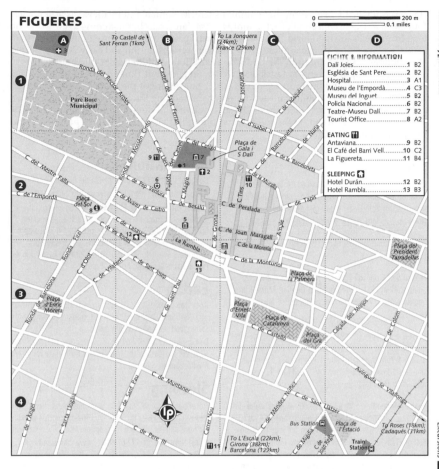

FIGUERES

0 — 200 m
0 — 0.1 miles

SIGHTS & INFORMATION	
Dalí Joies...........................1	B2
Església de Sant Pere.......2	B2
Hospital...........................3	A1
Museu de l'Empordà..........4	C3
Museu del Joguet..............5	B2
Policía Nacional................6	B2
Teatre-Museu Dalí............7	B2
Tourist Office...................8	A2

EATING	
Antaviana..........................9	B2
El Café del Barri Vell.........10	C2
La Figuereta....................11	B4

SLEEPING	
Hotel Durán.....................12	B2
Hotel Rambla...................13	B3

The stage area (level two), topped by a glass geodesic dome, was conceived as Dalí's Sistine Chapel. The large egg-head-breasts-rocks-trees backdrop was part of a ballet set, one of Dalí's ventures into the performing arts. If proof were needed of Dalí's acute sense of the absurd, *Gala Mirando el Mar Mediterráneo* (Gala Looking at the Mediterranean Sea) would be it. From the other end of the room, the work appears, with the help of coin-operated viewfinders, to be a portrait of Abraham Lincoln. One floor up (level three) is the Sala de Mae West, a living room where the components, viewed from the right spot, make up a portrait of Ms West: a sofa for her luscious, wet lips, twin fireplaces for nostrils, impressionist paintings of Paris for those come-to-bed eyes.

A separate section displays the magnificent Owen Cheatham collection of 37 pieces of jewellery in gold and precious stones designed by Dalí. Dalí did the designs on paper (his first commission was in 1941) and the jewellery was made by specialists in New York. Each piece, ranging from the disconcerting *Ull del Temps* (Eye of Time) through to the *Cor Reial* (Royal Heart), is unique. They changed hands several times until the foundation that runs the museum acquired them in 2001 for a cool €5.5 million. Entrance to Dalí Joies (Dalí Jewels) is by a separate door.

On La Rambla, the town's main boulevard about 100m south of the dazzling display of Dalían dizziness, lie what are, by comparison, two rather staid museums. The Museu de

233

l'Empordà is a worthy institution that combines Greek, Roman and medieval archaeological finds with a sizable collection of art, mainly by Catalan artists but including a few works on loan from the Prado in Madrid. The **Museu del Joguet**, Spain's only toy museum, has more than 3500 Catalonia- and Valencia-made toys from the pre-Barbie 19th and early 20th centuries. One wonders to what children the Groucho Marx doll would have appealed.

The sprawling 18th-century **Castell de Sant Ferran**, on a low hill 1km northwest of the centre, was built to withstand the most vicious of sieges but never got the chance to show its mettle. Built in 1750, it saw almost no action. After abandoning Barcelona, Spain's Republican government held its final meeting of the civil war in the dungeons on 1 February 1939. The Castell is still owned by the military, who don't at all mind divisions of tourists manoeuvring around inside.

Sights

Castell de Sant Ferran (☎ 972 50 60 94; www.les fortalesescatalanes.info/santferran.html; admission €2; ⏱ 10.30am-8pm Easter & Jul–mid-Sep, 10.30am-2pm Nov-Feb, 10.30am-2pm & 4-6pm rest of yr)

Dalí Joies (adult/student €6/4; ⏱ as for Teatre-Museu Dalí)

Museu de l'Empordà (☎ 972 50 23 05; La Rambla 2; adult/student €2/1; ⏱ 11am-7pm Tue-Sat, 11am-2pm Sun & holidays) Admission free with a Teatre-Museu Dalí ticket.

Museu del Joguet (☎ 972 50 45 85; www.mjc-figueres .net; La Rambla 10; adult/student €4.70/3.80; ⏱ 10am-1pm & 4-7pm Mon-Sat, 11am-1.30pm & 5-7.30pm Sun Jun-Sep, 10am-1pm & 4-7pm Tue-Sat, 11am-1.30pm Sun & holidays Oct-May)

Teatre-Museu Dalí (☎ 972 67 75 00; www.salvador-dali .org; Plaça de Gala i Salvador Dalí; adult/student €10/7, summer nights €11; ⏱ 9am-7.45pm Jul-Sep, 10.30am-5.45pm Tue-Sun Oct-Jun, summer nights 10pm-1am Aug) Admission includes entry to Dalí Joies. Night entry in August is limited and tickets must be booked ahead. Entry includes a complimentary glass of *cava*.

Information

Hospital (☎ 972 67 50 89; Ronda del Rector Aroles s/n)
Policía Nacional (☎ 091; Carrer de Pep Ventura 8)
Tourist office (☎ 972 50 31 55; www.figueresciutat .com/vis-info.html; Plaça del Sol; ⏱ 8.30am-9pm Mon-Fri, 9am-9pm Sat, 9am-3pm Sun Jul & Aug, 8.30am-8pm Mon-Fri, 9am-8pm Sat Sep, 8.30am-3pm & 4.30-8pm Mon-Fri, 9.30am-1.30pm & 3.30-6.30pm Sat Easter-Jun & Oct, 8.30am-3pm Mon-Fri Nov-Easter)

Eating

Antaviana (☎ 972 51 03 77; Carrer de Llers 5; meals €30; ⏱ Wed-Sun; ✕) A mix of Mediterranean cooking, with some good seafood and light meals.

La Figuereta (☎ 972 67 38 45; Carrer Nou 101; meals €25; ⏱ Tue-Sat, lunch Mon) Elegant little place for tasty Mediterranean cooking.

Sleeping

Hotel Durán (☎ 972 50 12 50; www.hotelduran.com; Carrer de Lasauca 5; s/d €75/107; ⛄ Ⓟ) The city centre's grand old hotel and the most attractive option. Also a fine restaurant.
Hotel Rambla (☎ 972 67 60 20; www.hotelrambla.net; La Rambla 33; s/d €50/75; ⛄ Ⓟ) Right in the heart of the city with comfortable, modern rooms. Larger ones cost a little more.

MONTSERRAT

Shimmering bizarrely in the distance as you drive the C-16 toll road between Terrassa and Manresa is the emblematic mountain range of Catalonia, Montserrat (Serrated Mountain). So dear is it to Catalan hearts that it has long been a popular first name for girls (generally Montse for short). Lying 50km northwest of Barcelona, the serried ranks of wind- and rain-whipped rock pillars (reaching a height of 1236m) were formed from a conglomeration of limestone, pebbles and sand that once lay beneath the sea. With the historic Benedictine monastery, one of Catalonia's most important shrines, perched at 725m on the mountain range's flank, it makes a great outing from Barcelona.

From the range, on a clear day, you can see as far as the Pyrenees, Barcelona's Tibidabo hill and even, if you're lucky, Mallorca.

A cable car, rack-and-pinion railway or your own wheels can be used to ascend the mountain as far as the monastery. From here, the main road curves (past a snack bar, cafeteria, information office and the Espai Audiovisual) round and up to the right, passing the blocks of the Cel.les Abat Marcel, to enter Plaça de Santa Maria at the centre of the monastery complex.

TRANSPORT

Distance from Barcelona 46km
Direction Northwest
Travel time One hour

Bus A daily bus (€43) from Barcelona with **Julià Tours** (Map pp298–9; ☎ 93 317 64 54; Ronda de l'Universitat 5, Barcelona) leaves for the monastery at 9.30am (returning at 3pm). The price includes travel, all entry prices, use of funiculars at Montserrat and a meal at the self-service restaurant.

Car Take the C-16. Shortly after Terrassa, follow the exit signs to Montserrat, which will put you on the C-58 road. Follow it northwest to the C-55. Then head 2km south on this road to Monistrol de Montserrat, from where a road snakes 7km up the mountain.

Train The R5 line trains operated by **FGC** (☎ 93 205 15 15) run from Plaça d'Espanya station in Barcelona to Monistrol de Montserrat up to 18 times daily starting at 8.36am. They connect with the rack-and-pinion train, or **cremallera** (☎ 902 31 20 20; www.cremalleradamontserrat.com), which takes 17 minutes to make the upwards journey and costs €3.80/6 one way/return. One-way/return from Barcelona to Montserrat with the FGC train and *cremallera* costs €8/14.40. Alternatively, you could get off the train a stop earlier at Montserrat Aeri and take the Aeri de Montserrat cable car (same price as *cremallera*).

TransMontserrat tickets (€18.40) include the train, *cremallera*, two Metro rides, the Espai Audiovisual and unlimited use of the funiculars. The TotMontserrat card (€31) includes all this plus museum entrance and a modest dinner at the self-service restaurant. Two further ticketing options are available for those who get to the *cremallera* under their own steam. The Combi 1 ticket (€12) includes unlimited use of the funiculars and entrance to the Espai Audiovisual, while the Combi 2 ticket (€24.75) also includes the museum entrance and a meal at the self-service restaurant. There are discounts for children, students and senior citizens on all the above fares.

The **Monestir de Montserrat** was founded in 1025 to commemorate a vision of the Virgin on the mountain. Wrecked by Napoleon's troops in 1811, then abandoned as a result of anticlerical legislation in the 1830s, it was rebuilt from 1858. Today a community of about 80 monks lives here. Pilgrims come from far and wide to venerate **La Moreneta** (Black Madonna), a 12th-century Romanesque wooden sculpture of Mary with the infant Jesus that has been Catalonia's official patron since 1881. A bit like children refusing to believe claims that Santa Claus does not exist, Catalans chose to ignore the discovery in 2002 that their Madonna is not black at all, just deeply tanned by centuries of candle smoke!

The two-part **Museu de Montserrat** has a collection ranging from ancient artefacts, including an Egyptian mummy, to occasional works by Caravaggio, Monet, Degas, Picasso and others, as well as a new collection of 17th- to 20th-century Orthodox church icons from Eastern Europe. The **Espai Audiovisual** is a walk-through multimedia space (with images and sounds) that illustrates the daily life and activities of the monks and the monastery's history.

From Plaça de Santa Maria you enter the courtyard of the 16th-century **basilica**. The façade, with its carvings of Christ and the 12 Apostles, dates from 1901, despite its 16th-century Plateresque style. For La Moreneta, follow the signs to the Cambril de la Mare de Déu, to the right of the basilica's main entrance.

The **Escolania** (reckoned to be Europe's oldest music school) has a boys' choir, the **Montserrat Boys' Choir**, which sings in the basilica once a day, Sunday to Friday, except in July and August. It is a rare (if brief) treat as the choir does not often perform outside Montserrat – five concerts a year and a world tour every two. The choir has sung hymns since the 13th century. The 40 to 50 *escolanets*, aged between 10 and 14, go to boarding school at Montserrat and must endure a two-year selection process to join the choir.

To see where the holy image of the Virgin was discovered, take the **Funicular de Santa Cova** down from the main area. You can explore the mountain above the monastery by a network of paths leading to some of the peaks and to 13 empty and rather dilapidated hermitages. The **Funicular de Sant Joan** will carry you from the monastery 250m up the mountain in seven minutes. If you prefer to walk, the road leading past the funicular's bottom station winds 3km up the mountain and around to the top station.

From the Sant Joan top station, it's a 20-minute stroll (signposted) to the **Sant Joan hermitage**; both the walk and the hermitage have fine westwards views. More exciting is the hour's walk northwest along a path marked with occasional blobs of yellow paint to Montserrat's highest peak, **Sant Jeroni** (1236m), from which there's an awesome sheer drop on the northern side.

Excursions

MONTSERRAT

Sights

Basilica (admission incl La Moreneta €5; 8am-8.15pm Jul-Sep, earlier closing rest of yr)

Cambril de la Mare de Déu (La Moreneta; 8-10.30am & 12.15-6.30pm Mon-Sat; 8-10.30am, 12.15-6.30pm & 7.30-8.15pm Sun & holidays)

Escolania on Montserrat (www.escolania.net; admission free; performances 1pm Mon-Fri, noon & 6.45pm Sun Sep-Jun) See latest performance times on the web page.

Espai Audiovisual (admission €2, with Museu de Montserrat free; 10am-6pm)

Funicular de Sant Joan (one way/return €3.90/6.30; every 20min 10am-5.40pm Apr-Oct, to 7pm mid-Jul–Aug, 11am-4.30pm Nov-Mar)

Funicular de Santa Cova (one way/return €1.61/2.60; every 20min 10am-5.35pm Apr-Oct, 11am-4.25pm Nov-Mar)

Monestir de Montserrat information office (93 877 77 01; www.abadiamontserrat.net; 9am-6pm)

Museu de Montserrat (93 877 77 77; Plaça de Santa Maria; admission €5.50; 10am-6pm)

Eating

Cafeteria Self-Service (meals €10-15; lunch) Downstairs from the snack bar near the top cable-car station, the cafeteria has standard self-service fare and great views.

Hotel Abat Cisneros (meals €25-30) The hotel restaurant is one of only two options for full, sit-down dining.

Sleeping

Cel.les Abat Marcel (93 877 77 01; per day for 2/4 people €47/€83; P) Comfortable apartments equipped with full bathroom and kitchenette. Smaller studios go for €32/38 for one/two people.

Hotel Abat Cisneros (93 877 77 01; s/d €51/89; P) The only hotel in the monastery complex, with modern, comfortable rooms, some looking onto Plaça de Santa Maria.

COSTA BRAVA

The rugged Costa Brava stretches from bland Blanes (about 60km northeast of Barcelona) to the French border. At its best it is magnificent. At its worst it fully lives up to its reputation as a beach-holiday inferno. Lloret de Mar and parts of the Golf de Roses are the worst offenders, where you can almost hear all that northern European flesh sizzling on the beaches in between lager top-ups. But don't run away! The bulk of the coast is one of nature's grand spectacles, with rugged cliffs plunging into crystalline azure water, interrupted at improbable points by ribbons of golden sand, tiny hidden coves and the shade of pine stands. Some of the towns have managed to retain great charm, and one of the most ancient sites of settlement in Spain, Empúries, is on the Costa Brava.

Driving is the easiest way to explore the coast, as getting about by bus can be complicated. What follows is a taster. To reach all these spots you need to reckon on at least one overnight stay. In July and August finding lodgings without a reservation can be problematic.

Leaving the strobe-light silliness of Lloret de Mar behind you, the road slices back inland into the coastal hills before setting you down in **Tossa de Mar**. A small white town backing onto

TRANSPORT

Distance from Barcelona Tossa de Mar 77km; Palafrugell 125km; Empúries 153km; Cadaqués 164km (or 199km via Empúries)

Direction Northeast

Travel time 1½ to 2¼ hours

Car The quickest way to reach any one of these destinations is to take the AP-7 motorway from Barcelona and peel off at exit 9 for Tossa de Mar, exit 6 for Palafrugell and around, exit 5 for L'Escala and Empúries and exit 4 for Cadaqués (via Roses). Alternatively you can follow the coast for all or parts of the trip. From Barcelona take the C-32 to Blanes and then single-carriage roads to Tossa de Mar via Lloret de Mar. The single-carriageway A-2 coast road is slower still. From Tossa it is possible to follow the coast (the initial 21km stretch to Sant Feliu de Guíxols is breathtaking) to Palafrugell and beyond.

Bus SARFA (902 302025; www.sarfa.com) runs buses from Barcelona's Estació del Nord to Tossa de Mar (€8.95, 1½ hours, seven to 18 times daily) and to Palafrugell (€13.70, two hours, seven to 13 times daily). Local buses connect to Calella, Llafranc and Tamariu. Up to four buses a day run from Barcelona to L'Escala and Empúries via Palafrugell (€15, 1½ hours). For Cadaqués, buses to/from Barcelona (€18.05, 2¼ hours) operate from two to five times daily.

View over the headland, with medieval defensive walls and tower, and beach of Tossa de Mar (opposite), Costa Brava

a curved bay that ends in a headland protected by medieval walls and towers, Tossa is an enticing location. Artist Marc Chagall called it his Blue Paradise. The place has sprawled since Chagall stopped by in the 1930s, but Tossa has retained the integrity of a beachside village.

The walls and towers on the headland, **Mont Guardí**, at the southern end of the main beach, were built in the 12th to 14th centuries. The area they girdle is known as the **Vila Vella** (Old Town). Wandering around Mont Guardí you come across ruins of a castle and a lighthouse; the sunsets here are superb. **Vila Nova** (New Town), a tangle of 18th-century lanes, stretches away from the old nucleus and makes for a pleasant stroll. The main beach, **Platja Gran**, tends to be busy. Further north along the same bay are some quieter, smaller beaches.

The 21km drive from Tossa to **Sant Feliu de Guíxols** is a treat, the most breathtaking driving stretch of the coast. From here the coast road continues through the not unpleasant Spanish resort area of Platja d'Aro, on through the more offensive Palamós and inland to **Palafrugell**, a local transport hub that funnels you into another prime stretch of the Costa Brava. Again, uncompromising rock walls are interspersed with coves and hideaways. Among the places you can fan out to are **Calella de Palafrugell**, **Llafranc**, **Tamariu**, **Aigua Blava** and **Fornells de Mar**. A coastal walking path links the first three.

Jagged cliffs and pine stands give way to a long stretch of beach beyond Sa Punta to **L'Estartit**, the diving centre of the coast fronted by the marine reserve of the **Illes Medes**. From here roads redirect you inland to **L'Escala**, a low-key resort town on the southern tip of the Golf de Roses bay, and the nearby ruins of **Empúries**. Founded around 600 BC, it was probably the first, and certainly one of the most important, Greek colonies in Iberia. It came to be called Emporion (literally 'market'). In 218 BC, Roman legions set foot on the peninsula here to cut off Hannibal's supply lines during the Second Punic War. By the early 1st century AD, the Roman and Greek settlements had merged. Emporiae, as the place was then known, was abandoned in the late 3rd century after raids by Germanic tribes.

A small **museum** separates the Greek town from the larger Roman town on the upper part of the site (the Museu d'Arqueologia de Catalunya in Barcelona, p121, has a bigger and better Empúries collection). Highlights of the latter include the mosaic floors of a 1st century BC house, the forum and walls. Outside the walls are the remains of an oval amphitheatre.

A string of brown-sand beaches stretches north from the ruins and leads to the cheerful 15th-century hamlet of **Sant Martí d'Empúries**. On Plaça Major four restaurant-bars compete for your business.

Next, head for the windswept **Parc Natural del Cap de Creus**. Apart from Spain's most easterly point (Cap de Creus), the area bursts with hiking possibilities, coves and the eternally attractive seaside town of **Cadaqués**, a strange mix of whitewashed fishing village and minor hedonists' hangout. The area was the stomping ground of Dalí and a host of other jet-set figures through the 1960s and 1970s. Today it is ideal for strolling, lazing around on nearby beaches and, in the evening, eating and drinking. It can get quite lively on weekends. A couple of kilometres away is **Port Lligat** and a house where Dalí spent much of his time (see Dallying With Dalí Delirium, p232).

Sights

Empúries (☎ 972 77 02 08; http://ftp.mac.es/empuries; adult/student €2.40/1.80; ◷ 10am-8pm Jun-Sep, 10am-6pm Oct-May)

Information

Cadaqués tourist office (☎ 972 25 83 15; www
.cadaques.org; Carrer del Cotxe 2; ◷ 9am-2pm & 4-9pm Mon-Sat, 10.30am-1pm Sun Easter-Sep, 9.30am-1pm & 4-7pm Mon-Sat Oct-Easter) Opening hours are unpredictable.

Tossa tourist office (☎ 972 34 01 08; www.infotossa.com; Avinguda del Pelegrí 25; ◷ 9am-9pm Mon-Sat, 10am-2pm & 5-8pm Sun Jun-Sep, 10am-2pm & 4-8pm Mon-Sat Apr, May & Oct, 10am-2pm & 4-7pm Mon-Sat Nov-Mar)

Eating

Ca l'Anita (☎ 972 25 84 71; Carrer de Miquel Roset 16, Cadaqués; meals €20-25; ◷ Tue-Sun) An ebullient, intimate spot that's a perfect place for grilled fish.

Casamar (☎ 972 30 01 04; Carrer de Nero 3, Llafranc; meals €30; ◷ Wed-Mon Mar–mid-Jan) All sorts of marvels pour out of the hotel's restaurant kitchen, from peach ravioli to succulent lamb ribs.

La Cuina de Can Simon (☎ 972 34 12 69; Carrer del Portal 24, Tossa de Mar; meals €45-50; ◷ Wed-Sat, lunch Sun; ✗) Tossa's culinary star in a former fisherman's stone house serves an imaginative array of creative local and Mediterranean cuisine, such as black rice with artichokes and shrimp dumplings.

Sleeping

Hotel Diana (☎ 972 34 18 86; www.diana-hotel.com; Plaça d'Espanya 6, Tossa de Mar; s/d €69/133, d with sea

COOKING UP A STORM

Once a simple bar and grill clutching on to a rocky perch high above the bare Mediterranean beach of Cala Montjoi and accessible only by dirt track from the town of Roses, 6km to the west, **El Bulli** (☎ 972 15 04 57; www.elbulli.com; Cala Montjoi; meal €200+; ◷ dinner Jul-Sep, dinner Wed-Sat, lunch Sun Apr-Jun; ✗) has metamorphosed into one of the world's most sought-after dining experiences, thanks to star chef Ferran Adrià (see p148 for more on him). His restaurant is known for its surprises, menus in which diners (maximum 50) are presented with a series of original and unpredictable dishes, ranging from foams and essences to perhaps one classically grilled local prawn. Some enigmatic words from Adrià about 'returning to cooking' in 2008 have unleashed all sorts of rumours, including that he might bow out of El Bulli. Fellow chef the Basque Juan Maria Arzak doesn't believe it for a minute and in one interview Adrià said he would retire from his *other* activities to devote himself exclusively to the restaurant. Fingers crossed!

view €169; ✗) A small-scale, older hotel fronting Platja Gran with 21 rooms, a Gaudí-built fireplace in the lounge, modernista décor and stained glass in the central covered courtyard.

Hotel La Residència (☎ 972 25 83 12; www.laresidencia
.net; Avinguda de la Caritat Serinyana 1, Cadaqués; s/d €70/91; ✗ P) Right in the heart of the town, with a dozen rooms ranging from simple doubles to extravagantly decorated suites.

SITGES

Jet setters, honeymooners, international gay partygoers and streams of others descend on this once-quiet fishing village from spring to autumn. Just 32km (a half-hour by train) southwest of Barcelona, Sitges boasts a long and sandy beach, groovy boutiques for *fashionistas*, a handful of interesting sights and nightlife that thumps from dusk till dawn. In winter Sitges can be dead and dreary, but it wakes up with a vengeance for Carnaval (see p11) in February, when the gay crowd puts on an outrageous show.

Sitges has been fashionable in one way or another since the 1890s, when it became an avant-garde art-world hang-out. It has been one of Spain's most unconventional, anything-goes resorts since the 1960s.

The main landmark is the **Església de Sant Bartomeu i Santa Tecla** parish church, atop a rocky elevation that separates the 2km-long main beach to the southwest from the smaller, quieter Platja de Sant Sebastià to the northeast.

Three museums, which offer a combined ticket (adult/child €6.40/3.50), serve as a timid counterweight to the hedonism. The **Museu Cau Ferrat** was built in the 1890s as a house-cum-studio by Santiago Rusiñol, a co-founder of Els Quatre Gats in Barcelona and the man who attracted the art world to Sitges. The house is full of his own art and that of his contemporaries. The interior, with its exquisitely tiled walls and lofty arches, is enchanting. Next door is the **Museu Maricel del Mar**, with art and handicrafts from the Middle Ages to the 20th century.

The **Museu Romàntic**, housed in a late-18th-century mansion, re-creates with its furnishings and dioramas the lifestyle of a 19th-century Catalan landowning family. It also has a collection of several hundred antique dolls – and some of them are mighty ugly! Many of the grand old residences dotted about the town were built in the 19th century by locals who made good (often in dubious business such as cotton-raising using slave labour) in South America and were commonly dubbed *Americanos* or *Indianos*.

At night, head down to the 'Calle del Pecado' (Sin St), actually Carrer de Marquès de Montroig and its extension, Carrer del 1er de Maig – wall-to-wall bars that will kick your Sitges nocturnal life off with decibels.

www.lonelyplanet.com

TRANSPORT

Distance from Barcelona 32km
Direction Southwest
Travel time Half an hour
Car The best road from Barcelona is the C-32 toll road. More scenic is the C-31, which hooks up with the C-32 after Castelldefels, but it is often busy and slow.
Train Four *rodalies* trains an hour, from about 6am to 10pm, run from Barcelona's Estació Sants to Sitges (€2.40, 30 minutes).

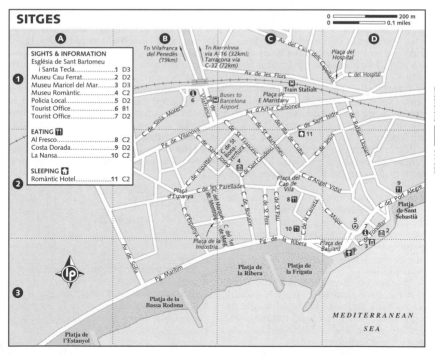

Excursions **SITGES**

239

Sights

Museu Cau Ferrat (☎ 93 894 03 64; Carrer de Fonollar; adult/child €3.50/1.75; ☻ 10am-1.30pm & 3-6.30pm Tue-Fri, 10am-7pm Sat, 10am-3pm Sun Oct-Jun, 10am-2pm & 5-9pm Tue-Sun Jul-Sep)

Museu Maricel del Mar (☎ 93 894 03 64; Carrer de Fonollar; adult/child €3.50/1.75; ☻ 10am-1.30pm & 3-6.30pm Tue-Fri, 10am-7pm Sat, 10am-3pm Sun Oct-Jun, 10am-2pm & 5-9pm Tue-Sun Jul-Sep)

Museu Romàntic (☎ 93 894 03 64; Carrer de Sant Gaudenci 1; adult/child €3.50/1.75; ☻ 10am-1.30pm & 3-6.30pm Tue-Fri, 10am-7pm Sat, 10am-3pm Sun Oct-Jun, 10am-2pm & 5-9pm Tue-Sun Jul-Sep)

Information

Policia Local (☎ 704 101092; Plaça d'Ajuntament)

Tourist office (☎ 93 894 50 04; www.sitgestur.com; Carrer de Sínia Morera 1; ☻ 9am-8pm Jul-Sep, 9am-2pm & 4-6.30pm Mon-Fri Oct-Jun)

Tourist office (☎ 93 811 06 11; Carrer de Fonollar s/n; ☻ 10am-1.30pm & 5-9pm Thu-Tue Jul–mid-Sep, 10.30am-2pm Wed-Fri, 11am-2pm & 4-7pm Sat, 11am-2.30pm Sun mid-Sep–Jun) A branch office.

Eating

Al Fresco (☎ 93 894 06 00; Carrer de Pau Barrabeig 4; meals €25-30; ☻ dinner Wed-Sun mid-Jan–mid-Dec ✗) Hidden along a narrow stairway that masquerades as a street, it serves light curries and other surprises.

Costa Dorada (☎ 93 894 35 43; Carrer del Port Alegre 27; meals €30; ☻ Fri-Tue, lunch Wed Jan-Nov) Old-world service in a 1970s atmosphere, perfect for seafood, paella and *fideuá* (similar to paella but using vermicelli noodles as the base).

La Nansa (☎ 93 894 19 27; Carrer de la Carreta 24; meals €30-35; ☻ Thu-Mon, closed Jan) Cast just back from the waterfront up a little lane in a fine old house is this seafood specialist that does a good line in paella and other rice dishes.

Sleeping

Romàntic Hotel (☎ 93 894 83 75; www.hotelromantic .com; Carrer de Sant Isidre 33; s/d €75/111) Three adjoining 19th-century villas, sensuously restored in period style, with a leafy dining courtyard. If they have no rooms, ask about their other boutique hotel, Hotel La Renaixença.

PENEDÈS WINE COUNTRY

Rivers of still white and bubbly, among Spain's best wines, spring forth from the area around the towns of Sant Sadurní d'Anoia and Vilafranca del Penedès. **Sant Sadurní d'Anoia**, a half-hour train ride west of Barcelona, is the capital of *cava*. **Vilafranca del Penedès**, 12km further down the track, is the heart of the Penedès DO region (*denominación de origen*, see p54), which produces light, still whites. Some good reds and rosés also gurgle forth here.

A hundred or so wineries around Sant Sadurní produce 140 million bottles of *cava* a year – something like 85% of the national output. *Cava* is made by the same method as French champagne (of course, the French harrumph at such observations) and is gaining ground in international markets. If you happen to be in town in October, you may catch the Mostra de Caves i Gastronomia, a *cava*- and food-tasting fest.

The epicentre of the Penedès wine-making district is the large, straggly Vilafranca del Penedès. Around the pleasant old centre spreads a less captivating and sprawling new town that seems like it's been under repair for years.

A block north of the tourist office, the mainly Gothic **Basílica de Santa Maria** stands at the heart of the old town. Begun in 1285, it has been much restored over the years. It is possible to arrange visits of the bell tower in summer at around sunset. Ask at the tourist office.

The basilica faces the combined **Museu de Vilafranca** and **Museu del Vi** (Wine Museum) across Plaça de Jaume I. The museums, in a fine Gothic building, cover local archaeology, art, geology and bird life, and also have an excellent section on wine.

TRANSPORT

Distance from Barcelona Vilafranca del Penedès 48km

Direction West

Travel time 30 to 45 minutes

Car Head west along Avinguda Diagonal and follow the signs for the AP-7 motorway, then take either the Sant Sadurní d'Anoia or Vilafranca del Penedès exits.

Train Up to three *rodalies* trains an hour run from Estació Sants in Barcelona to Sant Sadurní (€2.40, 40 minutes) and Vilafranca (€3, 50 minutes).

IN SEARCH OF THE PERFECT TIPPLE

To do a tour of the Penedès area (www.dopenedes.es) you will need your own transport. Do not expect to wander into any old winery. Many only open their doors to the public at limited times at the weekend, if at all. The more enthusiastic ones will show you around, give you an idea of how wines and/or *cava* (the Catalan version of champagne) are made and finish off with a glass or two. Tours generally last about 1½ hours and may only be in Catalan and/or Spanish. Groups must book. This list should get you started:

Cava Martín Soler (Map p242; ☎ 93 898 82 20; Puigdàlber; ☼ 9am-1pm & 3-7pm Mon-Fri, 10am-1pm Sat, Sun & holidays) Located 8km north of Vilafranca in an attractive 17th-century farmhouse surrounded by vineyards, this winery only makes *cava*.

Caves Romagosa Torné (Map p242; ☎ 93 899 13 53; www.romagosatorne.com; ☼ 10am-1pm & 4-7pm Mon-Sat, 10am-2pm Sun & holidays) This winery at Finca La Serra is on the road to Sant Martí Sarroca. Although it produces other wines, *cava* is again the star. If you get here, head on for a look at the village of Sant Martí Sarroca.

Codorníu (Map p242; ☎ 93 891 33 42; www.codorniu.es; Avinguda de Jaume Codorníu s/n, Sant Sadurní d'Anoia; ☼ 9am-5pm Mon-Fri, 9am-1pm Sat & Sun) Bottled for the first time in 1872, it remains one of the best-known wineries around. The Codorníu headquarters is in a modernista building at the entry to Sant Sadurní d'Anoia by road from Barcelona.

Freixenet (Map p242; ☎ 93 891 70 00; www.freixenet.es/web/eng/; Carrer de Joan Sala 2, Sant Sadurní d'Anoia; ☼ 1½hr tours 11am, noon, 1pm, 4pm & 5pm Mon-Thu, 10am, 11am, noon & 1pm Fri, 10am & 1pm weekends) Easily the best-known *cava* company internationally, Freixenet owns myriad wine producers in and beyond Catalonia.

Giró Ribot (Map p242; ☎ 93 897 40 50; www.giroribot.es; Finca el Pont s/n, Santa Fe del Penedès; ☼ 9am-2pm & 3.30-6.30pm Mon-Fri, 10am-2pm & 4-7pm Sat, 10am-2pm Sun) The magnificent winemaker's farm buildings ooze centuries of tradition, although today's products are partly the result of a process of modernisation that began in 1990. These vintners use mostly local grape varieties to produce a limited range of fine *cava* and wines (including muscat). The times given are for the shop. To visit the cellars, call ahead.

Jean León (Map p242; ☎ 93 817 74 51; www.jeanleon.com; Carrer del Comerç 22, Torrelavit; tour per person €3; ☼ 9.30am-5.30pm Mon-Sat, 9.30am-1pm Sun) Born in Santander as Ceferino Carrión in 1928, Jean León has led an adventurous life that led him to change his name, establish a star restaurant in Hollywood and then, from 1963, create his own top-notch wines in the heart of the Penedès. Using cabernet sauvignon and other grape types imported from prestigious vineyards in France, he has created a unique name in wines.

Nadal (Map p242; ☎ 93 898 80 11; www.nadal.com; El Pla del Penedès; tour per person €3; ☼ tours 11.30am, 3.30pm & 5.30pm Mon-Fri, 11.30am Sat, 10.30am & noon Sun & holidays) Nadal is just outside the hamlet of El Pla del Penedès and has been producing *cava* since 1943. The centrepiece is a fine *masia* (Catalan country farmhouse) where you can join organised visits that finish with a tasting.

Torres (Map p242; ☎ 93 817 74 87; www.torres.es; ☼ 9am-5pm Mon-Fri, 9am-6pm Sat, 9am-1pm Sun & holidays) About 3km northwest of Vilafranca on the BP-2121 near Pacs del Penedès, this is the area's premier winery. The Torres family tradition dates from the 17th century, but the family company, in its present form, was founded in 1870. It revolutionised Spanish winemaking in the 1960s by introducing new temperature-controlled stainless-steel technology and French grape varieties that helped produce lighter wines than the traditionally heavy Spanish plonk. Torres produces an array of reds and whites of all qualities, using many grape varieties, including Chardonnay, Sauvignon Blanc, Merlot, Cabernet Sauvignon, Pinot Noir and more locally specific ones such as Parellada, Garnacha and Tempranillo. The tour includes a kind of time tunnel in which you 'experience' climate and other changes that affect the vineyards.

Sights

La Botiga del Celler (☎ 93 890 45 36; Carrer de l'Ateneu 9, Vilafranca) This shop sells a fine selection of local wines and gourmet food products.

Museu de Vilafranca & Museu del Vi (☎ 93 890 05 82; Plaça de Jaume I, Vilafranca; adult/under 6yr/7-17yr €3/free/0.90; ☼ 10am-2pm & 4-7pm Tue-Sat, 10am-2pm Sun & holidays)

Information

Tourist office (☎ 93 818 12 54; www.turismevilafranca.com; Carrer de la Cort 14, Vilafranca; ☼ 9am-1pm & 4-7pm Tue-Fri, 10am-1pm Sat & 4-7pm Mon) A good source of information on wineries.

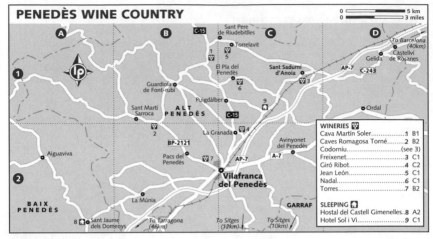

PENEDÈS WINE COUNTRY

WINERIES
Cava Martín Soler.................1 B1
Caves Romagosa Torné........2 B2
Codorníu..........................(see 3)
Freixenet..........................3 C1
Giró Ribot..........................4 C2
Jean León..........................5 C1
Nadal..............................6 C1
Torres..............................7 B2

SLEEPING
Hostal del Castell Gimenelles..8 A2
Hotel Sol i Vi.......................9 C1

Eating

Cal Ton (☎ 93 890 37 41; Carrer Casal 8, Vilafranca; meals €35-40; ⌚ Wed-Sat, lunch Sun & Tue) Hidden away down a narrow side street, Cal Ton has a crisp, modern décor and inventive Mediterranean chow.

Fonda Neus (☎ 93 891 03 65; Carrer de Marc Mir 14-16, Sant Sadurní d'Anoia; meals €20-25; ⌚ Mon-Fri, lunch Sun) This is a classic, knockabout Catalan eatery with local specialities in the heart of the *cava* town. It has a few basic rooms too (double rooms €47).

Sleeping

Hostal del Castell Gimenelles (☎ 977 678193; www .gimenelles.com; Sant Jaume dels Domeny; r €72-84; P) Five rooms with antique furniture arranged in a typical Penedès farmhouse and surrounded by vineyards, just west of the town of Sant Jaume dels Domenys.

Hotel Sol i Vi (☎ 93 899 32 04; www.solivi.com; s/d €62/83; P) Occupying a renovated *masia* (Catalan country farmhouse) in Subirats, 4km south of Sant Sadurní on the C-243a road to Vilafranca, Hotel Sol i Vi has spacious rooms, a pool, a restaurant and country views.

TARRAGONA

A hustling port city that in recent years has set new records in increased container traffic, Tarragona was once Catalonia's leading light. Roman and medieval vestiges testify to its two greatest epochs. The Romans established the city as Tarraco in the 2nd century BC, and in 27 BC Augustus elevated it to the capital of his new Tarraconensis province (stretching from Catalonia to Cantabria in the northwest and to Almería in the southeast). Abandoned when the Muslims arrived in AD 714, it was reborn as a Christian archbishopric in 1089.

The superb **Catedral** was built between 1171 and 1331 on the site of a Roman temple, combining Romanesque and Gothic features, as typified by the main façade on Pla de la Seu. The same combination continues inside in the grand cloister, with Gothic vaulting and Romanesque carved capitals. One of the latter depicts rats conducting what they imagine to be a cat's funeral, until the cat comes back to life! The rooms off the cloister house the **Museu Diocesà**, with an extensive collection ranging from Roman hairpins to some lovely 12th- to 14th-century polychrome woodcarvings of a breastfeeding Virgin. The interior of the cathedral, which is over 100m long, is Romanesque at the northeast end and Gothic at the southwest (a result of the prolonged construction period). The aisles are lined with 14th- to 19th-century chapels and hung with 16th- and 17th-century tapestries from Brussels. As a mark of reverence for St Thecla, Tarragona's patron saint, her arm is kept as a permanent and rather gruesome souvenir in the Capella de Santa Tecla on the southeast side. All sorts of tall tales abound about St Thecla, who was apparently so impressed by St Paul's preaching on virginity that she called off her impending wedding to follow his advice (and then him). Paul's teaching and her example were not always popular, and she escaped several attempts to have her put to death, and wound up living as a hermit.

The so-called Museu d'Història de Tarragona (History Museum) is actually an ensemble of elements that includes four separate Roman sites (which together with Roman sites around the province constitute a Unesco World Heritage site) and a 14th-century noble mansion, the **Museu Casa Castellarnau**. The mansion is furnished in 19th-century fashion and sheds light on how the other half lived through the centuries. For the Roman stuff, start with the **Pretori i Circ Romans**, which includes part of the vaults of the Roman circus, where chariots would thunder along in dangerous, and often deadly, races. The 300m-long circus stretched from here to beyond Plaça de la Font. Near the beach is the well-preserved **Amfiteatre Romà**, where gladiators hacked away at each other, or wild animals, to the death. In its arena are the remains of 6th- and 12th-century churches built to commemorate the martyrdom of the Christian bishop Fructuosus and two deacons, believed to have been burnt alive here in AD 259. There was certainly no lack of excitement in Roman Tarraco! East of Carrer de Lleida are remains of the **Fòrum Romà**, dominated by several imposing columns. The **Passeig Arqueològic** is a peaceful walk around part of the perimeter of the old town between two lines of city walls; the inner ones are mainly Roman while the outer ones were put up by the British in the War of the Spanish Succession.

The **Museu Nacional Arqueològic de Tarragona** gives further insight into Roman Tarraco, although most explanatory material is in Catalan or Spanish. Exhibits include part of the Roman city walls, frescoes, sculpture and pottery. A highlight is the large, almost complete *Mosaic de*

TRANSPORT

Distance from Barcelona 96km
Direction Southwest
Travel time One to 1½ hours
Car Take the C-32 toll road along the coast via Castelldefels or the AP-7 (if following Avinguda Diagonal west out of town).
Train At least 38 regional and long-distance trains per day run to/from Barcelona's Passeig de Gràcia via Sants. The cheapest fares cost €4.75 to €5.40 and the journey takes one to 1½ hours. Long-distance trains (such as Arco, Euromed and Altaria trains) are faster but more expensive – as much as €17.20.

The Romanesque and Gothic features of Tarragona's Catedral (opposite)

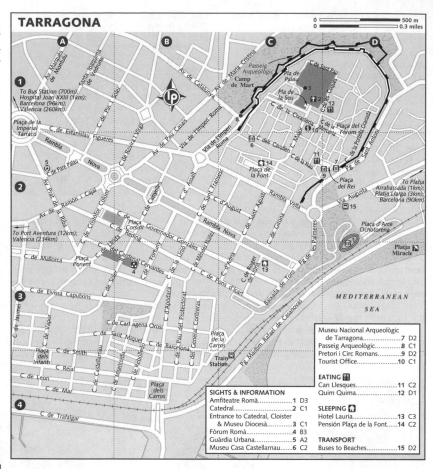

TARRAGONA

0	500 m
0	0.3 miles

Museu Nacional Arqueològic
de Tarragona...................**7** D2
Passeig Arqueològic...........**8** C1
Pretori i Circ Romans..........**9** D2
Tourist Office...................**10** C1

EATING
Can Llesques.....................**11** C2
Quim Quima......................**12** D1

SLEEPING
Hotel Lauria......................**13** C3
Pensión Plaça de la Font.....**14** C2

TRANSPORT
Buses to Beaches...............**15** D2

SIGHTS & INFORMATION
Amfiteatre Romà.................**1** D3
Catedral...........................**2** C1
Entrance to Catedral, Cloister
& Museu Diocesà.............**3** C1
Fòrum Romà......................**4** B3
Guàrdia Urbana..................**5** A2
Museu Casa Castellarnau......**6** C2

Peixos de la Pineda (Fish Mosaic) showing local fish and sea creatures that we can only dream about in these times of overfishing. In the section on everyday arts you can admire ancient fertility aids including an outsized stone penis, symbol of the god Priapus.

The town beach, **Platja del Miracle**, is clean but crowded. **Platja Arrabassada**, 1km northeast across the headland, is better, and the aptly named **Platja Llarga** (Long Beach), beginning 2km further out, stretches for about 3km. Local buses 1 and 9 from the Balcó stop on Via Augusta go to Platja Arrabassada and Platja Llarga.

About 11.5km southwest of Tarragona is Port Aventura, a massive and popular Disney-style theme park.

Sights

Amfiteatre Romà (☎ 977 24 25 79; www.museutgn
.com; Plaça d'Arce Ochotorena; adult/concession €2/1, incl all elements of Museu d'Història de Tarragona €8/4; ☼ 9am-9pm Tue-Sat, 9am-3pm Sun Easter-Sep, 9am-5pm Tue-Sat, 10am-3pm Sun & holidays Oct-Easter)

Catedral (☎ 977 23 86 85; Pla de la Seu; admission €2.40; ☼ 10am-1pm & 4-7pm Mon-Sat mid-Mar–May, 10am-7pm Mon-Sat Jun–mid-Oct, 10am-5pm Mon-Sat mid-Oct–mid-Nov, 10am-2pm Mon-Sat mid-Nov–mid-Mar)

Fòrum Romà (☎ 977 24 25 01; www.museutgn.com; Carrer del Cardenal Cervantes; adult/concession €2/1, incl all elements of Museu d'Història de Tarragona €8/4; 9am-9pm Tue-Sat, 9am-3pm Sun Easter-Sep, 9am-5pm Tue-Sat, 10am-3pm Sun & holidays Oct-Easter)

Museu Casa Castellarnau (☎ 977 24 22 20; www .museutgn.com; Carrer dels Cavallers 14; adult/concession €2/1, incl all elements of Museu d'Història de Tarragona €8/4; 9am-9pm Tue-Sat, 9am-3pm Sun Easter-Sep, 9am-5pm Tue-Sat, 10am-3pm Sun & holidays Oct-Easter)

Museu Nacional Arqueològic de Tarragona (☎ 977 23 62 09; www.mnat.es; Plaça del Rei 5; adult/senior & under 18yr €2.40/free; 10am-8pm Tue-Sat, 10am-2pm Sun Jun-Sep, 10am-1.30pm & 4-7pm Tue-Sat, 10am-2pm Sun Oct-May)

Passeig Arqueològic (www.museutgn.com; adult/ concession €2/1, incl all elements of Museu d'Història de Tarragona €8/4; 9am-9pm Tue-Sat, 9am-3pm Sun Easter-Sep, 9am-5pm Tue-Sat, 10am-3pm Sun & holidays Oct-Easter)

Pretori i Circ Romans (☎ 977 24 19 52; www.museutgn .com; Plaça del Rei; adult/concession €2/1, incl all elements of Museu d'Història de Tarragona €8/4; 9am-9pm Tue-Sat, 9am-3pm Sun Easter-Sep, 9am-5pm Tue-Sat, 10am-3pm Sun & holidays Oct-Easter)

Information

Guàrdia Urbana (☎ 977 24 03 45; Carrer de Pare Palau 7)

Hospital Joan XXIII (☎ 977 29 58 00; Carrer del Dr Mallafre Guasch 4)

Tourist office (☎ 977 25 07 95; www.tarragonaturisme .es; Carrer Major 39; 9am-9pm Mon-Sat, 10am-3pm Sun Jul-Sep, 10am-2pm & 4-7pm Mon-Sat, 10am-2pm Sun & holidays year round)

DETOUR: THE MONASTERIES ROUTE

The verdant oasis of La Conca de Barberà lies 30km west of Vilafranca del Penedès. Vineyards and woods succeed one another across rolling green hills (largely hidden from the ribbon of motorway that cuts through them), studded with the occasional medieval village and a trio of grand Cistercian monasteries (a combined ticket to all three is available for €7). With your own vehicle, it is possible to extend a Penedès wineries excursion to some of these magnificent sights.

Following the AP-7 motorway southwest from Vilafranca, take the AP-2 fork about 18km west, then take exit 11 north for the medieval **Reial Monestir de Santes Creus** (Royal Monastery of the Holy Crosses; ☎ 977 63 83 29; Plaça de Jaume el Just s/n; adult/child €3.60/2.40, Tue free; 10am-1.30pm & 3-7pm Tue-Sun mid-Mar–mid-Sep, 10am-1.30pm & 3-5.30pm Tue-Sun mid-Sep–mid-Jan, 10am-1.30pm & 3-6pm Tue-Sun mid-Jan–mid-Mar). Cistercian monks moved in here in 1168 and from then on the monastery developed as a major centre of learning and a launch pad for the repopulation of the surrounding territory. Behind the Romanesque and Gothic façade lies a glorious 14th-century sandstone cloister, chapter house and royal apartments where the *comtes-reis* (count-kings; rulers of the joint state of Catalonia and Aragón) often stayed when they popped by during Holy Week. The church, begun in the 12th century, is a lofty Gothic structure in the French tradition.

Back on the AP-2, travel another 22km to the medieval town of Montblanc, still surrounded by its defensive walls, and then L'Espluga de Francolí, beyond which you continue 3km to the fortified **Reial Monestir de Santa Maria de Poblet** (Royal Monastery of Santa Maria in Poblet; ☎ 977 87 00 89; adult/student €4.20/2.40; 10am-12.45pm & 3-6pm Mon-Sat, 10am-12.30pm & 3-5.30pm Sun and holidays mid-Mar–mid-Oct, 10am-12.45pm & 3-5.30pm Mon-Sat, 10am-12.30pm & 3-5.30pm Sun and holidays mid-Oct–mid-Mar), the jewel in the crown of the Conca de Barberà and a Unesco World Heritage site. Founded by Cistercian monks from southern France in 1151, it became Catalonia's most powerful monastery (it is said to be the largest Cistercian monastery in the world) and the burial place of many of its rulers. A community of Cistercian monks moved back in after the Spanish Civil War and did much to restore the monastery to its former glory after decades of ruin. High points include the mostly Gothic main cloister and the alabaster sculptural treasures of the Panteón de los Reyes (Kings' Pantheon). The raised alabaster sarcophagi contain such greats as Jaume I (the conqueror of Mallorca and Valencia) and Pere III.

Swinging away north from Montblanc (take the C-14 and then branch west along the LP-2335), country roads guide you up through tough countryside into the low hills of the Serra del Tallat and towards yet another Cistercian complex, the **Reial Monestir de Santa Maria de Vallbona de les Monges** (Royal Monastery of St Mary of Vallbona of the Nuns; ☎ 973 33 02 66; adult/child €2.50/2; 10.30am-1.30pm & 4.30-6.45pm Tue-Sat, noon-1.30pm & 4.30-6.45pm Sun & holidays Mar-Oct, 10.30am-1.30pm & 4.30-6pm Tue-Sat, noon-1.30pm & 4.30-6pm Sun & holidays Nov-Feb), where around 20 nuns still live and pray. You will be taken on a guided tour, probably in Catalan, in which it will become clear that it has even today not yet fully recovered from Civil War damage.

Eating

Can Llesques (☎ 977 22 29 06; Carrer de Natzaret 6; meals €15) Looks onto Plaça del Rei. House specialities include the *taula de formatges* (cheese platter).

Quim Quima (☎ 977 25 21 21; Carrer de les Coques 1bis; meals €35, menú del día €14.90; ⏲ Tue-Sat) This rambling medieval mansion with a charming courtyard is a fine setting for anything from fondue to crepes.

Sleeping

Hotel Lauria (☎ 977 23 67 12; www.hlauria.es; Rambla Nova 20; s/d €40/58; ✂ ⚑) Pleasant enough rooms with parquet floors, with a good location and a modest pool and sun deck.

Pensió Plaça de la Font (☎ 977 24 61 34; www.hotel pdelafont.com; Plaça de la Font 26; s/d €40/58; ✂) Reasonable pension with its own restaurant on a characterful, busy old town square.

Directory

Directory

TRANSPORT
AIR

After Madrid, Barcelona is Spain's busiest international transport hub and is easy to reach by air from anywhere in Spain, Europe or North America.

A host of airlines, including many budget airlines led by EasyJet, flies direct to Barcelona from destinations around Europe. One important exception is the budget airline Ryanair, which uses Girona and Reus airports (buses link Barcelona to both). Budget airlines work on a first-come, first-served basis: the earlier you book, the less you pay.

Most intercontinental flights require you to change flights in either Madrid or another major European hub.

Within Spain, Iberia, Air Europa and Spanair all have dense networks across the country and, while flights can be costly, there is no doubt that you can save considerable time by flying to Madrid and other major cities.

Other useful general sites that list competitive fares are www.expedia.com, www.opodo.com and www.planesimple.co.uk.

Airlines

Increasingly, airlines have abandoned their shopfronts in Barcelona. To contact them, you will have to go online, call the following numbers or try a travel agent. Most airlines have information desks at the airports they serve.

Air Berlin (AB; ☎ 902 320737, in Germany 01805 737800; www.airberlin.com) German budget airline with direct flights from cities all over Germany, as well as Amsterdam, Helsinki, London and Zürich.

Air Europa (UX; ☎ 902 401501; www.aireuropa.com) Flies to Barcelona from destinations all over Spain, as well as some European cities (including Paris and Rome) and American destinations, generally via Madrid.

Alpi Eagles (E8; ☎ in Italy 899 500 058; www.alpieagles.com) Flights from Venice and Naples to Barcelona.

British Airways (BA; ☎ 902 111333, in the UK 0870 850 9850; www.britishairways.com)

Continental (CO; ☎ 900 961266, in the US 1 800 523 3273; www.continental.com) Direct flights to Barcelona from New York (Newark).

Delta (DL; ☎ 901 116946, in the US 800 241 4141; www.delta.com) Flies from New York (JFK) to Barcelona, sometimes via Madrid.

EasyJet (U2; ☎ 902 299992, in the UK 0905 821 0905; www.easyjet.com) Flies to Barcelona from London (Gatwick, Stansted, City and Luton), Bristol, Liverpool, Newcastle, Basel, Berlin (Schönefeld), Dortmund, Geneva and Paris (Orly).

FlyGlobeSpan (Y2; ☎ in the UK 0870 556 1522; www.flyglobespan.com) Flights from Edinburgh and Glasgow to Barcelona.

Germanwings (4U; ☎ 91 625 97 04, in Germany 0900-1919100; www15.germanwings.com) Flights to Barcelona from Cologne-Bonn and Stuttgart.

Iberia (IB; Map pp294–5; ☎ 902 400500; www.iberia.es; Carrer de la Diputació 258; Ⓜ Passeig de Gràcia) Spain's national carrier.

Jet2 (LS; ☎ in the UK 0871 226 1737; www.jet2.com) A budget airline that flies from Leeds and Belfast to Barcelona.

Meridiana (IG; ☎ in Italy 199 111 333; www.meridiana.it) Flights from Florence, Pisa and Catania and connections throughout Italy.

MyAir (8I; ☎ in Italy 899 500 060; www.myair.com) A budget airline with flights to Barcelona from Venice.

Ryanair (FR; ☎ 807 220032, in the UK 0906 270 5656, in Ireland 0530 787787; www.ryanair.com) Flies to Girona from London (Stansted and Luton), Blackpool, Bournemouth, East Midlands, Glasgow, Liverpool, Dublin, Shannon, Brussels (Charleroi), Eindhoven, Düsseldorf, Frankfurt (Hahn), Karlsruhe, Milan (Bergamo), Paris (Beauvais), Pisa, Rome (Ciampino), Stockholm, Sardinia (Alghero), Venice (Treviso) and Turin. Also flies to Reus, 108km southwest of Barcelona, from London (Stansted and Luton), Dublin, Glasgow, Liverpool and Frankfurt (Hahn).

Singapore Airlines (SQ; ☎ 91 563 80 01; www.singaporeair.com) Flights from Barcelona to Singapore.

Sky Europe (NE; ☎ 807 001204, in Slovakia 02-48 50 48 50, in Hungary 06 1777 7000; www.skyeurope.com) Flights to Barcelona from Bratislava, Budapest, Krakow and Salzburg.

BOOKINGS ONLINE

Flights, tours and train tickets can be booked online at www.lonelyplanet.com/travel_services.

Spanair (JK; ☎ 902 131415; www.spanair.com) Flights from Madrid and other destinations throughout Spain, as well as direct flights from Dublin, Ancona (Italy), Copenhagen and Stockholm.

Sterling Airlines (NB; ☎ 91 749 66 43, in Denmark 70 10 84 84; www.sterlingticket.com) Flights from Copenhagen, Stockholm, Helsinki and other Scandinavian airports.

Swiss (LX; ☎ 901 116712, in Switzerland 0848 700700) Now owned by Germany's Lufthansa, Swiss sometimes has surprisingly good deals from Geneva and Zürich.

Thomson Fly (TOM; ☎ in the UK 0870 190 0737; www.thomsonfly.com) Flights from Coventry (UK) to Barcelona.

Transavia (HV; ☎ 902 114478, in the Netherlands 0900 0737; www.transavia.com) Low-cost flights from Amsterdam to Barcelona and Rotterdam to Girona.

Virgin Express (TV; ☎ 902 888459, in Belgium 070 353637; www.virgin-express.com) Regular flights from Brussels to Barcelona.

Vueling (VY; ☎ 902 333933; www.vueling.com) Barcelona-based budget airline with flights to Amsterdam, Brussels, Lisbon, Milan, Paris, Rome and a growing range of Spanish destinations.

Airports

Barcelona's **El Prat airport** (☎ 93 298 38 38; www.aena.es) lies 12km southwest of the city at El Prat de Llobregat. The airport building contains three terminals. Terminal A handles the bulk of international arrivals and departures by non-Spanish airlines. Terminal B handles international and domestic flights by Spanish airlines and a handful of other European airlines. Terminal C is largely for the Pont Aeri (Puente Aereo), the Barcelona–Madrid shuttle. A new south terminal, designed by local architect Ricardo Bofill, should be operational by 2007.

The arrivals halls are on the ground floor; departures are on the 1st floor. The **tourist office** (☎ 93 478 47 04; ☺ 9am-9pm) is on the ground floor of Terminal B. A smaller office on the ground floor of Terminal A operates the same hours. ATMs are scattered throughout all three terminals and currency exchange facilities are available at Terminals A and B. You'll also find post offices at these two terminals and car-rental agencies in Terminals B and C. *Consigna* (left luggage; open 24 hours, €4.10 per piece per day) is on the ground floor at the end of Terminal B closest to Terminal C. Each terminal has a lost-luggage office on the arrivals floor. You can also call **Iberia Handling** (☎ 93 401 31 29) for Iberia flights (Terminal A) and **Eurohandling** (☎ 93 298 33 30; Terminals A and B).

Girona-Costa Brava airport (☎ 972 18 66 00) is 12km south of Girona and about 80km north of Barcelona. You'll find a **tourist office** (☎ 972 18 67 08; ☺ 8am-8pm), ATM and lost luggage desks. **Reus airport** (☎ 977 77 98 32) is 13km west of Tarragona and 108km southwest of Barcelona. There's an ATM in the departure terminal. Ryanair flights serve both airports, which are more than an hour's bus ride from Barcelona.

Directory

TRANSPORT

GETTING INTO TOWN

Barcelona El Prat Airport

Transport from Barcelona's El Prat airport is proving increasingly inadequate to meet the growing flow of passengers.

The **A1 Aerobús** (Map pp298–9, pp296–7 & pp304–5; ☎ 93 415 60 20) runs from the airport to Plaça de Catalunya via Plaça d'Espanya, Gran Via de les Corts Catalanes (on the corner of Carrer del Comte d'Urgell) and Plaça de la Universitat (€3.60, 30 to 40 minutes depending on traffic) every eight to 10 minutes from 6am to midnight Monday to Friday (from 6.30am to midnight on weekends and holidays). Departures from Plaça de Catalunya are from 5.30am to 11.15pm Monday to Friday (6am to 11.30pm on weekends and holidays) and go via Estació Sants and Plaça d'Espanya. Buy tickets on the bus.

Getting to and from the airport by train is a minor odyssey now that work on the high-speed rail link between Madrid and Barcelona has interrupted services. This work could go on for years. Renfe's *rodalies* (*cercanías* in Spanish) runs a five-minute shuttle train between the airport and El Prat de Llobregat every 20 minutes. From there you wait up to 15 minutes for a connection by line C2 to Barcelona Estació Sants, Passeig de Gràcia (the most central stop) and beyond. As many as four trains run per hour to/from El Prat de Llobregat, from 6.46am to 10.47pm (from the airport), and 6.01am to 10.35 from Passeig de Gràcia. The question arises, if they can run a train to El Prat de Llobregat and then another from there to the airport (and vice-versa), why can't they just have a train service right through? All answers gratefully received. Reckon on close to an hour's travel time to/from Passeig de Gràcia. From Barcelona you must catch a train headed for Sant Vicenç or Vilanova (platform 5 at Estació Sants, from where it's two stops). A one-way ticket for this fun costs €2.40 (unless you have a multiride ticket for Barcelona public transport – see p254). For the same price you can opt for the temporary bus service between the airport train station and Estació Sants (Map pp296–7). It runs every half hour from 6am to 11pm and takes about 15 minutes.

The new Metro line (line 9) is (very) slowly being laid between the airport and the future high-speed train (AVE) station in the suburb of Sagrera.

A taxi to/from the city centre – about a half-hour ride depending on traffic – costs €18 to €20. There is generally no shortage of them. Occasionally, unscrupulous drivers overcharge, so keep an eye on the meter; fares and charges are generally posted inside the passenger side of the taxi. Parking is available at each terminal (€1.50 an hour to a maximum of €15 a day).

Mon-Bus (☎ 93 893 70 60) has regular direct buses from the airport to Sitges (€2.85). In Sitges, catch it at Passeig de Vilafranca near the taxi stand.

Alsa (☎ 902 422242; www.alsa.es) runs the Aerobús Rápid bus service several times daily from Barcelona airport to Girona, Figueres, Lleida, Reus and Tarragona. Fares range from €11.25/20.25 one-way/return to Tarragona up to €22.65/40.75 one-way/return to Lleida.

Girona-Costa Brava Airport

Sagalés (☎ 902 361550; www.sagales.com) runs hourly services from Girona-Costa Brava airport to Girona's main bus/train station (€1.75, 25 minutes) in connection with flights. The same company runs direct Barcelona Bus services to/from Estació del Nord bus station (Map pp290–1) in Barcelona (one way/return €11/19, 70 minutes), connecting with flights. Regular trains run between Girona and Barcelona (€5.45 to €6.25, up to 1½ hours). A taxi into Girona from the airport costs €15-18. To Barcelona you'd pay around €120. Parking costs an average €0.75 an hour or €7.50 a day.

Reus Airport

Buses make the run between Reus airport and Barcelona (Estació Sants) to meet flights (€11/18 one-way/return, 1½ hours). Other buses serve Reus and local coastal destinations. Check Ryanair's website for the latest timetables. There is limited free parking from 8am to 11pm.

BICYCLE

Bike lanes have been laid out along quite a few main roads (including Gran Via de les Corts Catalanes, Avinguda Diagonal, Carrer d'Aragó, Avinguda de la Meridiana and Carrer de la Marina) and a growing if ad hoc network of secondary streets, so it is possible to get around on two environmentally friendly wheels. Traffic-dodging can be a little hairy at times in the city centre. A waterfront path runs from Port Olímpic northeast towards the Riu Besòs. Scenic itineraries are mapped for bike-riders in the Collserola parkland.

You can transport your bicycle on the Metro except during rush hours on weekdays (ie not between 6.30am and 9.30am or 4.30pm and 8.30pm). On weekends and holidays, and during July and August, there are no restrictions. You can use FGC trains to carry your bike at any time and Renfe's *rodalies* trains from 10am to 3pm on weekdays and all day on weekends and holidays.

Rental

Rental options:

Biciclot (Map pp302–3; ☎ 93 221 97 78; www.biciclot .net; Passeig Marítim; per hr/day €5/€19; ☯ 9am-3pm & 4-7pm Mon-Fri plus 9am-3pm & 4-8pm Sat & Sun May-Oct, 10am-3pm Sat & Sun Nov-Apr; Ⓜ Ciutadella Vila Olímpica) Handy seaside location.

Ciclo Bus Barcelona (Map pp298–9 & pp302–3; ☎ 93 285 38 32; per hr/half-day/full day/week €4.50/11/15/56) Barcelona town hall lays on this bicycle hire service in three locations: Plaça de Catalunya, Plaça del Portal de la Pau (Monument a Colom) and Passeig de Joan de Borbó. You can also buy a card for 10 hours, to be used when you want.

ClassicBikes (Map pp298–9; ☎ 93 317 19 70; www.barce lonarentbikes.com; Carrer dels Tallers 45; per hr/day €6/16; ☯ 9.30am-2pm & 3.30-8pm) You can book a bike on the website, and has foldable bikes.

Purple Bike (☎ 661 891356; www.thepurplebike.com; per 3hr/day €9.90/19.90, subsequent days €12.90; ☯ 10am-8pm) Will deliver folding bikes to your hotel and pick up too. Book online or by phone.

Un Cotxe Menys (Map pp302–3; ☎ 93 268 21 05; www .bicicletabarcelona.com; Carrer de l'Esparteria 3; per hr/half-day/full day/week €6/12/16.50/65; ☯ 10am-2pm Mon-Fri; Ⓜ Jaume I) Also organises bike tours around the old city and port on weekends.

BOAT
Balearic Islands

Passenger and vehicular ferries operated by **Trasmediterránea** (Map pp290–1; ☎ 902 454645; www.trasmediterranea.es; Ⓜ Drassanes) to/ from the Balearic Islands dock around the Moll de Barcelona wharf in Port Vell. Information and tickets are available at the terminal building along Moll de San Beltran (Map pp290–1) or along Moll de Barcelona (Map pp290–1), or from travel agents. Standard fares for a 'Butaca Turista' (seat) from Barcelona to any of the islands are €44 on standard ferries or €70 on high-speed catamaran ferries. Cabins for up to four people are also available on overnight standard ferries.

Another company with links between Barcelona and the Balearic Islands is **Baleària** (☎ 902 160180; www.balearia.net).

Italy

The Grimaldi group's **Grandi Navi Veloci** (Map pp290–1; ☎ 902 410200, 93 443 98 98, in Italy 899 199 069; www1.gnv.it; Moll de San Beltran; Ⓜ Drassanes) runs a high-speed, roll-on-roll-off luxury ferry service from Genoa to Barcelona three times a week. The journey takes 18 hours and costs from €56 for an economy-class airline-style seat in low season to €242 for a single cabin suite in high season. **Grimaldi Ferries** (☎ 93 502 81 63, in Italy 081 496444; www.grimaldi-ferries .com) has a similar service between Barcelona and Civitavecchia (for Rome) up to six days a week, with a sailing time of 20 hours. An economy-class airline-style seat costs from €29 in low season to €79 in high season. Top-class cabins cost up to €528 per person in high season.

BUS
Barcelona

Transports Metropolitans de Barcelona (TMB; ☎ 010; www.tmb.net) buses run along most city routes every few minutes from 5am or 6am to 10pm or 11pm. Many routes pass through Plaça de Catalunya and/or Plaça de la Universitat. After 11pm a reduced network of yellow *nitbusos* (night buses) runs until 3am or 5am. All *nitbus* routes pass through Plaça de Catalunya and most run every 30 to 45 minutes.

BUS TURÍSTIC

This service, run by TMB (Map pp298–9), covers three circuits (44 stops) linking virtually all the major tourist sights. Tourist offices, TMB offices and many hotels have leaflets explaining the system. Tickets, available on the bus, cost €18 (€11 for children from four to 12 years) for one day of unlimited rides, or €22 (€14 for children) for two consecutive days. Buses run from 9am to 7.45pm and the frequency varies from every 10 to 30 minutes, depending on the season. Buses do not operate on Christmas Day or New Year's Day. Each of the two main circuits takes about two hours. The third circuit, from Port Olímpic to the Fòrum, runs from April to September and takes about half an hour.

TOMBBÚS

The T1 Tombbús (Map pp298–9) route, operated by TMB, is designed for shoppers and runs regularly from Plaça de Catalunya up to Avinguda Diagonal and then west to Plaça de Pius XII, where it turns around (€1.40). On the way it passes landmarks such as El Corte Inglés (several of them), Bulevard Rosa and FNAC.

Catalonia

Much of the Pyrenees and the entire Costa Brava are served only by buses, as train services are limited to important railheads such as Girona, Figueres, Lleida, Ripoll and Puigcerdà. If there is a train, take it – they're generally more comfortable and convenient. Various bus companies operate across the region. All of the following except Hispano-Igualadina and TEISA operate from Estació del Nord (see Long Distance, below):

Alsina Graells (☎ 902 330400; www.continental-auto.es) Part of the Continental-Auto group, it runs buses from Barcelona to destinations west and northwest, such as Vielha, La Seu d'Urgell and Lleida.

Barcelona Bus (☎ 902 130014; www.sagales.com in Catalan/Spanish) Runs buses from the capital to Girona (and Girona airport), Figueres and parts of the Costa Brava.

Hispano-Igualadina (Map pp290–1; ☎ 93 804 44 51; www.hispanoigualadina.net; Estació Sants & Plaça de la Reina Maria Cristina) Serves much of central Catalonia.

SARFA (☎ 902 302025; www.sarfa.com) The main operator on and around the Costa Brava.

TEISA (Map pp294–5; ☎ 972 20 48 68; www.teisa-bus .com; Carrer de Pau Claris 117; M Passeig de Gràcia) Covers a large part of the eastern Catalan Pyrenees from Girona and Figueres. From Barcelona buses head for Camprodon via Ripoll and Olot via Besalú.

Long-Distance

Long-distance buses for destinations within Spain leave from **Estació del Nord** (Map pp290–1; ☎ 902 260606; www.barcelonanord.com; Carrer d'Ali Bei 80; M Arc de Triomf). A plethora of companies operates to different parts of the country, although many come under the umbrella of **Alsa-Enatcar** (☎ 902 422242; www.alsa.es). For other companies, enquire at the bus station. There are frequent services to Madrid, Valencia and Zaragoza (up to 20 a day) and several daily departures to distant destinations such as Burgos, Santiago de Compostela and Seville.

Eurolines (www.eurolines.com), in conjunction with local carriers all over Europe, is the main international carrier. Its website provides links to national operators; it runs services across Europe and to Morocco from

Estació del Nord, and **Estació d'Autobusos de Sants** (Map pp296–7; Carrer de Viriat; M Sants Estació), next to Estació Sants Barcelona. For information and tickets in Barcelona, contact Alsa-Enatcar. Another carrier is **Linebús** (☎ 902 335533; www.linebus.com).

CAR & MOTORCYCLE
Driving & Parking in Barcelona

An effective one-way system makes traffic flow fairly smoothly, but unless you happen to have an adept navigator and a map that shows one-way streets you'll often find yourself flowing in the wrong direction. Driving in the Ciutat Vella (Old City) area is largely illegal, and is frustrating where permitted.

Limited parking in the Ciutat Vella is virtually all for residents only, with some metered parking. The narrow streets of Gràcia are not much better. The broad boulevards of l'Eixample are divided into blue and green zones. For nonresidents they mean the same thing: limited meter parking. Fees vary but tend to hover around €2.25 an hour.

Anything marked in yellow usually means you are permitted to stop for up to 30 minutes for loading and unloading (*càrrega* and *descàrrega*) only. Most of these zones operate from 8am to 2pm and 4pm to 8pm Monday to Saturday.

Parking motorbikes and scooters is easier. On occasion you'll see spaces marked out especially for bikes. Parking on the pavements is illegal, but many do it.

If you get towed, call the **Dipòsit Municipal** (car pound; ☎ 902 364116). Depending on where your car was nabbed, you will be directed to one of several pounds around town. You pay €137.50 for the tow and €1.80 per hour (maximum of €18 per day). The first four hours your car is held are free!

Driving to Barcelona

Barcelona is 1930km from Berlin, 1555km from London, 1145km from Paris, 1300km from Lisbon, 1200km from Milan, 780km from Geneva and 690km from Madrid.

The AP-7 *autopista* (motorway) is the main toll road from France (via Girona and Figueres). It skirts inland around the city before proceeding south to Valencia and Alicante. About 40km southwest of Barcelona, the AP-2, also a toll road, branches west off the AP-7 towards Zaragoza. From there it links up with the A-2 dual carriageway for Madrid (no tolls). Several other shorter tollways fan out into the Catalan heartland from Barcelona.

As a rule, alternative toll-free routes are busy (if not clogged). The A-2 is the most important. From the French border it follows the AP-7, branches off to the coast and then drops into Barcelona, from where it heads west to Lleida and beyond.

Coming from the UK you can put your car on a ferry from Portsmouth to Bilbao with **P&O Ferries** (☎ in the UK 0870 598 0333; www.poferries.com) or from Plymouth to Santander with **Brittany Ferries** (☎ in the UK 0870 366 5333; www.brittanyferries.co.uk). From either destination there is still a fair drive to Barcelona. Another option is to take a ferry to France or the Channel Tunnel car train, **Eurotunnel** (☎ in the UK 0870 535 3535; www.eurotunnel.com). The latter runs round the clock, with up to four crossings (35 minutes) an hour between Folkestone and Calais in the high season.

Vehicles must be roadworthy, registered and have at least third-party insurance. Ask your insurer for a European Accident Statement form, which can simplify matters in the event of an accident. A European breakdown assistance policy, such as the AA Five Star Service or the RAC Eurocover Motoring Assistance in the UK, is a good investment. European Union national driver's licences are accepted. Technically other nationalities require an international driver's licence, although in practice (eg when renting a car) this requirement is often overlooked.

Rental

Avis, Europcar, Hertz and several other big companies have desks at the airport, Estació Sants and Estació del Nord. Rental outlets in Barcelona include:

Avis (Map pp294–5; ☎ 902 180854, 93 237 56 80; www .avis.es; Carrer de Còrsega 293-295; Ⓜ Diagonal)

Europcar (Map pp294–5; ☎ 91 343 45 12, 93 302 05 43; www.europcar.es; Gran Via de les Corts Catalanes 680; Ⓜ Girona)

Hertz (Map pp294–5; ☎ 91 749 90 69, 93 217 80 76; www.hertz.es; Carrer de Tuset 10; Ⓜ Diagonal)

National/Atesa (Map pp296–7; ☎ 902 100101, 93 323 07 01; www.atesa.es; Carrer de Muntaner 45; Ⓜ Universitat)

Pepecar (Map pp298–9; ☎ 807 414243; www.pepecar .com; Plaça de Catalunya; Ⓜ Catalunya) Specialises in cheap rentals with a mix of cars (the Smart cars for two

people are the cheapest). There's a branch near Sants train station at Carrer de Béjar 68 (Map pp296–7), and another near the airport at the Hotel Tryp Barcelona Aeropuerto. If bookings are made far enough ahead, the cost can be around €10.50 a day.

Vanguard (Map pp296–7; ☎ 93 439 38 80; www .vanguardrent.com; Carrer de Viladomat 297; Ⓜ Entença) For motorbikes.

METRO & FGC

The easy-to-use **TMB Metro** (☎ 010; www.tmb .net) system has six numbered and colour-coded lines. It runs from 5am to midnight Sunday to Thursday, and from 5am to 2am on Friday, Saturday and days immediately preceding holidays. Line 2 has access for disabled people and a handful of stations on other lines also have lifts. Line 11, a short suburban run, is automated, and in the future the other lines will also run without the need of a driver. See p306 for a map of the Metro system.

Suburban trains run by the **Ferrocarrils de la Generalitat de Catalunya** (FGC; ☎ 93 205 15 15; www.fgc.net) include a couple of useful city lines. One heads north from Plaça de Catalunya. A branch of this line will take you to Tibidabo and another branch has a stop within spitting distance of the Monestir de Pedralbes. Some trains along this line continue beyond Barcelona to Sant Cugat, Sabadell and Terrassa.The other FGC line heads to Manresa from Plaça d'Espanya and is handy for the trip to Montserrat.

These trains run from about 5am (with only one or two services before 6am) to 11pm or midnight (depending on the line) Sunday to Thursday, and from 5am to 2am on Friday and Saturday.

TAXI

Taxis charge €1.45 flagfall (€1.55 from 9pm to 7am weekdays and all day Saturday, Sunday and holidays) plus meter charges of €0.78 per kilometre (€1 at night and on weekends). A further €3 is added for all trips to/from the airport, and €0.90 for luggage bigger than 55cm x 35cm x 35cm. The trip from Estació Sants to Plaça de Catalunya, about 3km, costs about €8. You can call a **taxi** (☎ 93 225 00 00, 93 300 11 00, 93 303 30 33, 93 322 22 22) or flag them down in the streets. General information is available on ☎ 010. The call-out charge is €2.93 (€3.66 at night and on weekends).

Fono Taxi (☎ 93 300 11 00) is one of several taxi companies with taxis adapted for the disabled. **Taxi Amic** (☎ 93 420 80 88; www .terra.es/personal/taxiamic) is a special taxi service for the disabled or difficult situations (transport of big objects). Book at least 24 hours in advance if possible.

Trixis

These three-wheeled **cycle taxis** (www.trixi .info) operate on the waterfront (noon to 8pm daily June to October). They can take two passengers and cost €10/18 per half-hour/hour. Children aged three to 12 pay half-price. You can find them near the Monument a Colom and in front of La Catedral.

TRAIN

The train is the most convenient overland option for reaching Barcelona from major Spanish centres such as Madrid and Valencia. It can be a long haul from other parts of Europe, where budget flights frequently offer a saving in time and money. For information on travelling from the UK, contact the **Rail Europe Travel Centre** (☎ in the UK 0870 837 1371; www.raileurope.co.uk; 178 Piccadilly, London W1V 0BA). For travel within Spain, information is available at train stations or travel agents. A network of local area trains known as *rodalies/cercanías* serves towns around Barcelona (and the air-port). Contact **Renfe** (☎ 902 240202; www .renfe.es) for information on these services.

A host of train types coasts the wide-gauge lines of the Spanish network. A saving of a couple of hours on a faster train can mean a big hike in the fare.

Most long-distance *(largo recorrido)* trains have 1st and 2nd classes (known as *preferente* and *turista*). Those running more than 400km are called Grandes Líneas. Common long-distance trains are the Talgos (Tren Articulado Ligero Goicoechea Oriol). They stop only at major centres and have extras such as TVs. The Talgo Pendular is a sleeker, faster version that picks up speed by leaning into curves. Some of these limited-stops services are classified Inter-City or InterCity Plus.

The high-speed Tren de Alta Velocidad Española (AVE) between Madrid and Lleida can, in theory, travel at up to 350km per hour. The line will extend to Barcelona and the French border (perhaps by 2009).

Another high-speed AVE train running on standard Spanish track, known as Euromed, connects Barcelona with Valencia and Alicante.

Autoexpreso and Motoexpreso wagons are sometimes attached to long-distance services for the transport of cars and motorbikes, respectively.

A *trenhotel* is a sleeping-car train with up to three classes: *turista* (for those sitting or in a couchette), *preferente* (sleeping car) and *gran clase* (sleeping in sheer luxury!).

TICKETS & TARGETES

The Metro, FGC trains, *rodalies/cercanías* (Renfe-run local trains) and buses come under one zoned-fare regime. Single-ride tickets on all standard transport within Zone 1 (which extends beyond the airport), except on Renfe trains, cost €1.20.

Targetes are multitrip transport tickets. They are sold at most city-centre Metro stations. The prices given here are for travel in Zone 1. Children under four years of age travel free. Options include:

- Monthly transport pass (€42.75) – unlimited use of all public transport.
- Targeta T-10 (€6.65) – 10 rides (each valid for 1¼ hours) on the Metro, buses, FGC trains and *rodalies*. You can change between Metro, FGC, *rodalies* and buses.
- Targeta T-50/30 (€27.55) – 50 trips within 30 days, valid on all transport.
- Targeta T-DIA (€5) – unlimited travel on all transport for one day.
- Two-/three-/four-/five-day tickets (€9.20/13.20/16.80/20) – unlimited travel on all transport except the A1 Aerobús; buy them at Metro stations and tourist offices.

Fines

The fine for being caught without a ticket on public transport is €40 – in addition to the price of the ticket. There's also a €30.05 fine for smoking on the Metro.

Estació Sants Train Station

The main international and domestic station is Estació Sants (Map pp296–7; Plaça dels Països Catalans; M Sants Estació), 2.5km west of La Rambla. Direct overnight trains from Paris, Geneva, Lisbon and Milan arrive here, as do services from various French cities and across Spain.

The Informació Largo Recorrido windows give information on all except suburban trains. The station has a tourist office, a telephone and fax office, currency exchange booths open from 8am to 10pm, ATMs and a consigna (left-luggage lockers; small/big locker for 24hr €3/4.50; ⏲ 5.30am-11pm).

TRAM

TMB (☎ 902 193275; www.trambcn.com) runs three tram lines into the suburbs of greater Barcelona from Plaça de Francesc Macià and are of limited interest to visitors. Another line runs from behind the zoo near the Ciutadella Vila Olímpica Metro stop to Sant Adrià via the Fòrum. All standard transport passes are valid.

PRACTICALITIES

ACCOMMODATION

Sleeping options range from down and dirty youth hostels for young party animals to grand old luxury hotels and glittering designer digs. The Sleeping chapter (p212) includes recommendations presented by district and in budget order. The emphasis is on midrange accommodation, but we have slipped in some of the city's cheapies and great top-range hotels as well.

High season is most of the time for most hotels, and when business is good many hotels do not alter their rates significantly during the year. There are slow moments, however. The depths of winter (late November to December, except Christmas, and mid-January to March) are quieter and hoteliers are often prepared to do deals.

BUSINESS HOURS

Generally, Barcelonins work Monday to Friday from 8am or 9am to 2pm and then again from 4.30pm or 5pm for another three hours. In the hot summer months, many work an *horario intensivo* (intensive timetable), from around 7am to 3pm.

Banks tend to open between 8.30am and 2pm Monday to Friday. Some also open from around 4pm to 7pm on Thursday evenings and/or Saturday mornings from around 9am to 1pm. See Post, p261, for post office opening times.

Museum and art gallery opening hours vary considerably, but as a rule of thumb most places are open between 10am and 6pm (some shut for lunch from around 2pm to 4pm). Most museums and galleries close all day Monday and at 2pm Sunday. For shop opening hours, see p201.

CHILDREN

One of the great things about Barcelona is the inclusion of children in many apparently adult activities. Going out to eat or sipping a beer on a late summer evening at a *terraza* (terrace) needn't mean leaving children with minders. Locals take their kids out all the time and don't worry too much about keeping them up late.

The daytime spectacle of La Rambla (p85) fascinates kids as much as adults. And while the latter might like to sneak a look at the Museu de l'Eròtica, kids will happily lose themselves in the Museu de Cera (wax museum; p87) further down the boulevard. Nearby, head to the top of the Monument a Colom (p86) for the views or the Golondrinas harbour tour boats (p81). The shark tunnel and children's activities at L'Aquàrium (p100) are guaranteed success. You might also score points with the nearby 3-D Imax cinema.

The Transbordador Aeri (p101) across the harbour between La Barceloneta and Montjuïc is another irresistible attraction, and you might even raise a smile on the Tramvia Blau, the blue tram that runs to the Tibidabo funicular station (see p112). While on Tibidabo, scare the willies out of your youngsters in the Hotel Kruger horror house at the Parc d'Atraccions amusement park (p115).

Of the city's museums, the ones mostly likely to capture children's imagination are the Museu Marítim (p92), the Museu de la Xocolata (p96) and the interactive Cosmo-Caixa (p113).

In summer, you will be rewarded by squeals of delight if you take the bairns to one of the city's pools (p197) or the beach (p101). In cooler weather, parks can be a good choice. A roam around Montjuïc, including exploration of its Castell (p119), should appeal. The sheer weirdness of Gaudí's Park Güell (p111) will have older children intrigued and everyone likes getting lost in the maze of the Jardins del Laberint d'Horta (p113). The Zoo de Barcelona (p99) is a universal child-pleaser.

You could take younger kiddies (maximum age 11) along to **Happy Parc** (Map pp294–5; ☎ 93 317 86 60; www.happyparc.com; Carrer de Pau Claris 97; per hr €4; ⏱ 5-9pm Mon-Fri, 11am-9pm Sat & Sun) for a play on the slides and other diversions.

For general advice on travelling with children, grab Lonely Planet's *Travel with Children*.

Baby-Sitting

Most of the mid- and upper-range hotels in Barcelona can organise a baby-sitting service. A company that many hotels use and that you can also contact directly is **5 Serveis** (☎ 93 412 56 76, 639 361111; Carrer de Pelai 50). They have multilingual baby-sitters *(canguros)*. Rates vary, but in the evening expect to pay around €7.50 an hour plus the cost of a taxi home for the baby-sitter.

Tender Loving Canguros (☎ 647 605989; www .tlcanguros.com) offers English-speaking baby-sitters for a minimum of three hours (€7 an hour).

CLIMATE

Barcelona enjoys a Mediterranean climate, with cool winters and hot summers. July and August are the most torrid months. Highs can reach 37°C. The seaside location promotes humidity, but sea breezes can bring relief. A hotel room with a fan or air conditioning can make all the difference to a good night's sleep.

In the depths of winter (especially in February) it gets cold enough (average lows of

6.7°C) for you to wish you had heating in your room, but by March things begin to thaw out. January tends to be sunny, though not warm.

Rainfall is highest in autumn and winter. In September and into October the city often gets a wash down in cracking, late-summer thunderstorms.

As Barcelona is downwind from the Pyrenees, cold snaps are always on the cards and the April-May period is changeable. At its best, May can be the most pleasant month of the year – clear and fresh.

COURSES
Language Courses

With its bilingual mix, Barcelona may not be the ideal location for embarking on Spanish (Castilian) courses, but there is no shortage of places to do so. The cost of language courses depends on the school, the length of the course and its intensity. Across Catalonia, more than 220 schools teach Catalan. Pick up a list at the **Llibreria & Informació Cultural de la Generalitat de Catalunya** (Map pp298–9; ☎ 93 302 64 62; Rambla dels Estudis 118; Ⓜ Liceu).

Non-EU citizens who want to study at a university or language school in Spain should have a study visa. These can be obtained from your nearest Spanish embassy or consulate. You will normally require confirmation of your enrolment and payment of fees, and proof of adequate funds to support yourself, before a visa will be issued. The visa will then cover only the period of the enrolment. This type of visa is renewable within Spain but, again, only with confirmation of ongoing enrolment and proof that you are able to support yourself.

Some schools that are worth investigating include:

Babylon Idiomas (Map pp294–5; ☎ 93 488 15 85; www .babylon-idiomas.com; Carrer del Bruc 65; Ⓜ Girona) This small school offers a high degree of flexibility – you can study for a week or enlist for a half-year intensive course in Spanish. The big selling point is class size, with a maximum of eight students per class. A week of 30 hours' tuition costs €235.

Escola Oficial d'Idiomes de Barcelona (Map pp298–9; ☎ 93 324 93 30; www.eoibd.es in Spanish; Avinguda de les Drassanes s/n; Ⓜ Drassanes) Part-time courses (around 10 hours a week) in Spanish and Catalan (around €165 for a semester) are offered. Because of the demand

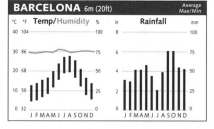

BARCELONA 6m (20ft)

for Spanish, there is no guarantee of a place. Generally there is no problem with Catalan.

International House (Map pp298–9; ☎ 93 268 45 11; www.ihes.com/bcn; Carrer de Trafalgar 14; Ⓜ Arc de Triomf) Intensive courses from around €370 for two weeks. It can also organise accommodation.

Universitat de Barcelona (Map pp298–9; ☎ 93 403 55 19 & www.eh.ub.es for Spanish, ☎ 93 403 54 77 & www.ub.edu/slc for Catalan; Gran Via de les Corts Catalanes 585; Ⓜ Universitat) Intensive courses (40 hours' tuition over periods ranging from two weeks to a month; €390) in Spanish year-round. Longer Spanish and Catalan courses are also available.

Other Courses

Antilla BCN Escuela de Baile (Map pp296–7; ☎ 93 451 45 64; www.antillasalsa.com; Carrer d'Aragó 141; term course, once a week €100; Ⓜ Urgell) The place to learn salsa and other Caribbean dance.

Cook and Taste (Map pp298–9; ☎ 93 302 13 20; www.cookandtaste.net; La Rambla 58; half-day workshop €50; Ⓜ Liceu) Learn to whip a paella or stir a gazpacho in this Spanish cookery school.

Dom's Gastronom Cookery School (☎ 93 674 51 60; domsgastronom1@yahoo.es; Passeig del Roser 43, Valldoreix; month of weekly classes from €85, groups catered for) Cordon bleu–trained chef Dominique Heathcoate holds cookery classes in anything from Catalan, Spanish and French cuisine to tapas and autumn mushroom cooking at her school just outside Barcelona. Valldoreix is about a 30-minute train ride from Plaça de Catalunya on the line to Sabadell and Terrassa and Dominique can arrange pick-up from the train station.

Escuela de Baile José de la Vega (Map pp296–7; ☎ 93 454 31 14; Carrer d'Aribau 19; Ⓜ Universitat) People come from all over town to learn to dance flamenco here.

Kedar – Centro de Yoga Satyananda (Map pp298–9; ☎ 93 301 89 17; www.kedarsatyananda.com; Carrer de Ferran 29; 1 class €10) Is all the excitement of Barcelona too much? Or have you decided to stay and go Zen for a while? Excuse the mixed religions, but here you can join classes in yoga and yoga nidra meditation.

CUSTOMS

People entering Spain from outside the EU are allowed to bring one bottle of spirits, one bottle of wine, 50mL of perfume and 200 cigarettes into Spain duty free. There are no duty-free allowances for travel between EU countries. For duty-paid items bought at normal shops in one EU country and taken into another, the allowances are 90L of wine, 10L of spirits, unlimited quantities of perfume and 800 cigarettes.

DISABLED TRAVELLERS

Things are slowly improving for the disabled, but much remains to be done. Some hotels and public institutions have wheelchair access. As of 2006 all buses are wheelchair accessible and all Metro stations should be by 2007. You can order special taxis; see p254. A campaign to make all street crossings in l'Eixample wheelchair-friendly is nearing completion.

Organisations

Accessible Barcelona (☎ 93 446 23 03; www.accessiblebarcelona.com) Craig Grimes, a T6 paraplegic and inveterate traveller, created this Barcelona-specific accessible travel site, easily the most useful doorway into the city for the disabled. Hotels are well researched and the company will help with transport and other aspects of your trip.

Accessible Travel & Leisure (☎ in the UK 01452-729739; www.accessibletravel.co.uk; Avionics House, Naas Lane, Gloucester GL2 2SN, UK). Claims to be the biggest UK travel agent dealing with travel for the disabled.

Institut Municipal de Persones amb Disminució (Map pp290–1; ☎ 93 413 27 75; Avinguda Diagonal 233). Has information for disabled people in Barcelona, although it is aimed mostly at permanent residents.

ONCE (Map pp296–7; ☎ 93 325 92 00; Carrer de Calàbria 66-76; Ⓜ Rocafort). The national blind people's organisation can help with information for the sight-impaired, including lists of places such as restaurants where Braille menus are provided. It has a guide to Barcelona in Braille.

DISCOUNT CARDS

The ISIC (International Student Identity Card; www.isic.org) and the Euro<26 card (for people under 26; www.euro26.org) are available from most national student organisations and can gain you discounted access to sights. Articket and Barcelona Card (see p80) each offer discounted entry to some sights.

ELECTRICITY

The electric current in Barcelona is 220V, 50Hz, as in the rest of continental Europe. Several countries outside Europe (such as the USA and Canada) use 110V, 60Hz, which means that some appliances from those countries may perform poorly in Barcelona. It is always safest to use a transformer. Plugs have two round pins, as in the rest of continental Europe.

EMBASSIES & CONSULATES

Most countries have an embassy in Madrid. Look them up under *Embajada* in that city's *Paginas Amarillas* (Yellow Pages). Various countries maintain consulates in Barcelona:

Australia (Map pp294–5; ☎ 93 490 90 13; Plaça de Gal .la Placídia 1; FGC Gràcia)

Canada (Map pp290–1; ☎ 93 204 27 00; Carrer d'Elisenda de Pinós 10; FGC Reina Elisenda)

France (Map pp298–9; ☎ 93 270 30 00; Ronda de la Universitat 22B; Ⓜ Universitat)

Germany (Map pp294–5; ☎ 93 292 10 00; Passeig de Gràcia 111; Ⓜ Diagonal)

Ireland (Map pp290–1; ☎ 93 491 50 21; Gran Via de Carles III 94; Ⓜ Maria Cristina)

New Zealand (Map p292; ☎ 93 209 03 99; Travessera de Gràcia 64; FGC Gràcia)

UK (Map p292; ☎ 93 366 62 00; Avinguda Diagonal 477; Ⓜ Hospital Clínic)

US (Map pp290–1; ☎ 93 280 02 95; Passeig de la Reina Elisenda de Montcada 23-25; FGC Reina Elisenda)

EMERGENCY

It cannot be stressed enough that newcomers to Barcelona must be on their guard. Petty theft is a problem in the city centre, on some public transport and around most main sights. Report thefts to the national police. You are unlikely to recover your goods but you need to make this formal *denuncia* for insurance purposes. To avoid endless queues at the police station (*comisaría*), you can make the report by phone (☎ 902 102112) in various languages or on the Web at www.policia.es (click on Denuncias). The following day you go to the station of your choice to pick up and sign the report, with-

out queuing. There's a handy **police station** (Map pp298–9; Carrer Nou de la Rambla 80; Ⓜ Paral.lel) near La Rambla. Otherwise, the main station dealing with tourists is at **Via Laietana 43** (Map pp298–9; ☎ 93 290 33 27). You could also try the **Guàrdia Urbana** (local police; Map pp298–9; La Rambla 43). The following are the main emergency numbers:

Ambulance	☎ 061
Catalan state police (Mossos d'Esquadra)	☎ 088
EU standard emergency number	☎ 112
Fire brigade (Bombers)	☎ 080, 085
Guardia Civil	☎ 062
Guàrdia Urbana	☎ 092
Policía Nacional	☎ 091

GAY & LESBIAN TRAVELLERS

Gay and lesbian sex is legal in Spain and the age of consent is 16 years, the same as for heterosexuals. Spain made history when the national parliament passed laws allowing same sex marriages in 2005. And Barcelona is set to host the 11th Eurogames, the European games for gays and lesbians, in July 2008.

Barcelona has a busy gay scene, but the region's gay capital is no doubt the saucily hedonistic nearby Sitges (p238), a major destination on the international gay party circuit. Gays take a leading role in the wild Carnaval celebrations there in February/March (p11).

The city's tourist board publishes *Barcelona – The Official Gay and Lesbian Tourist Guide* bi-annually. A couple of informative free magazines are in circulation in gay bookshops and bars. One is the biweekly *Shan-guide*. It is jammed with listings and contact ads and aimed principally at read-

CLEAN UP YOUR ACT

In January 2006 a controversial new law aimed at 'cleaning up' the streets of Barcelona went into effect. Wide-ranging rules give local police greater powers to deal with anything from prostitution and begging in the streets to graffiti and anti-social behaviour like drinking, fornicating and relieving oneself in the streets. Many of these problems are concentrated in the old town. Civil rights groups have decried measures to fine beggars and prostitutes. But anyone who has wandered around the Barri Gòtic late at night and been overwhelmed by the stench of urine and worse, or had to duck for cover as hordes of bare-chested, drunken stag-night revellers (mainly from the UK) charge through the streets, will no doubt be cheered. Barcelona has, since around 2000, gained a growing reputation as a cheap-end party town ideal for stag and hen nights, and the results in the city centre's streets have been sadly evident. Now, a quick pee, if you're caught, can cost €300. Drinking alcohol from bottles and cans while wandering the streets carries a fine of up to €1500. Walking the streets without a shirt (why do flabby, white men feel the need to share their visual riches with everyone else?) is also out. A romantic bout of sex in the streets, or being caught spraying graffiti, can cost up to €3000. Fines are applied on the spot. If you can't or won't pay, a still bigger one will arrive at your hotel.

ers in Barcelona and Madrid. The monthly *MENsual* (€2) is available at newsstands. There is an online version at www.mensual .com (in Spanish).

Also check out the following sites on the web:

Coordinadora Gai-Lesbiana (www.cogailes.org) A good site presented by Barcelona's main gay and lesbian organisation, with nationwide links. Here you can zero in on information ranging from bar, sauna and hotel listings through to contacts pages.

Corazon Gay (www.corazongay.com in Spanish) Gay personals and Internet search engine.

GayBarcelona.Net (www.gaybarcelona.net in Spanish) News and views and an extensive listings section covering bars, saunas, shops and more in Barcelona and Sitges.

Gays Abroad (www.gays-abroad.com) For gay men moving to Barcelona.

LesboNet.Org (www.lesbonet.org in Spanish) A lesbian site with contacts, forums and listings.

Nación Gay (www.naciongay.com in Spanish) News on the gay community across Spain.

Voz Gay (www.vozgay.com in Spanish) A Spanish community website with listings for the whole country.

Organisations

Casal Lambda (Map pp298–9; ☎ 93 319 55 50; www .lambdaweb.org; Carrer de Verdaguer i Callis 10; Ⓜ Uquinaona) A gay and lesbian social, cultural and information centre in the Ribera.

Coordinadora Gai-Lesbiana (Map pp290–1; ☎ 93 298 00 29; www.cogailes.org; Carrer de Finlàndia 45; Ⓜ Plaça de Sants) The city's main coordinating body for gay and lesbian groups. Some of the latter are to be found at Ca la Dona (see p265). It also runs an information line, the **Línia Rosa** (☎ 900 601601).

HOLIDAYS

For Barcelonins, the main holiday periods are summer (July and August), Christmas–New Year and Easter. August is a peculiar time as Spain largely grinds to a halt. Tourists flock in regardless of the heat, but many locals escape to cooler climes. Finding accommodation can be more difficult around Christmas and Easter. For information on the city's colourful festivals and other events, see p10. The following is a list of national public holidays:

New Year's Day (Any Nou/Año Nuevo) 1 January

Epiphany or **Three Kings' Day** (Epifanía or El Dia dels Reis/Día de los Reyes Magos) 6 January

Good Friday (Divendres Sant/Viernes Santo) March/April

Easter Monday (Dilluns de Pasqua Florida) March/April

Labour Day (Dia del Treball/Fiesta del Trabajo) 1 May

Day after Pentecost Sunday (Dilluns de Pasqua Granda) May/June

Feast of St John the Baptist (Dia de Sant Joan/Día de San Juan Bautista) 24 June

Feast of the Assumption (L'Assumpció/La Asunción) 15 August

Catalonia's National Day (Diada Nacional de Catalunya) 11 September

Festes de la Mercè 24 September

Spanish National Day (Festa de la Hispanitat/Día de la Hispanidad) 12 October

Constitution Day (Día de la Constitución) 6 December

Feast of the Immaculate Conception (La Immaculada Concepció/La Inmaculada Concepción) 8 December

Christmas (Nadal/Navidad) 25 December

Boxing Day or **St Stephen's Day** (El Dia de Sant Esteve) 26 December

INTERNET ACCESS

Internet centres abound in Barcelona. If you plan to take your portable computer, you may stumble on to wi-fi access in some parts of the city. A handful of hotels offer their guests wi-fi access and more offer high-speed modem access in rooms. A paying wi-fi service operates at the airport and train stations. The city operates wi-fi public access points across the city, but national competition rulings have restricted access to a handful of pages and services of the Ajuntament (City Hall). Some cafés (such as Starbucks) also offer pay-as-you-go wi-fi connections.

Internet Cafés

Barcelona is full of Internet centres. Some offer student rates and also sell cards for several hours' use at reduced rates. A handful of options follows:

Bornet (Map pp302–3; ☎ 93 268 15 07; www.bornet -bcn.com; Carrer de Barra Ferro 3; 1/5hr €2.60/10; Ⓨ 10am-10pm Mon-Fri, 3-10pm Sat & Sun; Ⓜ Jaume I)

Cybernet (Map pp296–7; ☎ 93 451 30 98; Carrer de Muntaner 127; per hr €1; Ⓨ noon-9pm; Ⓜ Hospital Clínic)

easyInternetcafé (Map pp298–9; ☎ 93 412 13 97; www .easyeverything.com; Ronda de la Universitat 35; per hr around €1.70, depending on demand; Ⓨ 8am-2am; Ⓜ Universitat) There is another branch at **La Rambla 31** (Map pp298–9; ☎ 93 318 24 35; Ⓨ 8am-2.30am; Ⓜ Liceu).

Internet MSN (Map pp294–5; Carrer del Penedès 1; per hr €1.20; Ⓨ 9.30am-2am; Ⓜ Fontana)

LOST PROPERTY

Centre d'Atenció al Client (☎ 93 318 70 74; Ⓜ Diagonal) TMB bus and Metro lost property, located within the Diagonal Metro station.

Oficina de Trovalles (Map pp298–9; ☎ 010; Carrer de la Ciutat 9; ☺ 9am-2pm Mon-Fri; Ⓜ Jaume I)

Taxis lost property (☎ 93 223 40 12)

MAPS

Tourist offices hand out free city and transport maps, but Lonely Planet's *Barcelona City Map* is better. Also handy is Michelin's ring-bound *Barcelona,* scaled at 1:12,000.

MEDICAL SERVICES

All foreigners have the same right as Spaniards to emergency medical treatment in public hospitals. EU citizens are entitled to the full range of health-care services in public hospitals, but you will need to present your European Health Insurance Card (enquire at your national health service before leaving home) and may have to pay up front and be reimbursed on returning home.

Non-EU citizens have to pay for anything other than emergency treatment. Most travel-insurance policies include medical cover.

For minor health problems you can try your local pharmacy (*farmàcia,* see opposite), where pharmaceuticals tend to be sold more freely without prescription than in places such as the USA, Australia or the UK.

If your country has a consulate in Barcelona, its staff should be able to refer you to doctors who speak your language. If you have a specific health complaint, obtain the necessary information and referrals before leaving home.

Some hospitals include:

Hospital Clínic i Provincial (Map pp296–7; ☎ 93 227 54 00; Carrer de Villarroel 170; Ⓜ Hospital Clínic)

Hospital de la Creu Roja (Map pp290–1; ☎ 93 507 27 00; Carrer del Dos de Maig 301; Ⓜ Hospital de Sant Pau)

Hospital de la Santa Creu i de Sant Pau (Map pp290–1; ☎ 93 291 91 91; Carrer de Sant Antoni Maria Claret 167; Ⓜ Hospital de Sant Pau)

MONEY

As in 11 other EU nations (Austria, Belgium, Finland, France, Germany, Greece, Ireland, Italy, Luxembourg, the Netherlands and Portugal), the euro has been Spain's currency since 2002.

Changing Money

You can change cash or travellers cheques in currencies of the developed world without problems (apart from queues) at virtually any bank or *bureau de change* (usually indicated by the word *canvi/cambio*).

Barcelona abounds with banks, many with ATMs, including several around Plaça de Catalunya and more on La Rambla and Plaça de Sant Jaume in the Barri Gòtic.

The foreign-exchange offices that you see along La Rambla and elsewhere are open for longer hours than banks, but they generally offer poorer rates. Also, keep a sharp eye open for commissions at *bureaux de change*.

American Express (Amex; Map pp298–9; ☎ 93 342 73 11; Rambla dels Caputxins 74; ☺ 9am-midnight Apr-Sep, 9am-9pm Mon-Fri plus 9am-2pm Sat Oct-Mar; Ⓜ Liceu) has a cash machine for Amex card-holders.

Credit/Debit Cards

Major cards, such as Visa, MasterCard, Maestro and Cirrus cards, are accepted throughout Spain. They can be used in many hotels, restaurants and shops. Credit cards can also be used in ATMs displaying the appropriate sign. Check charges with your bank. If your card is lost, stolen or swallowed by an ATM, you can telephone toll free to have an immediate stop put on its use:

Amex	☎ 900 994426
Diners Club	☎ 901 101011
MasterCard	☎ 900 971231
Visa	☎ 900 991124

Travellers Cheques & Travel Cards

These are a safe way of carrying your money because they can be replaced if lost or stolen. Most banks and exchange offices will cash them. Amex, MasterCard and Visa are widely accepted brands (the latter two also sold by Travelex). If you lose your cheques, call a 24-hour freephone number (☎ 900 994426 for Amex, 900 948973 for Visa, 900 948971 for MasterCard).

Get most of your cheques in fairly large denominations to save on per-cheque commission charges. Amex exchange offices do not charge commission to exchange travellers cheques (even other brands). Keep your initial receipt, along with a record of your cheque numbers and the ones you have used, separate from the cheques themselves. Take your passport when you go to cash travellers cheques.

Travelex (www.travelex.com) issues pre-paid Travel Cards and Cash Passports. Load funds onto the card before you travel and use it like any cash card in Visa ATMs worldwide. Funds are PIN-protected and losing your card does not mean losing your money.

NEWSPAPERS & MAGAZINES

A wide selection of national daily newspapers from around Europe (including the UK) is available at newsstands all over central Barcelona and at strategic locations such as the train and bus stations. The *International Herald Tribune*, *Time*, the *Economist*, *Der Spiegel* and a host of other international magazines are also available.

Catalan Press

El País includes a daily supplement devoted to Catalonia, but the region also has a lively home-grown press. *La Vanguardia* and *El Periódico* are the main local Spanish-language dailies. The latter also publishes a Catalan version. The more conservative and Catalan-nationalist-oriented daily is *Avui*. Another local Catalan daily, *El Punt*, concentrates on news in and around Barcelona.

English Press

The most useful publication for expats and blow-ins is *Barcelona Metropolitan*, with news, views, ads and listings information. *Catalonia Today* is a slim newssheet put out by the owners of *El Punt*.

Spanish Press

Conservative Spaniards tend to read the old-fashioned *ABC*, while most of the left-of-centre crowd study *El País*, which identifies with the Partido Socialista Obrero Español (PSOE). *El Mundo* prides itself on breaking political scandals but is not as good as it was. One of the best-selling dailies is *Marca*, devoted solely to sport.

PHARMACIES

Some 24-hour pharmacies:

Farmàcia Álvarez (Map pp298–9; ☎ 93 302 11 24; Passeig de Gràcia 26)

Farmàcia Clapés (Map pp298–9; ☎ 93 301 28 43; La Rambla 98)

Farmàcia Torres (Map pp296–7; ☎ 93 453 92 20; Carrer d'Aribau 62)

POST

Correus (Correos in Spanish; ☎ 902 197197; www.correos.es in Spanish), the national postal service, has its main office just opposite the northeast end of Port Vell at **Plaça d'Antoni López** (Map pp302–3; ☺ 8.30am-10pm Mon-Sat, noon-10pm Sun; Ⓜ Jaume I). A handy branch lies just off Passeig de Gràcia at **Carrer d'Aragó 282** (Map pp294–5; ☺ 8.30am-8.30pm Mon-Fri, 9.30am-1pm Sat; Ⓜ Passeig de Gràcia). Many other branches tend to open from 8.30am to 2.30pm Monday to Friday and 9.30am to 1pm on Saturday.

Stamps (*segells/sellos*) are sold at most *estancos* (tobacconists' shops) and at post offices.

Postal Rates

A postcard or letter weighing up to 20g costs €0.57 from Spain to other European countries, and €0.78 to the rest of the world. The same would cost €2.77 and €2.98, respectively, for registered (*certificado*) mail. Sending such letters *urgente*, which means your mail may arrive two or three days sooner than usual, costs €2.89 and €2.75, respectively. You can send mail both *certificado* and *urgente* if you wish.

Receiving Mail

Delivery times are similar to those for outbound mail. All Spanish addresses have five-digit postcodes; using postcodes will help your mail arrive a bit quicker.

Poste restante (*lista de correos*) mail can be addressed to you anywhere in Catalonia that has a post office. It will be delivered to the place's main post office unless another is specified in the address. Take your passport when you pick up mail. A typical *lista de correos* address looks like this:

Jenny JONES
Lista de Correos
08080 Barcelona
Spain

Amex card or travellers cheque holders can use the free client mail-holding service at the Amex office (opposite). Take your passport with you when you pick up mail. They only accept standard letters, not packages.

Sending Mail

Ordinary mail to other West European countries usually takes around three to four days, to North America and Australasia anything from one to two weeks.

RADIO

The Spanish national network, Radio Nacional de España (RNE), has several stations: RNE 1 (738AM; 88.3 FM) has general interest and current affairs programmes; RNE 3 (98.7 FM) presents a decent range of pop and rock music; RNE 5 (576AM) concentrates on sport and entertainment. Among the most listened-to rock and pop stations are 40 Principales (93.9 FM), Onda Cero (94.1 FM) and Cadena 100 (100 FM).

Those wanting to get into Catalan can tune into Catalunya Ràdio (102.8 FM), Catalunya Informació (92 FM) and a host of small local radio stations.

You can pick up BBC World Service (www.bbc.co.uk) on, among others, 6195kHz, 9410kHz and 15,485kHz (short wave). Voice of America (VOA) can be found on a host of short-wave frequencies, including 6040kHz, 9760kHz and 15,205kHz.

SAFETY

Petty crime and theft, with tourists the main prey, is a problem and the police seem unable to do much about it. The moment of most vulnerability is on arrival, when visitors are lumbered with luggage and often disoriented. Always keep a close eye on your belongings. This starts in the airport and continues on the trip into the city, especially on the trains.

Ciutat Vella, tourist sights and public transport are all hunting grounds. Tricks abound, and usually involve a team of two or more. While one distracts your attention, the other empties your pockets.

Prevention is better than cure. Where possible, keep only what you really need on your person. Never put anything in your back pocket; small day bags are best worn across your chest. Do not carry much cash at any one time. Money belts or pouches worn under your clothing are also a good idea.

Take particular care on and around La Rambla and stay well clear of the ball-and-three-cups brigades. This is always a set-up and you will lose your money (and maybe have your pockets emptied as you watch the game).

Never leave anything visible in your car, and preferably leave nothing at all. Foreign and hire cars are especially vulnerable. If you have a foreign or hire car, leave the glove box open to emphasise that there is nothing of value inside.

Violent crime is rarer than petty theft in Barcelona, although some thieves are not averse to using force on occasion.

You can take a few precautions before you even arrive in Barcelona. Inscribe your name, address and telephone number *inside* your luggage and take photocopies of the important pages of your passport, travel tickets and other key documents. Keep the copies separate from the originals and ideally leave one set of copies at home. This will make things easier if you do suffer a loss or theft. Take out travel insurance against theft and loss.

For reporting incidents and stolen items, see p258.

TAXES & REFUNDS

Value-added tax (VAT) is known as IVA (*impuesto sobre el valor añadido*, pronounced 'EE-ba'). On accommodation and restaurant prices, IVA is 7% and is usually – but not always – included in quoted prices. On retail goods IVA is 16%. IVA-free shopping is available in the duty-free shops at airports for people travelling between EU countries.

Non-EU residents are entitled to a refund of the 16% IVA on purchases costing more than €90.16 from any shop, if they take the goods out of the EU within three months. Ask the shop for a Cashback (or similar) refund form showing the price and IVA paid for each item and identifying the vendor and purchaser. Then present the form at the customs booth for IVA refunds when you depart from Spain (or elsewhere in the EU). You will need your passport and a boarding card that shows you are leaving the EU, and your luggage (so do this before checking in bags). The officer will stamp the invoice and you hand it in at a bank at the departure point to receive a reimbursement.

At Barcelona airport, look for the customs booth directly opposite the bar on the ground floor of Terminal A (by the arrivals doors). Branches of the Caixa and BBVA banks (both about 50m to the right of the customs window) will deal with Cashback refunds (7am to 11pm daily). Otherwise you can use the envelope provided to have the tax paid back to your credit card or by cheque.

TELEPHONE

The ubiquitous blue payphones are easy to use for international and domestic calls. They accept coins, *tarjetas telefónicas* (phonecards) issued by the national phone company Telefónica and, in some cases, credit cards. *Tarjetas telefónicas* come in €6 and €12 denominations and are sold at post offices and tobacconists.

Public telephones inside bars and cafés, and phones in hotel rooms, are nearly always a good deal more expensive than street payphones.

Codes & Dialling

To call Barcelona from outside Spain, dial the international access code, followed by the code for Spain (☎ 34) and the full number (including Barcelona's area code, ☎ 93, which is an integral part of the number).

The access code for international calls from Spain is ☎ 00. To make an international call, dial the access code, wait for a new dial tone, then dial the country code, area code and number you want.

International reverse-charge (collect) calls are simple: dial ☎ 900 followed by a code for the country you're calling: Australia (99 00 61); Canada (99 00 15); France (99 00 33); Germany (99 00 49); Ireland (99 03 53); Israel (99 09 72); New Zealand (99 00 64); UK (99 00 44 for BT, 99 09 44 for Cable & Wireless); or USA (99 00 11 for AT&T, 99 00 13 for Sprint and various others). You'll get straight through to an operator in the country you're calling. The same numbers can be used with direct-dial calling cards.

If for some reason the instructions above don't work for you, you can contact an English-speaking Spanish international operator on ☎ 1008 (for calls within Europe) or ☎ 1005 (rest of the world). For international directory inquiries, dial ☎ 11825. A call to this number costs €2!

Dial ☎ 1009 to speak to a domestic operator, including for a domestic reverse-charge call (*llamada por cobro revertido*). For national directory inquiries, dial ☎ 11818.

Mobile-phone numbers start with 6. Numbers starting with 900 are national toll-free numbers, while those starting with numbers between 901 and 905 come with varying conditions. A common one is 902, which is a national standard-rate number. In a similar category are numbers starting with 803, 806 and 807.

Mobile Phones

You can buy SIM cards and prepaid call time in Spain for your own national mobile phone (provided what you own is a GSM, dual- or tri-band cellular phone and not code-blocked). You need your passport to open any kind of mobile-phone account, prepaid or otherwise.

All Spanish mobile-phone companies (Telefónica's MoviStar, Vodaphone and Amena) offer prepaid *(prepagado)* accounts for GSM phones (frequency 900mHz). Phone outlets are scattered across the city. You can then purchase more time in their shops or by buying cards in outlets such as tobacconists.

US mobile phones generally work on a frequency of 1900mHz, so for use in Spain, your US handset will have to be tri-band.

You can organise mobile-phone rental at **Bright** (Map p292; ☎ 93 238 67 27; www .thebrightco.com; Carrer de Lincoln 1; FGC Gràcia). It has various plans to suit different needs, and also sells international calling cards.

Phonecards & Call Centres

Cut-price phonecards for international calls are available from many newsstands and tobacconists. You buy the card, dial a local or toll-free number and then follow the instructions – they can bring savings, especially if you are calling from a payphone. Compare rates (where possible before buying).

Call centres *(locutorios)* are another option. You'll mostly find these scattered about the old town, especially in and around El Raval. Check rates before making calls.

TELEVISION

Most TVs receive seven channels – two from Spain's state-run Televisión Española (TVE1 and La 2), three independent stations (Antena 3, Tele 5 and Canal Plus), the Catalan regional government station (TV-3) and another Catalan station (Canal 33). Most TVs will also receive the local city stations, Barcelona TV and Citytv. You may also get a couple of other local Catalan stations. The introduction of terrestrial digital TV is set to expand the number of local and nationwide stations available to viewers.

News programmes are a mixed bag, with at times inordinate concentration on crime and cats-up-trees stories. You can sometimes catch an interesting documentary or film (look out for the occasional English-language classic late at night on La 2). Otherwise, the main fare is a rather nauseating diet of soaps (many from Latin America), endless talk shows, reality TV and almost vaudevillian variety shows (with plenty of glitz and tits). Canal Plus is a pay channel dedicated mainly to movies: you need a decoder and subscription to see the movies, but anyone can watch the other programmes.

Many better hotels have cable or satellite TV, serving up the usual diet of BBC World, CNN, Eurosport and the like.

TIME

Spain (and hence Barcelona) is one hour ahead of GMT/UTC during winter, and two hours ahead during daylight saving (the last Sunday in March to the last Sunday in October). Most other Western European countries are on the same time as Spain year-round, the major exceptions being the UK, Ireland and Portugal, which are one hour behind. Spaniards use the 24-hour clock for official business (timetables etc) but often switch to the 12-hour version in daily conversation.

TIPPING

You are not expected to tip on top of restaurant service charges, but it is common to leave a small amount, say €1 per person. If there is no service charge, you might consider leaving a 10% tip, but this is not obligatory. In bars, Spaniards often leave some small change as a tip. Tipping taxi drivers is not common practice, but you should tip the porter at higher-class hotels.

TOILETS

There are so few public toilets in Barcelona that stopping at a bar or café for a quick coffee and then a trip to the toilet is the common solution to those sudden urges at awkward times. Make sure your chosen bar actually has a toilet before committing yourself!

TOURIST INFORMATION

Several tourist offices operate in Barcelona. A couple of general information numbers worth bearing in mind are ☎ 010 and ☎ 012. The first is for Barcelona and the other is for all Catalonia (run by the Generalitat). You sometimes strike English-speakers, although for the most part operators are Catalan/Spanish bilingual. In addition to the following listed tourist offices, information booths operate at Estació del Nord bus station and at Portal de la Pau, at the foot of the Monument a Colom at the port end of La Rambla. At least three others set up at various points in the city centre in summer.

Oficina d'Informació de Turisme de Barcelona (Map pp298–9; ☎ 93 285 38 34; www.barcelonaturisme.com; Plaça de Catalunya 17-S, underground; 🕑 9am-9pm;

Ⓜ Catalunya) The main Barcelona tourist information office, it concentrates on city information and can help book accommodation. Expect to queue.

Oficina d'Informació de Turisme de Barcelona (Map pp298–9; Carrer de la Ciutat 2; 🕑 9am-8pm Mon-Fri, 10am-8pm Sat, 10am-2pm Sun & holidays; Ⓜ Jaume I) A branch in the Ajuntament (town hall).

Oficina d'Informació de Turisme de Barcelona (Map pp296–7; Estació Sants; 🕑 8am-8pm Jun-Sep, 8am-8pm Mon-Fri plus 8am-2pm Sat, Sun & holidays Oct-May; Ⓜ Sants Estació) Train-station branch with limited city information.

Oficina d'Informació de Turisme de Barcelona (El Prat airport; ☎ 93 478 47 04; 🕑 9am-9pm) In the airport's Terminal B arrivals hall, it has information on all Catalonia. A smaller office at the international arrivals hall opens the same hours.

Palau de la Virreina arts information office (Map pp298–9; ☎ 93 301 77 75; Rambla de Sant Josep 99; 🕑 10am-8pm Mon-Sat, 11am-3pm Sun; Ⓜ Liceu) A useful office for events information and tickets.

Palau Robert regional tourist office (Map pp294–5; ☎ 93 238 40 00; www.gencat.net/probert; Passeig de Gràcia 107; 🕑 10am-7pm Mon-Sat, 10am-2pm Sun; Ⓜ Diagonal) A host of material on Catalonia, audiovisual resources, a bookshop and a branch of Turisme Juvenil de Catalunya (for youth travel).

TRAVEL AGENTS

Apart from the budget airlines serving Barcelona, the city is not a great source of cheap air travel. Travel agencies worth checking out are:

Halcón Viatges (Map pp294–5; ☎ 807 227222; www.halconviajes.com in Spanish; Carrer de Pau Claris 108; Ⓜ Passeig de Gràcia) Reliable chain of travel agents that sometimes has good deals. This is one of many branches around town.

Orixà (Map pp296–7; ☎ 93 487 00 22; www.orixa.com in Spanish; Carrer d'Aragó 227; Ⓜ Passeig de Gràcia) Good local agent oriented to independent travellers.

Viajes Zeppelin (Map pp296–7; ☎ 93 412 00 13; www.viajeszeppelin.com in Spanish; Carrer de Villarroel 49; Ⓜ Urgell) Small chain that often finds good-value fares.

VISAS

Spain is one of 15 member countries of the Schengen Convention, under which 13 EU member countries (the others are Austria, Belgium, Denmark, Finland, France, Germany, Greece, Italy, Luxembourg, the Netherlands, Portugal and Sweden) plus Iceland and Norway have abolished checks at common borders. Legal residents of one Schengen country do not require a visa for another Schengen country. Citizens of the UK, Ireland and Switzerland are also exempt. Nationals of the 10 countries that entered the EU in May 2004 (Cyprus, Czech Republic, Estonia, Hungary, Latvia, Lithuania, Malta, Poland, Slovak Republic and Slovenia) do not need visas for tourist visits or even to take up residence in Spain and other EU countries, but will not have the full freedom to work enjoyed by other EU citizens for several years. Nationals of many other countries, including Australia, Canada, Israel, Japan, New Zealand and the USA, do not require visas for tourist visits to Spain of up to 90 days.

All non-EU nationals entering Spain for any reason other than tourism (such as study or work) should contact a Spanish consulate, as they may need a specific visa.

If you are a citizen of a country not mentioned here, check with a Spanish consulate to see if you need a visa. The standard tourist visa issued by Spanish consulates is the Schengen visa (www.eurovisa.info), valid for up to 90 days. A Schengen visa issued by one Schengen country is generally valid for travel in all other Schengen countries. However, member countries may impose additional restrictions on certain nationalities. You should check visa regulations with the consulate of each Schengen country you plan to visit. The visas are not renewable inside Spain and no more than two will be issued in any 12-month period.

WOMEN TRAVELLERS

Women travellers should be ready to ignore stares, catcalls and unnecessary comments, although harassment is much less frequent than you might expect.

Think twice about going by yourself to isolated stretches of beach or lonely country areas, or down empty city streets at night. It's highly inadvisable for a woman to hitchhike alone – and not a great idea even for two women together.

Topless bathing is OK on beaches in Catalonia and also at swimming pools. While skimpy clothing tends not to attract much attention in Barcelona and the coastal resorts, tastes in inland Catalonia tend to be somewhat conservative.

Organisations

Ca la Dona (Map pp298–9; ☎ 93 412 71 61; http://cala dona.pangea.org; Carrer de Casp 38; Ⓜ Catalunya) The nerve centre of the region's feminist movement. It includes many diverse women's groups.

Centre Francesca Bonnemaison (Map pp298–9; ☎ 93 268 42 18; www.bonnemaison-ccd.org; Carrer de Sant Pere més baix 7; Ⓜ Urquinaona) A women's cultural centre that was established in 2003, more than 60 years after the building was ceded to the Barcelona city council on condition that it be used for that purpose. More than 80 women's groups and feminist associations work together to put on expositions, stage theatre productions and promote social groups.

Institut Català de la Dona (Map pp296–7; ☎ 93 495 16 00; www.gencat.net/icdona; Carrer de Viladomat 319; Ⓜ Entença) It can point you in the right direction for information on marriage, divorce, rape/assault counselling and related issues for long-termers, social activities, women's clubs etc.

WORK

Nationals of EU countries, Switzerland, Norway and Iceland may work in Spain without a visa, but for stays of more than three months they are supposed to apply within the first month for a residence card *(tarjeta de residencia)*. If you are offered a contract, your employer will usually steer you through the labyrinth of paperwork.

Virtually everyone else is supposed to obtain a work permit from a Spanish consulate in their country of residence and, if they plan to stay more than 90 days, a residence visa. Getting a work permit or residence visa is close to impossible unless you already have a job contract lined up. Quite a few people do work, discreetly, without bothering to tangle with the bureaucracy.

Doing Business in Barcelona

The main business district in Barcelona is along the western end of Avinguda Diagonal. The big banks cluster here with several major business-oriented hotels. Another centre of activity is the World Trade Center in Port Vell. A hi-tech district, known as 22@bcn, is slowly emerging in what was once the industrial area of Poblenou. The giant congress centre in Fòrum attracts international get-togethers on the northeast coast of the city.

People wishing to make the first moves towards expanding their business into Spain should contact their own country's trade department (such as the DTI in the UK). The commercial department of the Spanish embassy in your own country should also have information – at least about red tape.

In Barcelona your next port of call should be the **Cambra de Comerç de Barcelona** (Map pp294–5;

☎ 902 448448; www.cambrabcn.es; Avinguda Diagonal 452; Ⓜ Diagonal). It has a documentation centre and business-oriented bookshop, the Llibreria de la Cambra.

The Fira de Barcelona information office (see right) offers business services (communications etc), meeting rooms and other facilities for people working at trade fairs.

Problems with your portable computer? You'll find ads for English-speaking computer technicians in the free English-language magazine *Barcelona Metropolitan,* which can be found in English and Irish pubs and occasionally other central bars and cafés, cultural centres and tourist offices.

Many of the business-oriented hotels offer business centres (with computers and other office equipment), Internet access and in some cases secretarial services.

Employment Options

The easiest source of work for foreigners is teaching English (or another foreign language). Most of the larger, more reputable schools will hire only non-EU citizens who already have work and/or residence permits, but their attitude can become more flexible if demand for teachers is high and they come across someone with good qualifications. In the case of EU citizens, employers generally have no great problem in helping you through the bureaucracy.

Barcelona is loaded with 'cowboy outfits' that pay badly and often aren't overly concerned about quality. Still, the only way you'll find out is by hunting around. Schools are listed under *Acadèmies de Idiomes* in the yellow pages.

Sources of information on possible teaching work – school or private – include foreign cultural centres (the British Council, Institut Français etc), language schools, foreign-language bookshops and university notice boards. Cultural institutes you may want to try include:

British Council (Map p292; ☎ 93 241 99 72; www .britishcouncil.org/es/spain.htm; Carrer d'Amigó 74; Ⓡ FGC Muntaner)

Institut Français de Barcelona (Map pp294–5; ☎ 93 567 77 77; www.institutfrances.org; Carrer de Moià 8; Ⓜ Diagonal)

Institute for North American Studies (Map p292; ☎ 93 240 51 10; www.ien.es; Via Augusta 123; Ⓡ FGC Plaça Molina)

Translating and interpreting could be an option if you are fluent in Spanish (and/or Catalan) and a language in demand.

Another option might be au pair work, organised before you come to Spain. A useful guide is *The Au Pair and Nanny's Guide to Working Abroad,* by Susan Griffith and Sharon Legg. Susan Griffith's *Work Your Way Around the World* is also worth a look.

University students or recent graduates might be able to set up an internship with companies in Barcelona. The **Association of International Students for Economics and Commerce** (www .aiesec.org), with branches throughout the world, helps member students find internships in related fields. For information on membership, check out its website.

Exhibitions & Conferences

With more than 80 trade fairs a year and a growing number of congresses of all types, Barcelona is an important centre of international business in Europe. The **Fira de Barcelona** (Map pp304–5; ☎ 902 233200; www .firabcn.es; Plaça d'Espanya; Ⓜ Espanya) organises fairs for everything from fashion to technology, furniture, recycling, jewellery and classic cars.

The main **trade fair** (Fira M1; Map pp304–5) is located between the base of Montjuïc and Plaça d'Espanya, with 90,000 sq metres of exhibition space and a conference centre. Fira M2 (Fair No 2), southwest of Montjuïc, continues to expand and could total 120,000 sq metres by the end of 2007. The planned Metro line across the city from the airport will also stop at these trade areas.

On the waterfront, the **World Trade Center** (Map pp290–1; ☎ 93 508 80 00; www.wtc barcelona.com; Ⓜ Drassanes) at Port Vell offers a variety of meeting rooms and conference centres. The **Centre de Convencions Internacional de Barcelona** (CCIB; Map pp290–1; ☎ 93 230 10 00; www.ccib.es; Rambla de Prim 1-17) near the waterfront in the northeast of the city can host 15,000 people (see p102).

The **Barcelona Convention Bureau** (Map pp294–5; ☎ 93 368 97 00; Rambla de Catalunya 123; Ⓜ Diagonal) organises conventions and other events.

The Hotel Rey Juan Carlos I's private **Palau de Congressos** (Map pp304–5; ☎ 93 364 44 00; www.pcongresos.com in Spanish; Avinguda Diagonal 661-671; Ⓜ Zona Universitària) has a capacity of 2300.

Language

Language

It's true – anyone can speak another language. Don't worry if you haven't studied languages before or that you studied a language at school for years and can't remember any of it. It doesn't even matter if you failed English grammar. After all, that's never affected your ability to speak English! And this is the key to picking up a language in another country. You just need to start speaking.

Learn a few key phrases before you go. Write them on pieces of paper and stick them on the fridge, by the bed or even on the computer – anywhere that you'll see them often.

You'll find that locals appreciate travellers trying their language, no matter how muddled you may think you sound. So don't just stand there, say something! If you want to learn more Spanish than we've included here, pick up a copy of Lonely Planet's comprehensive but user-friendly *Spanish Phrasebook*.

SOCIAL
Meeting People
Hello.
¡Hola!
Goodbye.
¡Adiós!
Please.
Por favor.
Thank you.
(Muchas) Gracias.
Yes.
Sí.
No.
No.
Excuse me.
Perdón.
Sorry!
Perdón/Perdóneme.
Do you speak English?
¿Hablas ingles?
Does anyone speak English?
¿Hay alguien que hable ingles?
Do you understand?
¿Me entiende?
Yes, I understand.
Sí, entiendo.
No, I don't understand.
No, no entiendo.
Pardon?;What?
¿Cómo?

Could you please ...?
¿Puedes ... por favor?
  speak more slowly hablar más despacio
  repeat that repetir
  write it down escribirlo

Going Out
What's there to do in the evenings?
¿Qué se puede hacer por las noches?

What's on ...?
¿Qué hay...?
  locally en la zona
  this weekend este fin de semana
  today hoy
  tonight esta noche

Where are the ...?
¿Dónde hay ... ?
  places to eat lugares para comer
  nightclubs discotecas
  pubs pubs
  gay venues lugares gay

Is there a local entertainment guide?
¿Hay una guía del ocio de la zona?

PRACTICAL
Question Words
Who?   ¿Quién? (sg)
              ¿Quiénes? (pl)
What?   ¿Qué?
Which?   ¿Cuál? (sg)
              ¿Cuáles? (pl)
When?   ¿Cuándo?
Where?   ¿Dónde?
How?   ¿Cómo?
How much?   ¿Cuantos?
How many?   ¿Cuánto?
How much is it? ¿Cuánto cuesta?
Why?   ¿Por qué?

Numbers & Amounts

0	cero
1	una/uno
2	dos
3	tres
4	cuatro
5	cinco
6	seis
7	siete
8	ocho
9	nueve
10	diez
11	once
12	doce
13	trece
14	catorce
15	quince
16	dieciséis
17	diecisiete
18	dieciocho
19	diecinueve
20	veinte
21	veintiuno
22	veintidós
30	treinta
31	treinta y uno
40	cuarenta
50	cincuenta
60	sesenta
70	setenta
80	ochenta
90	noventa
100	cien
1000	mil
2000	dos mil

Days

Monday	lunes
Tuesday	martes
Wednesday	miércoles
Thursday	jueves
Friday	viernes
Saturday	sábado
Sunday	domingo

Banking

I'd like to change some money.
Me gustaría cambiar dinero.
I'd like to change a travellers cheque.
Me gustaría cobrar un cheque de viajero.

Where's the nearest ...?
¿Dónde está ... más cercano?

ATM	el cajero automático
foreign exchange office	la oficina de cambio

Do you accept ...?
¿Aceptan ...?

credit cards	tarjetas de crédito
debit cards	tarjetas de débito
travellers cheques	cheques de viajero

Post

Where's the post office?
¿Dónde está correos?

I want to send a ...
Quisiera enviar ...

fax	un fax
parcel	un paquete
postcard	una postal

I want to buy a/an ...
Quisiera comprar ...

aerogramme	un aerograma
envelope	un sobre
stamp/stamps	un sello/sellos

Phones & Mobiles

I want to buy a phone card.
Quiero comprar una tarjeta.

I want to make a ...
Quiero hacer ...

call (to ...)	una llamada (a ...)
reverse-charge/ collect call	una llamada a cobro revertido

Where can I find a/an ...?
¿Dónde se puede encontrar un ...?
I'd like a/an ...
Quisiera un ...

adaptor plug	adaptador
charger for my phone	cargador para mi teléfono
mobile/cell phone for hire	móvil para alquilar
prepaid mobile/ cell phone	móvil pagado por adelantado
SIM card for your network	tarjeta SIM para su red

Internet

Where's the local Internet cafe?
¿Dónde hay un cibercafé cercano?

I'd like to ...
Quisiera ...

get Internet access	usar el Internet
check my email	revisar mi correo electrónico

Transport

What time does the ... leave?
¿A qué hora sale el ...?

boat	barco
bus	autobús
bus (intercity)	autocar
plane	avión
train	tren

What time's the ... bus?
¿A qué hora es el ... autocar/autobús?

first	primer
last	último
next	próximo

Is this taxi free?
¿Está libre este taxi?
Please put the meter on.
Por favor, ponga el taxímetro
How much is it to ...?
¿Cuánto cuesta ir a ...?
Please take me (to this address).
Por favor, lléveme (a esta dirección).

FOOD

breakfast	desayuno
lunch	comida
dinner	cena
snack	tentempié
to eat/to drink	comer/beber

Can you recommend a ...?
¿Puede recomendar un ...?

bar	bar
café	café
coffee bar	cafetería
restaurant	restaurante

Is service/cover charge included in the bill?
¿Il servicio está incluido en la cuenta?

For more detailed information on food and dining out, see p48 and p140.

EMERGENCIES

Help!
¡Socorro!
It's an emergency!
Es una emergencia!
Could you help me please?
¿Me puede ayudar, por favor?
Where's the police station?
¿Dónde está la comisaría?

Call ...!
¡Llame a ...!

the police	la policía
a doctor	un médico
an ambulance	una ambulancia

HEALTH

Where's the nearest ...?
¿Dónde está … más cercano?

(night) chemist	la farmacia (de guardia)
dentist	el dentista
doctor	el médico
hospital	el hospital

I need a doctor (who speaks English).
Necesito un doctor (que hable inglés).

Symptoms

I have (a/an) ...
Tengo …

diarrhoea	diarrea
fever	fiebre
headache	dolor de cabeza
pain	dolor

I'm allergic to ...
Soy alérgico ...

antibiotics	a los antibióticos
nuts	las nueces
peanuts	los cacahuetes
penicillin	a la penicilina

GLOSSARY

Items listed below are in Catalan/Spanish (Castilian) where they start with the same letter. Where the two terms start with different letters, or where only the Catalan or the Spanish term is provided, they are listed separately and marked (C) for Catalan or (S) for Spanish. If an entry is not marked at all, it is because it takes the same form in both languages.

ajuntament/ayuntamiento – town hall

artesonado (S) – Mudéjar wooden ceiling with interlaced beams leaving a pattern of spaces for decoration
avinguda (C) – avenue

Barcelonin (C) – inhabitant/native of Barcelona
Barcino – Roman name for Barcelona
barri/barrio – neighbourhood, quarter of Barcelona

caganer (C) – crapper, a character that appears in Catalan nativity scenes
Call (C) – Jewish quarter in medieval Barcelona

capella/capilla – chapel
carrer/calle – street
casa – house
castellers (C) – human castle builders
cercanías (S) – local trains serving Barcelona's airport, suburbs and some outlying towns
comte/conde – count

església (C) – church

farmàcia/farmacia – pharmacy
festa/fiesta – festival, public holiday or party
FGC (C) – Ferrocarrils de la Generalitat de Catalunya; local trains operating alongside the Metro in Barcelona
fundació (C) – foundation

garum – a spicy sauce made from fish entrails, found throughout the Roman Empire
gegants – huge figures paraded at festes
Generalitat (C) – Catalan regional government
guiri – foreigner (somewhat pejorative)

hostal – commercial establishment providing one- to three-star accommodation

iglesia (S) – church
IVA – impost sobre el valor afegit/impesto sobre el valor añadido, or value-added tax

masia – Catalan country farmhouse

mercat/mercado – market
modernisme (C) – the turn-of-the-19th-century artistic style, influenced by Art Nouveau, whose leading practitioner was Antoni Gaudí
modernista – an exponent of modernisme
Mudéjar (S) – a Muslim living under Christian rule in medieval Spain; also refers to their decorative style of architecture

palau (C) – palace
passatge (C) – laneway
pension – commercial establishment providing one- to three-star accommodation
plaça/plaza – plaza
platja (C) – beach

Renaixença – Rebirth of interest in Catalan literature, culture and language in the second half of the 19th century
rodalies (C) – see cercanías

saló (C) – hall
sardana – traditional Catalan folk dance
s/n (S) – sin número (without number)

tablao – restaurant where flamenco is performed
teatre – theatre
terrassa/terazza – terrace; often means a café or bar's outdoor tables
turista – second class; economy class

Behind the Scenes

THE LONELY PLANET STORY

The story begins with a classic travel adventure: Tony and Maureen Wheeler's 1972 journey across Europe and Asia to Australia. There was no useful information about the overland trail then, so Tony and Maureen published the first Lonely Planet guidebook to meet a growing need.

From a kitchen table, Lonely Planet has grown to become the largest independent travel publisher in the world, with offices in Melbourne (Australia), Oakland (USA) and London (UK). Today Lonely Planet guidebooks cover the globe. There is an ever-growing list of books and information in a variety of media. Some things haven't changed. The main aim is still to make it possible for adventurous travellers to get out there – to explore and better understand the world.

At Lonely Planet we believe travellers can make a positive contribution to the countries they visit – if they respect their host communities and spend their money wisely. Every year 5% of company profit is donated to charities around the world.

THIS BOOK

This 5th edition of *Barcelona* was written by Damien Simonis. Damien also wrote the first four editions. The guide was commissioned in Lonely Planet's London office and produced by:

Commissioning Editors Stefanie Di Trocchio, Sally Schafer

Coordinating Editor Andrea Dobbin

Coordinating Cartographers Hunor Csutoros, Emma McNicol

Coordinating Layout Designer Katie Thuy Bui

Managing Cartographer Mark Griffiths

Proofreader John Hinman

Assisting Cartographer Marion Byass

Cover Designer Yukiyoshi Kamimura

Project Manager Fabrice Rocher

Managing Editor Bruce Evans

Language Content Coordinator Quentin Frayne

Thanks to Michala Green, Meagan Williams, Trent Paton, Sarah Sloane, Celia Wood, Sally Darmody, Jennifer Garrett, Helen Christinis, Chris Lee Ack, Mark Germanchis, Wayne Murphy, Julie Sheridan, Fiona Siseman, Karina Dea, Gerard Walker, Wendy Wright

Cover photographs Diamond windows and iron gate, Park Güell, Nikreates/Alamy (top); Diving World Championships, Manuel Blondeau/Photo & Co/Corbis (bottom); Chimney pots on the roof of Palau Güell, Neil Setchfield/Lonely Planet Images (back).

Internal photographs by Lonely Planet Images and Krzysztof Dydynski except for the following: p2 (#1) Anders Blomqvist; p13, p74 (#1) Damien Simonis; p49 Pascale Beroujon; p67 (#2) Martin Hughes; p74 (#2) John Hay; p157 Barbara Van Zanten; p171 (#1) Geoff Stringer; p178 (#1 &

#3), p243 David Tomlinson; p178 (#2) Martin Moos; p178 (#4) Bethune Carmichael; p232 John Banagan; p237 Stephen Saks; p20, p25, p26, p34, p45, p59, p67 (#3), p68 (#5, #6 & #7), p69 (#3), p70 (#2 & #3), p71 (#1 & #2), p72 (#3), p73 (#1 & #2), p74 (#3), p86, p98, p116, p123, p131, p137, p143, p167, p169, p170, p171 (#2 & #3), p172 (#1, #5 & #6), p173 (#2, #3 & #4), p174 (#1 & #2), p175 (#2 & #3), p176 (#3 & #4), p177 (#2 & #3), p190, p217 Neil Setchfield. All images are the copyright of the photographers unless otherwise indicated. Many of the images in this guide are available for licensing from Lonely Planet Images: www .lonelyplanetimages.com.

THANKS
DAMIEN SIMONIS

Keeping up with what's happening in Barcelona is a nonstop affair, and a task made easier and more enjoyable by the company of friends. Thanks to all those who have, over the two years since the last edition, shared tips and discoveries, or simply tagged along for a meal or a drink: Edith López García, María Barbosa Pérez and Enric Muñoz, Alfredo López and friends, Susan Kempster, Michael van Laake and Rocío Vázquez, Susana Pellicer (along with Albert and friends), Cristina Pedraza Sánchez, Peter (don't call me 'the Greek') Sotirakis, Ottobrina Voccoli, Teresa Moreno Quintana, Nicole Neuefeind, Armin Teichmann, José María Toro, Stephan Rundel, Simona Volonterio, Oscar Elias, Steven Muller and Veronika Brinkmann (fabulous fondue!), Monica Gispert, Geoff Leaver-Heaton, Grant Reid and Celine Garcia, Antonio Marin and Ana Pina, Ita Fàbregas, Antonio Campañá (and the SCIJ Espanya crowd), John Rochlin (and the folks of ASBA), Simona Volonterio, Ralf Himburg and Lilian Müller (thanks for the *calçotada!*) and the Thursday gang, Brian O'Hare and Marta Cervera (St Patrick's 2006 was memorable!), Damien Harris (the party man), and to all those met along the way.

As always, this is dedicated to Janique LeBlanc, who makes it all worthwhile.

OUR READERS

Many thanks to the travellers who used the last edition and wrote to us with helpful hints, useful advice and interesting anecdotes:

Therese Agståhl, Mikael Albrecht, Jen Allen, Yariv Alpher, Christine Ambrosini, Phil, Hilary & Pippa Andre, Rikard Åström, Alison Barber, Stephen Barnes, Alf Batchelor, Karen Boss, Jess Boydell, Brian Brennan, Henrik Brockdorff, Lisbeth Brunthaler, Nina Brydolf, Tina Buckley, Ruth Butland, Pat Byrne, Catherine Carter, Randall Chan, Cornelia Chan-Graschitz, Anna Cifani, Bjorn Clasen, Katherine & Cassie Clift, David Cox, Richard Coxon, Jake Crossley, Stuart Cunningham, Daniel Dahl, Roanna Dalziel, Annemieke Dekker, Marco Dellagati, Olive Donnelly, Luisa Doplicher, Su & Chris Dore, Steve Draper, Moniek Falke, Franziska Fleischli, Claire Fragonas, Max Francis, Mikey Mike Francis, Ariel Gejman, Lilian Grundström, Meunier Guillaume, Eric Halvorson, Alison Harris, Olaf Hauk, Cayla Henn, Sylvia Henriksen, Martin Hlawon, Sim Sim Hockney, Stefan Hofer, John Iaquinto, Annika Johansson, Hans Jonsson, Alex Kamenski, Mary Kauffman, Jakob Kejerud, Simon Kerby, Michael Kessler, Roni & Ayala Klaus, Robin Krieger, Chris Kurkjian, Rebekah Kvart, Tonko Lacmanovic, Cis Lebour, Beni Lew, Derek Manson-Smith, John & Diana Martin, Katherine Martin, Leigh Mayhew, Codrin Mihai, Steven Mirra, Phil Newnham, Judy Ng, Daniel Nilsson, Simón Nuñez, Bente Nystad, Robert Olsson, Karina Osgood, Adis Osmanovic, Patric Öström, Marie-Eve Paquette, Turid Pedersen, Tanya Pepper, Alexandra Prichard, Christopher Prusaski, Anita Raets, Emma Retson, Andres Roman, Lorenza Rossi, Xavier Ruiz, Ines Rybbelen, P Saillart, Paul Schilder, Frida Sellman, Britt-Marie Svensson, Carme Tapias, Emma Taylor, Fiona Thomson, Jason Thorpe, Naima & Oscar Tillman, Cari van Rood, Wim Vandenbussche, Helen Varley, Sue Vidovic, Kjell-Tore Waale, Ann-Marie Wall, Beth Wallace, Eva-Lena Weinstock, Pat & Derek Westcott, Cecilia Wrebström, Andrew Young, Åke Zander

SEND US YOUR FEEDBACK

We love to hear from travellers – your comments keep us on our toes and help make our books better. Our well-travelled team reads every word on what you loved or loathed about this book. Although we cannot reply individually to postal submissions, we always guarantee that your feedback goes straight to the appropriate authors, in time for the next edition. Each person who sends us information is thanked in the next edition – and the most useful submissions are rewarded with a free book.

To send us your updates – and find out about Lonely Planet events, newsletters and travel news – visit our award-winning website: www.lonelyplanet.com /feedback.

Note: We may edit, reproduce and incorporate your comments in Lonely Planet products such as guidebooks, websites and digital products, so let us know if you don't want your comments reproduced or your name acknowledged. For a copy of our privacy policy visit www.lonelyplanet.com/privacy.

ACKNOWLEDGMENTS

Many thanks to the following for use of their content:
Barcelona Metro Map © TMB 2006

Notes

Notes

Notes

Notes

Index

See also separate indexes for Drinking & Nightlife (p284), Eating (p285), Entertainment (p286), Shopping (p286) and Sleeping (p287).

000 map pages
000 photographs

SLEEPING

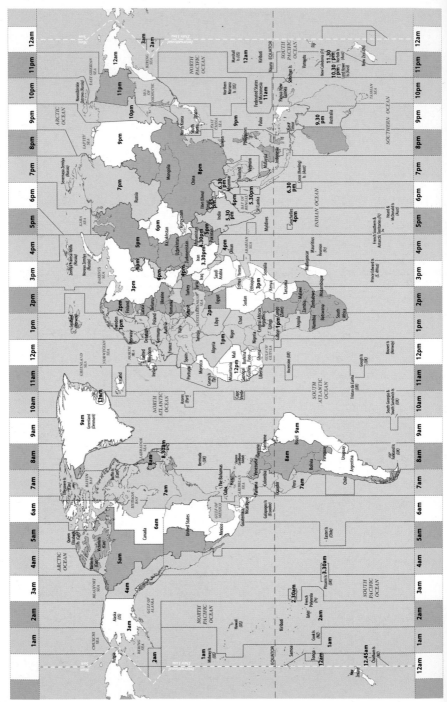

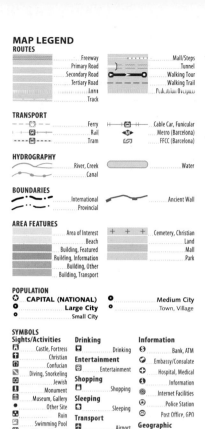

MAP LEGEND
ROUTES
............Freeway
............Primary Road
............Secondary Road
............Tertiary Road
............Lane
............Track
............Mall/Steps
............Tunnel
............Walking Tour
............Walking Trail
............Pedestrian Overpass

TRANSPORT
............Ferry
............Rail
............Tram
............Cable Car, Funicular
............Metro (Barcelona)
............FFCC (Barcelona)

HYDROGRAPHY
............River, Creek
............Canal
............Water

BOUNDARIES
............International
............Provincial
............Ancient Wall

AREA FEATURES
............Area of Interest
............Beach
............Building, Featured
............Building, Information
............Building, Other
............Building, Transport
............Cemetery, Christian
............Land
............Mall
............Park

POPULATION
⊙ ...CAPITAL (NATIONAL)
● ....Large City
○ ....Small City
● ....Medium City
○ ....Town, Village

SYMBOLS
Sights/Activities
............Castle, Fortress
............Christian
............Confucian
............Diving, Snorkeling
............Jewish
............Monument
............Museum, Gallery
............Other Site
............Ruin
............Swimming Pool
............Winery, Vineyard
............Zoo, Bird Sanctuary
Eating
............Eating

Drinking
............Drinking
Entertainment
............Entertainment
Shopping
............Shopping
Sleeping
............Sleeping
Transport
............Airport
............Bus Station
............Parking Area
............Taxi Rank

Information
............Bank, ATM
............Embassy/Consulate
............Hospital, Medical
............Information
............Internet Facilities
............Police Station
............Post Office, GPO
Geographic
............Lighthouse
............Lookout
............River Flow

Maps ■

SIGHTS & ACTIVITIES (pp78–124)
Casa Vicenç..............................1 D2
Museu i Centre d'Estudis de
l'Esport Dr Melchior Colet.....2 C5

EATING 🍴 (pp140–62)
Krampus..................................3 C2
Saüc.......................................4 D5
Via Veneto..............................5 A6

DRINKING 🍷 (pp164–86)
Berlin......................................6 D5
Bocayma.................................7 C4
Búcaro....................................8 D4
La Base...................................9 C5
Luz de Gas............................10 D5
Mas i Mas..............................11 B5
Otto Zutz...............................12 D3

ENTERTAINMENT 🎭 (pp188–98)
La Cova del Drac–Jazzroom.....13 A2
Luz de Gas ....(see 10)
Zac Club...............................(see 19)

SHOPPING 🛍 (pp200–10)
El Corte Inglés........................14 C5

SLEEPING 🛏 (pp212–24)
Aparthotel Silver.....................15 D2
Barcelona Apartments.............16 B3
Rent A Bedroom......................17 D1

INFORMATION
Bright.....................................18 D3
British Consulate......................19 C5
British Council.........................20 B4
Institute for North American
Studies.................................21 C3
New Zealand Consulate...........22 D4

L'EIXAMPLE

To Plaça de Rovira i Trias (275m)

Joanic

Fontana

Gràcia

Diagonal

Provença

Plaça del Doctor Ferrer i Cajigal

Plaça de la Virreina

Plaça del Diamant

Plaça de la Revolució de Setembre de 1868

Plaça del Sol

Plaça de Rius i Taulet

Plaça de la Llibertat

Plaça de Gal.la Placídia

Plaça de Narcís Oller

Plaça de Joan Carles I

Plaça de Raspall

See p292

See pp296-7

294

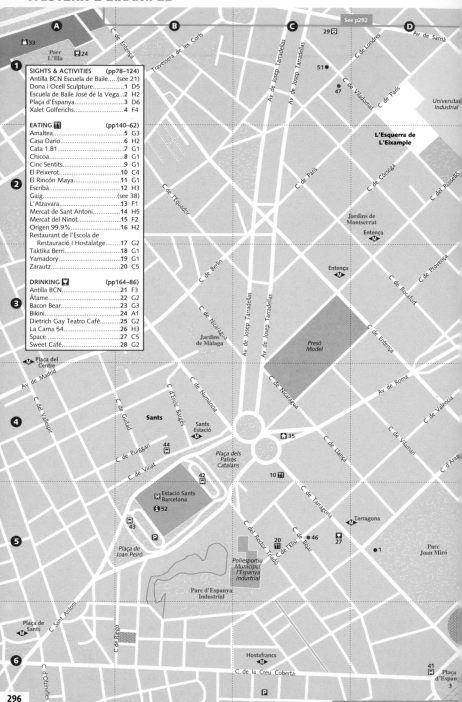

See p292

SIGHTS & ACTIVITIES	(pp78–124)
Antilla BCN Escuela de Baile	(see 21)
Dona i Ocell Sculpture	1 D5
Escuela de Baile José de la Vega	2 H2
Plaça d'Espanya	3 D6
Xalet Golferichs	4 F4

EATING 🍴	(pp140–62)
Amaltea	5 G3
Casa Darío	6 H2
Cata 1.81	7 G1
Chicoa	8 G1
Cinc Sentits	9 G1
El Peixerot	10 C4
El Rincón Maya	11 G1
Escribà	12 H3
Gaig	(see 38)
L'Atzavara	13 F1
Mercat de Sant Antoni	14 H5
Mercat del Ninot	15 F2
Origen 99.9%	16 H2
Restaurant de l'Escola de Restauració I Hostalatge	17 G2
Taktika Berri	18 G1
Yamadory	19 G1
Zarautz	20 C5

DRINKING 🍸	(pp164–86)
Antilla BCN	21 F3
Átame	22 G2
Bacon Bear	23 G3
Bikini	24 A1
Dietrich Gay Teatro Café	25 G2
La Cama 54	26 H3
Space	27 C5
Sweet Café	28 G2

0 | 400 m
0 | 0.2 miles

Plaça del
Doctor Ferrer
i Cajigal

Plaça del
Doctor
Lefamendi

Hospital
Clínic

Hospital
Clínic

Universitat
de Barcelona

L'EIXAMPLE

Urgell

Rocafort

To Inopia
(450m)

Espanya

Poble Sec

Av del Paral.lel

See pp304–5

TRANSPORT (pp248–55)
A1 Aerobús Stop (From Airport)..40 G4
A1 Aerobús Stop (From Airport)..41 D6
A1 Aerobús Stop (To Airport).....42 B4
Bus to Airport Train Station.......43 B5
Estació d'Autobusos de Sants....44 B4
National/Atesa.........................45 H2
Pepecar.................................46 C5
Vanguard...............................47 C1

ENTERTAINMENT (pp188–98)
Bikini ....(see 24)
Filmoteca.............................29 C1
Méliès Cinemes.....................30 G3
Renoir Floridablanca...............31 H4
Toros Taquilla Oficial..............32 H2

SHOPPING (pp200–10)
L'Illa del Diagonal..................33 A1

SLEEPING (pp212–24)
Hostal Cèntric.......................34 H4
Hostal Sofia..........................35 C4
Hotel Advance.......................36 H3
Hotel Axel............................37 H2
Hotel Cram...........................38 H1
Lodging Barcelona..................39 H1

INFORMATION
Cybernet..............................48 F1
Farmàcia Torres.....................49 G1
Hospital Clínic i Provincial........50 E1
Institut Català de la Dona........51 C1
Oficina d'Informació de Turisme
  de Barcelona.......................52 B5
ONCE..................................53 G5
Orixà..................................54 H1
Viajes Zeppelin.....................55 G4

297

Mercat de Santa Caterina

La Ribera

Plaça Antoni Maura

Plaça R. de Berenguer el Gran

Plaça del Rei

Plaça de la Seu

Plaça Nova

Església de Sant Felip Neri

Barri Gòtic

Plaça d'Urquinaona

Plaça del Patriarca

Plaça de Ramon Amadeu

Església Santa Anna

Av. del Portal de l'Àngel

Plaça de Rivadeneyra

La Rambla

La Rambla dels Estudis

La Rambla de Canaletes

Plaça de Catalunya

El Triangle

Plaça de Vicenç Martorell

Plaça del Bonsuccés

Jardins de la Reina Victoria

Rambla de Catalunya

Ronda de la Universitat

Universitat de Barcelona

Plaça dels Àngels

Plaça de Joan Coromines

Universitat Ramon Llull Communications Faculty

Plaça de Castella

Plaça de la Universitat

Universitat de Barcelona

Rambla de Catalunya

Gran Via de les Corts Catalanes

Plaça Goya

Ronda de Sant Antoni

Gran Via de les Corts Catalanes

See pp302-3
See pp294-5
See pp296-7

1

C de la Marina

Parc
Carles I

2

Ciutadella
Vila
Olímpica

See Port Olímpic Inset

3

Parc de Recerca
Biomèdica
de Barcelona

C del Gasòmetre

4

F

Port Olímpic

M de Gregal

43

M de Mestral

Port
Olímpic

Av Litoral

Ronda del Litoral

Torre
Mapfre

M de Marina

31

74

57

61

99

Platja de la
Barceloneta

300 m

0.2 milles

0

0

Hospital
del Mar

Parc de la

Edifici
Gas Natural

C dels
Pinzon

E

Universitat
Pompeu
Fabra

C de la Marina

C de Salvador Espriu

Plaça dels
Voluntaris

78

23

95

3

60

C de Edmon Trias
Fragat

Torrent

C de Trelawny

24

28

C de Salvador Espriu

Pg de Circumval·lació

Pg del Doctor Aiguader

Ronda del Litoral

C de la Marquesa

D

Cascada

Parc de la
Ciutadella

22

26

L'Umbracle

Estació
de França

de l'Atarazana

C d'Ocata

C de la Marquesa

C

Pg de Joaquim Renart

L'Hivernacle

Pg de Picasso

10

14

70

C de la Ribera

Former Mercat
del Born

C del Comerç

88

27

Pg de Lluís Companys

16

64

Plaça
Comercial

39

33

C de Rera Palau

Plaça
del Palau

B

Plaça
del Comerç

Pg de Lluís Companys

41

C del Comerç

Former Convent
de Sant Agustí

53

15

Plaça
de Pons i
Clerch

93

C del Comerç

C del Rec

65

Vermell

87

80

82

72

101

59

90

71

40

Plaça
de Santa Maria

C de Santa Maria

49

44

C dels Mirallers

9

C dels Flassaders

C de Montcada

86

81

48

C de Banys Vells

67

45

68

C dels Sombrerers

C del Portal Nou

55

C de Tantarantana

C de l'Allada

C de la Princesa

Ptge del Sabadell

21

C del Rec

18

19

50

C de l'Argenteria

46

89

84

47

96

A

Plaça de
Sant Pere

Pere Mitja

C del Rec Comtal

C d'En Llàstics

C dels Metges

C de Jaume Giralt

C del Portal Nou

Plaça de Sant
Agustí Vell

C dels
Carders

C dels Assaonadors

Pta d'En
Marcús

13

La Ribera

79

C de la Nau

C de l'Argenteria

Via Laietana

25

C del Sotstinent

Plaça de
Lluís el Piadós

1

2

See pp298-9

3

4

See pp296–7

C de la Bordeta

Gran Via de les Corts Catalanes

Plaça d'Espanya

Espanya

41

45

46

47

Plaça de l'Univers

C de la Bordeta

C de Sant Fructuós

Av de la Reina Maria Cristina

C de Mexic

48

Av de Rius i Taulet

C de Lleida

C de la Font Honrada

C del Mare de Déu del Remei

C de la Babila

C de Ricart

C de la Franca Xica

Barcelona Teatre Musical

Institut del Teatre

38

1

7

Plaça del Marquès de Foronda

Plaça de les Cascades

37

14

C de la Dàlia

19

Pg de les Cascades

Av del Marquès de Comillas

21

8

35

Mirador del Palau Nacional

17

Palau Nacional

15

Pg de Santa Madrona

Av dels Montanyans

4

25

Plaça del Pare Eusebi Millan

Antic Jardí Botànic

Jardins de Joan Maragall

Av de l'Estadi

C dels Tres Pins

20

Jardí d'Aclimatació

C dels Jocs de 92

12

Plaça d'Europa

Torre Calatrava

Pg de Minici Natal

Plaça de Nemesi Ponsati

6

Anella Olímpica

Carrer de Pierre de Coubertin

11

C Doctor Font i

18

Parc del Migdia

C dels Jocs de 92

Pg Olímpic

Montjuïc

13 Jardí Botànic

44

Pg de Migdia

3